THE TRIUMPH OF PIERROT

Harlequin.

THE TRIUMPH OF PIERROT,

The Commedia dell'Arte and the Modern Imagination

MARTIN B. GREEN & JOHN SWAN

Macmillan Publishing Company   New York

Macmillan Publishing Company
866 Third Avenue, New York, N.Y. 10022
Collier Macmillan Canada, Inc.

Library of Congress Cataloging-in-Publication Data

Green, Martin Burgess, 1927–
The triumph of Pierrot : the commedia dell'arte and
the modern imagination.
Bibliography: p.
Includes index.
1. Performing arts—History—20th century.   2. Theater
—History—20th century.   3. Commedia dell'arte—History
and criticism.   I. Swan, John C., 1945–   .   II. Title.
PN1581.G74   1986   790.2'09'04   85-23373
ISBN 0-02-545420-X

Macmillan books are available at special discounts for bulk purchases
for sales promotions, premiums, fund-raising, or educational use.
For details, contact:

Special Sales Director
Macmillan Publishing Company
866 Third Avenue
New York, N.Y. 10022

10 9 8 7 6 5 4 3 2 1

Designed by Jack Meserole

Printed in the United States of America

Permissions and credits appear on page 297.

For Carol Green and Susan Swan

CONTENTS

ACKNOWLEDGMENTS

I wish to acknowledge the help of several people in the Tufts Library, especially those at the Reference Desk and in the Inter-Library Loan department. In working on this book—as in all my other work—I have got cheerful, ready, and intelligent assistance, of the kind that makes work a pleasure. Without them, and others like them in libraries elsewhere, books would just not get written.

M.G.

For my part in this work I owe many debts, most of all to my co-author, whose lucid and commanding vision helped me immeasurably in shaping my own arguments. I am grateful also for the generous support of Wabash College and Dean Paul McKinney. Several of my Wabash colleagues have given me valued encouragement, and I offer particular thanks to Jim Fisher, himself the author of a wonderful commedia and an effective champion of the art, both on the stage and in the classroom. Thanks also to Elaine Greenlee for her skillful word-processing of an ungrateful manuscript; to Paul Mielke for his excellent picture-taking; to Dan Stepner in Boston for providing me with important materials; and to my fellow staffers at Lilly Library for their help and patience. Of course, this task would have been impossible for me without the steadfast support of my wife, Susan.

J.S.

INTRODUCTION

The commedia dell'arte is not an idea or a meaning, but a collection of images with many meanings. And though one *can* devise formulas that cover most of them, those formulas will be a bit vague and abstract. They *ought* to be abstract, and the reader *ought* to turn, baffled, to the images, to let them speak for themselves.

But does the commedia speak to us today? Its images are all around us; for instance, in cheap and ordinary Pierrot paintings, Columbine dolls, or the patterns on cushion fabrics. But we take such images for granted, as meaningless. They seem like fragments left behind by a whole that has long been broken up. The last time I was in London I walked along Piccadilly on a Sunday morning, when artists were arranging their pictures along the fence of Green Park, and one of them had dozens of Pierrot dolls for sale, each with his black teardrop under his eye, tumbled about on the pavement. If Fellini had come along with his movie cameras, he would have made them speak to us; but left to themselves, they were silent.

There are, of course, people who pay scholarly attention to the commedia. They attend revivals of the old plays and watch the performances of mimes and clowns with the knowledge of connoisseurs. But they clearly constitute a special case.

If we say the commedia speaks to people in general today, we must mean in ways different from theirs. Its ways are in fact today devious and subtle and oblique. Unlike the forty years from 1890 to 1930, ours is not a period when the commedia is a conscious presence and pressure on everyone of imagination. But in all periods of Western culture since the Renaissance—so we believe—the commedia has been a half-conscious presence. To be more precise, our society exerts certain pressures on our imaginations, resulting in certain moods and attitudes (to love, to death, to violence, to family happiness) for which the commedia provides the best imagery. These moods can all be described as consciously brittle. They include both gaiety and sadness, both exhilaration and terror, depending on the aspect of life encountered; but all commedia moods are characterized by a readiness for reversal, an insecurity about their source, a moral self-doubt—by a sense of the artifice of all emotion. To this feeling the commedia scenarios and modes of characterization correspond.

Some historians speak of an "oscillating temperament" as being dominant in Europe at the time the commedia arose there. In *The Waning of the Middle Ages*, Johan Huizinga says that people then moved abruptly from one emotion to another, from anger to fear, from joy to sadness, and that this mobility of emotion was encouraged by various social institutions, including fairs, charivari, and a certain kind of bell ringing. A town's church bells would sound the knell and then, immediately, ring in merry peals; bells of exhilaration would follow bells of despair. Huizinga says the effect must have been "intoxicating." And then there were the public processions, the lurid sermons of itinerant preachers, the public displays of mourning, and the commedia-style players at the fairs. Everything was presented to the mind in terms of violent contrast, and lent a tone of excitement and passion to everyday life—"a perpetual oscillation between despair and distracted joy, between cruelty and pious tenderness." (Huizinga, p. 10. I am indebted for this reference and for the next one to Norbert Elias, to Edmund Leites's *The Puritan Conscience and Modern Sexuality*.)

This mood or temperament is the very opposite of that fostered by the Puritans and their mercantile-bourgeois allies, when the latter won cultural hegemony in seventeenth-century Europe. It was that Puritan *steadiness* and self-respect which animated the builders of the modern world system. But in our day the oscillating temperament has again become prominent. Another historian of culture, Norbert Elias, says of Huizinga's people:

A moment ago they were joking, now they mock each other, one word leads to another, and suddenly from the midst of laughter they find themselves in the fiercest feud . . . the immense outbursts of joy and gaiety, the sudden flaring and uncontrollable force of their hatred and belligerence—all these, like the rapid changes of mood, are in reality symptoms of the same social and personality structure. (Elias, p. 200.)

One can surely see a likeness between this behavior and what is attributed to New Yorkers in Susan Sontag's *Trip to Hanoi*, and to Londoners in Doris Lessing's *The Golden Notebook*.

Our temperament or mood may resemble that of the age that produced the commedia. However, it does not necessarily follow that the literal imagery of the commedia is equally potent for us. Imagery is a matter of fashion; a tragic age will not respond to the tragic imagery of an age gone by. And in fact the commedia is less popular today than it was fifty years ago. But the imagery that *is* in fashion reveals, when probed, a hidden affinity with the commedia.

Let us begin by listing some rather heterogeneous items of the contemporary scene, which have in common a certain aggressive flamboyance: *The Rocky Horror Show*, Andrew Lloyd-Webber's operas, Provincetown in the summer, the Halloween parade in Greenwich Village, a good deal of Glitter Rock, and personalities like David Bowie and Mick Jagger. All these phenomena, very much of the 1980s, use the language of violence and sexual challenge and blend quite disparate elements by means of exaggerated style.

Then take a second list, of quite different items: the New York City Ballet, the American Repertory Theatre's version of Carlo Gozzi's *King Stag*, exhibitions of Picasso's acrobat and Harlequin paintings, any good revivals of Wedekind's or Berg's *Lulu*, or of Giraud's or Schoenberg's *Pierrot Lunaire*. These also can be seen as phenomena of the 1980s, but they are retrospective, and they are triumphs of taste in art. The original works were bold, experimental, disturbing, and that is still discernible, but as produced now they are controlled by a decorum and sophistication that separates them widely from the first list.

Third, one might make a list of contemporary artists and enterprises recognizably deriving from surrealism; using the word *surrealism* to cover all those tendencies in twentieth-century art that shock by disturbing one's sense of decorum, one's self-respect as an art lover, and finally one's sense of reality. Let us take David Hockney's 1980 designs for *Parade*, Poulenc's *Les Mamelles de Tirésias*, and Ravel's *L'Enfant et les sortilèges* as examples. One could add plays by Beckett, films by Fellini and Bergman, music by Cage, dance by Cunningham. In various ways, they all challenge our idea of reality. Surrealism has never been fully acclimatized in the Anglo-Saxon countries; critics have treated it as a temporary departure from the main enterprise of art. But if we look at European artists, at Western art as a whole, surrealism would seem to be the dominant movement since 1918. The artists of modern sensibility, even in the Anglo-Saxon countries, are largely surrealist in inspiration.

On the surface these three lists have only incidental points in common. But deeper down, we want to suggest, there is a substantial family resemblance that takes us back to the commedia. The items in the second list of course derive historically from the commedia; those in the first and third represent today what the commedia represented in the past. That is, they all represent a recoil from our society's dominant respectable values, and attack them by nonserious means. This last point distinguishes the commedia from other forms of radicalism, political or artistic. It may have fostered culturally significant entertainment enterprises and inspire in us a genuine aesthetic response. But there remains something nonserious in its intentions, something defiantly frivolous or sullenly crude, which distinguishes it from other forms of protest.

This nonserious dissent was true of the troupes of commedia actors who have performed throughout the Western world, beginning in Italy in the mid–sixteenth century. Those performers caught the attention of serious painters like Watteau and Picasso, and serious composers like Schoenberg and Stravinsky, but the key to their survival was their appeal to a less refined and less intellectual public.

Commedia belonged to the world of entertainment—to circus and carnival, not to the high arts like tragedy—but in certain periods, it burst out of its ghetto and invaded that other world. This it did in the period 1890–1930, which is the focus of this book. At such times the commedia style became visible in social life, especially in metropolitan centers. In the 1920s, for example, women's cosmetics and the hairstyles and clothes of both sexes directly copied the commedia.

These alterations of style, moreover, have deeper effects than one might suppose, morally, politically, historically. In *Children of the Sun* I followed the careers of some forty Englishmen born into the upper classes between 1900 and 1910. This was the generation for and about which Evelyn Waugh wrote his novels. It included similar writers, like Anthony Powell and Nancy Mitford, but also people who became famous in other, more political areas, like John Strachey, Randolph Churchill, Guy Burgess, and Donald Maclean.

The people of this generation perceived and conceived of one another in almost explicitly commedic terms. (I have taken the liberty of inventing the adjective "commedic.") The terms they actually used were those of the charade, the historical pageant and tableau, the fancy-dress ball, which they attended in the costumes their ancestors had worn in real life. Those ancestors seemed larger and more solid than their descendants. At the same time, being dead, they were less real. The younger generation saw themselves as permanently young—as supple, lightweight, underage. For these people the great schools and Oxbridge colleges, and the stately homes into which the most fortunate were born, and even the ceremonies of England's official life, all felt like a commedic backdrop and setting for their own antics.

The generation before theirs, the readers of Kipling, had begun to see England as a superlatively rich and dangerously vulnerable country; its southern counties especially were a kind of treasure house in which the great palaces of the nobility were so many crown jewels, each set in splendid lawns and formal gardens and picturesque villages. In the generation that came of age after 1918, this vision extended its authority but altered. The material aesthetic splendor glowed more richly, but its justifying moral righteousness faded. The crown jewels looked like loot. To be born the heirs to such loot induced a moral unease for which the commedia provided the natural imagery; and in fact you find such imagery just beneath the surface of Waugh's novels. Characters like Sebastian, Anthony, and Celia in *Brideshead Revisited* are Pierrot, Harlequin, and Columbine, as well as being representative of their class and generation.

To feel oneself to be a commedia character gives one a sense of self that is hard to combine with serious political commitment, as also with religious faith or with marriage and parenthood. But people of that generation did combine those things. Indeed, part of their interest for us is that they left plenty of evidence of *how* they yoked those incompatible drives together. Evelyn Waugh was converted to Roman Catholicism, married, and fathered several children. All these enterprises were clearly sincere, but at the same time in some sense absurd because his deepest sense of himself was commedic.

In the realm of politics and statecraft the most striking cases were Donald Maclean and Guy Burgess. The subjects of comic anecdotes since their schooldays at Eton and Harrow, they were converted to Communism at Cambridge and espoused Russia's world leadership. In the 1950s they finally defected to the Soviet Union, after having betrayed England's state secrets. They had long careers in the Foreign Office and the diplomatic services, despite good reason to suspect their disaffection and their inefficiency, because nobody could take them seriously—because they were felt to be *zanni*, the commedia buffoons. Can anyone, even now, take *them* seriously, even given the seriousness of their offense?

This is a single vivid case of the way ordinary moral and political values may be affected by (undermined by) the moods we call commedic. It would not occur to us to characterize the decade we live in primarily in commedic terms. In our day the commedic imagery is disguised, split apart, and recombined with other imagery, as we showed in the three lists with which we began. But the tendencies it expresses have not, they cannot, cease to function within us and to press upon our minds. Because the conditions under which we live make us see ourselves commedically.

For one thing, the threat of nuclear war, and the possibility of an end to history, undermine that sense of the future which is a necessary part of moral and political seriousness. There is an absurdity about the human situation that was never there before, and which will apparently never go away. We have to make our daily choices by reference to a future that may very likely never occur. This absurdity makes much ordinary seriousness, and many ordinary ambitions, ring hollow and weigh light. In this context, the white-faced, hollow-cheeked grimaces of Pierrot and the defiant and gross capers of Harlequin look to us like appropriate self-expression.

Another condition, not unique to our times but in some ways stronger than ever before, is the crowding in big cities, where people live in tall towers, increasingly dependent on unseen and uncontrollable machines. Sitting in a traffic jam at rush hour, pushing along Fifth Avenue at noon, or crowding into subway trains and elevators undermines one's sense of self—that liberal-individual sense of self which is necessary for the making of moral choices. When you feel reduced to being a body among a thousand bodies, subject to forces beyond your control (commedia acrobatics play upon this feeling) you feel like a laboratory rat forced to live in overcrowded conditions. We are told that traditional identities and traditional behaviors radically alter and that rat homosexuality and rat cannibalism greatly increase under such circumstances.

One striking example of that change in human societies also is the prominence of gay culture in most of our big cities. Historically, the commedia has always held a special attraction for gays, as we see in the work of both Diaghilev and Proust, and in the cult that has grown around them. Whether or not more people are homosexual than before, and whether or not people are more sexually aggressive and experimental than before, we are bound to feel as if they were, because of our new conventions of social expressiveness. This too makes the commedic styles attractive to us, both the strikingly epicene style of Pierrot and the gross sexuality of Harlequin.

And finally—though there are many other such conditions we could cite—there is the pervasiveness and insistence of the world of theater and performance today. For anyone who spends a lot of time in theaters—or watching TV or dancing at discos—the commedia must ring true. The disjunction and recombination of real life and stage life, so prominent in actors' experience, is just what the self-stylizations of the commedia express. *Le style, c'est l'homme,* in a morally subversive sense— people are to be known only as their styles; the criterion of sincerity becomes impossible to apply. An example is the regular partygoer who makes a habit of telling long jokes, who lives in part as a performer, and so needs to see himself in commedic terms. People in ordinary domestic life (celebrated in the Victorian novel) do not style themselves so sharply.

In the life situations for which our traditional morality is best suited, for every man there is a wife, for every woman a husband, and for every child two parents. The great fulfillments of life occur within the home, under the influence of those constellations. But as those situations become rare, and that morality fits a minority rather than a majority, people will find more meaning in commedic stories, which neither belong in the home nor allow for other generations (everyone is the same age in the theater). The erotic obsession of Pierrot for Columbine, the sado-masochism of Harlequin's protection/exploitation of Pierrot, and the half-heartbroken, half-deliberate infidelities of Columbine will assume greater validity.

These are some of the pressures (especially strong on those of us who live in big cities) in 1986, which ensure that the appeal of the commedia, however disguised its forms and substitutes, will never die. That appeal can be located in a pattern, of conscious pathos and reckless laughter, of bleak despair and passionate love of beauty, which lies below the surface of our rationalizations and our behavior. It lies quite close to the surface of much art: ballet, poetry, painting, fiction, music, film, and so on—both past and present. There is, as will be seen, good reason to argue that *the* mythos and ethos of art in itself—art considered apart from its social and moral purposes—is the commedia. The artist as artist is a performer, a purveyor of expressiveness, and so his experience is theatrical. He knows the excitement of applause and the self-accusation of heartlessness; he feels the emptiness of mere egotism following on the fullness of afflatus, and suspects that even his passionate loves have served the purposes of his precious talent. He sees himself, sooner or later, as Pierrot or Harlequin. To put it crudely, *all* art is commedic, all artists are comedians, and the purer the art is, the more intensely is that true.

In what follows, chapters 1, 2, 3, and 8 were written mostly by me, chapters 4, 5, 6, and 7 by John Swan; chapter 9 is the work of both of us equally.

Martin Green

THE TRIUMPH OF PIERROT

Chapter 1.

PIERROT AND HARLEQUIN, PICASSO AND STRAVINSKY

T HIS is a book about why Pierrot and Harlequin meant so much to Picasso and Stravinsky; about why there were so many *Saltimbanques* paintings and *Petrushka* ballets and *Pierrot Lunaire* compositions in the first decades of this century; why the great artists of modernism were so attracted to the forms and themes of the commedia dell'arte. Of course this attraction was only temporary—we are suggesting the limiting dates of 1890 and 1930 for the period during which it held, while modernism stretched beyond in both directions—but during that period the commedia turned up everywhere, fertilizing the minds of composers, painters, novelists, poets, in all the countries of the West. And this is all the more striking because so much in the modernist movement was highbrow, revolutionary, spiritually ambitious, while the commedia has always been lowbrow popular entertainment.

First of all, we must define or describe the commedia. But let us begin with a word of warning against even the process of definition. For not exactitude or serious meaning but nonsense, laughter, comedy in the sense of entertainment, is of the essence of this phenomenon. (That is just what fascinated the serious artists.) It is a subject easily violated by a history-of-ideas approach.

Therefore we will not systematically expound the history of the commedia here. A good deal about that history is only guessed at, because it was such an unofficial or antiofficial phenomenon. Even its emotional colors shifted. The characteristics of even Pierrot and Harlequin changed over time, and you can find the one figure so played as to have the other's (opposite) personality. Not to mention the shifts of names, which mean that what we here call Pierrot is sometimes Pedrolino, sometimes Gilles, or Pagliacci, or Petrushka, or other things. Besides, what matters to us is something the commedia shares with other forms of unofficial theater, as we shall see—with circus, carnival, pantomime, and the like. What we are interested in is the spirit of all "illegitimate" theater (that is, nonliterary theater) of which the commedia is only the most striking example.

So what was the commedia like in its original form? Let us take a very early and very simple scenario, *Li tre becchi, The Three Cuckolds.* (This is given in K. M. Lea's *Italian Popular Comedy,* vol. 2, pp. 582–84.) Let us imagine a simple trestle stage, bare benches for the audience, and a troupe of players who obviously belong to the poorest social class, however distanced they are from it by their special calling. They lack social refinement and literary education. For us, therefore, a book-reading public, they are socially remote, but the distance between them and us brings their expressiveness into sharper focus, lets them show us with acuteness and poignancy aspects of *our* experience hidden from us by our own conventions. They are in effect dumb, as far as *our* vocabularies go, but their dumb gesturing accompanies behavior so *like* our own that it makes our eloquent rationalizations transparent to us.

The play involves three couples and a young man called Leandro. The properties include a washing basket with sheets, a cask, a lemon chest, and a fire. In Act 1, the first couple, Coviello and Cintia, quarrel out of mutual jealousy. But when Cintia exits, Coviello reveals that he wants Flaminia, the wife of his neighbor Pantalone. He knocks on her door (the stage has three doors, one to each house) and the pair plan to get him smuggled into her house inside a chest of lemons. She persuades Pantalone to order such a chest for the kitchen, but Pantalone is himself pursuing an intrigue with Franceschina, the wife of Zanni. Then Leandro enters, amorous of Cintia, and the act ends with his entering her house. (We must of course flesh out this skeleton by imagining how each player corporeally characterizes or caricatures a certain human type—the feeble totterings of the old man, the proud bounciness of the young, the provocative walk and voice of the amorous woman, and so on.)

In Act 2, Zanni, who has carried Coviello into Pantalone's house in the lemon chest, congratulates himself on his own wife's fidelity (and his own freedom), but of course he is mistaken. While Franceschina "playfully" puts the cask over his head, Pantalone sneaks sniggering out of her house and back into his own. Then Flaminia persuades him, Pantalone, to cover his eyes, in amorous play with her, and while he is blinded, Coviello slips out of *her* house, laughing silently. And so on. The act ends with Pantalone and Coviello shouting "cuckold" at each other.

In Act 3, Franceschina borrows a laundry basket from Cintia.

Pantalone climbs in and hides himself under the sheets. Zanni, suspecting what is happening, prepares to empty the basket into a copper full of boiling water. Then he pretends to go away for the day, and Franceschina takes Pantalone into her house. Zanni rushes back, knocks on the door furiously, and prepares to burn the house down. All the couples come together to put the fire out, Leandro explains all the tricks they have been playing on one another, and they are restored to their respective spouses.

I chose this scenario to retell, in compressed form, because it is so much simpler than most. It is familiar to us as the kind of theater we call farce. The difference between the commedia and modern farce lies largely in the performers. The artists of the commedia wore traditional costumes and masks; each played the same role in all productions, and carried some variant on the traditional name for that role. They performed acrobatically, and interrupted the dialogue spontaneously, to show off their *lazzi,* their tricks. To make *Li tre becchi* represent the commedia tradition, we must imagine it played in that style; and we must add the later-developed figures of Pierrot, the love-struck simpleton and victim of life, Columbine, the light-minded sex object, and Harlequin, the brutal and cynical trickster; and the mutual dependency that underlies the conflicts of the three.

The commedia originated in Italy, and came to notice in the sixteenth century. It remained in popular favor there until well into the nineteenth century, according to Robert Storey. In 1611 Flaminio Scala published a collection of its scenarios. Each scenario was a sequence of traditional comic routines strung together by a "plot." The different figures were associated with different Italian towns and spoke in the appropriate local accents and dialects—they were local jokes. They played, in masks that expressed their characteristic traits, outdoors, in squares and at street corners. Each actor played the same role over and over, and became identified with it. They belonged together in permanent troupes, whose members often married, and the roles often passed from brother to brother or from father to son.

One of the most famous of these companies, the Gelosi, came to Paris in 1576, where they were called the Italian Comedians. They were, of course, culturally unlike the classical French theater, which in the seventeenth century played classical dramas by Corneille and Racine. But Molière was a contemporary who studied the Gelosi (he learned especially from the actor who played Scaramouche with them) and there was some interaction between them and his own troupe. In 1658 the Italian Comedians put on *The Stone Guest,* an episode from the Don

Juan legend; in 1665 Molière produced his play *Don Juan,* which includes the stone statue scene; and in 1673 *they* put on a version of the same scene, called *Suite du festin de Pierre.* Through Molière their kind of art entered into a (somewhat uneasy) alliance with high culture.

In France, a foreign country to them, the Comedians could not make use of their mastery of local Italian accents; and so they made more play with mime, and with stage machinery. Moreover, they were under the protection of the king, and cut off from the popular audience that had been their social root. This may help account for the melancholy and aestheticism we begin to associate with them in eighteenth-century France. We find that image primarily in Watteau's famous paintings of them, but essentially the same feeling for them is to be found in the earlier work of Watteau's master, Claude Gillot (1673–1722). Gillot was a designer for the Paris Opera, and he seems to have seen the Italian Comedians—as Watteau did—as embodying the self-consciousness of all theater, but theater at its most wistful, most reflective, most sad.

The term *commedia dell'arte* contrasted it with the *commedia erudita,* which was literary, written down, learned, legitimized comedy. The *arte* was the art of performance—at its purest, of dancing or acrobatics. In France the commedia was said to be *imprévue* or *à l'improviste*—improvised or spontaneous. That meant it could be played only by professionals, whereas amateurs, educated amateurs, could learn and recite lines from a script.

As we shall see, however, that contrast did not always hold true. There were conjunctions of the commedia with literature, especially for women. One commedia actress, Isabella Andreini, published her poems, *Rime,* in 1606, and *Lettere* in 1607; and another Elena Balletti, was welcomed to Paris in 1716 because she was the member of four "academies," those literary and learned societies that began in Renaissance Italy. (In modern times commedia actresses have had a special fascination for men of letters. One thinks of Hemingway and Dietrich, or of Mailer and Monroe, and Gypsy Rose Lee was both stripper and writer.) In fact, women found rare opportunities in the commedia.

In some troupes, impromptu verbal display was as important as mime, for both men and women. And that verbal impromptu ranged from the coarsely humorous to the learnedly euphuistic. The *graciosi* or lover pairs sometimes declaimed an elaborate love rhetoric.

Sometimes, moreover, when a group of intellectuals adopted some commedia troupe as their private preference, the plots were more elaborate and ambitious. In Lesage's *Harlequin Orphée fils* (1718) Harlequin plays a guitar to prove himself the son of Apollo; Columbine yields to him; Pierrot kills himself. The other two marry, but at their wedding Pierrot appears as a ghost and Columbine dies; Harlequin goes to hell in search of her. In Jean-Gaspard Deburau's *Le Marchand d'habits* (1842) Pierrot loves a duchess and is enabled to marry her when he kills an old-clothesman and dresses himself up as a grandee; but at the wedding the murdered man's ghost forces Pierrot to waltz with him and impales him on his own sword. Both these plots obviously invoked the same themes as classical drama, and Théophile Gautier compared the second one with Shakespeare. (His essay was entitled "Shakespeare aux Funambules," the last word being the name of Deburau's theater.) He called Deburau the most perfect actor who ever lived, and this one actor has been central to our idea of the commedia. Much that was otherwise amorphous crystallized in him.

In England there were no Italian players. The commedia figures came from France and were incorporated into the native pantomime. This move up north, from Italy to France, and from France to England, was typical of Renaissance luxuries, in food, perfumes, jewels, and clothes; and the commedia came as a Renaissance luxury, of entertainment. Pantomime is said to have won great public favor in London by 1723, and to have reached its peak of perfection a century later, in the clown Grimaldi. Many of its players and their playlets came from France.

One of the men in charge of Astley's renowned circus, Laurent, had been a famous clown in France, and his sons started the Théâtre des Funambules, where Philippe Laurent played Harlequin, and where Deburau made himself the greatest of recorded Pierrots in the 1830s and 1840s.

On Deburau we must dwell a moment, because he was a point of entry into literature for the commedia figures, a bridge by which they passed over from entertainment into high culture. This entry happened in Paris forty years before it happened in London, and that is a large reason why Paris was the great nineteenth-century capital of European art. In Théodore de Banville's poem "Pierrot" are the lines: "La blanche lune aux cornes de taureau,/Jette un regard de son oeil en coulisse,/À son ami, Jean-Gaspard Deburau." (The moon that's white with horns that bend,/Casts her glance into the wings,/At J. G. Deburau, her friend.) The moon and Pierrot were always linked. Both were emblems of fantasy, of "poetry"—that opposite to the realism of broad daylight, and to the gross fertility of the hot sun.

Born in 1796, Deburau arrived in Paris in 1814 as one of his father's troupe of tumblers and ropedancers. In 1825 he began to play Pierrot at the Funambules. He simplified the image of the character physically, and intensified it emotionally, by wearing a black skullcap in place of a floppy hat, and getting rid of the ruff around the neck. A group of lit-erary intellectuals discovered him, grew enthusiastic, and wrote scripts for him. Flaubert wrote *Pierrot au sérail* in 1840, Gautier, *Pierrot post-hume* in 1847. They became fascinated with the commedia in general. Gavarni drew a gallery of Parisian portraits as *L'Ecole des Pierrots* in 1851. Baudelaire and his friends rediscovered the greatness of Watteau as the painter of *Gilles* (recently renamed *Pierrot*) and *The Italian Comedians Leaving Paris*, and other paintings with no commedia subject but the same commedia spirit. Later in the century poets put the commedia into verse; in various ways this is true of Verlaine, Rimbaud, and Mallarmé. But the really striking case was Jules Laforgue, who habitually wrote about, *and as*, Pierrot.

There was a succession of famous Pierrot performers on the Paris stage. But Deburau seems to have presented the most various as well as the most intense version. Duchartre describes him as being "pale as the moon, mysterious as silence, supple and acute as the serpent, tall and straight as the gallows." The first is the aspect beautifully caught by Jean-Louis Barrault in the film about Deburau, *Les Enfants du Paradis* (U.S. title: *Children of Paradise*). But Deburau was also involved in violence, both on stage and off. He was charged with murder in 1836, and he played Pierrot as a murderer in some of his playlets.

This connection with crime is not unique in the commedia's history. A London pantomime of 1724 presented Harlequin as Jack Sheppard (the highwayman) in prison. Criminality is just the sharpest expression of the commedia's "illegitimacy." Gay's *Beggar's Opera*—and Brecht's *Threepenny Opera*—are commedic in spirit. Thus crime is an essential aspect of the commedia tradition as we inherit it today. Nevertheless, it makes sense to connect this aspect with Deburau in particular, and to stress its novelty in the mid–nineteenth century. Criminality does not seem to have been so important to the original Italian players—or, at least, not murder. The crimes we associate with the original com-media dell'arte are thievery and fraud. In the nineteenth century, more-over, this murder was further specified as big-city, newspaper-reported murder, and characteristically as "horrible." By the end of that century, the case of Jack the Ripper was adapted, again and again, for commedic purposes; a horrible crime, but also—in newsboy accents—"horrible crime!"; a "popular murder," responded to with emotional luxury but not with moral seriousness.

This is the second large-scale adaptation of the commedia tradition, after its eighteenth-century adaptation to court audiences, with the consequent association with rococo painting and music, and with ele-

gant melancholy. And the third adaptation—the female figure of incarnate sexuality, a destructive life force insusceptible of moral or rational
control—may also be associated with Jack the Ripper, for she is often
presented as his provocation or his ultimate victim. Frank Wedekind,
at the beginning of the twentieth century, introduced that female figure
and that kind of murderer, together, into his Lulu plays. In our century,
this also has been a part of the commedia tradition, though it was not
there before. Marilyn Monroe, for instance, is a commedic figure for us
because she embodied this idea.

The Revival of the Commedia

The history of the commedia before 1890 is significant for us mostly
because of the cult of the commedia thereafter. Up to 1890 Pierrot and
Harlequin had been popular entertainment for most serious artists (except for the group around Deburau) or else just episodes in the history
of art.

But in our period, Pierrot and Harlequin suddenly leaped to life in
everyone's minds, colors glowing, limbs moving, not as history but as
archetypes: forms both personal and impersonal that transcend psychology and history and all the categories of realism—the archetypes of art.

This phenomenon was part of the history of what we call modernism. At the end of the nineteenth century, Western culture began producing a revolutionary new kind of art, which was inspired by *modern*
experience (experience felt to be unlike that of the past) and which
rebelled against social norms and norm-subordinated art. When we turn
back to nineteenth-century novels, portraits, symphonies, we feel ourselves in a different world, in which half the detail given seems superfluous, and *from* which half the things that concern us in art seem to
be missing. And those changes in the arts have affected other parts of
our lives: the lettering and texts of our advertisements, the displays in
our shop windows, our dances and popular songs. But it is not only a
matter of artistic styles. There are also nonaesthetic modes of thought
and feeling that can be called modernist: a heavy stress on the erotic,
a conviction that God is dead, a general anxiety, a reverence for the
unconscious, a social and philosophical skepticism. So these ideas, too,
stand behind the word.

We are concerned with one phase in that great movement. Modernism began in a form we call symbolism (or *symbolisme*, because so
many of its ideas were defined in France and reached other countries
from there). This wave was indeed highbrow and solemn, and we can

take our examples of it from the operas of Wagner and the poetry of Wagner enthusiasts like Mallarmé. Then came that reaction against such solemnity which took the commedia as its banner imagery, a reaction whose myriad forms this book will describe. And then, at the end of our period, there came a turn toward something less playful, something more rigorous: an attraction to Communist politics or Roman Catholic religion, often. But the three waves were continuous, or overlapping; the one was not obliterated by the next, and some artists, like Picasso, went through several radically different phases while remaining modernists.

In parallel with the arts, social life-styles changed, especially in the big cities; and in this matter of social effectiveness, the commedia phase of modernism was more important than the other two. Commedia images like Pierrot and Harlequin became popular decorative motifs. Entertainments like the music halls in London, and (later) blues singing in America, became more generally popular than they were before. They came to represent art in general. And quite apart from entertainment, in the 1920s women wore something like clowns' makeup (circles of red on their cheekbones, white noses and chins) while the men had hairless faces and brushed their hair back to make a skullcap like Pierrot's. Reacting against Edwardian elaborateness, both men and women wore unisex clothes (for instance, pullovers) or sports clothes (simplifying the body to a single stroke of life) that made the two sexes look like each other, and like acrobats.

The 1920s was the time when this commedia stylization of social life was most pronounced, and most commented on, but it had begun earlier in this period. The first time an English lady was shown painting her face on stage was in Somerset Maugham's play *Lady Frederick*, which was performed in London in 1906. The spectacle caused a scandal, implying as it did not only that ladies painted, but that theatergoers took an interest in how they did so; but it was a mild and pleasurable scandal that was part of the Edwardian mood. That mood, long before the 1920s, was hedonist, theater-oriented, cosmetics- and artifice-oriented—commedic.

Gradually, during the years 1890–1930, this mood expressed itself in a fondness for the commedia images. This habit took hold, naturally, earlier and more completely in some places than in others. We can take an example from England and from literature, which took the commedia infection later than other arts in other countries. In 1926 Cyril Beaumont, who was then England's leading balletomane, published *History of Harlequin*. He described Pierrot thus: "The butt of fools, the sport of bullies, the vanquished in love—he has aroused sympathy from his first birthday. His pale, woebegone countenance, his listless air, the long drooping sleeves of his jacket—everything about him incites pity." He contrasts Harlequin, whose performance "consisted of a series of extravagant capers, of violent movements and outrageous blackguardisms. He was at once insolent, mocking, clownish, and, above all, obscene." (Beaumont, p. 25.) Beaumont's book treats Harlequin as a living person, whose century-long biography he is writing, in much the same style as Virginia Woolf used in her 1928 novel, *Orlando*. (That commedic novel is an adaptation of the archetypal figures to the subject matter of literature and history.)

Beaumont's book was dedicated to Osbert and Sacheverell Sitwell, and the latter contributed a long preface. Indeed, the Sitwells' own writings, and their life-style, were playfully fantastic in the same way. This preface draws connections between the commedia and many other things; for instance, the contemporary Russian ballet.

Sitwell describes as the masterpiece of painting in this century the curtain Picasso painted for Cocteau's ballet *Parade*, which modernized the insignia of the commedia by adding to the usual harlequin masks a Negro boxer, a Spanish guitarist, a cowboy, and a cowgirl. But Sitwell also connects Harlequin with the English music hall traditions of Dan Leno and Nellie Wallace, and with the circus clowns like Grock and the Fratellini brothers. He saw that the essence of the commedia was, and always will be, popular and commercial entertainment. We can associate it with any kind of "theater," even the highest kind: indeed, with any art form which parades its artifice, its untruth. But it is always rooted in that most vulgar and artificial of art forms, illegitimate theater. In our period, that art form came to stand for all the others.

"We cannot now imagine the theatre without Pierrot. He has become the personification of the artist in humanity, translated into the world of the theatre." So wrote Irene Mawer in *The Art of Mime*, published in London in 1932. Her rhetoric is sentimental, her account of Pierrot is only partial, and the whole Pierrot is only a part of the commedia dell'arte. But the quotation is interesting for our argument because of its date and because of the boldness of its claims. In 1932 Pierrot embodied the artist, all artists, in all humanity; he was the emblematic hero of sensibility.

Nowadays, we recognize, unthinkingly, Pierrot's image in advertising, in mime shows, as a decorative motif on shower curtains, tea cosies, men's ties, cheap pottery. In decorative and fantastic patterns—on the unregarded wallpaper of our lives—his image lies scattered all around us. But its *meaning?* It has no meaning now, for most of us. However, for forty years of modernism, things were very different.

And our explanation must begin with the eternal triangle of Pierrot, Columbine, and Harlequin. (The other commedia figures—the Dottone, the Punchinello, the Capitano, and so on—are peripheral.) Pierrot, at least in modern times, wears a black skullcap, white floppy pants and jacket, a pale, gaunt makeup. Harlequin wears tights, designed in contrasting diamonds of color, often spangled, and carries a stick. Columbine is sumptuously and sensually adorned. The naive, defenseless, moonstruck Pierrot adores the lovely Columbine, who has wit and feeling enough to appreciate his worth but is too light-minded to resist the coarse and brutal Harlequin, who is himself bound to Pierrot in a mocking, rueful, treacherous comradeship.

It is worth noting the antimarital and antifamilial tendency of this triangle. These three are in love with one another, sometimes erotically obsessed, but not joined in matrimony, much less in parenthood. Harlequin and Pierrot and Columbine as a constellation represent quite different values from the young father, mother, and child who shine through the Victorian novel as the ideal human group. This is the group to be seen at the end of Dickens's novels and, in their most powerful representation, in Tolstoy's *War and Peace* and *Anna Karenina.* Pierrot and Columbine cannot be imagined as having such a future. First of all, they are not "real," but also they are not "virtuous"—such an idea does not apply to them—and so they do not deserve happiness.

As for the scenarios in which the three main figures move together, they are often—in both the old commedia and its modern counterparts, like the early movies—only a series of standard situations, giving occasion for the players' best comic or sentimental routines. Quite often in sixteenth-century theaters or twentieth-century film studios the plot, indeed, the script, is no more than a sheet of paper pinned up in the wings, listing situations and routines; the lover hidden under the bed or singing a serenade; the visit to the dentist; the drunk accosting the policeman; the con men tricking each other; the imaginary ladder to climb or meal to eat; the somersault holding the full tumbler; the violin solo, half parody, half pathos.

But there are many other figures besides those three in the commedia gallery. There is Pantaloon, the miserly, overreaching, credulous, talkative old fool—the cuckolded husband par excellence. He was played in early movie comedies by W. C. Fields, Oliver Hardy, and John Bunny. There is the Doctor, the pretentious pedagogue who in the old days spouted Latin, but is still recognizable in Groucho Marx or W. C. Fields

in the twentieth century, blinding their victims with science. There is
the Captain, the bully and boaster, the would-be man of force; played
by Fields, Wallace Beery, and Ford Sterling. There is the pair of comic
servants—Laurel and Hardy, Chico and Harpo Marx. These were called
zanni in the old commedia, and zanies in modern times. And there are
other figures, so absorbed into our experience of entertainment that we
no longer think of them as belonging to the commedia—the clown of
the circus, often the subject of musical plays and films, and Punch and
Judy.

These figures, too, are not meant for happy marriage, or for parenthood, or for the virtues of citizenship. They do not belong in the same
part of our mind as our plans for our own futures. It is realistic or serious
art which mixes with our purposeful dreams. These figures preside over
that part of our experience and our selves which does not make any
sense—the part we laugh at or fear.

But the commedia is serious in its own way, indeed, revolutionary.
Deburau seemed—and this of course recommended him to his intellectual admirers—to represent the proletariat. His audience was proletarian, his theater was socially the opposite of the Comédie-Française (there
was often hostility between the two theaters), and the spirit of his performance seemed politically subversive in the atmosphere of mid-
nineteenth-century Paris, where revolution was never far from people's
thoughts.

There was also a touch of madness in Deburau's Pierrot, who seemed
driven to the verge of insanity by life's remorseless frustration of all his
desires. You went to his theater to laugh, and to admire his technique,
but you felt a sadness and a touch of horror as you watched. And that
mixture of feelings came to seem the purest form of the aesthetic experience. Such feelings formed a hinterland to Deburau's Pierrot performance, and became a foreground in, for instance, T. S. Eliot's early
poems, inspired by Laforgue.

Commedia Art as a Stage in Modernism

Eliot wrote Pierrot poetry up to the time of *The Waste Land*. His later
work, such as *The Four Quartets*, cannot be described in that way, though
the continuities are strong between that and the early poems. But in
this discontinuity and development, this continuity within change, Eliot
is representative of the artists of modernism as a whole, the painters
like Picasso, the composers like Stravinsky, the poets like Eliot himself.

The modernist artist's attraction to the commedia, we are suggesting, came between that first stage of modernism we call symbolism, and the one we might call rigorism—meaning by the last a commitment to theoretical rigor, to highbrow harshness, seriousness, and difficulty, either within art, like a commitment to cubism (Picasso) or atonalism (Schoenberg), or outside art, like a commitment to Communism (Brecht) or to Christianity (Eliot).

We see artists embracing these two kinds of rigor towards the end of this period. However, more important for the beginning of our argument is symbolism, the stage in the development of the modern that preceded the attraction to the commedia. We have to understand both its temporarily compelling power, in the years when every ambitious artist was a symbolist, and how its hegemony over the artistic mind of Europe was later subverted and dislodged.

Symbolism can be defined most simply as art built around symbols, which are images to which more than ordinary potency and significance are attributed and which become in some sense magical or religious. (Pierrot and Harlequin are not magical or religious; they are stereotypes rather than archetypes.) And it seems to us that the most fruitful way to think about the movement is to associate it with Wagner, with archetypes like Siegfried and Brünnhilde and Valhalla. Symbolism was a translation into terms the other arts could use of the effects which Wagner had achieved in his music dramas, effects which expressed the same general aspiration for art.

In philosophical terms, Wagner had aspired to give a voice, by the means of art, to the unconscious, to that stress on the life deep in man and nature which underlay and could undermine all the reason and morality. The unconscious has been the major preoccupation of European thought in the nineteenth and twentieth centuries, and Nietzsche hailed Wagner's music dramas as a translation of Schopenhauer's philosophy of the unconscious into intoxicating art. In his third "Untimely Meditation" he discussed Wagner's precursor; the fourth was on Wagner himself.

The music dramas expressed an enormous ambition, to displace religion (and any other contender for the throne of culture) and to replace it with art. Because it expressed this idea so powerfully, Wagner's music had a great influence on others. Gustav Mahler said, "There is only Beethoven and Wagner, and after them nobody." (Magee, p. 60.) People "made the pilgrimage" to Bayreuth, the "Holy Land" of the music dramas, and were "converted" to Wagner. Debussy, Mahler, Schoenberg, Berg, Massenet, all bore his imprint. Stravinsky (the commedia composer par excellence) was the only great composer of the generation just after Wagner who refused to acknowledge or manifest any debt.

But there soon came a general reaction against Wagner and against symbolism. The music dramas provoked disbelief and distaste, as well as reverence and pilgrimage. The creaking stage machinery of Bayreuth (the metaphorical as well as the literal—the home life of the royal pair, Richard and Cosima) came to seem in the worst bourgeois taste. Above all, the mythology Wagner worked with, the gods, giants, and dwarfs of the Ring, the Liebestod and the Rainbow Bridge, the swan knights and Grail ceremonies, went against the grain of the new taste. It was all too imposing, too ceremonial, too institutional. It did not suffi- ciently express the *critical* activity of the modern mind. Nietzsche re- belled when he saw the way the Wagnerian myth served the purposes of the Second Reich, set up in 1871. But even when separated from that particular politics, the myth remained "political" in the sense that it was an equivalent to, a substitute for, state power or church power. It was, in architectural terms, a cathedral, and that made many artists uncomfortable. They preferred the incomplete, the shifting, the crazily composite—a vaudeville program, not a cathedral service.

Wagner did not combine with his "unconscious" flow of melody the other element (of self-irony, self-parody, self-conflict, self-fragmentation) that is just as vital a component of the modern sensibility. The grand style had to be renounced, mocked, shattered; and the impulse to mock took its banner imagery from the commedia dell'arte. Diaghilev and his friends in the *World of Art* group in St. Petersburg were great admirers of Wagner; but their Ballets Russes, the supreme single mani- festation of the commedia in twentieth-century form, were brilliant fragmentary exotica—an anti-Ring. Commedia modernism was to be, paradoxically, vulgar.

The Shame of the Commedia

The traditional view of art's place within culture is suggested by the myth that Robert Payne retells in his book on Charlie Chaplin. Pan foolishly challenged Apollo to a test in music, Pan having been intoxicated by the incense burned to him by Midas the plutocrat. Of course Pan was defeated in the contest; Tmolus, the appointed judge, gave the prize to Apollo, and Pan went into hiding, in which he has remained. The commedia can be seen as a manifestation of the vulgar, Panic urges in man, and it has traditionally hidden its face before Apollo, the god of art, and before the Apollonian principle in culture.

In seventeenth-century France, Madame de Maintenon, who represented moral and intellectual seriousness at the court of Louis XIV, had the Italian players exiled from Paris to a distance of thirty leagues. She was the protectress of serious art, such as Racine's plays, and the Italian players were the enemy of art in that sense. They had been brought to Paris by the Medici family, when the latter married into French royalty, as one of their Italian luxuries. It is striking how intimately the Medici kings and queens wrote to their protégés about their private lives, but that intimacy is itself proof that the players stood outside all the structures of moral and political seriousness.

The same saving distance between the commedia and politics, between fantasy and reality, was maintained in other times and places; and the same superiority was attributed—by those in power in society—to politics and "reality." When in 1843 the king of Denmark built the Tivoli gardens (a center of commedia theater, and of commedic entertainments of all kinds) it was on the site of his capital city's old fortifications. Art danced over the field of battle. Georg Carstensen, who persuaded him to build the pleasure gardens, told Christian VIII that "where the people are kept amused, they forget politics," but it was understood that in case of war (when life gets serious) the theater buildings would be burned down, to rebuild forts there. Denmark drifted out of history's main currents and the gardens survived, preserving a strong tradition of commedia in Copenhagen, which Isak Dinesen in the twentieth century translated into literary form.

Thus the irreverent spirit of the commedia was lodged in the unofficial forms of culture and the low forms of art, in London's music halls as opposed to her great theaters. Only in modern times was it taken seriously, when art assembled an army sworn to take seriously whatever society did not. Then we find an eminently serious man like Schoenberg composing *Pierrot Lunaire*. The distance between pre-1890 manifestations of the commedia and those of our forty years is suggested by Robert Storey: "To move from the etiolated, wraith-like clown who wanders, moonstruck, in and out of the vague, disquieting harmonies of Schoenberg's expressionistic song-cycle to a quick and capricious buffoon of sixteenth-century Italy, who darts about a trestle stage in the glare of a bright noon sun, is to take a long step indeed, in point of both history and the imagination." (Storey, p. 3.) Why? Because Schoenberg's music aimed very high, artistically and culturally, while the traditional Pierrot did not.

In post-1930 art we again meet the commedia figures, mostly in low art forms, for instance, in the slapstick, transvestism, parody, and custard pie of television serials. Ambitious writers such as Doris Lessing make little use of that repertoire. But the forty-year triumph of Pierrot has left behind some traces; low forms are sometimes now employed by major artists. Today we can recognize the commedia's priapic treatment of sex not only in burlesque and vaudeville but in the fiction of Philip Roth, Norman Mailer, Kingsley Amis, and Vladimir Nabokov. If we compare their treatment of sex with that offered by comparably ambitious novelists of a hundred years ago, we shall see that the commedia sensibility has now become available to serious fiction writers. That sensibility was what we now call "male chauvinist."

Women were less differentiated than men in the old commedia; all women were Woman, whatever else they might be; and modern comedy films show a similar pattern, though less pronounced. Women were a prominent presence, but with a single significance of sexual identity; the actresses did not wear masks as the actors did, but were gorgeously dressed and frankly erotic. There were also the grotesques, some fat, some thin—Cinderella's sisters or Fellini's monsters. These were, at least in the old days, often men in drag, but the statement they made was still about women. As types we can distinguish the bold and experienced Columbine from the Inamorata, the sweet young thing destined to marry the *jeune premier*; the latter two together were the *graciosi*, both of them often inert figures, allowed to take center stage only for sentimental duets. But both women were sex objects.

As we have said, however, when compared with the legitimate stage, the commedia is seen to have given actresses more chance to become stars. (Even in legitimate theater, for example, in Shakespeare, women get more scope in comedy than in tragedy.) And when they did so, they represented much more than mere sex appeal. Thus Isabella Andreini, who belonged to Flaminio Scala's company in sixteenth-century Italy, was a Latin scholar, belonged to several academies, and was honored by Tasso. Silvia, of Riccoboni's troupe in eighteenth-century France, was a famous exponent of roles in Marivaux's legitimate plays. And Antonia Veronese, called Camille, was famous in the latter part of that century.

Actresses of this stature are sometimes referred to (as in Henry James's novel, *The Tragic Muse*), as Muses, because they embody the idea of art in all its dignity. Edmund Wilson used that term to describe Edna St. Vincent Millay, and it has perhaps been used more often about women writers. But Millay was an actress, too, and in fact Wilson used it apropos of her recitations of her own poetry. So it seems appropriate to use it here, for that commedia role which gave most initiative and dignity to women.

It was women like these who played the great tragedienne roles of nineteenth-century French theater, women like Rachel, Réjane, and Bernhardt, and who so impressed the nineteenth-century imagination. These actresses played classical roles, like Racine's Phèdre, which belonged to legitimate theater, but in themselves, as living legends, they belonged to the commedia. One might say that that so-often-replayed story of the whore with the heart of gold (embodied most perfectly in Dumas's play, *La Dame aux Camélias*) makes most sense if one takes the woman to be a star actress rather than a mere whore. Women writers of the nineteenth century were particularly fascinated by this actress figure, as we see not only in George Sand's work, but also in George Eliot's (Lydgate's French actress in *Middlemarch*) and in Charlotte Brontë's (Lucy Snow's visit to the theater in *Villette*). Indeed, such actresses sometimes played the literal Pierrot; Bernhardt appeared in *Pierrot, assassin de sa femme,* and Jane May in *L'Enfant prodigue.*

And when the serious novel makes this use of the actress—as a figure of semicriminal daring—we see an example of just how the light-minded commedia has often served the more serious half of our culture, how ideas were mirrored to and fro between them.

Strategically speaking, the low forms were accommodated to high ambitions above all by means of parody, irony, and fragmentation. These three artistic strategies obviously have a lot in common. You parody something just by fracturing it, and you ironize just by juxtaposing fragments. The three can be grasped as a single complex pattern, the one feature implying or involving the others. (Sometimes indeed, as in some Diaghilev ballets, this pattern amounts to a simply exotic and elaborate framing, which alienates the action and allows the audience a freer response, but explicit irony and parody are rarely far to seek.) This is perhaps the best guide, at the level of form, to the presence of the commedia sensibility in a given artist, and it can be pointed to in Stravinsky and Picasso. But it is easiest to demonstrate in a literary case, the French Pierrot poet, Jules Laforgue.

There is a special interest for us in Laforgue's parodic play about Hamlet; for *Hamlet* may fairly be taken to represent the serious drama, and thus the opposite of the commedia, of Harlequin and Pierrot. This opposition has often been remarked, because of the comparable life span of the two kinds of theater. Allardyce Nicoll in his *The World of Har-*

lequin points out the opposite careers of the two figures, Hamlet and Harlequin. 1601 was the date both of *Hamlet*'s composition, and of the first datable painting of Harlequin; 1611 saw Scala's book of commedia scenarios, and 1623 Shakespeare's First Folio. But Hamlet is a character and a play, indeed a *tragedy;* Harlequin is a role and an entertainment—something much lower down the culture hierarchy. One belongs to Apollo, the other to Pan. Laforgue, however, though a highbrow artist, may be said to turn Hamlet into Harlequin in his play; to subdue the official high-culture genre, tragedy, to at least the appearance of entertainment.

His Hamlet is no tragic prince, but an ignominiously comic figure (minutely described to resemble Laforgue himself), a Deburau, a sad but vicious clown, a Pierrot or Harlequin. Jean-Louis Barrault (a versatile actor, who has played Shakespeare's Hamlet, *and* Laforgue's Hamlet, *and* Deburau's Pierrot) described Laforgue's play as "variations on *Hamlet,* written by Hamlet himself." (Arkell, p. 191.) Laforgue's Ophelia is called Lili, and could remind us of Nabokov's Lolita; Hamlet says Ophelia isn't a real name but pure theater. It belongs with Cordelia, Lelia, Coppelia, Camelia—all names from the commedia tradition. Laforgue takes from Shakespeare's tragedy only the graveyard scene and the scene of Hamlet's play. Fragments are all he needs. His dialogue is full of provocative anachronisms, and there is also some deliberate ugliness; Hamlet gratuitously kills a bird. And by the end Hamlet becomes a sort of 1890s aesthete or decadent. He dies with Nero's words on his lips: *"Qualis artifex pereo"* (What an artist dies in me).

By engaging in parody of this crude kind, Laforgue proclaims his affinity, his preference, for low culture, which is typical of commedia modernists even at their subtlest. (One thinks of T. S. Eliot's *Sweeney Agonistes,* and parts of *The Waste Land.*) Another notable motif of the low genres after 1890 was the Fun Factory. This phrase is the title Fred Karno gave to his establishment in Camberwell, London, in the 1890s, where he trained several troupes at a time in mainly wordless slapstick—with some song-and-dance burlesque—and sent them out to variety theaters and music halls to perform. Among the big names that emerged from that training were Max Miller, Stan Laurel, Harry Weldon, and Charlie Chaplin. And later in his career Chaplin found another fun factory in the Mack Sennett studios, where he began his Hollywood work. But the phrase can be taken, metaphorically, as a powerful image of all art, as seen by a commedia artist.

This image reminds us also of the original commedia, which also had numbers of actors each doing his special tricks, with only a dictatorial director to impose some order on them, because there was no script, no author, no meaning, no message. This is clearly the very opposite of the image of art we associate with, say, Emerson's poems, or *Walden*, or, for that matter, Michelangelo painting the Sistine Chapel ceiling—the solitary artist wrestling heroically with giant themes.

Commedia also makes something of a cult of laughter, of which we can see literary equivalents in Kipling, Wodehouse, and Waugh. Pierrot is not only a figure of fun; since T. S. Eliot was in his early years, like Laforgue, a Pierrot poet, clearly Pierrot is not merely popular entertainment. One side of him, as we have said, is highly aesthetic, wistful, elegant, graceful. There is also, on the other side, the commedia's aptitude for themes of madness and murder. Pierrot and Harlequin can be terrifying. Nevertheless, the idea of laughter as a cult does lead us to something generally true about the commedia, and that is its conscious brittleness of mood, its promise of change, its instability, its artificiality.

This separates the commedia decisively from serious art. If we compare this artificiality with the sort of moral realism represented by *War and Peace*, we see that Tolstoy included in his novel, or took account of, every kind of experience. If a given scene in that novel makes the reader think of some other experience which has escaped the control of Tolstoy's philosophy, upsets the broadly understanding mood the artist is putting him into, then that constitutes a criticism of the novel—the novelist has failed.

Commedia art is the reverse. It promises to fill to the brim a cup which almost any other experience, mood, or truth would shatter. It is an art that Truth in any of its aspects would shatter. This is another way that it announces itself illegitimate, unrespectable. The cult of laughter, the invitation "Let's laugh as hard as we can," extended by for instance Evelyn Waugh in his humorous work, can emblemize that implicit trespass against Truth, that artificiality and incipient pathos.

Motifs and Forms

Because of that untruthfulness, that artifice, some commedia figures call for both laughter and tears at the same time, and for the fear of violence, and for the charm of romance—all together. The incompatibility of the various responses amplifies that pathos of artifice. Perhaps the most famous single example of this is the tragic clown—in opera, Rigoletto and Pagliacci, in film, Giulietta Masina. (She consciously followed Chaplin in *La Strada*, and Chaplin himself was a great tragic clown.) In literature we find this effect in Nathanael West's *Miss Lonelyhearts* and *The Day of the Locust.*

We have just alluded to one of the contemporary artists most concerned with clowns—the filmmaker, Federico Fellini. He has made a television program, *The Clowns,* about living clowns, and has built his finest films around the great female clown, Masina. And his work reminds us of another feature of this kind of art, the circular parade of figures. Very often his films end with such a procession of seriogrotesques—*Amarcord, La Dolce Vita,* 8½, *Juliet of the Spirits, The Clowns.* The actors, and the people they represent, display themselves. They are actors displaying their skills, their beauty, or their challenging deformity, but they are also people humbly acknowledging their own shame or triviality.

Such a parade (typically associated with fairground music, played on a concertina or a merry-go-round machine) corresponds in literature to a circular convention of plot. In Arthur Schnitzler's play and film *Reigen (La Ronde),* an erotic chain—each beloved becoming a lover in his/her turn—ends where it began (Schnitzler also wrote on specifically commedia subjects). This can be seen also in Evelyn Waugh's "entertainment" fictions, which return at their ends to their starting points, and parenthesize themselves in artifice. Such a circle or cycle stresses recurrence and aesthetic form, at the cost of moral purpose or rational meaning. It also stresses theatricality, the transiency and ignobility (and charm) of performance, an idea which pervades all commedia art. Another example is the parade of artists before a performance, a self-advertisement to a prospective audience at a fair, which is often used in other films, like Fassbinder's, and in ballet, as in Cocteau's *Parade* and Stravinsky's *Petrushka.*

Ballet is one of the art forms most completely animated by the commedia spirit, especially in its love of low aesthetic effects lifted up to the heights of elegance. The dazzling success of Diaghilev's Ballets Russes throughout Europe and America between 1905 and 1925 altered the idea of art for artists in nearly every field, and is one of the most important examples of the triumph of Pierrot. As we shall see, that ballet company did learn literally from the commedia tradition, and every aspect of its art—plot, music, costume, and the inner life of the company—expressed that idea.

We have already mentioned other forms that are linked to the commedia as distinct from legitimate theater—circus, carnival, freak shows, pantomime, interludes, acrobatics. Let us dwell on only one more such, marionettes, which perhaps represent the idea of stereotypes more clearly than any other form. Their inhumanity constitutes a hollow space, inside which the human meanings reverberate and swell to thunder, and the audience that identifies with them feels those meanings become larger than life. Duchartre, writing in 1929, describes the marionette theater as the last vestige of the commedia, and Irene Mawer (in 1932) says, "They are more passionate than rhetoric, more comic than farce, and, with it all, they hold some hidden secret charm which is indefinable and secret." (Mawer, p. 59.)

Both writers take an elegiac tone, about marionettes as about the commedia figures. But modern television has given us popular marionette shows (the most famous being the Muppets). There is in fact a striking contemporary fascination with puppets, as we see in the androids of the science fiction films *Blade Runner* and *Alien*. In the time that Duchartre and Mawer were writing, it seemed that such imaginative forms were dying, overcome by the hegemonic powers of legitimate theater, which served the purpose of the bourgeois class. Before 1890 only eccentric geniuses like Kleist and Hoffman took an interest in puppets, and even in the 1890–1930 period it could seem that only artists cared for them. But now, at the end of the twentieth century, it is legitimate theater that looks fragile, like so many other institutions of Western culture.

Sightings

In this last part of our first chapter, one or two other ways to approach the commedia are offered, in the spirit of surveyors or gunnery officers trying to determine exactly where the target lies. The first of them has to do with religion.

The commedia was never a religious form, or group of forms. One of the ways it distinguished itself from symbolism was in its secularization of the modernist mood, its renunciation of the spiritual-religious ambitions of the great symbolists. This change is something we see with special clarity in Russia, in the transition from the symbolist modernists led by Vyacheslav Ivanov to the commedia modernists led by Mikhail Kuzmin. The latter group, the Clarists or Acmeists, turned away from the religious aspirations of the symbolists, and indeed away from all cultural responsibility, toward a bittersweet immoralism. They were semiofficially dubbed Decadents; and in a sense (though that term is too loaded for general use) one can say that the commedia movement everywhere was Decadent.

But if commedia art was not itself religious, it did quite often *go with* religion in the artist—it often found a rather incongruous partner in piety and even ecclesiasticism. Thus one justification for using the term Decadent about them is to evoke the memory of those artists of late nineteenth-century Paris (and elsewhere) who combined aestheticism, and indeed immoralism, with religiosity; who can therefore, if rather luridly, illuminate this part of our pattern for us. We are thinking here of novelists like J. K. Huysmans (À rebours/Against the Grain) and Joséphin Péladan (Le Vice suprême/The Supreme Vice) and of composers like Erik Satie; who was deeply influenced by those writers, and who for some years maintained a Rosicrucian chapel of his own, in that same spirit of mingled piety and parody. One Satie scholar has described Péladan's fiction as having an atmosphere of incense, lubricious mysticism, exotic perversion, and hermaphrodite frolics. (Harding, p. 24.)

Musically speaking, however, Satie was strongly attracted to Gregorian chant—both as something from the past to appreciate and as a style to compose in himself—and this represents that more serious and dignified side to this religiosity. He combined a love of this traditional and austere music with other defiantly modernist and frivolous or self-destructing styles. And in this combination or alternation of the grandly traditional with the irreverently experimental; and in the combination of the religiously noble with the amorally cynical or absurdist; he was again typical of the commedia artists.

In the most brilliant and serious cases, for example, Igor Stravinsky and T. S. Eliot, the turning away from symbolism to the commedia implied splitting the heritage of symbolism into two parts—separating the religion from the art—and then in some sense confiding or consigning the religious concerns to a church, the Anglican or Russian Orthodox Church. These ecclesiastical bodies have the dignity of a tradition, an orthodoxy, that is cultural but also mystical. Each is a repository of art and taste (of a specifically religious kind) but it is not ultimately susceptible of criticism on aesthetic grounds, even when by aesthetic we mean something morally sincere and intense. Then, having handed over the weightier part of his conscience, his seriousness, to a church, the artist is free in his art to be as experimental, absurdist, surreal, as the other half of his temperament demands.

As the names of Stravinsky and Eliot alone indicate (and we could add W. H. Auden, Aubrey Beardsley, Georges Rouault) we do not mean that this division is a cheap escape from moral or aesthetic problems. On the contrary, this is, in them, as noble and serious as any resolution of those problems, anywhere in the history of art. Stravinsky and Eliot did not cast off their religious loyalties when they began to compose, nor did they resign their critical intelligence when they went to church. On the other hand, there are many levels of dignity in art, and the same choice plays itself out in other cases in cruder terms; as for instance in Edith Sitwell and Evelyn Waugh.

In some commedia artists, of course, the impulse to parody religion outweighs the reverence. This was true of Diaghilev, who shocked Stravinsky by proposing to choreograph the Mass, and turn it into another Ballet Russe. It was true of Cocteau, despite his strenuous efforts to take Christianity seriously. It was true of Buñuel.

Among actors, it is generally acknowledged that we often find the same paradoxical and sometimes superstitious devotion; symbolized perhaps by the crucifix in the dressing room, as a signal of a side of life deeply remote from that of the makeup box and the curtain call; remote but complementary, psychologically necessary to sustain a personality so constantly exposed to storms of destabilizing excitement. Again there are differences of level in this art-and-religion separation and recombination; from dignified figures like Sir Alec Guinness, whom one can imagine in terms similar to Eliot and Stravinsky, to more doubtful cases of hectic and overpublicized conversions and lucky-charm rosaries and holy water.

There are thus several ways in which commedia artists divide and recombine art and religion. And there are exceptions to and dissents from that pattern. Picasso and Schoenberg, for example, do not fit. Picasso seems to have had no element of religion in him; Schoenberg's religion was too strong to play partner to commedia art.

Nevertheless, when we compare commedia with the artists of the erotic movement, or to those with primary affiliations to the folk, or to the socialist realists, we do see this pattern stand out in this group. One might say that in their houses a winding passage often leads one from the studio to the chapel, and takes one not only from art to religion, but from experimental art to traditional.

The idea of decadence suggests to us also the decay of European civilization, its coming to an end, its moral and political exhaustion. This was an idea which pressed upon the commedia artists (as upon most artists), and upon the audiences for the commedia movement. Their art was not political or realistic, but it was significantly a reaction to the world around them, and it is possible to sketch in the vision of that world which several of them shared.

This vision focused upon cities rather than on the countryside. Nature was present to them under the aspect of parks. Within the cities it focused upon the affluent quarter, the people who patronized theaters, concerts, galleries, though also upon the artists' quarter, those who worked in the theaters, concerts, galleries. Slum streets were often brought into stylized focus as backdrops for lurid violence, murder, riot, prostitution. Suburban streets are likely to be even more stylized as backdrops to bland meaninglessness, vacuous recurrence, and routine. Factories might be fancifully evoked as temples of Moloch and houses of Juggernaut.

But the single image that meant most to commedia artists is the public square with colonnaded or pedimented buildings at right angles to one another, with flights of steps and statues, fountains and flowers, an Arch of Triumph or a Bronze Horseman; an empty space to be filled with a parade or a revolution, or with a crowd of singers or dancers. This image of high civilization could be localized in any of the West's big cities, and in the next chapter we shall localize it in Paris, Munich, St. Petersburg, London, and New York. But there is one other city, where not so much took place that concerns us as historians of the commedia, but that was the ideal setting and that most haunted the minds of our artists, the city of decadence par excellence—Venice.

The Jewel of the Adriatic, encrusted with the loot of centuries of empire, the city of lagoons and gondoliers, of St. Mark's and the Lido, above all the city of water and mists; melting back into water and light, both by illusion of reflection, and by fact of settling and sinking; succumbing to the mists with their hint of disease and epidemic.

Over and over again in modern art, Venice has been evoked as the splendid backdrop to decay and death. Evelyn Waugh, in *Brideshead Revisited*, evoked first Oxford, then Brideshead, then Venice as increasingly gorgeous and guilty playgrounds for gilded youth. Thomas Mann—perhaps thinking of Mahler, certainly thinking of himself—wrote about a great decadent artist choosing death in Venice. Then there was the Visconti film of Mann's story, and Franz Werfel, in his novel *Verdi*, wrote about Wagner's death in Venice.

For Diaghilev, in some ways the most intensely commedic figure in this whole book, Venice was a favorite city, and it was in every way appropriate that he found his death in Venice, in 1929. Superstitious as he was, it had been prophesied to him that he would meet his death on water, and for that reason he had refused to go to sea. He had lost Nijinsky because he let him sail to South America alone, or rather with a woman—but it was Venice, a city really on the water despite its appearances of being on solid ground, that he should have feared. But even had he known, he, like Mann's character, Aschenbach, would perhaps have accepted his fate—have chosen death as the price of love-and-art-and-Venice. He was buried there, and his own grandiose apostrophe to the city was carved upon his tombstone; though in true commedic fashion the pomp of his funeral was interrupted by the rivalrous histrionics of his young disciples, his *zanni*.

But Venice is our backdrop, above all because of all those paintings—by Guardi, Bellotto, Canaletto—which have made that image, that vision, of a city of splendor shimmering toward and away from us the emblem of all our ambivalent feelings about our civilization. Pride alternates with self-doubt, a sense of splendor alternates with a sense of theater, a sense of its centuries-old solidity with a sense of its paper-thin impermanence. Emblematically, every time that a curtain rises in a European theater, we see, or expect to see, that vision of Venice. And so, since the commedia *is* theater, this story is played out against that backdrop.

Chapter 2.
THE SPREAD OF THE COMMEDIA, 1890–1930

G RADUALLY, half the artists of Europe, and the United States, fell under the fascination of the commedia in the period from 1890 to 1930. The process began in Paris, spread to Munich and St. Petersburg and later to London and New York. We say "spread" partly to mean the way this message was communicated from city to city, but partly to suggest the variety of forms taken by this cult of the commedia.

France

At the beginning of our period the supreme reputation among the forward-looking citizens of the poetry scene in Paris was Wagner's. Romain Rolland said that in the 1880s, "Writers not only discussed musical subjects, but judged painting, literature, and philosophy from a Wagnerian point of view." And Proust's friend Léon Daudet said, of a slightly later period, "We studied his characters as if Wotan held the secret of the world, and Hans Sachs were the spokesman for free, natural and spontaneous art." (Magee, p. 88.) Thus *symbolisme* was in full swing among the avant-garde.

The artists who interest us moved from Wagnerism toward the commedia more quickly than others. One such group were the contributors to *La Vogue*, an avant-garde literary magazine that began in Paris in 1886. A central figure was Jules Laforgue, the most important French Pierrot writer. The magazine was founded by Léo d'Orfer, who was Laforgue's admirer, and edited by Gustave Kahn, who was his great friend. The first issue included work by Verlaine, Rimbaud, Mallarmé, and Villiers de L'Isle-Adam. In its first year *La Vogue* published much of Laforgue's best work, plus Rimbaud's *Illuminations*. One of the literary innovations it promoted was *vers libre*, a verse form associated with the Pierrot sensibility, brought into English verse above all by T. S. Eliot, who took it from Laforgue. Kahn and Rimbaud also experimented with vers libre, but Laforgue carried the experiments to perfection. For most of these writers, Wagner was a great enthusiasm.

But a revolt against Wagner and *symbolisme* began in the 1890s. Indeed, many of the French had always found Wagner's mythology repellent, and Wagnerism ridiculous. Verlaine, though he had included three Wagner poems in his *Amours*, was quite satirical about the Wagner enthusiasm. He published his sonnet "Parsifal" in the *Revue Wagnérienne*, but he objected to that publication's "Germanism"; he referred to the symbolists as "cymbalists," and said, *"Schopenhauer m'embête un peu"* (Schopenhauer's a bit of a bore). (Martin, p. 242.) His is the dandified tone of a Laforgue, of a Pierrot, confronted with the pomp of Bayreuth. Artists in France (and elsewhere) were reacting away from that enthusiasm for the all-embracing myth, toward fragmentation, irony, parody, play—and the imagery of the commedia which carried that mood.

The great poet of this fragmentation was Jules Laforgue (1860–1887), who in fact died before our period began, but was still becoming known. Much of his work was still finding first publication—even in Paris, his own city. His was a shy and evasive personality. He identified himself not by ordinary self-commitments, but by a series of links with literary figures (for instance, with Hamlet, and with the Jacques of *As You Like It*) and above all with the Pierrot of the commedia.

Laforgue was a queer mixture of primness and irreverence, of profound anarchism and buttoned-up social correctness—a surreal "clergyman," as the French use that word. As such he reminds us of his Anglo-American disciple, T. S. Eliot, and his composer contemporary, Erik Satie. (The latter worked with Diaghilev and Cocteau, and in the 1880s played piano in the Montmartre cabaret, Le Chat Noir, a commedia establishment. It featured a Pierrot painting by Wilmette, whose Pierrots were to be seen in many Montmartre cabarets then.) This human type, socially elusive, psychologically eccentric, intellectually oblique, with abysses of metaphysical melancholy within, and lifelines of frail humor, hypersensitive and hypersubtle, is perhaps the characteristic type behind commedia art. And one way to diagnose it is as "unmanly"; that is, those broad, warm, genial gestures and opinions by which a man asserts his membership of the club of men are so alien to individuals of this type that they go about the world masked and muffled, denying even their gender identity. (They deny their other social identities, too, or assert only blatant travesties, like "le clergyman," but their denial of gender best accounts for their buttoned-up self-denial.) And since the cult of manliness (and womanliness) was an essential part of the public art of the nineteenth century, the denial of manliness was an essential part of commedia modernism.

Laforgue's first book was called *Le Sanglot de la Terre (The Earth's Sob)*, and he worked on it between 1878 and 1881. This was portentous in scope and tone (he was hoping to be "the prophet of a new era") and one might call this Wagnerian or *symboliste* poetry. But the Laforgue we are interested in began with his next book, *Les Complaintes* (1885), self-mocking adaptations of popular songs.

Laforgue defined the difference between his two books of poetry thus: "I was once a tragic Buddhist and now I am a dilettante Buddhist." (Smith, p. 6.) ("Buddhist" here signifies a disillusioned alienation from every kind of action and engagement.) W. J. Smith says the change from the first style to the second is enormous, and yet, also, "merely a shift in tone. The poet treats the same major themes but in a minor key [in the second book], the macrocosm is reduced to microcosm; the instrument is smaller, but capable nevertheless of vibrant echoes. The pale, serious young organist in the loft is replaced by the nimble, playful, sentimental organgrinder on the street-corner." (*Ibid.*, p. 18.)

What Smith describes is of course a shift from Wagnerian *symbolisme* to the commedia style of fragments and irony. Laforgue himself said, "Before I became a dilettante and a pierrot, I sojourned in the cosmic." (Arkell, p. 162.) The change in him can be pinpointed with unusual preciseness—it occurred at a Paris street carnival on September 20, 1880. This was where Laforgue conceived the idea of his *Complaintes*, poems that imitate carnival music with great sophistication, and have been compared by critics with blues music. His journal notes on the carnival begin with the clowns and mountebanks he saw there, the pimps and whores. They progress to notes on the merry-go-rounds and the drunkenness, the smell of the lamps, the cries of the barkers, the melancholy of the barrel organs. "And high up the virgin and eternal stars. Stray, strange, planet." (Smith, p. 85.) This commedia conjunction of phenomena constituted the realm of Laforgue's poetry.

Laforgue forthwith identified with all Pierrots and all clowns. He wrote to a friend in 1882, "Don't you love the circus? I've just spent five consecutive evenings there. Clowns seem to me to have arrived at real wisdom. I should be a clown, I've missed my true calling." (*Ibid.*, p. 242.) Many of his poems are written in Pierrot's voice and from Pierrot's point of view: "The Complaint of Lord Pierrot," "Marriage Complaint of Pierrot," and so on. And he was seen that way by his friends. When a critic compared his work with Tristan Corbière's, Gustave Kahn said that the latter was only a Harlequin (a wry and agitated joker) while Laforgue was a Pierrot, an artist sensitive to everything.

In six weeks, in 1885, Laforgue wrote the whole book, *L'Imitation de Notre-Dame la Lune (The Imitation of Our Lady the Moon)*, which is all about various Pierrots, some of whom wear scarab rings and some, dandelion buttonholes. The moon of his title was an image Laforgue associated closely with the commedia, while he treated the sun as source of grossness and contamination—gross vitality or gross corruption. Smith says, "The bone-white face of Pierrot, as expressionless as it is timeless, is the image of the full moon. It is also a death's head animated by feeling." (Smith, p. 39.) Watteau's *Gilles* has one of those moon-round faces, and Watteau was a painter often associated with Laforgue, both for his commedia subjects and for his emotional resonance. (George Moore called Laforgue the Watteau of the *café-concert.*)

This seems a long way away from Wagner and symbolism. But Laforgue was so powerful an influence on later poets (Eliot called him "if not quite the greatest French poet after Baudelaire . . . certainly the most important technical innovator.") (Eliot, p. viii.) because he preserved, in parodic form, the enormous ambitions of symbolism. He had read Schopenhauer and Hartmann, the philosophers of pessimism. He often quoted Schopenhauer's lines "Life is an evil. The end of the world will mean the salvation, the deliverance of humanity." (Arkell, p. 32.) But he also believed in the unconscious, as the life-force opposite to, and a salvation from, reason, logic, consciousness. "Its principle is the anarchy of life: let it lead us where it may, let us delight in the limitless treasures of our senses and bedeck our dreams with flowers during the short time that is left to us." (*Ibid.*, pp. 140–41.) In his early stories we see the hero in a state of "delicious enervation, enjoying the vague sensation of his mind dissolving into a thousand kinds of floating reverie, of his whole identity being atomised and scattered through nature . . ." (*Ibid.*, p. 26.) The similarity to Proust is not a mere coincidence, as we shall see.

And if Schopenhauer was Laforgue's philosopher, his poet was Baudelaire, the prophet of Wagnerism in France. But Laforgue described Baudelaire's poems as being "as vague and inconsequential as the flutter of a fan, as equivocal as make-up, so that the bourgeois who reads them asks: 'So what?' " (*Ibid.*, p. 108.)

This makes us see Baudelaire as a commedia poet, and as the precursor from whom Laforgue was to learn so much, as a disreputable poet. The opposite kind of poet—the respectable kind—Laforgue found in Victor Hugo, the official "great poet" of France then. He described Hugo's poetical practice as "seating himself every day at the organ," and spoke of "the ennui of those periodical paving stones rolled down from the customary Sinai." (Ramsey, p. 93.) It was just because one could see Wagner too as "seating himself every day at his organ" that Laforgue was not Wagnerian. When he treated Wagner's themes and motifs, he made fun of them. In Laforgue's version of *Lohengrin*, the amorous knight resists Elsa's caresses, embracing his pillow instead, which transforms itself into a swan.

Laforgue was wholeheartedly and indiscriminately parodic, even when he admired. We have described his parody of *Hamlet*, which did not prevent him from identifying himself with Hamlet. He mocked his hero, Baudelaire, too, in his *Des Fleurs de bonne volonté*; and another of his heroes, Flaubert, in "Salomé." For Laforgue, and for other poets of the Pierrot sensibility, like T. S. Eliot, parody and irony are not modes of disengagement from an idea; indeed they are modes of engagement with it. That is why the Pierrot figure, which is self-parodic, is so attractive to them.

Laforgue's influence was intense and widespread, especially in the second half of our period, and even amongst Anglo-Saxons. Eliot spoke of his own case as "a sort of possession by a stronger personality." Ezra Pound loaded the pages of *The Little Review* with Laforgue poems. Hart Crane wrote "Locutions de Pierrot" and "Chaplinesque" (full of Laforguisms) in the 1920s. And so on.

Of contemporaneous writers the one Laforgue reminds us of most, by biographical link and similarities of sensibility, is Marcel Proust. The latter was a few years younger, and did not belong to the same social world, but we must name him here, to suggest how wide this mood spread in Paris then. The special interest of this link lies, in part, in its element of paradox—for Proust was not a Pierrot writer. In some ways, for instance in the massiveness of his form and the elaborateness of his discourse, he was quite the reverse of the fragmentary and ironic commedia.

Up to a point one could say that Proust was not a Pierrot in what he wrote so much as in what he was. He, like Laforgue, had been a pupil of the Lycée Condorcet—one of the famous Paris lycées, which trained the intellectual elite. And we see in the memoirs of his earliest friends that they saw Proust even then—implicitly—as a Pierrot figure. His lycée classmate Daniel Halévy calls him "a disturbed and disturbing archangel," and makes us see him as a Pierrot, "with his huge Oriental eyes, his big white collar and flying cravat." (Painter, p. 78.) A somewhat older friend, Gaston de Caillavet, wrote a Columbine play in the

1890s in which he asked Proust to play Pierrot, saying "You'd be just right for the part, you're so pale, and your eyes are so big." But, Proust's biographer tells us, he refused to act on stage a character that he was already playing in real life. (*Ibid.*, p. 102.)

As a boy he was hypersensitive and precocious; and the combination of those two qualities is a psychological recipe for the Pierrot type. But above all—because this is so important an item in his whole generation's rebellion against their fathers' culture—at the root of Proust's sensibility, like Laforgue's, lay a rebellion against manhood—against the manly identity assigned the young boy by nineteenth-century culture, embodied in his parents. Such rebellion was everywhere, as we shall see, an implication of the cult of Pierrot. When Proust's father died, in 1903, he told a friend that he had been the "dark side" of his father's life—the disappointment, the tragedy. We may understand this to mean both the anxiety all the family felt about his various debilities of health and willpower: his extravagance, his feverish social ambitions, his refusal to make a career—and his more essential refusal to be manly. His homosexuality, and even more his interest in other men's homosexuality, was only the most blatant example.

This refusal was not in every way defiant or aggressive. Proust felt a yearning as well as a rebellion—a nostalgia for that solid world he'd left. But he was *himself* a commedia artist—see, for instance, the brilliance and profusion of his parodies—just as he was *himself* a homosexual. (By stressing himself I mean to distinguish the "dandy" elements in his great novel from the bourgeois elements—putting it crudely, I am pointing to the parts about "Marcel" and Charlus and the decadents, as distinct from the parts about his parents and grandparents.) We can also see this commedia character to Proust's art represented in Marcel's passion for the theater, a passion established before he ever entered one. Acting was "the first of all its numberless forms in which Art itself allowed me to anticipate its enjoyment." (Proust, p. 91.)

So there in the Paris of the Belle Epoque, between the just-dead Laforgue and the always sickly Proust, the air was haunted by that ironic nostalgia for a rococo past, that camp appreciation of grandes dames, that pallid mask of the anguished dandy, which the commedia dell'arte has always represented.

Germany

Now, translating thought into geographical movement, we go east from Paris and Montmartre across the map of Europe. In the case of Germany, the poetry scene we are interested in is to be found in Schwabing, the artists' quarter of Munich, around the year 1900. It was a more playful and hopeful scene than Paris—a carnival scene. And it was more localized. Whereas the commedic artists of Paris mingled on the Champs-Elysées as so many Pierrots in the crowd, those of Munich confined themselves to one northern suburb of the city, where they were dominant. What Schwabing then meant to German artists of every kind, and its meaning was deeply felt, was a socially realized province of the commedia.

Franziska zu Reventlow (1871–1918), "the queen of Schwabing," "the spirit of Carnival," settled in Munich in 1895. It had long been the city of her dreams, both because she wanted to become an artist, a painter, and because she was morally and socially rebellious. She came of a conservative and aristocratic family: her sister became a nun, two of her brothers became members of the Reichstag: and she waged a fierce struggle against her parents throughout her adolescence. Naturally, art and rebellion went hand in hand for her, as for many young people who came to live in Schwabing then.

One of them, Hans Brandenburg, poet, novelist, theorist of Modern Dance, entitled his memoirs *München Leuchtete (Munich Gleamed)*, taking the phrase from Thomas Mann. Brandenburg, like Mann, came to Munich as to a vision of art and freedom. He says that in 1903, when he was seventeen, there was no other place to go if you wanted to be a poet. He came from the Rhineland, in the west of Germany. Reventlow came from Lübeck in the north, which also produced, amongst Schwabingites, Thomas and Heinrich Mann, and Erich Mühsam, the anarchist writer of poems, plays, and satires.

For them, for all Germany, Munich was the South. It lay, they said, halfway along a line from Berlin to Rome, geographically and symbolically. It was the antithesis of Prussian Berlin, which was all discipline and militarism, embodied in a blond, blue-eyed, long-skulled physique. The people of Bavarian Munich were dark-eyed, Italianate, Catholic peasants, with a preindustrial culture of festivity. They were, the intellectuals said, still a people, not a proletariat.

Their tradition of festivity, of periodic carnivals, saturnalia, days of public license, was much prized by the artists of Schwabing (who were themselves, of course, rootless rebels from all over Europe). The carnivals were especially associated with the week before Lent, called Fasching, and with the beer-drinking feasts of October. But the carnivals had spread out from those two centers, to cover the whole year, and the Schwabingites both organized their own equivalents (the students of medicine had their annual ball, the students of law had theirs) and participated in the peasant originals, in the villages near Munich.

At the artists' balls, people wore fancy-dress costumes (notably in Roman, medieval, and Greek-myth styles) of which Pierrot/Harlequin/Columbine were the prototypes. In her autobiographical novel, *Ellen Olenstjerne,* Reventlow described herself dancing the week of Fasching in Pierrot costume. Life as Pierrot or Columbine was her alternative to, her deliverance from, the social and moral bondage she could not tolerate.

Schwabing was a year-round Fasching for Reventlow and, partly thanks to her, for others also. She was not a remarkable writer, but she was a remarkable personality, beautiful and elegant—a pure blonde, of aristocratic manners—and at the same time an intellectual, or at least a woman of ideas. Incapable of moral or practical prudence, she re-embodied the old idea of the hetaera, the free courtesan, promiscuous and yet honorable. (Her equivalents on the Paris poetry scene were Colette, the novelist and vaudevillian, and Suzanne Valadon, the painter and model. We must let Reventlow represent them and their counterparts in St. Petersburg, London, and New York.)

Reventlow lived from hand to mouth. She is said to have moved house thirty times during her years in Schwabing. For a time she lived *à trois* with Franz Hessel, a Jewish Pierrot writer, and the Bogdan von Suchocki, a Balkan adventurer. She took acting lessons and played soubrette parts; she appeared as a ropedancer in many South German country fairs. She dreamed of committing herself to a circus life and envied Frank Wedekind when he got attached to the Herzog Circus. In her 1918 novel, *Das Geldkomplex,* she said she had been a circus *Jongleur* (juggler) half her life.

Her fame derived largely from her erotic freedom. Hessel described her as a *grosse Liebesheroine* (a great love heroine) and she can be aligned directly with Hemingway's Brett. In her own day she was often compared with Wedekind's Lulu, whom Karl Kraus summed up, in a phrase that applied equally well to Reventlow, as *"eine Herrin der Liebe, die alle Typen des Männlichen kannte"* (a queen of love, who knew every type of manliness). She did in fact cruise bars, and paid house calls, sometimes as Domina, with a whip. She was a heroine of sexual freedom, and, in her own way, of women's liberation. In 1899 she wrote an essay, "Hetaerae oder Viragines?" ("Courtesans or Viragoes?"), in which she dissented from orthodox political feminism in favor of a sharp gender differentiation of social roles which yet gave women sexual freedom.

She was a combination of the Columbine and the Muse, or more generally an incarnation of the commedia mood, in its gaily sad but profound rebelliousness. In her letters and her fiction, for instance, she assigns people fanciful names ("Monsieur" or "Adam") which, like "Harlequin" or "Pierrot," both disguise and stylize their identities. (Social and psychological detail stripped away, they are reduced to a simple line of characteristic behavior.) And she was a powerful presence among the artists and intellectuals of Schwabing. For instance, both Rilke and Mann were impressed by her, several famous intellectuals were amongst her lovers, and she is depicted in dozens of stories and poems.

The most striking single case seems to occur in Wedekind's plays about Lulu, and his work generally. Naturally it is impossible, and of no importance, to be sure it is Reventlow and not some other free woman who is the "original," but she embodied the idea that inspired *Lulu*. In the play's prologue, which is also a parade, such as we meet in Blok's *Balaganchik* and Cocteau's *Parade*, we hear the themes of commedia modernism, in a rather raw-toned version, defying legitimate theater and respectable culture. We hear the Animal Trainer say (and in the original it was Wedekind himself who delivered these lines):

> Proud gentlemen and ladies who are gay
> Step right inside to look around the zoo
> With burning pleasure, icy shudders too,
> Here where the soulless brute creations play
> . . . .

Nowadays Ibsen and serious drama is popular but:

> What do these plays of joy and grief reveal?
> Domestic beasts, well-bred in what they feel,
> Who vent their rage on vegetable fare
> . . . .
> The wild and lovely animal, the true,
> Ladies and gentlemen, only I can show you.
>
> (Wedekind, pp. 101–102.)

Then Lulu, the Earth-Spirit, is carried on stage by the Strong Man, and is described to us as a serpent. In Act 1, we see her having her portrait painted in Pierrot costume, and she is contrasted, in her amoral sensuality, with paler, more conventional women. Later we see her with a variety of men, then with lesbian women, and finally she meets her death at the hands of Jack the Ripper. This is commedia melodrama. Wedekind worked on his famous series of plays, in Schwabing, between 1892 and 1901, just when Reventlow was the talk of the town, and it is almost certain that he had her in mind. Wedekind, who was seven years older than Reventlow, had also rebelled against his family (as had so many Schwabingites.)

The playwright was, like Reventlow, fascinated by circuses, about which he began to write as early as 1887, calling attention to the physical and sensual perfection (and the moral nullity) of both animal and human performers. (This is part of the commedic pathos.) He came to Munich in 1891, and made friends with Willie Morgenstern, a famous mime and clown, who introduced him to Schwabing. In 1892 he moved to Paris, where he immersed himself in the nightclub life, and when Schwabing's famous nightclub Die Elf Scharfrichter (The Eleven Hangmen) opened in 1901, Wedekind introduced to Munich the Paris tradition of satirical song, himself playing the guitar and singing.

In literary terms, the figure of Lulu owes something to Zola's amoral actress, Nana, but it also derives from a novel and pantomime called *Lulu*, by Félicien Campaur, which Wedekind saw in Paris. He himself devised ballet pantomimes, the quintessential commedia form. There was one called *The Fleas*, about an animal trainer called Pantaleone (a commedia name), and another called *The Emperor of Newfoundland*, with a weight-lifter hero.

But if it is interesting for us to see the literary precedents from which Lulu derived, it is more so to see her literary successors and progeny. These include Heinrich Mann's Lola (in *Professor Unrat*, made famous in the film *The Blue Angel*) and Nabokov's Lolita (or his Margot in *Laughter in the Dark*). Nana, Lulu, Lola, Lolita—from Paris, Munich, Berlin, Hollywood, this series of Columbine figures passed through Schwabing about 1900. And associated with it was the nightclub satiric song, which Erich Mühsam, and later Bertolt Brecht, took over from Wedekind. In *The Threepenny Opera*, this commedic genre mated again with the eighteenth-century parodic commedia vein in which John Gay had written *The Beggar's Opera*.

Commedic pathos and serious eroticism went together. Schwabing prided itself on being able to accommodate every mood, frivolous and serious. Hessel's characters, in his 1913 novel, *Der Kramladen des Glücks*, praise the famous Schwabing street, the Ludwigstrasse, as an avenue down which one could expect to see Dionysus come, or Iokanaan, or a sandaled Jesus.

All the arts were practiced there, the dance, music, painting—the famous Blaue Reiter group of abstract painters, for instance, included Kandinsky and Marc. And of the many Schwabing writers, we now know best the names of Thomas Mann, Heinrich Mann, and Rainer Maria Rilke.

Like Proust, Mann was an ironic bourgeois who celebrated both the flowering of the late nineteenth century and its decadence. But when we turn from Paris to Munich, from Proust and Laforgue to Reventlow and Wedekind, we are mainly struck by a difference between the two. The French poetry scene was more concentrated in its irony, narrower in its mood, while the Germans still proclaimed the possibility of health. Munich's Faschingfeste proclaimed a less ironic gaiety that need not be despairing; a more German faith in life.

Reventlow herself belonged to the commedia side of Schwabing. She left Munich in 1910 to enter into a farcical marriage with a farcical baron who was being forced by his family (he preferred his Italian laundress) to marry an aristocrat in order not to forfeit his inheritance. And at the time of her death, in 1918, she was considering a world tour in a circus act, as the target of knives thrown at her by a Chinese acrobat. Both of these were commedic life gestures.

In her own writing, she had always belonged to the commedia and practiced a French wit. Her fiction, and her letters, were nearly all light, ironic, parodic, fragmentary. Her more talented protégé, Hessel, also left Schwabing for France, literally and symbolically. He moved to Paris in 1906, and became a middleman between French and German culture. Later a friend of Walter Benjamin, he translated Proust into German with him, and wrote impressions of city life, both in Paris and Berlin, which Benjamin much admired. His was a true Pierrot sensibility: melancholic, recessive, hypersensitive.

Thus we see how German commedia resembled the French variety, but was mated with something almost the opposite, in Schwabing. And for the next phase of the commedia's career in this period we can look east again, across Austria, Poland, and much of European Russia, to St. Petersburg.

Russia

What had happened in France in the 1880s and 1890s was directly echoed in Russia. (Germany was less important to the commedic Russians.) We might put it with only slight exaggeration that what happened in Paris was echoed in St. Petersburg, for the commedia movement had a narrow social focus.

We can take D. S. Merezhkovsky (1865–1941) as the great bringer of the news of *symbolisme* from France to Russia. In 1892 he published a volume of verse called *Symbols*, and in 1893 a volume of criticism called *On the Reasons for the Decline of, and on New Trends in, Contemporary Russian Literature.* These two together raised him to the leadership of the modernist movement in Russia.

He was a symbolist, and never graduated to the second, commedic phase of modernism, to parody, irony, and fragmentation. His first trilogy of novels (published 1892–1904) was entitled *Christ and Anti-Christ,* and it dramatized the conflict between Christianity and paganism, as that occurred in the eras of Julian the Apostate in Rome, Renaissance Florence, and Peter the Great of Russia.

But our interest focuses on that modernist rebellion against symbolism which took the commedia as a source for its imagery. The St. Petersburg poet and café performer, Mikhail Kuzmin (1872–1936), is the first important leader to be named. As for a date, we can take 1910 as important in the history of this rebellion, as being the date both of Tolstoy's death, and of the publication of Kuzmin's poetic manifesto, "Of a Beautiful Clarity," from which the Clarist or Acmeist movement in poetry took its name. Kuzmin protested here, and in his creative work, against the cloudy portentousness of the symbolists, and asked poets to paint city scenes and dandy portraits, expressed in colloquial but witty and elegant language—to write about Chablis on ice, the taste of toasted buns, and "the spirit of trifles, airy and exquisite." (Kuzmin, p. xii.) Many Russian writers were scandalized by this frivolity. Gorky, who stood for political commitment, said the commedia writers produced *articles de Paris* (luxury items).

Kuzmin was not so preeminently a Pierrot poet as Laforgue (he was more like the dandy English poets of the 1890s), but he did use commedia imagery, and other people used it to describe him. In 1906 he wrote a poem about the intoxicating lips of Pierrot (he was a defiant homosexual, and associated the figure of Pierrot with the young men he loved) and about the capricious pen of Marivaux, and the dazzle of *The Marriage of Figaro.* He made a cult of eighteenth-century elegance; in Akhmatova's *Poem Without a Hero,* Kuzmin appears masked as Cagliostro in the "hellish harlequinade," while the poem's central woman figure is presented as a Columbine. Above all, he expressed the commedia sensibility, whether or not he used the images. Vladimir Markov says Russian readers were enchanted by Kuzmin's ambivalent blend of "transparent sadness" and triumphant life affirmation, of delicate sensuality and smiling regret for the passing of "all dear and fragile things." He was not a sage but a seducer, a *charmeur* (a word Diaghilev used about himself, too), and this defiant practice of charm was a new thing in Russian literature. (Kuzmin, p. xii.)

In his novel *Wings*, Kuzmin's characters spend some time at a Wagner festival in Bayreuth, on their way to Italy, and ultimately to Alexandria, the source and haven of sensual joy for them. They love *Tannhäuser* and *Parsifal* and feel profoundly excited and moved by them, but they cannot accept—they cannot understand—the way Wagner contrasted desire with renunciation and then resolved the conflict in favor of the latter. This is all the more a problem for them in that the boy in their group is being guided, past shyness and shame, to a homosexual relation with the man. The climax of the story is to be the triumph of sex, of forbidden desire. Thus for them there was an extra reason to rebel against Wagner and symbolism. Wagner was for them a master of art, and a magician of love, but one they had to reject.

A good year to associate with Russian commedia is 1910, because it was the year that Anna Akhmatova and Nikolai Gumiliev, two of the leading poets in the Clarist movement, were married. Gumiliev (1886–1921) was something of a Harlequin of poetry, and Akhmatova (1889–1966) was indisputably a Columbine, and belongs among the leading commedia poets.

Pushkin (their hero because of his dandy or rococo elements) had been a pupil at the Tsarskoe Selo Lycée, as were Akhmatova and Gumiliev in their day, and he is often mentioned in her verse, as is the eighteenth-century palace and its rococo gardens.

One of Gumiliev's teachers there had been Innokenti Annenkov, a formalist and imagist poet, and it was he who inspired Akhmatova to write. (These close early relationships, often associated with school, are typical of this literary movement, as we saw in France. Two or three of the gymnasia in Moscow and St. Petersburg numbered among their pupils most of the leaders of symbolism, futurism, Clarism, formalism, etc., and some of those leaders were working on their careers while still in school.)

In 1910, therefore, many Russian artists were making choices about which way to go, now that realism was passé and the initial enthusiasm for symbolism was waning. The period from 1912 to 1922 has been called the remarkable decade in Russian poetry, and René Wellek says the battle lines were drawn about 1910. (Wellek, p. 32.)

The area in which we see the choice made for the commedia most clearly is naturally enough the theater. In 1910 Vsevolod Meyerhold, the great director, danced Pierrot in Fokine's production of the ballet *Carnival*. This was at a ball organized by the St. Petersburg journal *Satiricon*. Columbine was danced by Karsavina, and Florestan by Nijinsky. Meyerhold had acted a commedia character in 1903, in Franz von

Schönthan's *The Acrobats,* and again in 1906, in Alexander Blok's *Balaganchik (Fairground Booth).* For his experimental studio work and writing, he took the commedia nom de plume Dr. Dapertutto.

Blok himself, on the other hand, finally chose against the commedia. In 1914 he wrote in his journal the phrase "the poison of modernism," and followed it with a hostile criticism of Meyerhold's productions. Blok felt that commedia art neglected or insulted the human experience it used as its subject matter. (Tjalsma, p. 23.) He complained of the "aestheticism" of *Apollon,* the journal of Gumiliev, Kuzmin, and the Clarists. In 1921 he wrote an article against them, entitled "Without Divinity, Without Explanation." He named himself a symbolist, and linked the Clarists to decadence. On the other hand, he had earlier written a lot of commedia poetry and the important play, *Balaganchik,* in which he mocked symbolism from the commedia point of view.

The writers we are concerned with have also been grouped together as "The Petersburg Poets" because of their enthusiasm for that city. This was a nostalgic enthusiasm for the eighteenth century, too. St. Petersburg had been revealed to them as a neoclassical theater backdrop in various paintings reproduced in Diaghilev's *Mir Iskusstva (The World of Art).* Bakst and Benois there depicted the city in self-consciously eighteenth-century style, and Kuzmin translated their vision into poetic pastiche. In fact, an elegant kaleidoscope of old and new suits a commedia sensibility, and St. Petersburg was also a strikingly modern city then, often called the Northern Paris. The Singer Sewing Machine Building had a revolving sphere on top of it, the Hotel d'Europe was the height of modern luxury, and the Wandering Dog Café, frequented by Kuzmin, Akhmatova, and other writers, was one of Europe's famous literary nightclubs.

Kuzmin was composer, playwright, and singer, as well as writer, and all the poets of this group had something of the theater in their temperament and in their idea of literature. The Wandering Dog, opened in 1912, was a low, dark basement, with the windows boarded up and the walls painted with fantastic birds and flowers. It had been decorated by Sergei Sudeikin, husband of the dancer Olga Sudeikina, and designer for the Maryinsky Theater and later for Diaghilev's Ballets Russes.

H. J. Tjalsma says, "It was a time when Meyerhold sent his actors scurrying through the theatre audience and when the exuberance of the Modernist stage seemed to burst over into the life of the city. For instance, there is the theatrical and bloodless duel fought by Nikolai Gumiliev and Maximilian Voloshin, a young Symbolist poet who was connected with *Apollon.* . . . One of the most notorious affairs of the day involved an odd love-triangle among Kuzmin, Vladimir Knyazev, and Olga Sudeikina." (Tjalsma, p. 69.) This affair, and other similar ones in which Kuzmin was involved, formed the subject matter of two famous Russian poem cycles: Kuzmin's own *A Trout Breaking Ice* and Akhmatova's *Poem Without a Hero.*

Knyazev, a young officer, who had been Kuzmin's lover, left him for Olga Sudeikina, but committed suicide, in 1913, because he saw her with another man, who is generally supposed to have been the poet Blok. There were many other complications (Sudeikina was a close friend of Kuzmin, but also of Akhmatova, who was apparently herself attracted to Knyazev) and there are problems in interpreting the historical references in the poems, on which scholars disagree. What matters to us is the *tangle* of amorous relations, a tangle that bulked larger than the love relations themselves, even for the participants, a tangle that transgressed against every law, moral and emotional, so much as to involve the participants in unreality—as in a painful and sordid commedia imbroglio. A similar tangle inspired Blok's commedia play, *Balaganchik.*

In *Poem Without a Hero,* Akhmatova names Sudeikina as Columbine, as a St. Petersburg doll, a goat-legged bacchante, and so on. In fact Sudeikina had danced in a faun ballet; she was also a well-known fashion model and singer who often performed at the Wandering Dog. She appeared, for instance, in Kuzmin's play *Venetian Madness.* The commedia was one of her enthusiasms, and she was painted in commedia costume by her husband.

Part 1 of Akhmatova's poem is entitled "The Year 1913: A Petersburg Tale," and the action is set in a white, mirrored hall to which come commedia maskers out of the past:

> Here's one as Faust, there's one as Don Juan
> As Dapertutto [Meyerhold] as Iokanaan
> The most modest as the Northern Glahm
> Or as Dorian, the murderer.

Knyazev (helplessly yearning for Sudeikina's love) is referred to as the dragoon Pierrot. (Akhmatova, p. 6.)

In this poem, Kuzmin is reproached, accused. He had written the foreword to Akhmatova's first book of poems, but her judgment is harsh against him:

> Old Cagliostro is fooling around
> That most elegant Satan
> Who does not weep for the dead with me

Who does not know what conscience means
And why it exists. (Op. Cit.)

And in another poem about the Wandering Dog, entitled "Cabaret
Artistique," Akhmatova had expressed similar feelings much earlier:

We're all Drunkards here, and Harlots
How wretched we are together
. . . .
I have put on a narrow skirt
To show that my lines are trim
. . . .
O heavy heart, how long
Before the tolling bell?
But that one dancing there
Will surely rot in hell.

(Kunitz and Hayward, p. 5.)

This poem is dated January 1, 1913, to refer again to Knyazev's suicide,
and probably also to Kuzmin's Satanism.

Kuzmin's novel, *Wings*, had come out together with his book of
poems, *Alexandrian Songs*, in 1906. The novel first appeared in a journal but had several book editions before 1921. It caused a scandal because of its homosexuality; but also because in it a girl commits suicide
for love of a man who prefers boys, and who is as icily indifferent to
her death as he had been to her love. This satanic pride was one of the
elements in Kuzmin's very incisive personality. He was an immoralist.
Gide's book *L'Immoraliste* came out in 1902, and there are traits of Kuzmin's
intellectual life that recall Gide's, but his personality recalls rather that
of Proust's most famous character, the Baron de Charlus.

The sort of scandal that forms the subjects of these poems and novels, that seems to threaten the stability of all sexual and even all moral
relationships, had of course its parallels in the Paris and Munich and
London of the time. In Paris we can limit our reference to Proust's great
novel, and to the homosexual intrigues that it reveals everywhere in
society as it unfolds. In London we can point to the scandal surrounding Somerset Maugham's marriage and the Harold Nicolson marriage.
The stories of the quarrels between the Tolstoys undermined the myth
of marriage from the opposite direction: the heroes of a sexually orthodox love story were seen to have ended in mutual hatred. The commedia genre was congenial to those who had lost faith in marriage.

Akhmatova became an extremely popular poet in Russia early on,
and the object of a cult. Her impact on poetic taste has been compared

with Rilke's, because the songlike clarity of both poets' work drew readers' favor away from the cloudily symbolist poets like Stefan George in
Germany and Alexander Blok in Russia. After Akhmatova's *Rosary* was
published, lovers used her verses in their letters and played games of
completing her couplets when given the first line. She was the first woman
to create strings and cycles of love lyrics, and to identify herself with
the adventure of romantic love. (In America the equivalent figure was
Edna St. Vincent Millay—also a commedia poet.) There were more
paintings, sculptures, photographs, and poems about her in Russia than
about any other poet. A book called *The Image of Akhmatova* came out
in 1925. This suggests another way in which a poet can be commedic—
by playing a public, almost a self-advertising role.

This is most easily understood in women poets, but there have been
masculine equivalents. In any case, Akhmatova's conscious role playing—especially as "nun and whore"—fascinated the public. She applied
that phrase to herself, and it was taken up by both her admirers and her
enemies. It made her, if not precisely a Columbine, then a kind of Muse,
a theatrical "star," a public symbol of love like an actress.

England

The Wagner enthusiasm was established in England during the twenty
years before World War I. Mahler conducted the first full season of
Wagner in German at Covent Garden in 1892. In 1903 two cycles of
The Ring were staged there—indeed, of seventy-seven performances that
season, twenty-nine were of Wagner. This was the era of symbolism in
England. But after 1918 Wagner was just another composer. After 1918
the commedia dell'arte excited the avant-garde, and the theater belonged to the Ballets Russes—especially their *Petrushka*—and to the long-
running 1920s production of *The Beggar's Opera*.

The group of English modernists we want to focus on were not
Wagnerians but commedia enthusiasts—the Sitwells and their friends.
The crucial period might be said to run from 1918 to 1923. On Armistice
Day, 1918, Osbert and Sacheverell Sitwell gave a party in their house
in Chelsea. It was primarily for Daighilev and his dancers of the Ballets
Russes, recently arrived in England, but members of the Bloomsbury set,
the most prestigious of young intellectuals, were invited to meet them.
The occasion is an emblem of the Sitwells' whole enterprise of intro-
ducing the spirit of the commedia into the English intellectual establishment. It was here that J. M. Keynes, the economist, first met the

ballerina Lydia Lopokova, whom he later married, a union that brought financial patronage to the ballet in England.

Our other date, 1923, was the year of the second performance of Edith Sitwell's later book of poetry, *Façade*. This was a commedia occasion at which the poet declaimed her modernist, semi-Dada poems through a mask, to music composed by William Walton, before an elite audience, and in an atmosphere of elitist scandal. Diaghilev was one of those who attended, and he commissioned Sacheverell Sitwell and Lord Berners (another of the Sitwells' composer friends) to work on a ballet for him (*The Triumph of Neptune*, performed three years later).

Dominated by these siblings, English commedia had a country-house character. The Sitwells were the three children of a rich baronet of eccentric temperament but conventional opinions. They were unhappy with their family and social equals, and interpreted their suffering as a call to become artists. They dramatized their sense of being different (in matters of physical appearance, too) into challenging poses and costumes. Edith said, "If one is a greyhound why try to look like a Pekinese? I am as stylized as it is possible to be—as stylized as the music of Debussy or Ravel." She claimed to be the first person to paint her nails silver or wear jet and ivory bracelets. She had brocade dresses designed for her, with narrow bodices, long skirts, wide sleeves, to which she added enormous jewels and high turbans. (Glendinning, p. 53.) She and her brothers were often depicted by the fashionable young photographer Cecil Beaton.

Beaton tells us that:

[Osbert] encouraged his sister Edith, whom I now considered the most remarkable and beautiful-looking human object I had ever seen, to pose for me. With her etiolated Gothic bones, her hands of ivory, the pointed, delicate nose, the amused, deep-set eyes, and silken wisps of hair, I considered she must be more remarkable than any model that I would ever have the fortune to find. Edith became a most willing subject for my camera. She posed wearing a flowered gown like Botticelli's Primavera; she sat on a sofa wearing a Longhi tricorne and looking like a Modigliani painting; she lay on the floor on a square of chequered linoleum disguised as a figure from a medieval tomb, while I snapped her from the top of a pair of rickety house-steps. At Renishaw Hall, the Sitwell house in Derbyshire, the ivy-covered ruins, the stone terraces ornamented with large Italian statues, and the tapestried rooms, made wonderful backgrounds for pictures of her. Here was the apotheosis of all I loved. With an enthusiasm I felt I could never surpass, I photographed Edith playing ring a ring of roses with her brothers.

(Beaton, p. 42.)

This kind of living theater is always commedic, because of its artificiality, its self-alienation, its touch of self-parody. Though the Sitwells did not characterize themselves literally as Pierrot, Harlequin, and Columbine, they did play equally artificial parts, equally stylized, and gay-in-their-grief.

They were moreover very alert to the more sordid and proletarian side of the commedia tradition. In *For Want of the Golden City*, Sacheverell Sitwell describes an early memory of Pierrots on the seaside trestles at the resort of Scarborough. He recalls that one of the performers was a rich man who paid for the privilege of dressing and singing as a woman. He hints at sexual scandal, and goes on to recall the French writer Colette with her lesbian lover at Dieppe, watched jealously by her husband. He passes from that to the castrati singers of Italy, and returns to the English music hall stars, George Robey and Little Tich, a dwarf. Sitwell compares the latter's long boots (which so stabilized him that he could lean forward and touch the stage with his nose) with the long shovel hat of Don Basilio in the commedia. He insists on the sinister side to Little Tich's talent, and tells of his strange friendship with that other dwarf, the painter Toulouse-Lautrec. (Sitwell, *Golden City*, pp. 186–87.)

This pattern of allusions and ancedotes (typical of the way Sitwell constructed his books) shows us how fully he had mapped out the commedia sensibility. The Sitwells were great admirers of English music hall performers like Nellie Wallace, and for that reason felt themselves to be closer to "the people" than left-wing writers. They liked grotesque events and personalities and read newspaper reports on mass murders avidly. And they insisted on the parodic connections between that and the opposite pole of the commedia sensibility, the love of lyric grace and exquisiteness. Edith put nightmares next to fairy tales in her books of poems; and Sacheverell (in the passage just discussed) described Dicky Flexmore, a nineteenth-century clown who brilliantly burlesqued the serious ballet dancing of Jules Perrot (whom Sitwell ranked with Nijinsky). Perrot was a great artist, but Flexmore was a great *commedic* artist, because he parodied Perrot.

Her title *Clowns' Houses* suggests the influence of the commedia on Edith Sitwell's poetry; another collection, by her and Osbert, was entitled *Twentieth Century Harlequinade;* and an early book of Sacheverell's was *The Hundred and One Harlequins*. This debt was often remarked on. In his introduction to the 1938 *Oxford Book of Modern Verse*, W. B. Yeats said about the two halves of Edith's dream world, "In its first half, through separated metaphor, through mythology, she creates, amid crowds and scenery that suggest the Russian ballet and Aubrey Beardsley's final phase, a perpetual metamorphosis that seems an elegant artificial childhood; in the other half . . . a nightmare vision, like that of Webster, of the emblems of mortality." (Glendinning, p. 4.) Both halves of that split were to be found in the commedia entertainments of, for instance, Deburau. The emphasis on childishness is one we have not made explicit so far, but it is closely allied to something we have already met.

We remarked, apropos of Akhmatova and Gumiliev, how often artists of this sensibility formed the attachments significant for their artistic lives during their time at school, who in some sense became their artistic selves while at school. The same is true of French, German, and English versions of the type. The Sitwells banded together in the nursery to defy the modern world, and their writings only continued that defiance. The Sitwells' friend, Cyril Connolly, wrote at length about the life-determining character of his and his friends' experience at Eton; and in America Edmund Wilson, Scott Fitzgerald, and John Peale Bishop formed themselves at Princeton, and wrote about school and college life. This implies a narrow focus of social experience, and an upper-class one; for a further dimension of the phenomenon is that these were all socially privileged childhoods. The overt intention of such art is to cherish the experience of childhood in criticism of adulthood. There seems to be a consonance between the commedia sensibility and this direction of sympathy and kind of social experience.

Edith was the most famous of the three, but from our point of view, her brother Sacheverell is even more important. He was best known for his books on baroque painting, sculpture, and architecture, the modern English taste for which he largely created. His empathy for the commedia is shown through his appreciations of Watteau. In *The Dance of the Quick and the Dead,* the section entitled "Episodes of Gilles" begins by describing Watteau's famous painting of Gilles.

In this painting Gilles's clothes, Sitwell says, are soaked in moonlight. "He stands for the artifice of night in this sunset landscape. . . . This may be a pool of moonlight, or the light of candles on the stage. . . . Like the mask of Shakespeare, his face is so round and even, so hung upon the ears. . . . A miraculous emptiness lies upon those moonlit clothes." In other pictures, we feel Watteau to be an onlooker, a disillusioned commentator. "But in this, the account of the illusions is still to be given. They are still to come upon that unclouded face." (Sitwell, *Quick and the Dead,* pp. 67–68.) And this emptiness was true of Watteau himself at his best, Sitwell thinks. He put all his personality into his pictures; his own self was silent.

Then Sitwell goes on to describe a pier theater in the North of England, where in summer he saw Pierrots perform; but he describes it in winter, with the sea surging furiously around all four sides of the pavilion, and even underfoot, among the rusted bolts and stays. The whole theater rocks to and fro, and shudders from the waves. "Their impact is like thunder, under earth, among the iron churns . . . no more dramatic introduction into artifice could be imagined than this closed theatre in the middle of the sea." (*Ibid.*, pp. 67–68.)

A later book, *The Cupid and the Jacaranda,* begins with a long piece on another Watteau painting, *L'Embarquement pour Cythère,* and on Watteau's general preoccupation with theater. Then comes "Pierrots on the Sands," in which Sitwell gives us another personal reminiscence of his boyhood fascination with the commedia. "I remember coming up the steep wood, the hanging wood where there are so many dead husks of bluebells, where you look down and see the lake between the trees, and thinking of Mezzetin [a commedia character portrayed by Watteau] in his black mask. I cannot have been more than 14 or 15 years old. I mention this because I believe it to be unusual and peculiar, and because I wonder if there is a young boy anywhere in Europe or America today who dreams of such subjects and characters, or has even heard of them." (Sitwell, *Cupid,* p. 21.) The boy looked up at the trees, and thought about Fragonard's paintings of leaves; art and nature enhanced each other.

Sitwell says that the poetry we find in Watteau's painting derives from the shock of meeting actors outside a theater, out in nature—"comedians out of the theatre, lying on the shores of the lake, or in wild, overgrown corners of the garden. It is the overlapping of one life into the other that makes the fascination." (*Ibid.*, p. 28.) This is a fine statement of the significance of what we have been calling commedia. "This subject, in all its ramifications and subdivisions, is what I mean by 'theater'; and, poetry apart, it has been one of the passions and intoxications of my life. . . . I am drawn in lesser degree to 'straight' plays than to ballet, opera, and comedy." (*Ibid.*, p. 26.)

Among the friends and allies of the Sitwells at this time was the novelist and controversialist Wyndham Lewis. He represented a more European aspect of the commedic enthusiasm—what Oskar Schlemmer, the painter, called "the spirit of antipathos." Schlemmer taught at the Bauhaus in its first years after World War I, and said that that institution was as a whole possessed by this spirit of revulsion against pathos, pity, sympathy; a spirit of exultation in machinery, farce, violence, laughter, and aggressive harshness. (He named Dada as among the symptoms of this spirit, and one can indeed find this pathos/antipathos element in the works of Tristan Tzara, one of the founders of Dada.) (Trotter, p. 73.)

He published a volume of short stories, *The Wild Body* (1927), which was built around a narrator called Ker-Orr, who names himself as "a conscious barbarian," and "a soldier of humour." (He describes himself as a large blond *clown*, and a blending of William Blake with an American boxer.) "But all the fierceness has been transformed into *laughter* . . . I am *never* serious about anything. I simply cannot help converting everything into burlesque patterns. And I admit that I am disposed to forget that people are real." (Lewis, p. 4.)

One of the most striking stories, "The Cornac and His Wife" (originally titled "Les Saltimbanques"), describes a family troupe of commedia performers in Brittany who hate their audience violently, which attracts Ker-Orr. "Why always violence?" Ker-Orr asks. "For my reply here I should go to the modern circus or to the Italian Comedy, or to Punch. Violence is of the essence of *laughter*. . . . It is the *grin* upon the Deathshead." (*Ibid.*, p. 158.)

Elsewhere in the same book he connects the commedia and laughter with puppets, and with the primitive and religion. "All religion has the mechanism of the celestial bodies, has a dance." The commedia characters perform their life gestures over and over again, indeed eternally. "They are not creations but puppets. You can be as exterior to them, and live their life as little, as the showman grasping from beneath and working about a Polichinelle." (*Ibid.*, p. 234.) And Lewis, or Ker-Orr, goes on to apply this idea of art to eighteenth- and nineteenth-century works (not only Dickens and Dostoevsky's novels, but Boswell's *Life of Dr. Johnson*), showing us how completely this twentieth-century taste differs from the humanism it replaced.

America

By the time we reach the second half of the 1920s, the echoes of Wagner are growing faint and even the commedia figures have faded. They were now a generation old, associated with the 1890s, which made them all too familiar. Because of its nonideological character, its lack of content, this iconography had less staying power than others. It depended heavily on its charm; when that was gone, artists looked for substitutes in their work—even when they themselves remained Pierrots in their hearts. However, we can still find clear traces of the commedia in the work of one group of American writers.

The first part of Edmund Wilson's *American Earthquake* (pieces originally published in *The New Republic* and elsewhere) is entitled "The Follies," and covers the second half of the twenties. It contains a number of essays on murder cases, a number on nightclubs, some essays on Stravinsky, a good number on vaudeville, and many on the Ziegfeld Follies. (Wilson and his friends were as upper-class as the Sitwells, but their commedia took place on Broadway—as seen by smart college boys.) This range of topics, when canvased by a mind as acute and experimental as Wilson's, can serve as a model of commedia thinking, applied to New York in the twenties. It represents that fragmentary, ironic, and parodistic temperament of which the commedia figures are the emblem.

In 1924 Wilson went to California to try to persuade Chaplin to dance in a ballet that Wilson was designing for the Ballets Suédois. It was to be called *Cronkhite's Clocks,* and to include a black comedian, seventeen other performers, typewriters, a movie machine, a radio, a phonograph, a telephone, an alarm clock, riveters, a jazz band, and electromagnets. It was to express New York City, and Leo Ornstein, the Russian modernist, was composing the music. Chaplin declined, on the grounds that he only appeared in shows he himself had devised. But the project reminds us of *Parade* and shows us Wilson as the American Cocteau, the impresario of modernist commedia. (He says he "enormously enjoyed" Cocteau's ballet performed by the Ballets Suédois, *Les Mariés de la Tour Eiffel.*)

In that same year the Provincetown Players put on Wilson's *The Crime in the Whistler Room,* his play in praise of rebellious youth, which contained a full-length portrait of Scott Fitzgerald and a partial one of Edna St. Vincent Millay. Wilson was much involved with theater, and notably illegitimate theater, then. He tells us (in his book *The Twenties*) that he "adored Yvette Guilbert, whom I regarded and still regard as one of the great French artists of her time"; and it is also notable how often he quotes and parodies popular songs of the period, which are in no sense great art. (Wilson, *The Twenties*, p. 88.) It was theater itself, in the sense Sacheverell Sitwell defined it for us, that fascinated Wilson.

In 1927 he spent the summer in Provincetown, in Eugene O'Neill's house, and began his book on literary modernism, *Axel's Castle,* with essays on six major symbolist writers. But he also visited Boston for the political demonstrations against the condemnation of Sacco and Vanzetti that year. He was becoming more political. And in 1929, finishing that book and his novel, *I Thought of Daisy* (also about the twenties) he divorced his actress wife, Mary Blair, and suffered a nervous breakdown.

He was rejecting the enthusiasms of the previous decade. The final version of *Axel's Castle* was completed in a mood quite unsympathetic to modernism. Wilson was already on the way to *To the Finland Station* and Leninist Communism. Thus his life illustrates the thesis we advanced, that at the end of this period the commedia sensibility was often subdued to, and replaced by, a new rigorism.

How much Wilson and his friends were of the commedia at the beginning of the decade can be seen in his discussion of Fitzgerald's early work in 1922. He pointed out that in *This Side of Paradise*, the hero, Amory Blaine, cast himself as a playboy but mocked himself for being only that. Blaine was romantic but cynical about romance, bitter as well as ecstatic, astringent as well as lyrical. (Wilson, *Light*, p. 31.) This is the familiar commedia ambivalence of feeling which Wilson is naming for us, a recognizable version of commedia characters and romance, though with no explicit reference.

However, when Wilson turns to Fitzgerald's second novel, *The Beautiful and Damned*, he invokes explicit commedia imagery to interpret it, saying that Fitzgerald's "characters—and he—are actors in an elfin harlequinade; they are as nimble, as gay and as lovely—and as hardhearted—as fairies; Columbine elopes with Harlequin on a rope-ladder dropped from the Ritz and both go morris-dancing amuck on a case of bootleg liquor; Pantaloon is pricked with an epigram that withers him up like a leaf; the Policeman is tripped by Harlequin and falls into the Pulitzer Fountain." (*Ibid.*, p. 32.) This is a commedia style in literary criticism.

In the first part of the 1920s, moreover, Wilson was in love with a Columbine-Muse—Edna St. Vincent Millay. He tells us, in his memoir of her, that they first met at an after-show party in Greenwich Village, to which she came from directing her own Pierrot and Columbine play, *Aria da Capo*. (Wilson was "thrilled and troubled" by this little antiwar play.) (*Ibid.*, p. 748.) She looked to him like a schoolgirl in her shabby dress, until she recited her own poems. Then she became a Muse. Her long, solid, and lovely throat and high, broad brow became suddenly prominent and impressive. Her poems were published in *Vanity Fair*, where Wilson and his Princeton friend John Peale Bishop were editors, and both fell "irretrievably" in love with her.

When she sailed to Europe in 1921, they took her out to dinner together, and then sat with her on her daybed, Bishop holding her upper half and Wilson her lower, making polite pleasantries about which had the advantage—a very commedic love situation. He concludes his memoir with someone else's vignette of Millay running round the corner of MacDougal Street in the Village, flushed and laughing, "like a nymph," with her hair swinging, and pursued by the dramatist Floyd Dell, also laughing. This is the Millay who presented herself to the reading public in A Few Figs from Thistles as an ever-fleeing and challenging Daphne, a poster image of romantic love.

She used to refer to Wilson and Bishop, when they were her twin suitors, as the "choirboys of hell," no doubt alluding to something in them intellectually prim and socially protected. Certainly it was striking how much they—and Fitzgerald also, to name only the most famous of their friends—kept together, still Princetonians after many years out of college.

They all tried to escape from realism when they wrote fiction, by introducing episodes of balletlike fantasy. Fitzgerald did this most obviously in stories like "A Diamond as Big as the Ritz," but also in the early novels. And even in his most mature work, this hope echoes in his prose and gives the narrative much of its charm. His titles are commedic phrasings of gaiety-and-sorrow, fantasy-and-satire, and similar phrases are integrated into the narrative of The Great Gatsby; for instance, the famous final paragraph.

We think of Wilson as predominantly a critic, and forget his fiction, and even more his plays. But he described himself as always "particularly susceptible to the theatre," and drama was linked to commedia modernism for him. The third of his plays, Beppo and Beth, has the most commedic title, and a commedic plot, but the first two are on the whole more successful. The Crime in the Whistler Room included two characters, embodiments of the commedia mood of the 1920s, who represented Scott Fitzgerald and Edna Millay. The girl, Bill, represents proletarian vitality. Her father is a rogue huckster, now selling correspondence courses. And Simon Lacy (Fitzgerald) represents radical protest. He is a gifted writer who is always getting into scrapes and fights with authority because of his generous but undisciplined heart. He tells Bill his novel plot, which is pure commedia of the grisly kind: a Pierrot figure, coming to New York from somewhere out west, complains of seeing skeletons everywhere—riding taxis, eating in restaurants. And when a millionaire gives him a soft job, he finds he has turned into a skeleton himself. It is characteristic of commedia art—we see this in ballets—to include a fable (or puppet play or dance) in parallel with a more realistic version of the same story. The fable (in theater works perhaps performed on an inner stage) represents an intenser artistic truth.

Wilson's next play, This Room and This Gin and These Sandwiches, is written in praise of Greenwich Village and the Provincetown Players. They figure as the spirit of generous protest in the corrupt city of New York; and as a commedia troupe, all picturesque personalities, who act upon one another. Wilson appears as a stuffy architect, in love with another version of Millay. She tells us, "Dan [the director] wants to declare Greenwich Village an independent republic. . . . He wants to have a ceremony with spaghetti and red ink on top of Washington Arch and send up a fleet of toy balloons . . . to the music of a hurdy gurdy. . . . I'll go up on a wire like one of those angels they have on Italian saints' days—scattering paper roses." (Wilson, *Plays*, p. 221.) This is a commedia ceremony and commedia politics—unrealistic, but poignantly moving. And in personal and artistic life, the strains of conflict and frustration among the actors again give their gaiety the transparency of pathos.

In his novella, *I Thought of Daisy*, Wilson presents similar people (Millay this time is called Rita, and is contrasted with a showgirl, Daisy) but pays more descriptive and analytic attention to the social setting. Both women are commedic types. Daisy is a Columbine, Rita is a Muse, like Isabella Andreini. And the sharp contrast which Wilson stresses between the two is even more commedic. (He does the same in other fiction, like "The Princess with the Golden Hair.") The two women are presented to us within separate frames, as picturesquely as Petrushka and the Moor in their fair booths.

When the narrator goes to the Village party at which he first meets both women, the scene is described in commedic terms. "I saw lettuce-green cocktail glasses, a bruised mulberry batik behind a divan and, on the wall, a set of framed designs for the costumes of some ballet, vivid tinselly golds, blues, and purples. And there were girls, like the colored sketches, in the brightest make-up and clothes, with red silk roses of Cuban shawls and silver turbans and red hair and black arching Russian eyebrows beautifully pencilled on." (Wilson, *Galahad*, p. 55.) The ballet backdrop is transferred to social life in the Village—we are shown life becoming commedic. But if, against this background, the shabby and serious Rita looks at first sight out of place, we soon realize that she is the very spirit of the occasion.

Millay, a commedia personality, grew up the oldest of three sisters in a poor and fatherless household, and remained strongly attached to her mother and sisters. This was very unlike Edith Sitwell's situation, given the Millays' poverty and Edna's attachment to her mother, but there is a likeness in the way the siblings (and Mrs. Millay seems to have been in effect an older sister) formed themselves into a party defying the rest of the world.

Millay came to Greenwich Village in 1917, when she joined the Provincetown Players. She soon became a public symbol of that township of crooked streets of red-brick, low-rent houses, the capital of that counter-America that lived in defiance of Wall Street and Main Street, government and Mrs. Grundy. In 1919 she joined the Theatre Guild and played Columbine in Benavente's *The Bonds of Interest,* from which she went on to direct her own *Aria da Capo.*

Aria da Capo is a picturesque commedia fable. The stage, we are told, is set for a harlequinade, and Pierrot and Columbine are dressed "according to tradition," except that he is in lilac, she in pink. They sit on delicate chairs and dine on macaroons, caviar, peacocks' livers, and persimmons. Their flirtation is interrupted by the inner fable with the antiwar message, but that is delivered in equally commedic style.

Millay's later poetry does not employ commedia imagery much. But she was a commedia poet in the way she presented herself to her public, the way she dramatized herself. *A Few Figs from Thistles* had the famous poems (first and second extracts, respectively):

> I burn my candle at both ends;
> It will not last the night;
> But, ah, my foes, and, oh, my friends—
> It gives a lovely light.

And also:

> Safe upon the solid rock the ugly houses stand:
> Come and see my shining palace built upon the sand!

These manifestos of defiant frivolity were much quoted, and indeed imitated by other poets. And in *The Singing Woman from the Wood's Edge* we read, "What should I be but a harlot and a nun?" (Millay, p. 127.)

Such gestures, and the popular response they received, must remind us of Akhmatova. Like her, Millay became a theatrical star of "love"— of romantic adventures—a public symbol. Floyd Dell called her "the gamine of Greenwich Village," and said she was at moments a scared little girl from Maine, and then "an austere immortal." (Gould, p. 85.) Wilson saw the same split in her, the same alternation of roles: harlot and nun, Muse and schoolgirl.

There was something similar in Fitzgerald. Joan Allen has pointed out, in *Candles and Carnival Lights*, that his sensibility was organized around the polarity between church and carnival. That polarity is often to be found in artists of commedic sensibility; Evelyn Waugh's first novel, *Decline and Fall*, ends with the image of a merry-go-round, while the sanctuary light is the key image of *Brideshead Revisited*.

The last writer in the group we are discussing, Ernest Hemingway, seems quite different. He did not go to Princeton, nor did he write about his schooldays. Implicitly, he claimed to have had an unsheltered youth, in which he tested himself against hardships, and acquired hunting skills, in woods and rivers. It was a democratic, adventurous, noncommedic youth like that of Twain's boy heroes—the kind felt to be prescriptively American.

Nevertheless, there was a significant friendship between him and Fitzgerald, a significant alliance between him and Wilson. The latter said, as early as 1924, that Hemingway's prose was "of the first distinction." And we can see the connection between this judgment and Wilson's enthusiasm for the commedia, when we notice that one of his words of praise for Hemingway's prose is "naive." (Wilson, *Light*, p. 119.) It was a very artful simplicity he was acknowledging. Nick Adams, Hemingway's early hero, has in his way the revulsion from experience, the conscious artistry in life, the artificial naiveté of a Pierrot. (In a different way, these things are true of Fitzgerald's heroes, too.) Hemingway's definition of heroism as grace under pressure is one which could also be applied to Deburau's Pierrot. There is something movingly and expressively silent about both forms of manhood—an alienation from ordinary feelings and relationships which makes them poignantly attractive to others.

By the time Wilson had finished writing *Axel's Castle*, he was quite out of sympathy with its subject—the great symbolist writers Yeats, Valéry, Proust, Eliot, Joyce, and Stein. He begins with a chapter entitled "Symbolism," but its tone is often very impatient. About Valéry he says, "It seems to me that a pretence to exactitude is here used to cover a number of ridiculously false assumptions, and to promote a kind of aesthetic mysticism rather than to effect a scientific analysis." (Wilson, *Castle*, p. 82.) And the effect of Eliot's literary criticism is "to impose on us a conception of poetry as some sort of pure and rare aesthetic essence with no relation to any of the practical human uses." (*Ibid.*, p. 119.)

This is not, of course, a rebellion against symbolism (aesthetic ambition) in the name of the commedia (aesthetic play) but a rejection of both the ambition and the play in the name of logical and moral rigor.

"The interminable and finespun solicitude with which Proust caresses his friends in his letters . . ." (*Ibid.*, p. 169.) "We may come to feel a little impatient at having our attention so continually solicited for valetudinarian neurotics." (*Ibid.*, p. 188.) While Valéry's persona, M. Teste, "gives us the creeps."

Here at the end of our period Wilson (and of course he stood for and influenced many others) had had enough of both early phases of the modernist movement. He discussed only symbolism, because only that had an ideology, an aesthetic, an epistemology; but what he says applies also to that more fragmentary, ironic, and parodic modernism that had in fact shaped his own vision and experience during the 1920s. The commedia was being banished in the name of moral rigor.

Chapter 3.

DIAGHILEV AND COMMEDIA BALLET

T HE GOSPEL of the commedia was propagated more effectively by the ballet than by any other art form, and by the Ballets Russes de Sergei de Diaghilev more effectively than by any other ballet company. In any complete history of the commedia influence on ballet, we should devote space to Frederick Ashton's work in England, and to the Ballets Suédois of Rolf de Maré, but for our purposes we need to simplify. This part of our story will therefore be told in terms of a small and unified group.

The gospel spread from St. Petersburg to Paris, to London, and to New York, not of course by means of sermons, nor even by means of ideas in any ordinary sense, but by splendidly sensual images: the mass whirling and stamping of the Polovtsian Dances, which burst open the confines of the nineteenth-century theater; the lurid red-orange and blue-green contrasts of Bakst's designs, which seared the European eye like a glimpse of the Sahara at noon; the ambiguous sexuality of Nijinsky, wearing a choker of pearls around that long and muscular throat. Once these images had established their dominance in the imagination of the audiences, which they did almost immediately in 1909 and 1910, the mind of the West was changed. A new gaudy aestheticism lodged within it—a commedic attitude to life.

The story fits very neatly into the chronological limits we have suggested, beginning in the 1880s and ending in 1929 with Diaghilev's death. Prince Lieven, one of the most reliable witnesses to the Ballets Russes story, says that its most important phase was its first, from 1885 to 1911. If so, it begins with a group of students, indeed schoolboys, in St. Petersburg. Again Russia is an important location, and again schooldays are an important part of the artist's life; moreover, these schoolboys were, like those we met before, of a highly privileged class. This group originally comprised Alexander Benois, Konstantin Somov, Dmitri Filosofov, and Walter Nuvel, and one or two others who need not concern us. Apart from their work on the Ballets Russes, and other Diaghilev enterprises, Benois's later career was as an art historian, Somov became a painter of portraits and of eighteenth-century scenes, Filosofov became a philosopher of religion; and Nuvel ended up serving Diaghilev in his company.

Benois was the central and in some sense dominant figure who instructed the others in the taste they shared and propagated. The descendant of Italian and French artists settled in Russia, he was perhaps the spirit of the Silver Age, of aesthetic St. Petersburg, incarnate. His parents' family (large, rich, happy) was quite at home in St. Petersburg, but had their own definition of "being Russian." Benois complained that people thought Rimsky-Korsakov composed Russian music because he used exotic and barbarous folk elements, while Tchaikovsky was dismissed as "European," though he was in fact just as Russian and a far better composer. (Nabokov also protested against similar definitions of "Russian" culture.) Benois and Nabokov thought that being Russian and being from St. Petersburg meant being more refined than other Europeans, not less. Thus in his catalogue for the Diaghilev exhibit of Russian paintings in 1906, Benois described the work of St. Petersburg artists as "a rather literary art, for we are in love with the refinements of days gone by, lost in dreams of the past, and pledged to the cult of all that is intimate, precious, and rare." (Buckle, *Diaghilev*, p. 94.)

But this elegant taste operated upon national and popular materials. It seems that Benois told Prince Lieven that his life as a man of taste was determined by his boyhood experience of Harlequin mimes at the Egarev Fair, whose performance he later reproduced on his puppet theater at home. In this version of the commedia story, Petrushka and Harlequin are both servants of Cassandre and in love with his daughter, but Petrushka is the violent one. He plots against Harlequin, kills him, and cuts him up. A fairy reassembles the broken body and gives Harlequin a magic baton, with whose aid he can now jump into a mirror, disappear down a trap, appear out of a fire, and so on. (Benois as a boy prayed to be given such a baton—and found it in art.) Sent to hell, Harlequin is rescued by Cupid, who marry him to the girl, and transform his enemies into animals. Though different in plot line, this Petrushka is the original of the famous ballet Benois created for the Ballets Russes, with the help of Stravinsky, Fokine, and Diaghilev.

Other boys and young men gathered around this group, who called themselves the Pickwickians and who developed a strong group personality, with high and intimidating standards of taste. According to Prince Lieven, they severely condemned "anything they considered devoid of talent, insincere, lacking in artistic truth." (Lieven, p. 36.) Nabokov uses the same phrasing about his own life, and applies it to things outside the ordinary limits of aesthetics. He came from the same class, the same generation, and the same world of ideas—the poetry scene of Russian culture in Silver Age St. Petersburg.

One of the first of the new recruits was Léon Bakst (born Rosenberg), who designed the costumes and decor, which, at least in the first years of the Ballets Russes, were what everyone talked about most. And then there was Sergei Diaghilev himself, who entered the group as Filosofov's country cousin. Though both these recruits were destined to more brilliant individual achievements than the original Pickwickians, they felt at first inferior, and perhaps never entirely overcame that feeling. Certainly they were for a long time treated and referred to with a certain condescension.

It is perhaps not irrelevant that Bakst was a Jew and Diaghilev was a homosexual; but what was crucial was a certain flamboyance, which Bakst displayed in his paintings, and Diaghilev in his manners and conduct. They both overdid things; and in a group like the Pickwickians, that was a fatal weakness. (For us it is more like a strength—it makes them more commedic.) Arnold Haskell says (no doubt reporting Nuvel's opinion) that Diaghilev was never the equal of the others in knowledge and taste. Moreover, he dressed flamboyantly, in top hat, monocle, fancy waistcoat, and fur coat, and he behaved flamboyantly, pursuing fashionable acquaintances and flaunting his familiarity with them.

Bakst had his talent as a painter—his lush and lurid fantasies of color. Diaghilev had his talent as an impresario—what Benois called his "unique speciality—namely will-power." (Buckle, *Nijinsky*, p. 17.) But within the group what counted above all was taste, understood as something politically quiet and morally conservative, although—within those limits—very bold and emancipated and above all sophisticated. Bakst and Diaghilev were never as secure in their taste as Benois was in his, although Diaghilev learned how to outface, and overcome, on occasion, his "superiors." And this insecurity remained an important fact. The Pickwickians, properly speaking, ceased to function before the Ballets Russes were constituted, and Benois was largely out of touch with Diaghilev after 1911, but there was always a somewhat similar high-taste "committee" around the impresario, an aesthetic conclave out of whose deliberations the new ballets were born. (Stravinsky, later, belonged to such a committee.) Diaghilev was sometimes delegated by his superiors. He sometimes mediated between them and his dancers and between them and his public.

When Diaghilev arrived in St. Petersburg and made the acquaintance of Benois and the rest, he listened rather than talked. He had been living in Perm, a country town a thousand miles from the capital, the epitome of provinciality, and allegedly the original of the town in Chekhov's *The Three Sisters*. He had been living in the house of his grandfather, a man of great and guilty piety who made huge donations to the church in expiation of his sin in deriving his wealth from selling vodka (he had the state monopoly in vodka). His family took action to prevent his giving away the whole family fortune. Stories about Diaghilev's grandfather are told in one of Leskov's novels, written when Leskov was under the influence of Tolstoy, and he belongs to the Tolstoyan, and not the Diaghilevian, world.

Thus there was social guilt and religious enthusiasm in Diaghilev's family past. And his aunt Anna, the mother of Filosofov, had been a political rebel of the 1860s who risked severe punishment by the czarist government. But Diaghilev and his friends rejected political and religious modes of action and instead expressed their protest against the status quo through aesthetic means, giving to the aesthetic a scope and depth usually reserved for politics and religion.

Diaghilev was the greatest commedic personality of the century, and demands description. He had an unusually large head and his mother died after giving him birth because the delivery was so difficult. His face was notable for its plumpness and bloom, with red lips and perfect white teeth. Lieven speaks of his "animal-like gaiety," and says that when he laughed you saw the back of his throat. (Lieven, p. 29.) He had fleshy hands, whose fingers pointed backward. Later in life, he had a single streak of silver in his hair, for which he was given the nickname Chinchilla. Arnold Haskell says he was a dandy in his bearing, as well as in his taste in clothes. (Haskell, p. 25.) And Lieven described his quiet drawl and tone of weary boredom.

Stravinsky described him as haughty, arrogant, and snobbish; a typical Russian *barin*, or noble; with "a nature strong, generous, and capricious; with intense will, a rich sense of contrasts, deep ancestral roots." (*Atlantic Monthly*, 1953.) He called himself a sensualist, and accepted the charge of decadence. This meant that he dressed, ate, and entertained himself extravagantly, and that he was homosexual.

In 1890 he and Filosofov made a tour of Europe, going to Berlin, Paris, Venice, and Vienna, where they heard *Lohengrin*. Wagner was one of the greatest enthusiasms of the Pickwickians, and especially of Diaghilev. He used to perform arias from Wagner operas. He and his cousin were apparently at this time lovers, and we can compare this Wagnerian and homosexual *Kulturwanderung* with the one Kuzmin describes in *Wings*. Diaghilev had hopes of a career as a singer and an arranger of music, but the Pickwickians told him he didn't have the talent. Having inherited a modest fortune in 1893, he began to collect paintings instead.

He was very aware of movements and personalities in other countries that were sympathetic to his own; above all, of the Decadents. In 1897, he met Aubrey Beardsley in Dieppe, and in 1898, Oscar Wilde in Paris. Diaghilev was frequently compared with Wilde. Stravinsky, for instance, makes the comparison, and they were alike in physique, in dress, and in manner. More important, of course, they were alike as homosexuals and as impresarios of the somewhat camp taste that they imposed on artistic society.

As a young man, Diaghilev wrote his stepmother, to whom he was devoted, "I am firstly a great charlatan, though con brio; secondly, a great *charmeur*; thirdly, I have any amount of cheek; fourthly, I am a man with a great amount of logic, but with very few principles; fifthly, I think I have no real gifts. All the same, I think I have found my true vocation—being a Maecenas. I have all that is necessary save the money—*mais ça viendra.*" (Haskell, p. 87.) The style is of course Wilde's (it sounds like his "I can resist everything except temptation.") But the content is more impressive, for this self-analysis was brilliantly borne out by Diaghilev's subsequent career.

He imposed himself on the connoisseurs and the artists he admired like a charlatan and a *charmeur*. Benois said, "There was one thing lacking in the artists of that generation who have become world-famous: they lacked the spirit to fight and impose themselves." (We can guess that he was thinking of himself, among others: he says he always resisted discipline and reacted against practical purpose.) "This spirit Diaghilev possessed in the highest degree, so that we can say he too had his speciality, namely will-power. . . . This powerful manipulation of men obliged creative artists to become the obedient executants of their own ideas under his despotic sway." (Buckle, *Nijinsky*, p. 16.) To take an early example, Diaghilev wrote to Rimsky-Korsakov in 1908, "How I need and crave to see you! How many tears and supplications I have prepared, how many bright and irrefutable arguments! . . . I shall hypnotize you with arguments that . . ." (Buckle, *Diaghilev*, p. 103.) His arguments' intention, on this occasion as on so many others, was to justify cuts in Rimsky-Korsakov's music to suit the purposes of Diaghilev's ballet.

And the most interesting word in his self-description, from our point of view, is "charlatan." (It means both "pretender-fraud" and, by origin, "commedia impresario"; the commedia players used to appear on

carts at street corners.) Thus Diaghilev saw himself in implicitly commedia terms even before he took any interest in the commedia tradition
or ballet. It was his strength, vis-à-vis the Pickwickians, that he was a
performer in the comic grotesque pantomime that they merely appreciated as connoisseurs. But it is also worth noting the acuteness and fullness of his self-knowledge, a power of understanding that Diaghilev was
apparently able to turn on other people too. Benois attributed to him a
psychiatrist's power of diagnosis; he saw other men's weaknesses and was
able to turn them to his advantage. This helped him in his often un-
savory dealings with patrons and rivals, but also perhaps explains the
paralytic spell he was able to cast on some of his favorites, such as Nijinsky.

But the Diaghilev enterprise (a venture in the public advertisement
and enforcement of the Pickwickians' taste) explored other fields before
it found the one destined to give it free play and triumph. It took the
form, first, of the art magazine *Mir Iskusstva (The World of Art)*, which
was modeled to some degree on English art magazines of the 1890s like
The Yellow Book and *Studio*. Edited by the Pickwickians in committee,
but with Diaghilev presiding, it was beautifully printed, and up to the
minute in taste. Buckle says that Diaghilev's achievement just as a propagandist for impressionist and post-impressionist painting in Russia is
not to be despised. (Buckle, *Diaghilev*, p. 80.) He promoted Degas, Sisley,
Renoir, Picasso, from the first issue of the magazine in 1898. In Volume
11, numbers 8 and 9, he reproduced seven Gauguins, one Cézanne, one
Lautrec, three Vuillards, two Bonnards, one van Gogh, and one Matisse.

The magazine's creed was of course defiantly "aesthetic." The year
it began was the year Tolstoy published his antiaesthetic manifesto, *What
Is Art?*, and the Diaghilev enterprise as a whole was the very opposite
of Tolstoy's Christian moralism. It is appropriate to think of the two as
the leaders of two heterogeneous armies battling each other. Diaghilev's
first editorial dealt with the Tolstoyan accusation that their taste was
"decadent," and claimed total moral freedom for the artist. "The artist
is confined in a mysterious way. . . . The creator must love only beauty.
He must commune only with beauty, when his divine nature is manifest. . . . The reactions of art to earthly difficulty are not worthy of
the soul of the Divinity. . . . The sole function of art is pleasure, its
only instrument beauty. . . . It is blasphemous to force ideas." (Haskell, p. 114.) He named Tolstoy as the inventor of the chains from which
he was freeing art.

Repin, a friend of Tolstoy, and a famous painter of the generation
before Diaghilev, wrote to *Mir Iskusstva*, denouncing its enthusiasm for

Degas, Monet, and others as all part of a gigantic aesthetic fraud. He wanted Russian art to concern itself with Russia, and with Russia's social problems, not to imitate France, or to join in an international aestheticism. The Russian press accused *Mir Iskusstva* of corrupting Russian youth; on the other hand, the czar subsidized it to the extent of 10,000 rubles a year for five years. Like all Diaghilev's enterprises, the magazine flourished on the support of the rich and the scandal of the naive.

Then in 1899 Diaghilev got his foot in the door of the Imperial Theaters, when Prince Volkonsky was appointed their director. Volkonsky assigned Diaghilev a new production of the ballet *Sylvia,* and he assembled Benois, Bakst, and Serov, another painter, to work on it. The Pickwickians were already fans of the ballet, their attention having been called to it primarily by Benois. But Diaghilev's flamboyance and arrogance provoked so much hostility in the Imperial Theaters that he was demoted and finally fired, amid a good deal of scandal.

In many ways the Russian ballet was, though conservative, the finest in Europe. The dancers were thoroughly and expertly trained, and the productions were lavishly financed. This was because the ballet company belonged to the state, or rather, to the czar. The dancers and choreographers did not need to compete in the marketplace for an audience. There were state schools, which the dancers entered as children, and once they became artists of the Imperial Theaters, they were in effect civil servants, with generous salaries, security of tenure, and an early pension. Ballet was not a mere adjunct to opera and drama in the Imperial Theaters, as it sometimes was in Paris. Every Wednesday and Sunday those theaters were set aside for ballet performances. The disadvantage was that they were also the private property of the Imperial family, whose members had access to the wings and dressing rooms, and who often chose a mistress from among the dancers. And the social or at least financial respectability of the ballet, which contrasted sharply with the position of other dancers in Russia, and dancers in other countries, brought with it the disadvantage that the same people stayed in authority for generations, and new ideas were not welcomed. Marius Petipa, for instance, was dance master in St. Petersburg for the second half of the nineteenth century and into the twentieth.

Like ballet elsewhere in nineteenth-century Europe, Russian ballet made women central. The ballerinas danced on their toes, and connoisseurs appreciated their sustained pirouettes and above all their elevation. The dancers defied gravity, and in some sense transcended corporeality. At their best, they were ethereal, and the ballet was magical. (We see the same in the New York City Ballet as developed by

Balanchine; whereas the Diaghilev Ballets Russes were in some ways different, as we shall see.)

Men dancers were mostly supportive, and though they had a tradition of expressive mime, that was somewhat separate from their dancing. It was not unusual for a man's role to be split between two performers, the older of whom did the mime, while the younger danced the romantic parts and lifted the ballerina. This fitted in with a general tendency to break up the story and the flow of the dance into a series of separate numbers.

The tradition of mime was kept alive by a series of Italian teachers, who constituted an ever-renewed contact with the commedia tradition. Russian ballet owed a debt to Denmark and France, but above all to Italy—and Italy meant the commedia and the mime tradition. When Virginia Zucchi danced in St. Petersburg for the season of 1885, she electrified everyone with her dramatic and mimic power, which was enhanced by the crude and unrealistic props she had to work with. Benois saw her and remembered her all his life as incomparable. The memory inspired him when he was devising ballets for Diaghilev. Diaghilev also considered it a great coup when in 1911 he persuaded Enrico Cecchetti to give lessons to his company; and when Cecchetti grew too old, in 1921, another Italian, Carlotta Brianza, took over.

Thus the state of ballet in Russia before Diaghilev could perhaps be described as "academic," but the standards maintained within those confines were higher than they were elsewhere. It had a tradition of professional expertise, like those in commedia companies like the Gelosi. Diaghilev combined those high standards with all the bright varieties of modernism, and with the spirit and topics of the commedia.

But that was to come later. Disappointed in this first attempt to bring new ideas into the ballet, Diaghilev turned his talents to organizing exhibitions of Russian paintings, first in St. Petersburg, and then in Paris. In 1905, a year of revolution in Russia, he mounted a very large exhibition of Russian portraits in the Tauride Palace in St. Petersburg, which he personally had borrowed from their owners, on a tireless series of journeys all over Russia. At a testimonial dinner in his honor, he made a speech that expressed some of his commedic ideas about history and art. These portraits, he said:

are only a grandiose summing up of a brilliant, but, alas! dead period of our history . . . we cannot any more believe the romantic heroism of terrifying helmets and heroic gestures. . . . We are witnesses of the greatest moment of summing up in history [he is referring to the revolution] in the name of a new and unknown culture, which will be created by us, and which will also sweep us away. That is why, without fear or misgiving, I raise my glass to the ruined walls of the beautiful palaces, as well as to the new commandments of a new aesthetic. The only wish that I, an incorrigible sensualist, can express, is that the forthcoming struggle should not damage the amenities of life, and that the death should be as beautiful and as illuminating as the resurrection.

(Haskell, pp. 160–61.)

This is a typically aesthetic piece of "political" thinking by a commedia sensibility.

In Paris, as he had in St. Petersburg, Diaghilev made as much of the art of exhibiting as he did of the objects displayed. He spent lavishly, and invented boldly, to modify the rooms assigned him, with drapes and false perspectives and theater architecture. He went to great lengths to hire the most impressive building, and to invite important guests to the opening night, so that the premieres were brilliant occasions and constituted a festival in the life of the city. He so presented art as to make it an occasion for a rich civilization to congratulate itself. This was the way the Imperial Theaters presented their dance company, also, but Diaghilev was more inventive, more au courant, more brilliant— and more raffish.

All Paris talked about his Russian paintings, and again about the Russian concerts he brought there in 1907 and 1908, at which he presented Chaliapin to the West and made him the most famous basso in the world.

Thus by 1909 Diaghilev was famous as the impresario of Russian art to the West, and the ballet seemed just the next in the series of excitements he was bringing every year. Benois dryly describes the Ballets Russes as just one phase in Diaghilev's export campaign.

But it was something much more than that when, in May, 1909, at the Théâtre du Châtelet, he presented his dancers, including Nijinsky and Karsavina, in a program of Benois's *Le Pavillon d'Armide*, *Les Sylphides*, with Pavlova and Nijinsky, Fokine's ecstatic version of the Polovtsian Dances, and Ida Rubinstein as Cleopatra.

In *La Pavillon d'Armide*, a young nobleman is invited to spend the night in a pavilion hung with Gobelin tapestries, by a sinister Marquis/magus. André Levinson, the ballet critic, compared this figure with Dapertutto (the E. T. A. Hoffmann character whose name Meyerhold borrowed for his nom de plume) and he is the first of many masks inside which we sense Diaghilev, for the Marquis in effect seduces the young man. Levinson calls him a mixture of dream magician and genuine devil, though with beautiful old-fashioned manners.

(Levinson, p. 9.) It is important to note how much the Pickwickians loved Hoffmann because his stories of magicians and hypnotists, dolls that come alive, and dollmakers in league with the devil, are a romantic version of the commedia.

The young man falls asleep, and in his dream, Armida steps down out of the tapestry and dances with him. One of her slaves is Nijinsky, who was sumptuously dressed in a skirt, with a feminine choker of pearls wound around his throat. (The story was taken from one by Gautier, the ballet lover of the mid–nineteenth century, and it has overtones of sexual ambivalence.) When the young man awakes, he realizes he has been dreaming, but then finds or is given Armida's shawl, which is lying where he saw her drop it in his dream.

The first aspect of ballet that everyone responded to was sensual splendor and lurid exoticism. As Benois said (of *Schéhérazade*, the following year), "From the stage there seem to pour spicy, sensuous aromas, and the soul is filled with alarm, as you realize that here, following the festival, behind these extraordinarily sweet images, must flow rivers of scarlet blood." (Lieven, p. 33.) His immediate reference there is to the execution of a slave (again played by Nijinsky) but more generally the reference is to the sadism behind the sensationalism of so many of the early Diaghilev ballets.

Though Paris found all this "so Russian," Prince Lieven points out that it seemed as exotic and new to Russians as to anyone else. Indeed, official Russia was hostile; the embassies wherever Diaghilev played were told not to lend countenance to the Ballets Russes. And even nonofficial Russians expected a single ballet to last all evening. This succession of glittering visions, and "the gorgeous decor, the choice of music other than ballet music, the daring, sometimes frenzied choreography," were as much of a shock to them as to Western Europeans. (*Ibid.*, p. 21.) It was at best St. Petersburg, not all Russia, and only the commedic avant-garde in that city, which was ready for this kind of "amoral" art.

The theatrical renaissance had occurred in Russia long after the nineteenth-century renaissance in the other arts, and in an atmosphere of moral rebellion—in the Silver Age of Russian culture, as opposed to its Golden Age. Literature had been heavily moral and political in nineteenth-century Russia (even Tolstoy had been found a frivolous novelist by the critics of the 1860s) and painting and music had followed the same pattern of development. But in the twentieth century, Meyerhold in theater and Diaghilev in ballet were flamboyantly aesthetic. Russia suddenly became the homeland of modernist art. Benois explained the triumph of the Ballets Russes in Paris, the enthusiasm of the Western audiences, by saying that Russians still believed in "art"—still knew the great Dionysiac inspiration.

Those first ballets were not all, taken individually, commedic; but taken together, as a program played by the Ballets Russes, their exoticism and sensationalism became just the colors of Harlequin's bright diamonds. For the exoticism was framed by other elements in the ballet performance and experience. One was the excitement of the dancers themselves, in Paris for the first time, and another was the wholesale improvisation necessary at the last minute. Diaghilev insisted on making changes to the stage machinery at the Châtelet, and on partly redecorating the auditorium. As Benois said, those engaged in the Diaghilev enterprise felt themselves to be conquistadores, usurpers, adventurers in the realm of art.

Moreover, that first night in Paris was a great social occasion, designed as carefully as the dances themselves. Diaghilev had entertained the appropriate critics in advance, and complimentary tickets had been sent to representatives of foreign governments and of other dance companies. Most strikingly, Gabriel Astruc, the Paris impresario with whom Diaghilev worked, had given front-row seats to beautiful actresses, alternating the blondes with the brunettes. Thus the auditorium became a stage, and everyone was everyone else's audience.

The dancers were a huge success immediately; notably with the homosexual intellectuals of Paris, including Cocteau, Robert de Montesquiou, Reynaldo Hahn, and Proust; but also with the leaders of fashion, like Madame de Greffulhe and Boni de Castellane. (These are figures best known to us now as the originals of the characters in Proust's fiction, but then they were leaders of Paris social life—figures in a real-life fiction.) And soon the inner circle of enthusiasts got to know the company socially, and found their way to the wings. Cocteau and Valentine Gross (who made drawings of all the dancers) have left us vivid descriptions of finding Nijinsky exhausted and panting on the boards after an apparently effortless leap from the stage into the wings. And this particular perception of the ballet, from the wings, was the crucial, the commedic, perception. Standing there, one saw both the ease and magic of a transcendent art, and its artifice, its strain, its fraud.

In 1910, Diaghilev took his dancers back to Paris, and in 1911 also on to London, where their social success was just as great. Le Figaro had cried in 1909 (under the headline "Le Gala Russe"), "Quelle soirée, quelle salle, quelle assistance!" and in 1911, in a similar vein, Diaghilev cabled Astruc from London, "Announce unparalleled triumph. . . . Audience indescribably smart." (Buckle, Diaghilev, pp. 143, 205.)

The newspapers and fashionable magazines like *The Lady* and *The Queen* were full of praise in superlatives, and the big stores changed their styles immediately, especially in imitation of Bakst's designs. Dress materials and patterns, upholstery, furnishings, all were affected within the season. Fashionable ladies began to wear jupe-culottes, turbans, and bandeaux with single peacock feathers affixed—anything that could be called "Persian." Designers in all sorts of materials mated blue with green, and red with orange, for the first time. Rooms were furnished with divans, alcoves, censers, and gaudy striped cushions on black or purple floors. Buckle says Bakst created a harem in every home; London became commedic. Strong and exotic perfumes, like sandalwood and patchouli, which had been the mark of the cocotte, were now bought by women of fashion. Poiret was the first couturier to sell scents, and he gave them Eastern names like Maharajah. The furniture windows of Heal's store and Harvey Nicols' were transformed, and Cartier's jewelry became more massive and colorful. Women wore ropes of pearls, with tassels of seed pearls, set off with coral and onyx, and tassels were attached to everything. And what was most striking was that this smart-set excitement was linked to artistic experiments that captured the imaginations of the most discriminating.

In the world of letters, as we have seen, the Sitwells and the Bloomsbury group were most responsive. Clive Bell, author of *Civilization*, and brother-in-law to Virginia Woolf, wrote, "Let us dance and sing, then, for singing and dancing are true arts, useless materially, valuable only for their aesthetic significance. Above all, let us dance and devise dances—dancing is a very pure art, a creation of abstract form." (Cohen, p. 15.) We read of many of Bloomsbury's devised dances in memoirs about them; for instance, the occasion on which J. M. Keynes danced the cancan at 45 Gordon Square with Lydia Lopokova. Virginia Woolf describes such a dance in her first novel, *The Voyage Out*. "The tune changed to a minuet; St. John hopped with incredible swiftness first on his left leg, then on his right; the tune flowed melodiously; Hewet, swaying his arms and holding out the tails of his coat, swam down the room in imitation of the voluptuous dream dance of an Indian maiden dancing before her Rajah." (Woolf, p. 166.)

Other literary figures on the edge of Bloomsbury shared the enthusiasm. Rupert Brooke wrote to his friend Eddie Marsh about the Russian dancers, in 1911, "They, if anything can, redeem our civilization. I'd give anything to be a ballet-designer." (Buckle, *Diaghilev*, p. 236.) Lady Ottoline Morell got to know Diaghilev and Nijinsky socially, and because she was also the friend of D. H. Lawrence we have a description of another of those devised dances at her house in his novel *Women in Love*. "A servant came, and soon reappeared with armfuls of silk robes and shawls and scarves, mostly Oriental, things that Hermione, with her love for beautiful extravagant dress, had collected gradually. . . . It was finally decided to do Ruth and Naomi and Orpah. Ursula was Naomi, Gudrun was Ruth, the Contessa was Orpah. The idea was to make a little ballet, in the style of the Russian Ballet of Pavlova and Nijinsky." (Lawrence, pp. 83–84.) Lawrence, of course, saw such dancing as part of the decadence into which his doomed pair, Gudrun and Gerald, were sinking. (The healthy kind of dancing we see in Anna's and Ursula's dancing in *The Rainbow*, which derives from German expressionist dance.)

And traces of this influence are widespread in the descriptive vocabulary of the time. Take the adjective "Russian" in T. S. Eliot's lines "Grishkin is nice, her Russian eye/Is underlined, for emphasis" and in Edmund Wilson's "girls with wonderfully drawn Russian eyebrows."

But all such matters of social decor and "influence" must be comparatively superficial or peripheral manifestations of the commedia idea. To see this idea given aesthetic profundity, we should turn to *Petrushka*, performed in 1911, and one of the greatest of all Diaghilev's triumphs. Edith Sitwell said, "This ballet, alone among them all, shatters our glass house about our ears and leaves us terrified, haunted by its tragedy." She explained it to her readers by making long quotations from Rimbaud and Laforgue—"In *Petrushka* we see mirrored for us, in those sharp outlines and movements, all the philosophy of Laforgue, as the puppets move somnambulistically through the dark of our hearts." (Hamm, p. 188.)

Stravinsky composed the score and Fokine the choreography, but the ballet is described (by Prince Lieven) as the triumph of the Pickwickians. Certainly Benois seems to have been responsible for the story line and decor, which derived ultimately from the fairground puppets he had seen as a child. Like so many boys of his class and generation, he had been given a puppet theater of his own, on which he re-created such performances. This puppeteering seems to have been a determining experience of creative art for him, as for others. It seems that at the end of the nineteenth century, the haute bourgeoisie of Europe began to take into their houses puppet theaters that had belonged to the fairgrounds and the people. Playing with them became as determining an experience for the aesthetes among the next generation as playing with soldiers was for the more military and playing shop was for certain others. Benois set up his theater (in which he played every part, and others were allowed only to be audience) in the same Red Room in his family home where later the Pickwickians held their meetings. (The Nijinsky children also saw the fairground puppets enact this story, but their family was not rich enough to give them a theater of their own, so they acted the parts.)

The scenario presents a fairground with a crowd of holidaymakers and three puppets, each in his booth: Petrushka (though he acted like Harlequin in the original story, he turns into Pierrot in the ballet), the Blackamoor (the Harlequin figure), and the Ballerina. They are owned by a Charlatan or Showman—another Hoffmann figure. Petrushka loves the Ballerina, and his love arouses him to nearly human life, but she prefers the simpler, cruder Blackamoor. Petrushka's intelligence and sensibility make him ridiculous to a superficial creature like her. Petrushka provokes the Blackamoor, fights him, and is slain. The Charlatan, who comes to pick up Petrushka, explains to the crowd that there is no call for grief, because Petrushka was only a doll. But suddenly, as a climax to the story, the spirit of Petrushka appears above his booth, accusing the Charlatan of a lie, of denying his immortal soul. In his love he had been alive.

One reason why this story was so moving to those who loved the Ballets Russes was that it mirrored the central emotional drama within the company—the relationship between Diaghilev and Nijinsky. Diaghilev, the great impresario and charlatan, had taken his leading dancer as his lover. By general agreement, Nijinsky delivered a marvelous performance as Petrushka, but of a kind never seen before. Lieven called it expressionistic dancing: angular, doll-like, and terre-à-terre. Nijinsky really looked like a puppet trying to become human. Lieven also calls Petrushka the first ballet tragedy in history. Cyril Beaumont, praising Nijinsky also, ascribes his poignant effect to what he had sacrificed as a dancer through his self-stylization—his sacrifice of his "fascinating features" and slanting eyes, for instance. Lieven suggests that Nijinsky might have justifiably leaned over the literal footlights, like Petrushka over his booth, and asked Diaghilev, "What have you done to my immortal soul?" (Lieven, p. 146.)

Whatever view we ourselves take of the relationship between the two men, it remains important that people intimate with the ballet company, like Beaumont and Lieven, should have seen it in these melodramatic terms. Nijinsky was apparently a strikingly ineffectual personality offstage, even before he began to display the symptoms of his eventual madness. He was, by most people's account, silent, evasive, uninformed. People like Benois, Stravinsky, and Lieven assert confidently that he had no mind, and no personality offstage. One gets a different impression from the book by his sister, Bronislava, and one can imagine that aristocrats of taste like those three formed a formidable audience for a self-doubting nonintellectual. But whatever he could have been under other circumstances, it seems established that the Nijinsky of the Ballets Russes was a doll-like Petrushka figure.

And Diaghilev was a possessive and paralyzing Charlatan. He surrounded Nijinsky with his protection, his gifts, his education. He gave him a complete set of *Mir Iskusstva* to study, and the catalogues of his exhibitions, but he also surrounded him with surveillance (Diaghilev's personal servant kept constant watch on Nijinsky) and carried him off at the end of rehearsals so that no one else should get close to him, especially no woman. Diaghilev was not only a homosexual but a propagandist for homosexuality as beneficial to an artist. (*Ibid.*, p. 258.)

There were, moreover, sadistic elements in Diaghilev's personality. He enjoyed frustrating and mystifying others; above all, he often said (not only about Nijinsky) that he could make anyone into a great dancer, whenever he wanted to. "I could make a plate dance if I wanted to. I do not discover, I invent." (*Ibid.*, p. 247.) This was part of his Nietzschean bravura: "The weak must perish, not be helped. . . . One must be above the petty squabbles and cares of mankind. . . . I want to leave them open-mouthed." (*Ibid.*, p. 253.) And thus people watching Nijinsky saw him as Diaghilev's creation, as Petrushka was the Charlatan's.

It is notable how often Nijinsky danced the part of a slave or a doll in these ballets. Besides being Armida's slave, he was Cleopatra's, and then, in *Schéhérazade*, he was slave to Zobeide, and a specifically sexual toy. And in *Petrushka* he was a doll. Nuvel pointed this out to Diaghilev with some malice, saying that he hoped that he would free Nijinsky some day. (Buckle, *Nijinsky*, p. 124.) Diaghilev was very sensitive to the suggestion that he was a slavemaster and dictatorial manager. Stravinsky jokingly made that assertion about him, and it has been suggested that the monstrous Manager figures Picasso constructed for *Parade* (in committee with Stravinsky and Cocteau) were a thrust at Diaghilev.

Later, Nijinsky was succeeded in Diaghilev's favor by other young dancers, notably Massine, Dolin, and Lifar. With all of them he instituted, or tried to, the same possessive and pedagogical relationship that he had had with Nijinsky. He took Massine around the art galleries of Florence, refining his taste, and at the same time invited him to devise new ballets for the company. But when he suspected Massine of amorous relations with two women, he had him followed by three pairs of detectives. When he thought he knew which girl was guilty, he had her brought to his hotel, drugged, stripped, and thrown into Massine's room, for him to find. Thus the commedia story line, with its Pierrots and Harlequins dancing at the Charlatan's command, was always eloquent to the Diaghilev audience, whether the dependent figures were a doll, a slave, an acrobat, a literal Pierrot, or a ghost, as in *Le Spectre de la rose.*

Buckle has given us an interesting account of Nijinsky's performance in the last-named ballet. (*Ibid.*, p. 192.) "Nijinsky instinctively realized that he must de-sex himself, soften every line, keep continually swinging, curving and circling like a leaf caught in a whirl of wind. . . . The most thrilling attribute of Nijinsky's performance was its strangeness—a quality of movement like the soaring song of the great castrati." (*Ibid.*, p. 193.) And many connoisseurs (for instance, Fokine) remarked on Nijinsky's inaptitude for conventionally noble or heroic roles. Though an attractive figure, and not effeminate, he was not suited to the traditional princely hero roles of ballet. One dimension of his pathos, his individuality, as a dancer, was precisely his distance from ordinary manliness. That individuality, plus his extraordinary technical and imaginative gifts were at the core of the Ballets Russes' glamor.

The story of *The Firebird* also makes use of the Hoffmann figure of the wizard/impresario. (So of course does the later *La Boutique Fantasque*, a remake of *Die Puppenfee*, which Bakst had designed; it is a typical ballet subject.) The story that Stravinsky and the committee concocted was something of a mishmash of folk elements, but according to a more coherent version, the Firebird is a village girl with a great gift for the traditional skill of colorful embroidery. When traveling merchants visit her village, they suggest that she come to the city, where rich people will appreciate and reward her skill. But she says she belongs where she was born, where her ancestors have lived and are buried. Then the sorcerer, Kotschei, begins to practice his deceptions upon her, promising every dazzling prize, but in vain. In fury, he transforms himself into a black dragon-bird, and her into a firebird with brilliant feathers like her own embroidery. Clutching her in his claws he rises into the air above the village. But she, in despair, plucks out her own brilliant feathers, which fall to earth for men to find. In other words, the folk arts of rural Russia, taken to the metropolis by an impresario like Diaghilev, leave behind brilliant but tragic mementos in the form of these ballets. This is implicitly a commedia story about theater.

The explicit commedia references of *Petrushka* were repeated in other Diaghilev ballets, including some of his most brilliant successes. There was, for instance, *Le Carnaval* (1910), danced to Schumann's music, with a Pierrot, a Harlequin, and a Columbine. Adrian Stokes has eloquently evoked the magic of that ballet in *Tonight the Ballet.* There was *Pulcinella* (1920), the fruit of a visit paid to Naples by Diaghilev and Stravinsky, and always a favorite. And there was *Parade* (1917), the occasion of scandal when it was first given in Paris.

Here the audience saw three samplings of the acts or turns at a traveling fair, each performer giving a brief preliminary performance outside his little booth in order to draw in the crowds. One is a Chinese conjurer, one a "Little American Girl" like Annie Oakley, and the third act is a pair of acrobats. They are driven to perform by their Managers, who are figures of harsh dominance, scolding the actors and exhorting the potential audience. The situation is therefore quite like that in *Petrushka.* The Managers wear towering cubist constructs as costumes, which leave only their arms and legs free to move. The score, by Satie, is also cubist, in that the music is interrupted by reproductions of modern noises, like sirens, drills, and machines. At the end the putative audience drifts away, having seen enough of the "parade" outside the booths without going in and paying. Cocteau said *Parade* ought to "distill all the involuntary emotions given off by circuses, music halls, carousels, public balls, factories, seaports, the movies, etc., etc." (Axsom, p. 59.) This is of course what Laforgue tried to do in his verse.

There are, then, cubist elements in the costumes, music, and choreography, and they work against the commedia elements, of dance and theater. Kirstein complains that the "dancing had been allowed to degenerate into shuffling, painting into artificial cubist chaos, music into carefully negligible noise." (Kirstein, p. 299.) But not everything is cubist. Picasso's overture curtain is an enormous commedia painting of two Harlequins (representing himself and Cocteau) with their friends, sitting around a table, and looking across at another group, comprised of a horse with circus wings strapped around its belly, an acrobat ballerina, and a monkey whom she is helping to climb a ladder, preparatory, no doubt, to walking a tightrope. In other words, the Harlequins, at whom the theater audience gazes when the *rideau rouge* goes up, are seen to be themselves gazing at another group of performers, who are still more travestied by their work as performers. The theme is, once again, theatricality, the pathos of the artist, who can only speak out indirectly, in performance, and whose best work—to be seen only inside his theater—will always be neglected for the external and superficial.

Just before the end, an insolent placard appears, saying, "The drama, which did not take place for those people who stayed outside, was by

Jean Cocteau, Erik Satie, Pablo Picasso." And the curtain makes clear the intimate connection of the commedia iconography with the cubist rigor that was coming into fashion.

There were of course far more ballets with non-commedia scenarios, but quite a few of them were nevertheless commedia cognates. One example is the eighteenth-century rococo fantasy *Le Pavillon d'Armide*. Benois said he intended this ballet to recall "the fêtes of the Sun King, whom I greatly admired and to whom I had dedicated several paintings." (Kochno, p. 7.) We have already seen the affinity that existed between the commedia and the rococo. By the same token, some of the early nineteenth-century set ballets, like *Giselle* and *Le Spectre de la rose*, were also rococo in spirit; the frame surrounding the romantic action reduced the latter to a decorative motif. (Both derive from ideas by Théophile Gautier, the nineteenth-century purveyor of commedia taste, who admired Deburau/Pierrot and helped write *Giselle* for the dancer Grisi.) And then the Oriental exotica, as already pointed out, were in effect commedia pantomimes (though of course given the benefit of extraordinary taste).

For many viewers, the ballet subject did not matter, because the ballet performance turned anything into "art," into theatricality. In *Tonight the Ballet*, Adrian Stokes writes, "For Ballet technique, in the perfect outwardness of its stylized forms, is akin to the dominant Mediterranean mode of projecting emotion as we find it in Mediterranean visual art . . . romantic impulses attain a concrete and definite fulfillment within the ballet framework without loss of their fluent strengths." (Stokes, p. 36.) The ballet, he says, restores to us the commedia masks, the Italian temperament. Thus it was only rarely that Diaghilev attempted something radically unlike the commedia, as he did in *L'Après-midi d'un faune* and *Le Sacre du printemps*, with their anthropological primitivism.

Indeed, in saying "radically unlike," we are leaving out of account the cultural character of the company, which stamped even *L'Après-midi d'un faune* with a somewhat rococo or commedia character. (This treatment of primitive material distinguishes Diaghilev from the German expressionist dancers.)

And this commedia character was not merely a matter of the sexual scandal of Nijinsky's performance, or of the aesthetic preferences of Diaghilev and the committee of taste makers who surrounded him. It was a matter even more of the economic character of the Diaghilev enterprise, and of the company's life-style. From 1909 on, they lived in hotel rooms, out of half-unpacked trunks, under threat of bills that got paid by somebody else and at the last minute.

Diaghilev took ballet away from the social respectability of the Imperial Theaters of St. Petersburg, back to the raffishness of the circus. There are many anecdotes of him on a first night having to appeal to a friend who had already taken a seat among the audience, asking for money to pay some importunate dun or theater official who would not allow the curtain to rise until he was satisfied.

Nijinsky's mother, who had had to dance in a circus (her husband, himself a famous leaping dancer, preferred the freedom of circus work) had made every sacrifice to get her son into the Imperial Theater schools, and was dismayed to see him link his fortune to Diaghilev's. Bronislava Nijinska tells us her parents worked in a *café chantant* for a time, and her father at the Folies Bergères, and the children learned juggling and somersaults from their parents' colleagues before getting into the Imperial schools. There was moreover a strong sense of the difference in dignity between these different kinds of entertainment. Vaslav thought his father's famous leaps were more a matter of acrobatics than of dance, and both he and his sister felt it a sad comedown for Pavlova that she had to appear in music halls. And yet the Ballets Russes dancers had to do that too, on occasion. But Diaghilev found for his Ballets Russes a social space between, or rather above, both the music hall and the Imperial Theaters. It was not socially respectable, but it was aesthetically triumphant.

Diaghilev lived extravagantly and improvidently, both as an individual and as a company director. The company kept no books for many years, and such accounts as there were later were sketchy. The contracts were between individual dancers and Diaghilev himself. Prince Lieven points out that Diaghilev conducted a business that, in 1911, had a budget of two million gold francs, with no books, no regular support, and no capital. He relied on creating an atmosphere of supra-commercial triumph around his company, which would bring in sufficient audiences and, more important, the subventions of the rich. To create that atmosphere, he had to have prestige but also publicity; and so he needed both sexual-moral scandals and intellectual-aesthetic controversies. There were sexual scandals in 1911 when Nijinsky was dismissed from the Imperial Theaters for wearing an indecent costume, and in 1912 in Paris when he simulated orgasm on stage in *L'Après-midi d'un faune*. Diaghilev had to have new painters and composers with new ideas all the time, and to produce extraordinary effects that would start people talking. All this was both genuinely exciting to the artists involved, and also alarming and dissatisfying.

Thus in the history of ballet from 1850 to 1980, from Petipa to

Balanchine, the Diaghilev years were an interlude of insecurity and instability, of glamour and squalor—of show business—when ballet was closer to circus, to carnival, than it had been before and was to be after. Often the dancers performed next to performing apes, dialect comedians, ventriloquists, leaders of sing-alongs. They had fifteen minutes to distill their magic, after which it was dispelled, but that transiency or transparency was congenial, since their genius was theatrical.

And then there were some very theatrical personages associated with the Ballets Russes, who brought the spirit of the commedia into real life. K. F. Valz, a theater technician whom Diaghilev brought from Russia with him, wore high heels, rouged cheeks, and dyed hair, and succeeded in looking fifty at the age of seventy-two. Baron Gunsburg, the Jewish financier, traveled with the ballet and lived for it. Gabriel Astruc and Diaghilev himself were *lions comiques,* to use the music hall term for comically grand personages. They brought the theater into the street. Moreover, some of the "public" who most attached themselves to the ballet were just as theatrical; for instance, Robert de Montesquiou (Proust's Baron de Charlus), who did a lot to spread the fame of the dancers in fashionable Paris; and Jean Cocteau, who already then wore rouge and lipstick and tried to persuade Nijinsky to follow his example. That is why the Ballets Russes carried the commedia infection so powerfully everywhere; whatever the company danced, the audience got the message, both of the beauty and richness of art (of fantasy and taste) and of its fragility and falsity—a tension of contradiction between art and other, moral and social, values.

"Classical" ballet, as performed earlier in the Imperial Theaters in St. Petersburg, and later by the New York City Ballet, was purer in its taste, less self-divided and self-exhibiting. Such ballet appropriately represents and dignifiedly belongs to the capital city of a great empire. Though remote from power and administration, and much more from politics, economic conflict, industrial dispute, such ballet constitutes an alternative occupation of the mind for the citizens of the metropolis, and just by its remoteness constitutes an alternative space.

Indeed, it is a fantasy *for* the ruling group—the rich men of the city. Suzanne Gordon brings out that point well in her book on contemporary ballet, *Off Balance.* She suggests the source and orientation of the magic of ballet in power relations—in the gratification of a male consciousness of power by the spectacle of female grace attenuated to an extreme. For she also shows us the source of that shimmering and diaphanous quality in the anorexic thinness of the dancers' bodies, "alarmingly frail and curiously defeminized." (Gordon, p. 91.)

It was the same in Imperial Russia. The Imperial Theaters and their schools belonged to the czar, and he and his family and friends enjoyed visiting them. Prince Lieven tells us that "A charming picture greeted [visitors] in the practice halls of the schools. Young girls about fifteen to eighteen in tutus with bare arms and shoulders, without make-up, were grouped here and there at the side of the hall, whispering and sometimes laughing together." (Lieven, p. 65.) The Diaghilev ballet presented a more disturbing and scandalous picture, less flattering to the visiting potentates from the outside.

Margot Fonteyn has drawn attention to the similarities between Petipa, the *maestro* of the Imperial ballet, and Balanchine, for instance, the shape of their careers (settling in a foreign country for a long career as dance master to a great company) and in the character of their taste (their avoidance of strong emotion directly expressed in dance). (Fonteyn, p. 198.) Diaghilev was very different, in his peripatetic career and in the various scandals that surrounded him. His was a much more flamboyant accusation of the power structure and respectability of his society; accusing it both by his proud self-separation from it, and by his embodiment of a comparable corruption. His ballet was like Deburau's Funambules; that of the other two ballet-masters was more like the Comédie-Française.

Perhaps the most striking similarity between Petipa and Balanchine (and of course there are many disparities, and it does not seem that Petipa was as great an artist) is that both built ballet companies and ballet traditions around *women* dancers. Balanchine often said that ballet is a feminine art, for men to appreciate—a ballet is like a rose, like a woman. Men dancers, for him and for Petipa, are comparatively minor; both in the more literal sense of their stage function, where they support the women, and also in the sense of their emotional significance; the men seem somewhat peripheral to the idea "dancer," at least to its severer tensions. They are, for instance, allowed more sexual freedom, and more fullness of body.

This is of course in striking contrast with the Diaghilev ballet, where the young men, Nijinsky, Massine, Dolin, Lifar, were each in turn the focus of attention, for the company and for the audience. Some of the great women stars, like Pavlova and Kschessinska, avoided dancing for Diaghilev just because they knew that they would be edged out of the spotlight. The great exception, Karsavina, seems to have survived in the company because she was something of an intellectual, and found a comradeship of the mind with the men. Lieven tells us that Diaghilev disliked women and treated them with contempt. He held marriage to

Family of Saltimbanques

Fokine and Fokina in *Carnival*

Nijinsky in *Schéhérazade*

Diaghilev and Cocteau

Stravinsky and Nijinsky

[RIGHT] Charlie Chaplin
[BELOW, LEFT] "Little Tich"
[BELOW, RIGHT] Buster Keaton

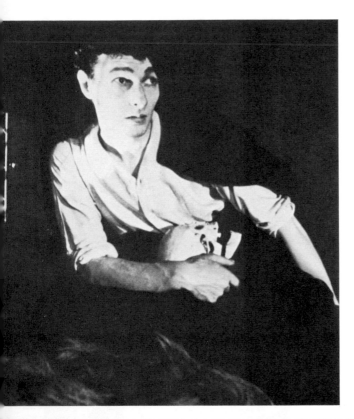

[LEFT] As Laforgue's Hamlet
[BELOW] As a real-life Pierrot
in a crowd of pretenders

be dangerous to a man of talent, and held that homosexuality was necessary to an artist. Certainly the Ballets Russes were a showcase for masculine beauty, and this again illustrates the different context into which he put ballet—the different cultural alliances he chose, compared with those chosen by the other two great ballet masters. They allied themselves to basically conservative forces in their societies. The Diaghilev ballet made its alliance with the subversive elements in culture; in a patriarchal society sexual desirability is more appropriately attributed to women.

The other contrast it is important to draw is between the Diaghilev ballet and the Modern Dance movement, which arose at roughly the same historical moment. This movement was led by Rudolf von Laban and Mary Wigman, and flourished in Germany.

Diaghilev talked about these dancers to a reporter in December 1928: "Their effort to heighten the possibilities of that sublime instrument which is the human body altogether deserves our approval. Yet their crusade against the 'outdated' classical dance led choreography into a blind alley from which it has not yet escaped. Germany has dancers who can move admirably, but they do not know how to dance." (Kochno, p. 286.) For him, all true dance, all art, was essentially theatrical and commedic.

Lincoln Kirstein, long associated with Balanchine and the New York City Ballet, has also made some pungent criticisms of Wigman and von Laban. Kirstein's aesthetic criterion is the same as Adrian Stokes's—the "produced" quality of the achieved work of art, which he finds in ballet dance and not in modern dance. (This is the criterion that makes commedia superior to other forms of theater.) Stokes describes Columbine's dancing feet in *Carnaval* (quoting Gautier, in fact) as like steel arrows rebounding quickly from a marble pavement, a kind of dancing which yet suggests the dancer's earthiness far better than "the heavy, barefoot or sandaled dancer, the expressionist dancer, who slowly enacts a kind of dream, whose movements imply that the stage is but a poor substitute for greenswards and woods." (Stokes, p. 38.) The same antagonism was felt by the dancers themselves. Bronislava Nijinska tells us that when she and her brother saw Isadora Duncan dance in 1908, he declared such childish hoppings and skippings could not be called art; and she herself was fiercely scornful of the Jaques-Dalcroze eurythmics when Diaghilev took her to see them at Hellerau.

The difference between the two schools, between commedia and anticommedia, is named by the ballet enthusiasts as visibility versus viscerality. From the other point of view, it is a difference between a series of external accomplishments and the expression of a unified center. Von

Laban set up an opposition between the five senses known to science, and the single, dancer's, sense of the environment, which apprehends everything as a whole and responds to it as a whole.

From the point of view of cultural history, perhaps the most important way to think of the difference is as two responses to the shared perception of social and political history as tragic. Diaghilev accepts the bitter ironies of modern life, allows them to fragment aesthetic and philosophic form, embraces all the jaggedness and compensates us for it with moments of glorious fantasy. The decadence von Laban rejects as "the Queen of the Night," Diaghilev makes a cult of. Von Laban turns away from all that irony and jaggedness and looks for a new faith in the intrapersonal depths of the individual dancer and in the interpersonal relations of the dancing group. He looks for new truth; Diaghilev, being a commedia artist, embraces old falsehood (in order to transcend it).

All ballet has something of this commedia character. Prince Lieven says:

There is no place on earth so strange, unreal, and fantastic as a ballet stage during an interval . . . [or the sight of] a sylphide, her face rudely daubed with wet white and streaming with large beads of perspiration. She is still panting, and looks serious, pathetic. (Lieven, p. 352.) [We see a dancer] the embodiment of flight, extraordinary buoyancy, a joy of life. Her number comes to an end. With graceful leaps and the same happy smile she flies towards the wings and with one last bound reaches the blue shadows . . . and falls exhausted on the floor . . . a little heap of tulle. Her poor weak body is shaken by her quick, uneven breathing. With face drawn after the exertion, she looks like an animal at bay.

(*Ibid.*, p. 356.)

On the question of makeup, Bronislava Nijinska describes the first time her face was painted, for a performance of *Die Puppenfee* in 1905, while she was still a child dancer. It was done by Bakst himself. He drew two bright red circles on her cheeks, and long lashes on her cheeks. Then the child looked at herself in the mirror, transformed. That moment, when one becomes unreal, becomes a figure in other people's fantasy, is repeated all the time in ballet and commedia. Suzanne Gordon describes watching two dancers rehearse a romantic pas de deux as one of the oddest experiences she ever had. "Coupling to the music, they stared past each other, through each other, over each other, straining for a glimpse in the mirror, making this lyrical dance an almost comic parody." (Gordon, p. 26.) Surely ballet is the most beautiful of the arts, but—as the modern dancers complained—that beauty can involve the neglect or denial of other values, such as truth. Benois said that all the time he worked on a ballet he was as in a dream. "The actualities of life seemed colourless and dead." (Lieven, p. 78.) And if this was true of classical ballet, it was much more true of Diaghilev's commedic enterprise.

Throughout his career, Diaghilev stayed in touch with the friends he had joined in St. Petersburg in the 1880s, the Pickwickians; but they did not agree with all he did. Benois disapproved of most of Diaghilev's work of the 1920s, when he seemed to be driven by a craze for modernity at all costs. Prince Lieven says that many Russians thought Diaghilev was taking a decadent parody of their ballet to the West, and he indicates that he sees some truth to that charge. Levinson distinguished the "Russian ballet's tinselled decor and exotic trappings" from the "golden essence of the art."

More discreetly, they disapproved of the sexual and financial scandals surrounding the Ballets Russes. Stravinsky said, "It is impossible to describe the perversity of Diaghilev's entourage—a kind of homosexual Swiss Guard." (Spencer and Dyer, p. 67.) He tells how at a rehearsal at Monte Carlo he found the pianist distracted, and saw that he was gazing love-struck at a soldier in uniform, murmuring, "I long to surrender myself to him." Stravinsky and Benois were, like Nabokov, men who found marriage in better taste than promiscuity and homosexuality. They were even, or so they claimed, men of religion. In general, they looked backward, nostalgically. Benois said, "My whole outlook on life is to an extreme degree sentimentally reminiscent. I find it hard to destroy even an old slip of paper. After all, the past is the only real thing in life, the future does not exist and the present is merely fiction." (Lieven, p. 269.) They were classical conservatives.

In all these ways, Diaghilev was certainly different. He looked toward the future, eager to ally himself with it (though of course he also looked back to the past with great appreciation). Generally speaking, he was cruder; he was unlike his friends in his passion to *épater le bourgeois*. But that crudity was the condition and expression of his energy, the energy with which he propagated the taste he shared with them. That crudity also made him more completely a man of the commedia. They maintained a distance from that world, they were its scholars. He was immersed in it.

There were many continuities between his first years and his last, and between him and the Silver Age poetry scene. One of the painters whose work he took to Paris (before he became a ballet impresario) was Sergei Sudeikin. This man was the husband of Olga Sudeikina, the central figure in the scandal of Knyazer's suicide, which inspired the poetry of Kuzmin and Akhmatova. In later years he designed ballets for Diaghilev. In 1914, Sudeikin designed *La Tragédie de Salomé* for the Ballets Russes (story by Wilde, sets inspired by Beardsley). He was, we are told by his second wife, for some time very close to Diaghilev. And that second wife, for a time dressmaker for the Ballets Russes, in the 1920s left Sudeikin to become Madame Stravinsky. These people constituted a (somewhat commedic) social world.

In 1925, Diaghilev found a permanent home for his company in Monte Carlo. He produced several ballets of a frivolous kind, about the seaside or about holidays or sports. But at the very end, just before his death in 1929, he produced two more substantial works. One was *Ode*, a largely Russian production, with an idea taken from Lomonosov, designed by Tchelitchev, and composed by Nicholas Nabokov. The other was Stravinsky and Balanchine's *Apollon musagète*, which pointed the way to the new classicism that was to be practiced by the New York City Ballet.

His own life, however, and his death, had the same features of the sumptuous and the sordid, the pathetic and the absurd, the same commedia features, as before. He had adopted three new, very young favorites, Boris Kochno, a poet; Serge Lifar, a dancer; and Igor Markevich, a composer. And when he died, in Venice on holiday, Kochno and Lifar were with him, and quarreled ludicrously over his heritage. His body was taken out to a cemetery in a black-and-gold gondola, but Lifar leaped into the grave and made a scene at the interment. Buckle tells us that when Nijinsky died, in 1950, Balanchine refused to be a pallbearer because he feared Lifar would make a similar commedic scene there too. This illustrates once more the difference in taste between the Diaghilev enterprise and what succeeded it. (Buckle, *Adventures*, p. 42.)

For the more grand, if grandiloquent, aspect of the Diaghilev enterprise, we can turn to Serge Grigoriev, the company's regisseur. When he first visited Diaghilev's grave, some time after the death, he says, "It was a wonderful sunny day. A deep silence reigned, the silence of cemeteries on still, fine days. Opening my eyes after a minute, I read the words cut on his tombstone. 'Venise l'Inspiratrice Eternelle de nos Appaisements [Venice, Our Eternal Fount of Consolations] Serge de Diaghilev 1882–1929.' " (Grigoriev, p. 262.)

Chapter 4.

MASKS, MIMES, AND MEYERHOLD: COMMEDIA IN THE THEATER

The public comes to the theatre to see the art of man, but what art is there in walking about the stage as oneself? The public expects invention, playacting and skill. But what it gets is either life or a slavish imitation of life. Surely the art of man on the stage consists in shedding all traces of environment, carefully choosing a mask, donning a decorative costume, and showing off one's brilliant tricks to the public—now as a dancer, now as the intrigant at some masquerade, now as the fool of old Italian comedy, now as a juggler.

(Meyerhold, *The Fairground Booth*, 1912, in Braun, *Meyerhold*, p. 130.)

W HATEVER the transformations imposed upon the "old Italian comedy" by the great revolutionaries in art, literature, music, and the ballet, it is well to remember that it was originally a very specific form of theater. It is significant, therefore, that some of the most vital, influential creators of modern theater embrace the old comedy (and its close cousins in the circus and the carnival) not only as raw material for new images and angles, but also as a gaudy storehouse of techniques for movement and acrobatics and of plots and characters.

Theatricality is of the essence in modernism, and it is not surprising that its literally theatrical form is, like the other modernist modes of expression, more or less traceable to Wagnerian and symbolist roots. The prophetic director Adolphe Appia projected a new world of lighting, design, and movement in the early nineties, taking Wagner as his inspiration. The signal champions of the new commedia all felt his influence and that of others of Wagnerian bent, but they also turned to the commedia. They did this in very different ways, despite much cross-pollination. Gordon Craig's vision of the masked, "depersonalized" actor

79

exerting supreme self-control, fueled by his scholarly resuscitation of the original commedia and of puppetry, is quite unlike Meyerhold's demand for masterfully acrobatic, assertively "grotesque" actors in his commedia transformations of Russian classics. Max Reinhardt's lush and tender baroque commedia bears little resemblance to the sharp ambiguities generated in Pirandello's commedic turns, to say nothing of the commedia in the raw cabaret satire of Brecht. The differences are vast, but these men, and many others, all went to the same storehouse for inspiration in their struggles for a new theater.

The figures of Pierrot, Harlequin, Columbine, and their fellows and their tricks are always more than incidental, more than casual decoration; for the revolutionaries their presence always celebrates or at least underlines the essential theatricality of the dramatic experience. The characters and symbols of commedia were central to the life of the Ballets Russes, but for the contemporary modernists of the theater, above all for Vsevolod Meyerhold, commedia was the wellspring of theatrical technique and much that was most telling in his dramatic vision. Considering the range and variety of the invention of the great Russian director, his eager absorption of bits and pieces from the theater of the East as well as the West, it may seem an overstatement to place the commedia so close to the center of his inspiration—but that kaleidoscopic taste was itself characteristic of the new commedists.

The scholarly and critical rediscovery of this master in the past two decades, after years of near-oblivion instigated by his murderer, Stalin, has made it possible to see the evidence of Meyerhold's work in a remarkable abundance of material that not long ago was considered to be lost forever. The vein of commedia runs bright throughout that evidence and Meyerhold's entire career.

Meyerhold's Early Career

Meyerhold's career, and his revolt against theatrical naturalism, began in the very home of such naturalism; indeed, in the breeding ground of its most vital and influential modern form. In the fall of 1896, the twenty-two-year-old son of an affluent distiller from the small town of Penza entered the drama school of the Moscow Philharmonic Society, having foresworn law school in favor of life in the theater. His principal teacher was Vladimir Nemirovich-Danchenko, brilliant and demanding crusader for naturalism in acting, who instilled in this star pupil a "literary grounding" and the ability to analyze character. In Meyerhold's words, "Above all, he was concerned with the internal justification of the role.

He demanded a clearly outlined personality." (Braun, *Theatre*, p. 21.)

In March 1898, Meyerhold graduated, winning the school's silver medal. The other winner of this highest honor was Olga Knipper, who was to become the wife of Chekhov. They both followed their teacher in a venture that was to become the most famous and enduring theatrical institution of twentieth-century Russia. In June 1897, Nemirovich-Danchenko and a well-to-do merchant and theater reformer, Alexeyev, who had adopted the name Stanislavsky, made the decision to embody their agenda for a new Russian drama in an entirely new theatrical enterprise, which became the Moscow Art Theater. In Stanislavsky's words:

We protested against the old manner of acting, against theatricalism, false pathos, declamation, artificiality in acting, bad staging, and decor conventions.

(Gorchakov, p. 21.)

The company was in revolt *against* "theatricalism" and "artificiality," in the ossified forms characteristic of the theatrical establishment. Thus Meyerhold's path began in a direction away from an externalized, conventionalized theater, and though there were many twists to that path, he always followed it.

His career with the Moscow Art Theater (or Moscow Popular Art theater, as it was first called, reflecting its populist spirit) began brilliantly. Not only did he enjoy the high esteem of both cofounders, but he quickly won the warm regard of Chekhov, particularly with his portrayal of the rebellious and sensitive young Treplev in *The Seagull*, the work destined to be the "signature" of the Moscow Art Theater. Even at this point, however, Meyerhold was having his difficulties with the tenets of theatrical naturalism, and later he was to call Chekhov himself as witness against the excesses of Moscow Art realism.

For Meyerhold, Chekhov was the creator of a "theater of mood" rather than of naturalism. He quotes him as asserting that "The stage demands a degree of artifice . . . the stage reflects the quintessence of life and there is no need to introduce anything superfluous on to it." The key "Stanislavskian" playwright thus became the ally of the antinaturalist, even the symbolist, for the young Meyerhold. However exaggerated this may be, it is true that Meyerhold and Chekhov remained friends until the dramatist's death in 1904, and that the younger man sought and learned from the master's advice.

In that auspicious first season Meyerhold played seven good roles besides that of Treplev, including one in Goldoni's *La locandiera*, a commedia play. In January 1901, he created the role of Baron Tusenbach in the premiere of *Three Sisters* in Petersburg. During its run he happened to witness the violent suppression of a mass student demonstration by police and soldiers in front of Kazan Cathedral. The experience prompted a letter to Chekhov heated by Meyerhold's revolutionary spirit:

I want to burn with the times. I want all servants of the stage to recognize their lofty destiny. I am disturbed at my comrade's failure to rise above narrow caste interests which are alien to the interests of society at large. Yes, the theatre can play an enormous part in the transformation of the whole of existence.

(Braun, *Theatre*, p. 26.)

Meyerhold's belief in the political and social power of the theater came early and remained unshaken, and it must always be taken into account in any understanding of his aesthetic theatricalism. For him the aesthetic framing that was essential to his direction and which he had in common with all of the commedia modernists led to an assertive, message-laden form of people's theater.

His strong concern for politics clashed with the company's concentration upon the world of the playhouse, despite its strain of populism. When the company decided to mount Nemirovich-Danchenko's new play *In Dreams* before the first play of Maxim Gorky, this rift widened. Gorky's *Philistines* was a celebration of the new proletarian ideal, which attracted the strong support of Meyerhold and the other company activists. Tensions in the company rose to the breaking point. When *In Dreams* was hissed on opening night, Stanislavsky inevitably blamed Meyerhold for having arranged for the insult. This was untrue, but the great parting of the ways had begun.

By the time *Philistines* finally was performed, near the end of the 1901–1902 season (with Meyerhold playing the lead), a group of the young activists, including Meyerhold, had tendered their resignations from the company. In August 1902, Meyerhold and a fellow defector set up shop in the city of Kherson, a port on the Dnieper near the Black Sea. Chekhov worried, writing to Olga Knipper, "I'd like to see Meyerhold and cheer him up. It isn't going to be easy for him in Kherson." But by late September Meyerhold and fellow defector Kosheverov were able to telegram his news of the "huge success" of their *Three Sisters*: "Beloved author of melancholy moods! You alone give true delight!" (*Ibid.*, p. 28.)

In the first season the Kherson theater ran through the whole four-year repertory of the Moscow Art Theater and a good deal else. The fledgling director naturally relied on his schooling, and later he admitted that he had begun "in slavish imitation of Stanislavsky":

In theory I no longer accepted many devices of his directing and regarded them critically, but in practice, starting out, I timidly followed in his footsteps . . . I do not regret it because this period did not last long.

(Rudnitsky, p. 28.)

The new company garnered much favorable notice as well as good audiences, in part because of this attachment to the methods and repertory of Stanislavsky. The province had not before been exposed to the art of the Art Theater. But Meyerhold was already very much his own man, and he quickly put his own ideas to work along with his Moscow training. Schnitzler (*The Last Masks*), the Polish Decadent Przybyszewski, Tolstoy, Sudermann, and then Gorky's *The Lower Depths* and Maeterlinck's *The Intruder* were performed, as Meyerhold moved to embrace new forms of drama, particularly the symbolist.

Meyerhold Meets Pierrot

For us, however, the most significant production of the first Kherson season, so successful that one local newspaper called it "a *chef d'oeuvre* of the director's art," was that of *Acrobats*, an obscure melodrama about circus life by the contemporary Austrian, Franz von Schönthan. Meyerhold translated the work into Russian in collaboration with one of the actresses of the company and added to it considerable directorial notes. In line with his naturalist training, he insisted on "a complete illusion of reality," with much painstaking attention to the details of on- and offstage circus life. This was not mere backsliding: Here realism *is* theatricalism. Meyerhold's instructions include a long list of the necessary circus props and posters; much effort was demanded for a real onstage audience in as good an approximation of proper perspective as could be managed; the juggler wore a "Neapolitan costume" and "a real clown's costume" was required for the central character, the defeated old clown Landovsky.

Landovsky was played by Meyerhold himself, and, as Rudnitsky convincingly argues, the part was extremely important to him:

This was an old Pierrot who had already been through the bitterness of failure, but was still trying to overcome fate, and who therefore exaggerated his worth out of self-importance. . . . "I need only make my entry and they'll laugh. My comic entry! What a laugh there will be! I know there will be four encores!" It is easy to imagine Meyerhold as Landovsky, tall, supple, melancholy and ridiculous, white face, long thin nose, uneasy eyes, a forced grimace of a smile. In this part Meyerhold acquired a new sense of his own physical gifts.

. . . Everything his great teachers and he were used to considering his defects—insufficient good looks, peculiar timbre of voice, a tendency to sharp, eccentric characterization—everything he had previously to overcome . . . now came to his aid, "furthered" the role and enhanced it with a nervous, haunting melancholy. Without a doubt this part predisposed Meyerhold for many years in favor of Pierrot.

(Rudnitsky, p. 32.)

Rudnitsky sees that in his direction of and portrayal in *Acrobats*, Meyerhold was sounding "one of the most important themes of great twentieth-century art." He notes its presence in Blok, Stravinsky, Chaplin, Jean-Louis Barrault, Carné, up through Bergman, Fellini, and Böll—all, of course, relevant to commedia modernism. He connects the figure of the clown with the theme "of a pathological confrontation":

Art in its simplicity and naiveté face to face with the overcomplicated life of our time. By returning again and again to their dying clowns, artists, poets, actors and directors were not declaring the surrender of art; on the contrary, they were affirming its immortality.

(*Ibid.*, p. 33.)

Braun also takes notice of the new uses for "the once rollicking clown Pierrot," traces the transformation back to Deburau, and summarizes that:

Over the years he became the new Everyman, the hapless butt of every cruel jest that an inscrutable fate chose to play on him.

(Braun, *Theatre*, p. 30.)

It may be true that Meyerhold's Landovsky and Stravinsky's Petrushka rely to a degree on the "simplicity and naiveté" of their central images, but it is not the art that is naive and simple; this is obvious enough in the expressively and masterfully framed ballet Pierrot, but it is also already the case in the Pierrot of the still-green Meyerhold. There is assertion and strong self-consciousness lurking in these modern Pierrots. Their creators stand behind and even inside them; even in their melancholy and their futility, these Pierrots have power.

Meyerhold's intimacy with the character of Pierrot emerged vividly in his acting of the part in Kherson. That he retained this identification as an actor apart from his directorial role is made clear in Bronislava Nijinska's striking description of his performance as Pierrot in another context in her *Early Memoirs*. In 1910, when Fokine created his *Carnaval*, danced to Schumann's romantically commedic music, for a charity masquerade ball, he was able to cast all the key "Diaghilevtsky-Fokinisty"

(Leontiev as Harlequin, Karsavina as Columbine, Nijinsky as Florestan, Bekefi as Pantalon). Several young Maryinsky Theater artists were also given roles, among them Nijinsky's younger sister as Papillon, who reported in some detail about the "unforgettable" Pierrot, Meyerhold:

Each of his appearances onstage produced an effect. First, only his leg would appear through the slit of the drape in a *grand développé*, then slowly the whole white body would emerge, the long arms made even longer by long, hanging, white sleeves. Sometimes Pierrot would simply peer through the openings, showing only his white face beneath the conical white hat. . . . Walking cautiously on tip-toes, flapping his long white armlike wings high above his head, he held his little white hat with which he hoped to catch the butterfly, me.

(Nijinska, p. 287.)

This was Meyerhold's only performance as a dancer, and Fokine himself wrote that the novice had much difficulty in his timing and entrances at first:

But by the third rehearsal our new mime had blossomed forth, and on the night he gave a marvelous portrayal of the sorrowful dreamer, Pierrot.

(Braun, *Theatre*, p. 71.)

In 1905 Meyerhold played his own Pierrot in his landmark creation of Blok's *Fairground Booth*; as will be apparent, that Pierrot, the centerpiece of one of the fullest and earliest expressions of the revolutionary new commedia, was much of a piece with these other characterizations.

Schönthan's *Acrobats* had given Meyerhold the opportunity to express his growing fascination with the world of symbolism in the intense realization of a single commedia character in a naturalist setting. Meyerhold's attachment to symbolism and to the commedia were connected, especially at this early stage, for the same reasons that drew the Decadents and others of the symbolist persuasion to these bright manifestations of a pure theater. Harlequin and Columbine and especially Pierrot mimed their way into these hearts because they brought with them centuries of nostalgia, tragicomic emotions, hidden terrors and yearnings. They were natural fodder for those who sought (paraphrasing the original Decadent manifesto of 1886) an art that connected sensory appearance with primordial ideas.

Meyerhold and Moscow

During his seasons in the provinces, Meyerhold gradually acquired a large reputation among the symbolists and others back in Moscow and Petersburg as he continued to be resolutely adventurous, presenting, among other things, Gorky's politically potent *Summer Folk* and Wedekind's *The Concert-Singer,* in his own translation. (This latter choice reveals his lively interest in the café commedia of the West.)

Soon Meyerhold was back in Moscow, named by Stanislavsky to be director of the new Moscow Art Theater Studio, which was an expansion of the Art Theater and an attempt on the part of the (also adventurous) realist to open his art and his company to the new stirrings in drama. The Studio offered Meyerhold important opportunities for development, and there is good evidence that brilliant work was done in preparing an extremely stylized version of Gerhart Hauptmann's *Schluck and Jau,* set by Meyerhold in the "periwig age" of Louis XVI, inspired by Diaghilev's famous exhibition of the portraits of Russian nobility. Meyerhold also plunged into work on Maeterlinck's *The Death of Tintagiles.* The Belgian playwright was the very center of the symbolist movement in drama, and Meyerhold believed that his plays should inspire the audience to "a quivering astonishment at what is, a religious veneration and acceptance."

As it happened, no public ever had the chance to experience this particular explosion, because no completed production ever emerged from the Theater Studio. For all their mutual respect, Stanislavsky and Meyerhold were simply too far apart to patch up personal differences and to seek a new theater together.

The head of the literary advisers to the Studio was Valery Bryusov, symbolist playwright and essayist whose antirealist essay "The Unnecessary Truth" had been widely influential among the symbolist-minded after its publication in Diaghilev's *World of Art (Mir Iskusstva)* in 1902. In Meyerhold's words, Bryusov "demanded the rejection of the futile 'truth' of the contemporary stage in favour of *conscious stylization*" to express the real truths beneath the surface. Meyerhold quoted Bryusov directly in his own essay, published about 1907, "The New Theatre Foreshadowed in Literature," as asserting "the theatre's sole obligation is to assist the actor to reveal his soul to the audience." (Braun, *Meyerhold,* pp. 37–38.) Meyerhold took Bryusov's declaration a step further to claim primacy for the director in the process of transforming the surface into symbols of the depths:

I would expand Bryusov's thoughts as follows: *the theatre must employ every means to assist the actor to blend his soul with that of the playwright and reveal it through the soul of the director.*

At first, the break between Stanislavsky and Meyerhold resulted in an announced delay in the opening of the Meyerhold productions. But it was to be a lifelong break—almost. At the end, in 1938, Stanislavsky invited Meyerhold to collaborate with him on a production of *Rigoletto*. It is fitting that Verdi's highly theatrical tragedy of the court jester would be the final meeting ground for the two great directors. For both it was their last production; as Stanislavsky approached death he attempted to have Meyerhold appointed his successor, and one of his assistants reported that he said of his great adversary, "Take care of Meyerhold; he is my sole heir in the theatre—here or anywhere else." (Symons, p. 26.)

The Fairground Booth

The Theater Studio failed, but Meyerhold's reputation as the new voice of the Russian avant-garde in matters dramatic had made him a sufficiently hot property to attract Vera Komissarzhevskaya, the great dramatic actress often regarded as Russia's answer to Duse. The two years, 1906–1907, that this relationship managed to survive saw much tension and failure, but it was also a time in which Meyerhold plunged into the theater of mood and stylization with unprecedented boldness, drawing inspiration from all the winds of modernism and also from Japanese theater, winning intermittently the cooperation of Komissarzhevskaya and her company.

The most significant event of these two seasons in Petersburg was a production that was both symbolist and a striking satire of symbolism. On December 30, 1906, a double bill opened on the stage of the theater on Ofitserskaya Street. The first play was Maeterlinck's *Miracle of St. Anthony*. The second was the premiere of Alexander Blok's first play, *Balaganchik*, translated variously as *The Fairground Booth* or *The Puppet Show*. In his seminal essay of 1912 named after the play, Meyerhold gives his version of the importance of puppet theater and of the comic power of masks and gestures and movement, with specific reference to the commedia:

If you examine the dog-eared pages of old scenarios such as Flaminio Scala's anthology, you will discover the magical power of the mask.

(Braun, Meyerhold, p. 131.)

He describes the setting for his *Fairground Booth* and outlines the contemporary fate and the promise of the farce:

Banished from the contemporary theatre, the principles of the fairground booth found a temporary refuge in the French cabarets, the German *Überbrettl*, the English music halls and the ubiquitous "varieties." If you read Ernst von

Wolzogen's *Überbrettl* manifesto, you will find that in essence it is an apologia for the principles of the fairground booth.

(*Ibid.*, p. 136.)

Wolzogen, so important to Arnold Schoenberg's commedia, published that "manifesto" in 1902. As Meyerhold indicates, the Berlin director provided him with highly useful underpinnings to his developing notions of comic stylization and of the grotesque:

Grotesque (Italian—*grottesca*) is the title of a genre of low comedy in literature, music and the plastic arts. Grotesque usually implies something hideous and strange, a humorous work which with no apparent logic combines the most dissimilar elements by *ignoring their details and relying on its own originality, borrowing from every source anything which satisfies its joie de vivre and its capricious, mocking attitude to life.*

(*Ibid.*, p. 139.)

For Meyerhold, this kind of comic freedom "reveals the most wonderful horizons to the creative artist," and he insists that Wolzogen's limitation of his definition to "low comedy" is unjustified, claiming its power for tragedy as well:

The grotesque has its own attitude towards the outward appearance of life. The grotesque deepens life's outward appearance to the point where it ceases to appear merely natural.

(*Op. cit.*)

In this essay, Meyerhold summons Pushkin, Wedekind (despite his "lack of taste"), Edgar Allan Poe, and "above all, of course," E. T. A. Hoffmann to the defense of his claims for the depth and sweep of the grotesque. He links the grotesque intimately with the notion of stylization:

Without compromise, the grotesque ignores all minor details and creates a totality of life "in stylized improbability" (to borrow Pushkin's phrase). Stylization impoverishes life to the extent that it reduces empirical abundance to topical unity. The grotesque does not recognize the purely debased or the purely exalted. The grotesque mixes opposites, consciously creating harsh incongruity and relying solely on its own originality.

(*Ibid.*, p. 138.)

The essay was written, most probably, in 1911, which allows for five years of hindsight, but it stands as an accurate summing of the lines of intention that went into that 1906 production of *Fairground Booth*—and more than that, as a declaration of aesthetics that reflects to a remarkable degree the basic assumptions governing the whole of Meyerhold's career.

Blok and *Balaganchik*

Alexander Blok was the light of Russian lyric poetry, the young and brilliant creator of a new, intense romanticism that, especially in the *Beautiful Lady* poems, seems to inhabit a world utterly different from that of the farce, even the farce made new in his collaboration with Meyerhold. But the passion in the poetry was fueled by powerful emotion that could make a revolution in the theater. In 1917 Blok wrote of *The Fairground Booth* that it "emerges from the depths of my soul's police department." (Rudnitsky, p. 104.) Earlier he wrote of "attacks of despair and irony" that accompanied the romantic strain of his poetry, "which had their outcome in my first experiment in drama." And at the time of the dress rehearsal for the opening of *Fairground Booth*, Blok wrote a letter to Meyerhold in which he gave perfect expression to the revolutionary's belief in the power of farce:

Any farce, mine included, strives to be a *battering ram*, to break through the lifeless. The farce embraces and comes forward to meet, discloses the frightful and perverted caresses of matter, as if sacrificing itself to it, and now this stupid, dull matter gives in, begins to trust it, and climbs into its arms . . . matter has been fooled, rendered weak and defeated. In this sense do I "accept the world"—the entire world, with its stupidity, stagnation, dead and dry colors— only to trick this bony old bitch and make her young. In the embraces of a fool and a farce the old world will wax beautiful and grow young, and its eyes will become clear, fathomless.

(*Ibid.*, p. 105.)

Blok's faith in this power had its roots in his own romanticism and symbolism. He had imbibed the romantic fascination with puppets and commedia through the worlds of Kleist, Jean Paul, and others, including the layers of ambiguity that the basic commedia trio had acquired, especially the close relationship of Harlequin and Pierrot. He was aware not only of Maeterlinck, but also of the briefly but widely popular *King Harlequin* of Lothar, premiered in 1902 and immediately translated from the German.

A Blok lyric of 1902 presents a masquerade ball with the Harlequin-Pierrot-Columbine triangle; a poem of 1903 depicts Columbine and Harlequin with tambourines; and there is another about the buffoon who is keeper of both wisdom and foolishness. A 1904 Harlequin is "lost in his own despair," and the previous year the poet signed a letter to his bride, "Your jester, Your Pierrot, Your scarecrow, Your fool." (Hackel, p. 18.) *Fairground Booth* itself began as a poem, the play being a puppet show seen by the boy and girl of the poem. (Read, pp. 1–2.) The poem and the play had behind them the real-life romantic triangle of Blok, his wife, and Andrei Biely, his friend and fellow symbolist. Blok's distress at his wife's affair with Biely (whom she left in 1904 for a stage career, for a time in Meyerhold's troupe) found some artistic outlet in the triangle of the play, with himself as Pierrot and Biely as Harlequin.

The 1905 revolution played havoc with Blok's personal form of symbolist religiosity, and by 1906 his distrust of mysticism had grown to an alienation that led him to describe it as nothing more than a literary device, a refinement inherited from the West that in religion was a source of hysteria, deception, and emptiness. This, too, is reflected in the satire in *Fairground Booth*. (Kluge, p. 59.)

For Blok, then, this play was a particularly important battering ram, a complex public declaration, satire against the mystical symbolism that was most closely identified with his art, expression of personal disillusionment, and a celebration of a new, energetic strain of theater. "When I ridicule what I hold most sacred—*I suffer*," he wrote to Biely in 1907 (Hackel, p. 15.), and part of the strange richness of the play is that it is no simple apostasy; the light rhythms of the farce are reinforced by a deeper round of feelings:

In the first scene . . . there is a long table covered with a black cloth reaching to the floor. . . . Behind the table sit the "mystics," the top halves of their bodies visible to the audience. Frightened by some rejoinder, they duck their heads, and suddenly all that remains at the table is a row of torsos minus heads and hands. It transpires that the figures are cut out of *cardboard* . . . The actors' hands are thrust through openings in the cardboard torsos, and their heads simply rest on the cardboard collars.

(Braun, *Meyerhold*, p. 141.)

A double illusion is asserted, celebrated—the illusion of the "mystics," theater as illusion:

The action begins at a signal on a big drum; music is heard [written by Kuzmin] and the audience sees the prompter crawl into his box and light a candle . . . by the window is a round table with a pot of geraniums and a slender gilt chair on which Pierrot is sitting. Harlequin makes his first entry from under the Mystics' table.

(*Ibid.*, p. 71.)

And here Meyerhold quotes Biely's description of the acting:

All the characters are restricted to their own typical gestures: Pierrot, for instance, always sighs and flaps his arms in the same way.

But Pierrot was played by Meyerhold himself, and even in the gestures the identification was sharp and personal, a Pierrot with a difference. In the words of one witness, Sergei Auslender:

He is nothing like those familiar, falsely sugary, whining Pierrots. Everything about him is sharply angular; in a hushed voice he whispers strange words of sadness; somehow he contrives to be caustic, heart-rending, gentle: all these things yet at the same time impudent.

(Braun, *Theatre*, p. 70.)

The "Mystics" are awaiting the appearance of Death in the form of a beautiful woman; Pierrot, garbed "like all Pierrots," lives in hopes of his Columbine. When she arrives, the Mystics see the Death they expect, while Pierrot protests that this person, silent and dressed in white, is indeed his Columbine. She speaks in recognition, but before he can take comfort in this, Harlequin, "eternally youthful, agile, and handsome," appears from under the table of the discomfitted Mystics to whisk her away. Suddenly the scene changes, and Pierrot is sitting "on the bench where Venus and Tannhäuser usually embrace," while a masked ball goes on about him. Pierrot tells us that when Harlequin carried Columbine off in a sleigh, she abruptly turned into a cardboard doll. Both now bereft, Harlequin and Pierrot sing and dance through the snow to comfort themselves.

Later, a procession of masked figures carrying torches leaps and prances on stage, and Harlequin steps forth from the group to greet the coming of spring. Declaring, "I will breathe your spring/Through your window of gold!," he leaps through the window—which turns out to be only a painted paper scene and is ripped open in his fall through it. The beautiful woman returns, this time carrying a scythe, and the masked crowd is frightened, but once again Pierrot sees his Columbine in her, and so she is, as morning light floods in to make the ominous scythe disappear and the life appear in her cheeks. Pierrot, about to find his happiness, seeks to embrace his Columbine, but he is interrupted by the "Author."

At the center of most of the action has been a little booth erected upon the stage, a small stage itself, with its own curtain, prompter's box, and proscenium arch. In an area beside the booth and the footlights, in an intermediary position between the audience and the events on the stage-within-a-stage, this "Author" has observed "his" play with much consternation and protest at the violence being done to his creation. But at this final moment of would-be embrace, the Author sticks his head between Pierrot and Columbine and proclaims a happy ending to his tale. As he tries to join their hands, all the scenery, which had been lowered into place in full view of the audience, is suddenly pulled up. The maskers and Columbine disappear, and Pierrot is alone on a bare stage. The actress Valentina Vergina described the scene:

The curtain fell behind Pierrot-Meyerhold and he was left face to face with the audience. He stood staring at them, and it was as though Pierrot was looking into the eyes of every single person. . . . There was something irresistible in his gaze. . . . Then Pierrot looked away, took his pipe from his pocket and began to play the tune of a rejected and unappreciated heart. That moment was the most powerful in his whole performance. Behind his lowered eyelids one sensed a gaze, stern and full of reproach.

(Braun, *Theatre*, pp. 67–72.)

The reaction of audience and critics to the premiere and to the whole run was very satisfactorily appropriate to the advent of something so utterly new: nearly violent scandal in the audience, derision from the critics, outrage from the playwright's betrayed fellow symbolists—and, from many young radicals, deep enthusiasm.

In 1910, Blok referred to his art, his "magic world," as a "puppet show, where I myself act a part side by side with my superlative dolls (*ecce Homo!*)." Even his landmark poem of the Revolution, *The Twelve*, has clear thematic links with *Fairground Booth;* one Russian Critic, Gorodetskii, noting that "the harlequinade is one of Blok's favourite leitmotivs," went so far as to claim *The Twelve* as another one (Hackel, p. 58.), an idea that strains the harlequinade to the point of complete formal abstraction. These affinities aside, the mainstream of Blok's art turned away from that of Meyerhold, to a preference, as he once put it, for "healthy realism, Stanislavsky, and musical drama." (Braun, *Meyerhold*, p. 117.)

But for Meyerhold *The Fairground Booth* was a moment of profound discovery, the realization of an artistic identity that had begun to emerge in earnest three years before in his provincial staging of *Acrobats*. On this December night the modernist commedia was brilliantly and fully brought to life in Vera Komissarzhevskaya's theater. All the important elements were there, constructed upon the basic commedia trio, their traditional images and roles both preserved and exploited. Here was the overt theatricality, the defiance of the naturalistic illusion that was grounded upon the open relationship between performer and audience in the circus, in vaudeville, and in the commedia itself through all its earlier transformations. And here was a "modernist" narrative line, full of abrupt discontinuities and vivid images that jostle against one another and shift freely between literal narrative and a more covert symbolist (or mock-symbolist) coherence. The ironic framing, the stage-within-a-stage, and the play-within-a-play, all act to force the audience into new relationships with the play and its participants. It all takes place within the context of farce; and farce, in allusion, in fragments, in ironic exploitation of the form, was to remain close to the center of the theater of Pirandello, Beckett, and Pinter, as well as Brecht.

Meyerhold and Komissarzhevskaya parted company in 1907. The differences between them had been exacerbated by critics and theater politics, but their disagreement was basic enough to make the break inevitable, anyway.

Evreinov

However, Komissarzhevskaya chose as Meyerhold's replacement another devotee of the commedia dell'arte, Nikolai Evreinov. Evreinov was founder of the Theater of Antiquity, devoted to the revival of earlier forms of drama. The company managed to mount impressive cycles of medieval drama and works from the Spanish Golden Age, and they planned a season of commedia dell'arte, though it never came off. Evreinov was, like Blok, Meyerhold, Andreyev, Alexander Tairov, and so many others at that time, deeply interested in the commedia. He once declared, "I am Harlequin and as Harlequin I shall die" (Golub, p. 35.), and through the first turbulent decades of the century in Russia, he managed to live up to the claim.

In his childhood Evreinov was (like Benois and Nijinsky) so fascinated with puppets, and particularly the Petrushka puppet of the fairground booths, that he badgered his parents into acquiring all available versions of this Russian folk Pierrot, so that he and his brother could mount puppet shows with multiple Petrushkas. In his adulthood Evreinov said, "least of all would I like to be considered a serious man" (*Ibid.*, p. 13.), and he led a flamboyant, consciously self-dramatizing existence, somewhat in the manner of his idol, Aubrey Beardsley. But he did desire very much to be taken seriously as an artist, to be the object of both adulation and consternation. As a director, as writer of some thirty plays, and as theoretician, he lived as a harlequin but tried also to carry the day as a major thinker, promulgator of the theory of "monodrama," the "theater for oneself," and also "the theatricalization of life" (the title of one of his books). For him the goal of the theater was:

> to clothe life in holiday clothes, to color it with the colors of the theater, to return it to its former theatricality. Out of this, life would become not only more beautiful, but also easier: theater will heal the wounds that life sustains.
>
> (Mead, p. 22.)

Evreinov was very much of his time. His theory of the "mono-drama," of presenting the drama from the perspective of a single actor whose consciousness of the events would become that of the audience, was similar to Fyodor Sologub's "Theater of One Will" and also reflected in Gordon Craig's Moscow Art Theater production of *Hamlet*. His devotion to theatricality was similarly echoed by many of the revolutionaries who believed intensely that a new theater had much to teach life, Craig, Meyerhold, and Georg Fuchs among them.

Evreinov experimented with monodrama in the theater of Mme. Komissarzhevskaya, and he did not stay very long, either. He pursued his vision in the Theater of Antiquity, in his essays, and perhaps most importantly in his association with a famous Petersburg cabaret theater, the Crooked Mirror, for which he wrote a number of harlequinades. The most famous of these are *A Merry Death* (1908) and the more substantial *The Chief Thing* (1919). In this the central character, Paraclete, dons several disguises, revealing himself, finally, as Harlequin in a speech celebrating the power of commedia:

> We are all here! . . . count: Harlequin, Pierrot, Columbine, and The Doctor from Bologna. . . . We have been resurrected, my friends. . . . We are risen anew! And not for the theater alone, but for life itself, which is unsavory without our pepper and salt and sugar!
>
> (Segal, p. 135.)

The Chief Thing was widely produced; the Theatre Guild presented it in New York in 1926, and it received literally hundreds of performances in avant-garde theaters in Paris and elsewhere. Meyerhold knew Evreinov's work, even referred to it with approval in his writing. In the early twenties, when Evreinov's career was at something of an ebb, Meyerhold offered him a position of importance as a director, but he refused it. When the Crooked Mirror company toured Poland in 1925, very unsuccessfully, Evreinov broke with the group for good and left for Paris, where he stayed until his death in 1953.

There are similarities between Evreinov's commedia and that of

Meyerhold. In the last speech of *A Merry Death,* Pierrot refers to the author, "who preaches that nothing in life is worth taking seriously." (Segal, p. 129.) Meyerhold's often-quoted remark from late in his life, "I know for a fact that what is said in jest is often more serious than what is said seriously" (Field, p. 322.), also reveals the ironist. But they took their jesting in very different directions. Meyerhold was not interested in dressing life in holiday clothes; he put the holiday clothes on his characters to make a new commedia, to strip drama to its essentials and bring new forms out of the old.

Meyerhold and St. Petersburg

Meyerhold's career continued to flourish. He was appointed to the position of director and actor in the Petersburg Imperial Theaters in 1908. Here he began his collaboration with the artist and designer Alexander Golovin, one of the most brilliant of the Diaghilev *World of Art* circle, soon to create the settings for the premiere of Stravinsky's *Firebird* and, for the next ten years, to be a vital participant in Meyerhold's Imperial Theater productions. It is apparent in Golovin's designs for the costumes for Meyerhold's *Don Juan* of 1910 and for his great production of Lermontov's *Masquerade* in 1917 that the artist imbibed the commedia atmosphere as readily as his colleague.

The new appointment called for far fewer productions than had generally been demanded of him in his previous posts, and Meyerhold seized the opportunity to exercise his innovative spirit in moonlighting. He put into practice his belief that small, flexible companies were necessary to the advance of the art through experimentation, instituting a theater studio in his own home in 1908, which included a commedia-derived course in "plastic gymnastics." He also participated in the creation of The Strand, which was conceived as Petersburg's answer to Wolzogen's Berlin *Überbrettl* and to the Moscow cabaret theater club, The Bat. It had a formal intimate theater component as well as a late-night program of satire, and for the theater's opening Meyerhold directed three short works, a "folk farce" by Peter Potemkin called *Petrushka,* a buffoon play by Count Vladimir Sollogub called *Honor and Vengeance,* and an adaptation of Poe's *The Fall of the House of Usher.* It turned out very quickly that the theater format was too demanding for Petersburg's cabaret audience—The Strand closed in a week—but the late-night program, the Crooked Mirror, turned out to be much more successful. It expanded to become the cabaret theater so important to Evreinov, and in various formats survived until 1931. In 1909 a program of

"Parisian Grand Guignol" was presented by the theater owner and producer Benjamin Kazansky; it included a "sensational melodrama" on circus
life, written by Meyerhold, called *The Kings of the Air and the Lady from
the Box,* based on a Danish short story. It shows his fascination with
the vivid dramatic possibilities of the circus. At about the same time he
also made a translation (from the German) of a Kabuki play.

On the side of theory, he published his important essay on the history and technique of the theater, and he also translated, again from
the German, two essays of Gordon Craig, published in Petersburg in
1909. There are many points of similarity between the theories of Craig
and the practice of Meyerhold, especially in the use of masks, and in
their interest in puppets and techniques of stylization. But they were
very different personalities and very different artists, and for all his exploration of the world of the original commedia, for all the pioneering
research published in his journal, *The Mask,* Craig did not seek to make
a modernist commedia. He sought rather to reclaim the stage for analogues to the original commedia and other forms of "pure" theater.

Craig was not the only prophet exerting an influence upon Meyerhold
at this time, as is clear in his significant essay on *Tristan und Isolde,*
published in 1910 and occasioned by his operatic debut, in his Imperial
Theater role, at the Maryinsky Opera in October 1909. His response to
Wagner, both in his prose and this great production, reflected his
commedic preoccupation:

If an opera were produced without words it would amount to *a pantomime.* In
pantomime every single episode, each movement in each episode (its plastic
modulations)—as well as the gestures of every character and the groupings of
the ensemble—are determined precisely by the music, by its changes in tempo,
its modulations, its overall structure. . . . So why don't operatic artists make
their movements and gestures follow the musical tempo, the tonic design of
the score, with mathematical precision?

(Braun, *Meyerhold,* pp. 80–81.)

He answers his own question with the assertion that the operatic singer
bases his acting upon the libretto rather than the music. Because the
libretto is nearly always based on realistic conventions, the singer is drawn
into a realism that is fatal to the total impression of the opera. The
conclusion is clear and very much in line with Meyerhold's sense of all
theater:

Stylization is the very basis of operatic art—*people sing.* Therefore no elements
of real life should be introduced; as soon as stylization and reality are juxta-

posed, the *apparent* inadequacy of stylization is revealed and the whole foundation of the art collapses.

(*Ibid.*, pp. 81–82.)

This was true of his approach to that which was already literally commedia, or had elements thereof, as it was of other material. His transformation of Arthur Schnitzler's pantomime, *The Veil of Pierrette,* into *Columbine's Scarf* in 1910 is a case in point. Schnitzler shared the taste for the soft-edged, sentimental, and morbid commedia of the Decadents, the Pierrot out of which Schoenberg made *Pierrot Lunaire*— a characteristic image out of his story "Mother and Son" has a woman's countenance like that of "a hanged Pierrot." This tone was characteristic of Schnitzler's little pantomime, but in Meyerhold's hands pale, flowing morbidity in three scenes became a jarring, grotesque progression of fourteen. In the words of a contemporary:

In vain Columbine tries to escape from her prison, from the ghastly dead body. Gradually, she succumbs to madness; she whirls in a frenzied dance, then finally drains the deadly cup and falls lifeless beside Pierrot.

(Braun, *Theatre,* p. 103.)

Meyerhold mixed the commedia of the cabarets with that of the German Romantics, but the result, with its overt, sharply etched theatricality, was modernist commedia. The vividly ugly, Gogolesque designs for the production were by Nikolai Sapunov, a young (and tragically short-lived) artist with an eye for the grotesque much like that of the director.

Dr. Dapertutto

Legally, the involvement of an Imperial Theaters' director in outside ventures constituted a breach of contract, but Meyerhold's understanding boss, Telyakovsky, merely asked him to take on a pseudonym to avoid public difficulties. The name, suggested by Meyerhold's friend the poet musician Mikhail Kuzmin—writer of the novel *Wings* and center of the famous love triangle described in Chapter 2—was Dr. Dapertutto, after the menacing, powerful magician created by E. T. A. Hoffmann. The image and the sense of the artist's power suited Meyerhold so well that the name came to represent him in his daring side ventures up to the Revolution. Dapertutto, the wizard creator of a beautiful woman who steals the shadows of men, is also an expressive link in the tradition of the artist as puppeteer, the director and his puppets.

The experiments with pantomime, masks, and improvisation that were the work of Dapertutto were not confined to him; Rudnitsky describes this symbiosis:

It soon became clear . . . that there existed an unbreakable bond between Doctor Dapertutto and Vsevolod Meyerhold, that the bold, daring and risky experiments created in little cabaret-type theaters were precursors of the confident and large-scale solutions for the shows on the Imperial stage. Dr. Dapertutto and Vsevolod Meyerhold assisted each other. Doctor Dapertutto, who directed enthusiastic amateurs and shy students, was the author of sudden impromptus and unexpected sketches for the mature, well-thought-out creations of Meyerhold the director, who worked with professional, experienced actors.

(Rudnitsky, p. 147.)

This is the reverse of the original commedia dell'arte pattern, in a sense: After all, only the professionals, the masters of the art, could be granted the freedom of impromptu theater, while amateurs were carefully chained to the text, the *commedia erudita*. Given the necessities that Meyerhold confronted, and transformed into virtues, this is no real paradox. But it has a specific relevance, because the director, influenced by his reading of Gozzi, as well as by his surroundings, sought an ever more important place for improvisation in the performance of his actors.

His famous production of Molière's *Don Juan* at the Alexandrinsky is a case in point. It opened on November 9, 1910, to a full house, despite the fact that it was the day of Tolstoy's funeral, a day of deep national mourning. Meyerhold argued that Molière believed, as he did himself, that the fairground stage and popular theater, rather than the formal proscenium framework, was the way of true theater. Meyerhold himself both exploited the proscenium arch—with a breathtakingly ornate, huge false frame devised by Golovin—and overcame it, with a forestage thrusting outward. He also employed the simple tactic of keeping the houselights up, except for specific dramatic effects, in order to diminish the formal separation from the audience.

True to the image of Meyerhold the puppet master, he choreographed in great detail the movements of the cast, making them move to the dance rhythm of the accompanying music of Rameau. But in the midst of all this he placed the figure of Sganarelle, whose vast bulk, in the Dottore tradition, was attended by proscenium servants—added to the cast by Meyerhold—"liveried little blackamoors" who, in Golovin's words, bustled about "like kittens," lighting candles, ringing bells, and announcing events. It was with the Sganarelle that Meyerhold made room for improvisation; he was played by Konstantin Varlamov, a large and much loved old character actor with a notoriously bad memory, and also a serious heart condition. The director turned these liabilities to brilliant account by making the production dance and bustle around him, and by allowing him a freedom that would have been outrageous in hands less ready for improvisation. The description of one witness is expressive:

Raising the lantern to eye-level, he looks for his friends in the auditorium; then his gaze halts: "Ah! Nikolai Platonovich! . . . How do you like our play? I don't know about you, but it suits me fine! By the way, don't forget that you're having a bite with me on Tuesday, will you, old chap?" . . . He spots a friend sitting with a young lady: "Ah! So that's your better half. You take her out to the theatre, but you hide her away from me. . . . Tut, tut! Ivan Ivanovich, you should be ashamed of treating an old man like that!"

(Braun, *Theatre*, pp. 112–13.)

Varlamov could bring all this banter off without destroying the character of Sganarelle, and he was a universal success. Meyerhold did not have nearly so unanimous a critical press; Benois entitled his review "Ballet at the Alexandrisky," which was fair enough, considering the director's bow toward the comédie-ballet of the French baroque theater He also attacked the production as an "elegant fairground show," a *balagan*, using the word much as Russians today would use it to dismiss something as cheap circus trickery. Meyerhold turned the scornful remark into praise, the highest praise the modern commedist could desire, when he used it as the point of departure for "The Fairground Booth," the seminal essay that is in many ways the manifesto of the theater of this greatest of modern commedists of the stage.

Meyerhold still pursued his commedia most directly in his Dapertutto role, and he had allies, such as Vladimir Solovyov, himself a young director, critic, and playwright who created a harlequinade, *Harlequin, the Marriage Broker*. This was performed often by Meyerhold, Solovyov, and a group of like-minded people who in 1912 formed a new "Fellowship," this time at the Finnish seaside resort of Terioki. In his own description of his production of Solovyov's harlequinade, Meyerhold made the specific connections between the pantomime, improvisation, and the grotesque that, once again, project a commedia ideal that was to underlie all of his work:

The harlequinade was written in the form of a pantomime because, more than any dramatic form, the pantomime is conducive to the revival of the art of improvisation. In the pantomime the actor is given the general outline of the plot and in the intervals between the various key moments he is free to act *ex improviso*. However, the actor's freedom is only relative, because he is subject to the discipline of the musical score. The actor in a harlequinade needs to possess an acute sense of rhythm, plus great agility and self-control. He must develop the equilibrist skills of an acrobat, because only an acrobat can master the problems posed by the grotesque style inherent in the fundamental conception of the harlequinade.

(Ibid., p. 121.)

These are the demands upon the actors in Meyerhold's later production of Crommelynck's *Magnanimous Cuckold*, Mayakovsky's *Mystery-Bouffe*, *The Bedbug*, and *The Bathhouse*, Griboyedov's *Woe from Wit*, his versions of Lermontov and Ostrovsky, and his epochal transformation of Gogol's *The Inspector General*, among other landmarks of early Soviet theater. In September 1913, with the aid of friends, Meyerhold was at last able to open his own reasonably permanent theater studio in Petersburg with the express purpose of pursuing these commedic ideals.

Paris and Film

In the spring before this, Meyerhold made his first and only trip abroad for the purposes of practicing his craft, and it deserves brief mention because it was the only time Meyerhold had serious contact with modern revolutionaries with a commedic bent outside of Russia. Contact was made, naturally enough, by virtue of his sometime membership in the Diaghilev circle; Ida Rubinstein invited him to Paris to direct her in D'Annunzio's heavily perfumed *La Pisanelle, ou la mort parfumée*, drama in verse with (very effective) music by Pizetti, sets by Bakst, and choreography by Fokine. The production enjoyed a large commercial success, and Meyerhold was glad for the chance to direct a large cast—around two hundred actors and dancers—but largeness and excess seemed to be the salient features of the project. Meyerhold did not get along well with Rubinstein, but he did come in fruitful contact with D'Annunzio himself, with the redoubtable actor of extravagant decadence, Edouard de Max, also in the play, and, most important, with Guillaume Apollinaire, who became a friend.

In Paris, probably through Apollinaire and his friends (and the young Abel Gance, a member of the *Pisanelle* cast), Meyerhold seems to have been brought to an appreciation of the possibilities of film. As late as the previous year he had dismissed the young medium as "a shining example of the obsession with quasi-verisimilitude." (Braun, *Meyerhold*, p. 135.) By 1915 he was at work on his film version of Wilde's *The Picture of Dorian Gray,* with himself as Lord Henry Wotton and Varvara Yanova in a pants role as the ever-young Dorian. The film, now lost, was regarded by those who saw it as the most brilliantly innovative of early feature films. According to film historian Jay Leyda, Meyerhold's approach to movement was "ready-made" for the cinema; the Soviet filmmaker Kuleshov later adapted Meyerhold's stage movement explicitly to his own use. For Leyda, *Dorian Gray* was "undoubtedly the most important Russian film made previous to the February revolution." (Leyda, p. 81.) Meyerhold's 1918 lecture on the film shows an extraordinary awareness of the unique demands and restraints of the medium that was still dominated by actors who merely carried their stage behavior into the film studio. He also wrote perceptively about the power of film captions, their function in the rhythmic punctuation of the narrative. For him, these titles should not explain—the clarity of the action should make that unnecessary—but they should be used "for the sake of the evocative power of the words." (Braun, *Meyerhold,* p. 310.) This usage parallels that in several places of Meyerhold's stage productions, and it anticipates the placement of titles and placards by Brecht, who also sought to underline the theatricality of the narrative.

The Studio, Masquerade, and Revolution

If Meyerhold thought to expand his career westward by virtue of his Parisian success, he must have been disappointed; a production of his was seen in Paris again only seventeen years later, and he was not in attendance. But back in Petersburg the studio that Meyerhold founded started life with a devoted group of faculty and students. The curriculum consisted at first of "musical reading in the drama" taught by Gnesin; the history and technique of commedia dell'arte, taught by Solovyov, and stage movement, taught by Meyerhold himself. Meyerhold's own class, according to a student, was actually a class in acting and directing, with exercises that clearly harmonized with the commedia studied: "Exercises were transformed into etudes, and from etudes arose the pantomimes." (Symons, pp. 64–65.) Several of Meyerhold's exercises made their way into the "classic" pedagogy of all aspiring actors; several also served him in the system of expressive exercises and gymnastics he was later to christen biomechanics.

In February 1914, the studio began publication of the journal devoted to the cause, *The Love for Three Oranges—Doctor Dapertutto's Journal,* named after the Gozzi *fiaba teatrale,* which was freely translated by Meyerhold, Solovyov, and Konstantin Vogak for the first number.

This adaptation was taken up by Prokofiev for his major contribution to modern commedia. Meyerhold urged the work upon the composer just before the latter's departure for America in 1918. (Braun, *Theatre*, p. 126.) Gozzi was the natural focal point of the journal because he, too, had been engaged in the noble cause of bringing the almost moribund commedia dell'arte back to life in the eighteenth century. The editors included more Gozzi in later issues, as well as new versions of Plautus and Tieck and history pieces and reviews. Poetry that caught their spirit was also included: the work of Blok, Akhmatova, Balmont, Fyodor Sologub, and others. The editorial board even managed to stage two of Blok's plays from his period of collaboration with Meyerhold, *The Unknown Woman*, and *The Fairground Booth*.

The triumph of these last years before the Revolution, the theatrical event with the largest place in the history of the time, was the production of Lermontov's *Masquerade*, which opened at the Alexandrinsky on February 25, 1917, the day the first shots of the Revolution were fired in St. Petersburg. The play had behind it five years of preparations, rehearsals, interruptions—but was finally mounted on only eighteen days' notice, under the threat that the financial backing for it was about to disappear. It demanded a cast of over two hundred, as well as lavish sets and costumes, brilliantly conceived by Golovin. In the words of the harshest critic, Kugel, the director built the production "like a Pharaoh building his Pyramid," (Rudnitsky, p. 231.) and indeed Meyerhold poured all of his labor and vision into the work, including the products of his commedia teaching, for the huge cast required recruits from his studio and other drama schools, as well as the whole Alexandrinsky company.

Lermontov's drama is a sustained attack on the extravagance and dissoluteness of upper-crust Petersburg of the 1830s. Much of the key action takes place in the course of two splendid masked balls, which gave the director much room for commedia spectacle. The masks allowed for a broad display of grotesque stylization, most memorably in the ominous Stranger, the figure of vengeance. Meyerhold converted the play's static five-act structure to ten scenes, which moved swiftly and seamlessly from one to another with the use of overlapping lines and exquisite drop curtains. Despite the elegance and opulence of his production, Meyerhold penetrated to the bitter satire that was the original heart of the work.

Despite the attacks on those who hated the extravagantly decadent image of society that Meyerhold projected, and those who simply hated the extravagance of the production (some four thousand design sketches were produced by Golovin), *Masquerade* was the kind of success that defines a new era or at least generates a new literature. The new era was at hand in another sense. A witness to the opening days of performance remembered, "There was shooting in the streets. A bullet killed a student in the vestibule of our theater." Golovin recalled that they worried (needlessly) that the fighting would cause the premiere to fail; he and Meyerhold "ran across the Nevsky under fire" (*Ibid.*, p. 223.) on their way to the theater.

Meyerhold certainly had his ties to the world that was perishing, but he embraced the Revolution enthusiastically and openly, long before this could have been regarded as the opportunistic thing to do, long before most of the Russian intelligentsia around him believed with any seriousness that the Bolsheviks would prevail. Whatever compelled Meyerhold to believe, his belief was certainly consistent with his sympathies as expressed in the 1905 revolution and with his general stance against established traditions in culture. In 1926 the Soviet writer A. V. Lunacharsky discussed Meyerhold's belief in the Revolution in terms useful to the understanding of the attraction of the specifically commedic artist to the upheaval:

The connection between Meyerhold's theater and the Revolution is very simple and, I might say, primitive. . . . Revolution is bold. It likes innovation, it likes brightness. Tradition does not envelop it the way it does the theatrical Old Believers, and therefore it accepts readily that expansion of realism which, essentially, lies well within its province. It may accept fantastic hyperbole, caricature, all sorts of deformations, if such deformations . . . further the expression of internal real essence by way of artistic transformation.

(*Ibid.*, p. 248.)

This does not take into account the fact that the modernist vision of the artist Meyerhold remained in tension with the new socialist vision and, fatally, with the politicians who promoted it. But it does make clear the place of farce, even Meyerhold's brand of it, in the revolutionary society. In December after the fateful October 1917, Meyerhold staged Ibsen at the (ex-) Alexandrinsky; in the following April the theater presented an unsuccessful version of Tolstoy's play-legend *Peter the Baker,* and in May Meyerhold staged Stravinsky's short opera after Hans Christian Andersen, *The Nightingale.* Stravinsky must have recognized in Meyerhold his kin in modernist commedia, because he specifically asked him, through Golovin, to stage the work; for his part, Meyerhold regarded Stravinsky as the most important modern composer. Meyerhold rose easily to the challenge of the work's ornateness, the stylization, and to the music above all. To frame the musical theatricality of the experience, the director placed music stands with scores before each of the opera's performers, stands that they carried about with them as they moved according to the action. But even the leading characters were extremely limited in their movement, and silent extras were used to mime most of the plot.

Meyerhold and Mayakovsky

In 1918 Meyerhold did join the Bolshevik Party, and he accepted a position as director and organizer that put his talents to work as an agitator and propagandist for the new age. But it is important to understand that Meyerhold the propagandist was essentially different from the state functionary that the term brings to mind; he was propagandist for his own vision of a new world, and the focal point of his energy and vision remained the stage. He was hardly alone in this. Blok turned from the inward lyricism of his early days to the burning message of *The Twelve*, and Vladimir Mayakovsky, like Meyerhold, welcomed the Revolution early and turned his extravagant muse entirely to its service. His purely poetic talent may have been betrayed by his decision to turn out simple didactic verse and rhyming slogans for the cause, but his bent for sharp caricature and for being, in the (admiring) words of Osip Mandelstam, "the traditional carnival barker" made him a potent revolutionary playwright—and, in collaboration with Meyerhold, an immortal one.

    Mystery-Bouffe was staged on the first anniversary of the Revolution. Rudnitsky described the work as "the *first* fully and thoroughly political play in the history of Russian theater." It was also quintessential modernist commedia, a jarring, intentionally crude assembly of scenes pitting the "unclean" proletariat against the "clean" exploiters, portrayed as clownlike fools and knaves. The sets were futurist sketches, the atmosphere of the whole a mixture of the circus and the political rally. The commedia emerges clearly in Rudnitsky's catalogue of the work's first-act "attractions":

1. The clownlike entrance of the fisherman and the Eskimo. . . . 2. The Frenchman's expository monologue. 3. Two paired clownlike entrances (the pair of Australians; the Italian and the German). 4. The fencing duel between the Italian and the German. 5. An acrobatic trick: the merchant falling onto the head of the Eskimo. 6. The parade of the clean and the unclean. 7. The rally scene. 8. Farce: commencement of the construction of the Ark.

(Rudnitsky, p. 254.)

It is important to remember that in 1917 not only did the Revolution occur but also the premiere of *Parade*, by Cocteau, Satie, Picasso, and the Diaghilev circle—also a parade of "attractions," also a daring and scandalous fruit of collaboration by the commedist inventors of the avant-garde. The specific use of that circus and variety term "attractions" in this context belongs to Sergei Eisenstein, Meyerhold's greatest disciple and one of the greatest of filmmakers. He claimed the term for the new drama, as meaning "any aggressive element of theater" in his brilliant declaration of his own theory, "A Montage of Attractions," published five years after this, two after he had left Meyerhold's studio.

With *Mystery-Bouffe*, farce, in its most colorful, impudent expression, asserted itself against tradition, both as embodied in the overthrown society and in the conservative traditions of the theater. In the Prologue to the play the "unclean" literally tore posters from other Petersburg theaters to shreds. Meyerhold thus stood in opposition to both the State Drama Theater, formerly his Alexandrinsky, and, in more complex ways, to the Art Theater of Stanislavsky and Nemirovich-Danchenko. Because the new drama was identified with "the people" and performed, as so many of Meyerhold's experimental efforts were, by amateurs, this opposition of the conservative and the revolutionary was in a sense another expression of the old tension between the "legitimate" stages and those of the fairground and the street. But Meyerhold, as newly appointed head of the theatrical department (with much power, but not over the major Moscow and Petersburg theaters), was far too much the professional himself to want this division:

The theatrical specialist ought to transmit carefully all his technical achievements into the hands of the new actor from the proletariat. Therefore, it is not in our interest to chase the specialists from the field of the theatrical arena.

(*Ibid.*, p. 262.)

Meyerhold plunged into the new age more boldly than anyone else; he was the first inspiration, the strongest force in that golden age of the theater that was the first Soviet decade, the age of Vakhtangov, Tairov, Mikhail Chekhov, the rededicated Stanislavsky, and the brilliant assembly of Meyerhold's own actors, writers, and artists. Meyerhold, however, was a true modernist, an artist whose aesthetic was steeped in ironic perception rather than simple affirmation. He insisted on his search for new ways of making his audiences see beyond their social and political masks. He had no interest in abetting the process of imposing a new set of illusions on the people, however promising the forms appeared at the time.

The three historic Meyerhold-Mayakovsky collaborations illustrate clearly the consequences of sustaining the modernist vision within a revolution that was rapidly betraying itself. The 1918 *Mystery-Bouffe* was a major success, but of course its satiric energies were directed outward, at the oppressive capitalists; the similarly successful 1921 restaging featured Clemenceau and Lloyd George among the "clean" clownlike oppressors. The 1928 *Klop*, or *The Bedbug*, has targets much closer to home. A man and a bedbug attached to him are accidently frozen, then found and revived fifty years later. In the first part of the work, the prefrozen man and his manicurist bride and their friends present abundant opportunity for a devastating satire of the new Soviet petite bourgeoisie and the corruptions of economic opportunists during the period of the New Economic Policy. The second part of the play shows a spotless, technologically and socially advanced Soviet society that treats its finds, a petty and wretched man and his bug (*bourgeoisius vulgaris*), with a humane contempt. The targets of the satire were legitimate enough in official eyes, but Mayakovsky and his director injected more than a little parody into the idealized, antiseptic future state, and there is a moment of unsettling pathos when the displaced ex-functionary, doomed never to find a place in society because he has lost his party card, lets out a long howl of loneliness and despair. To be sure, the production was a popular success and the play has had many revivals, but there was also much concerned puzzlement about the real targets of the many farcical elements and some semiofficial anger at the distortions and stylizations that clouded the beautiful future (and at the raucous, jauntily dissonant music by a little-known young composer whom Meyerhold had first hired as theater pianist, Dmitri Shostakovich).

Despite the controversy, Mayakovsky was inspired by the success of *The Bedbug* to set to work immediately on another play, *The Bathhouse*, produced in 1930 by Meyerhold, complete with fireworks and a circus. The author's most brilliant play, *The Bathhouse* focuses its satire on the corrupt, self-important, narrowly conformist denizens of a Soviet government office. There are also futurist elements in this work: a time machine (created by an honest, hardworking Soviet citizen) and the Phosphorescent Woman, the emissary from the future (played by Znaida Raikh, Meyerhold's wife). The play has its good proletarians and its proper Communist future (the Phosphorescent Woman whisks the good people off to the year 2030), but its farcical bureaucrats were too much for the censors, who demanded many cuts before passing the work for performance, and for the critics, who heaped abuse upon the writer and director for their misrepresentation of Soviet officialdom. Mayakovsky had placards hung from the sets with slogans attacking, again, the Art Theater, the Bolshoi, and other manifestations of the traditional and the realist. This, of course, produced another set of enemies.

The ironic "Back to the Classics!" placard of *The Bathhouse* was the real policy which for strategic reasons Meyerhold pursued in his last decade, including a *Lady of the Camellias.* But Meyerhold had always gone with a will back to the classics, and many of his versions thereof in the golden twenties were, given his sometimes radical transformations, brilliant examples of modernist commedia. The Belgian contemporary Fernand Crommelynck did not qualify as a "classic" playwright, but his *Le Cocu magnifique* (usually called *The Magnanimous Cuckold*) attained that position in Meyerhold's version, and the innovations in that landmark production occurred in varying degrees in all of his versions of older drama. The play opened in Moscow in April in 1922, and it signaled a new revolution in several areas of theater simultaneously, a revolution with its roots in the commedia and its seeds in *The Fairground Booth* of 1905. Meyerhold made a brilliant farce out of a strange tale of a man so obsessively jealous of his beautiful wife that he forces her to go to bed with every man in the village in a futile attempt to unmask her imagined "real lover." To underline the husband's foolishness, the director had the husband undercut his impassioned monologues by rolling his eyes, belching, and doing acrobatic tricks as he delivered them.

Government Inspector

Four years later Meyerhold accomplished this commedic alchemy with a genuine classic, one of the most beloved and tradition-encrusted staples of the Russian repertoire, Gogol's *The Government Inspector* (*Revizor,* also commonly translated as *The Inspector General*). This rich comedy is built upon the panic, hypocrisy, and social chicanery let loose when Khlestakov, a petty clerk from Petersburg, visits a provincial town and is taken to be the dreaded inspector general conducting his investigation of the local bureaucracy under cover of a disguise.

The director sought to achieve an unexpectedly dark effect, an effect not only other than comic, but also something colder and grander than the merely didactic. His approach was to create a new commedist bag of tricks. The obvious arsenal would not do, because the impact of the play had already been blunted by a long tradition of vaudeville tricks and stock comic characters. Meyerhold warned his actors, many of whom had been trained in commedia by him, in terms that must have sounded paradoxical:

We must avoid, in particular, anything which smacks of buffoonery. We musn't take anything over from commedia dell'arte but try to present everything in a tragi-comic fashion. The course to be held is one which leads towards tragedy.

(Worrall, p. 76.)

"Towards tragedy" actually meant revelation of the emptiness in the bustling hypocrites' lives, an emptiness portrayed in the most palpable way in one of the most penetrating, and quintessentially commedic directorial strokes in all of theater, the image which Meyerhold created at the final moment of the play.

If Meyerhold wanted to break from traditional commedia and vaudeville stock, he did so by turning to the modern versions of the same stock. His actors were exhorted to take Charlie Chaplin and Buster Keaton as their models, and there are strong echoes of other figures from the cinema, such as a Keystone Kops routine when the Mayor goes mad and has to be straitjacketed in the final episode.

As he had done with the works of Lermontov, Schnitzler, and others, Meyerhold restructured the play entirely, turning the five acts into fifteen vividly stylized episodes, each with its own title (such as "Filled with Tend'rest Love," "Bribes," "Mr. High Finance," "Embrace Me Do," "Unprecedented Confusion"), a vaudeville-theatricalist technique also used by Brecht. The modern commedia invested the character of Khlestakov also; the director transformed him from the simplistic swindler to an ever-changing, vaguely frightening figure of what Boris Alpers called "social masks." The photographs of Erast Garin in the role show him in a top hat and square-rimmed glasses with a cane, a composition of sharp angles and awkward lines, compressed energy and abrupt movements. In his shifting "masks" he moved from shabby dress to uniformed spit and polish, to Petersburgian dandyism, his spectacles changing from square to round-rimmed in the process.

Pantomime and the related technique Meyerhold called "pre-acting," preparing an effect with an expressive gesture or a pause, were very important in the molding of this elusive character, constantly the object of the manipulations and the dreams of the other characters, just as he manipulated them. One of the most famous moments revealing this relationship was the "Bribes" scene, in which Meyerhold turned what was originally a series of bribery episodes into a single visually stunning, comic yet frightening ritual. Khlestakov sat stage center facing a row of doors to the rear, which resembled eleven coffin lids standing on end. From them emerged first eleven gloved hands, each with a packet, followed by the eleven bodies, moving robotlike, chanting simultaneously what Worrall describes as "an eleven-part fugue for voices on the theme of bribery." (*Ibid.*, p. 90.) Khlestakov advanced to each hand in turn, picking off the bribes in rigid sequence, imitating a mechanical doll, with staring, expressionless eyes, working a "bribery machine" as an assembly line—ten years before Chaplin's machine-man sequence in *Modern Times*.

Meyerhold imposed radical changes upon Gogol's original—changing locations, as well as altering the rhythms, the structure, and the central characters of the play. But he insisted that it was all to restore the spirit of the original; the result was controversial, but it was also immediately and overwhelmingly successful. It was, even with all of the literal commedia images carefully translated, the fully realized commedia modern theater. This is nowhere more clear than in that final image, after the tumultuous, panicked departure of all the cast after the reading of the fatal letter announcing the arrival of the *real* government inspector:

In the middle of the hitherto empty stage, and forming a half circle across its width, were fully clothed, life-size dummies, every one of which was a replica of a character in the play. They stood as if caught in a moment of life, mostly in grotesque attitudes, standing, kneeling, gesturing, grimacing. It was as if Death had come to each, unexpectedly, as he might to victims of a volcano disaster.

(*Ibid.*, p. 94.)

Of all the century's commedia revolutionaries, Meyerhold most completely fulfilled the role of commedia modernist in his life and in his growth as an artist. There is an extraordinary passage in Eisenstein's memoirs that both captures his deep, complicated adoration of the man— it was Eisenstein who rescued many of his papers and preserved them from Stalin's planned oblivion—and "places" Meyerhold within his own experience of modernism:

Now, I have seen a few things in my time: I've spent an afternoon at Yvette Guilbert's apartment, where she sang for me and talked about her art; I've spent days on a movie set with Charlie Chaplin. I have heard Chaliapin sing and watched Stanislavsky act. . . . I've discussed . . . the meaning of theater with Luigi Pirandello; I've seen Raquel Müller in Reinhardt's productions . . . I've seen Chekhov, Vakhtangov, Fokine's ballet . . . Karsavina . . . I've seen Al Jolson, and George Gershwin playing "Rhapsody in Blue"; the three-ring circus of Barnum and Bailey and flea circuses in the sideshows; I've seen Primo Carnera knocked out of the ring by Max Schmeling with the Prince of Wales in a ringside seat; I've seen Mardi Gras in New Orleans. I've worked at Paramount Studios with Jackie Coogan; I've heard Yehudi Menuhin play at

Tchaikovsky Hall; I've had dinner with Douglas Fairbanks in New York and lunch with Rin-Tin-Tin in Boston; . . . I've gone car-racing with Greta Garbo and taken Marlene Dietrich to the bullfights.

But not a single one of these impressions can ever compare with the impressions made on me by those three days of rehearsal for *The Doll's House* in that hall on Novinsky Boulevard. I remember shaking all the time. It wasn't the cold, it was the excitement, it was nerves stretched to the limit . . . Meyerhold!

(Schmidt, pp. 7–8.)

Other Commedists: Reinhardt

Vsevolod Meyerhold is the exemplar of the commedia modernist on the home ground of the commedia dell'arte, the theater; but it is important to remember that there were other significant exponents of this form of theatricalism who used it to change the shape of modern drama. Beyond Meyerhold's fellow Russians there was, of course, Craig, with his strong scholarly and antiquarian interest in the commedia, an interest which fed his influential theories of acting and design. However, to take the cue from Eisenstein's catalogue, there were more visible proponents of both the antiquarian and modernist commedia. Max Reinhardt was more the former than the latter, at least in the fact that he directed his energies in this area more into revival and preservation of the old forms than into exploiting them to make a new kind of theater. He was a serious collector of rare books and artifacts of the commedia; at Leopoldskron he gathered paintings and sculpture of commedia figures. (Leisler, p. 3.)

Reinhardt was for much of his long career perhaps the most celebrated director in Europe and America, and his use of commedia did give its images and its tricks much circulation. He was attracted, naturally, to the flair and improvisatory nature of the form, and although he did not resort to actual improvisation, he used the gestures and acrobatic movements in controlled composition. In 1911 he directed the gorgeous and fantastic *Turandot* set to the music of Busoni, and he turned to Molière several times, utilizing great commedians like Viktor Arnold and Max Pallenberg. His most famous commedia effort was probably the 1924 production of Goldoni's *The Servant of Two Masters*, with the great family of actors, the Thimigs, and the music of Mozart. This was especially influential because it traveled the world over and gave exposure to commedia in places like the United States, where it heretofore had

had little play. Reinhardt's favorite play, A *Midsummer Night's Dream*, allowed him opportunity for commedic touches—they are certainly present in his famous 1935 film of the play. With the important exception of his mounting of the Strauss-Hofmannsthal *Ariadne auf Naxos*, however, most of Reinhardt's commedia is built on his unironic nature, his love of the images and the gay freedom, as projected in their more sentimental eighteenth-century forms, especially. Even in *Ariadne* he creates that commedia more or less intact; it is the context into which Hofmannsthal places it that renders it "modern," gives it the distance, the ironic self-reflection of the modernist commedia. A comparison of production photographs of Meyerhold's work with, say, some of the Thimigs or Nanette Fabray in Reinhardt's Goldoni shows us utterly different commedic worlds.

Pirandello

Another of Eisenstein's memorable names is Pirandello, who was indeed a commedia modernist in his enduring fascination with improvisation, with a highly self-conscious theatricalism, and with the basic issues of character and identity. The fixed, vividly distinctive identities of commedia *zanni* provided the modernists with a pattern for this exploration because of the multiple masks and roles taken on by these characters, with the original theatrical identity still intact underneath. Arlecchino's various disguises and roles and even his varied fates do not alter the particular relationship he has with the audience and with the rest of the commedia cast. This relationship and the equally vital connection (and distance) between the commedia figure and the actor playing him, whose identity is especially distinct because of that fixed identity underlying his theatrical role, was central to Pirandello. Like Stanislavsky, he believed intensely in his actors living inside their roles and becoming thereby utterly faithful to them. But like Meyerhold, he rejected the goal of naturalism that this, for Stanislavsky, implied. The 1930 *Tonight We Improvise* faced this version of the problem of theatrical illusion with a divided character:

The actor playing Ricco Verri had two distinct roles: the Leading Actor and Verri. The actor's consciousness of his own separate identity from each of the characters was obligatory, even as the roles became blurred during the course of the play when the Leading Actor began to assume the identity of Verri. Pirandello deliberately added to the confusion by having the actor playing the Leading Actor use his own name, deluding the audience into believing that the actor had in reality assumed Verri's identity. But the role of the Leading Actor was prescribed by the text; any resemblance between the character of the Leading Actor and the actor performing the role was purely coincidental.

(Sogliuzzo, p. 40.)

This is a strong echo of Meyerhold's actor-playing-actor mocking his role in *Magnanimous Cuckold*. Pirandello knew the traditions of commedia well, and they were important to him in his drive to relieve Italian theater of the excesses of sentimentality and other burdens from nineteenth-century performance practice. This too had its parallel in Meyerhold's revolt against that heritage in Russian theater. There are early faithful versions, but more important are the later bits and pieces of the commedia in Pirandello, often present only as a general acrobatic theatricality or an air of improvisation and trick playing along the course of a plot—none of which was actually impromptu. *Henry IV* (1922) can be seen as a sustained exercise in modernist harlequinade, with the central figure taking on, in madness first real then feigned, the character of the eleventh-century German emperor. As all the characters around him are drawn into playing the roles he, in his role as emperor, expects of them, many commedia roles are played out: there are the Dottore, the lovers, various servants, and the all-important masks. Loss, or absence, of identity, false identity, madness, all parade in vividly theatrical form in "Henry's" charade and in the arranged masquerades and small plays that he orders within that charade. The power of the mask is evoked when the (otherwise nameless) "Henry" is trapped within his Arlecchino-madman mask. The aging beauty Matilda remembers:

I shall never forget that scene—all our masked faces hideous and terrified gazing at him, at that terrible mask of his face, which was no longer a mask, but madness, madness personified.

(*Ibid.*, pp. 169–70.)

One might call this existential commedia, a play of masks that forces the viewer to examine, to doubt, the essential human identity itself. Pirandello's most famous work, from the year before *Henry IV*, 1921, is existential commedia in this sense; the *Six Characters in Search of an Author* force the question of their existence; they are essence without existence, puppets without a puppet master, but they insist on their existence, their desires, their rights. And the author arranges it so that the audience must struggle with them both as what they are and, literally, as characters with an author. This is another form of the sharp ambiguity of identity so prevalent in modernist commedia, another look at Petrushka come alive to mock his puppet master.

Brecht

For Brecht the theatricality of commedia had, in the main, other uses than this existential play; he framed the illusion, drew a sharp distinction between it and reality in order to force the viewer out of the illusion back into a deeper reality. Like Pirandello, he insisted on the framework, on the ultimate theatricality of the experience of drama, but unlike the Italian master he sought continuously to break the illusion spun by the drama, never to exploit the ambiguities, the blurred edges between emotional commitment to an illusion and to reality. He was influenced, at a distance, by Meyerhold's similar politically oriented theatricalism. In the twenties the visits of the Moscow Art Theater with Stanislavsky made a considerable impression on the Germans, but the younger artists were more influenced by what they learned of Meyerhold (and also of Tairov, with his version of constructivism and his use of commedia images).

That which is most truly commedic about Brecht comes out of his cabaret aesthetic, the vaudeville turns, the jaunty doggerel, the quick changes, and the use of placards to underline and define those changes. Brecht's fascination with the circus and its clowns was akin to that of Picasso and his friends, although it was perhaps a more studied admiration, as expressed in a diary entry from September of 1920:

I went with Brustle and saw an eccentric clown of immense stature who shot at the lights with a little pistol, banged himself on the head, developed a large bump, sawed it off and ate it. I was enchanted: there's more wit and style in that than in the entire contemporary theatre.

(Ewen, p. 32.)

Like Meyerhold, he had a deep commitment to popular theater, to the simple peasant and the worker, and the presence of their images and their values within Brecht's cabaret-like context makes something new of it; the "decadence" of such a framework is filled with political energy. This is most memorably true of the Weill collaborations, *The Threepenny Opera* and *The Rise and Fall of the City of Mahagonny*, which are rife with modernist transmutations of the commedia. Brecht's theories of "Epic Opera," of the place of music in drama, and his approach to acting, the inculcation of basic, expressive gestures, the theory of

Verfremdung, deliberate distancing, all are importantly related to commedia, as is his use of broad, but sharply stylized satire.

Still, Brecht's often overriding concern for social and political meaning took him some distance from the commedic impulse, even when many of the techniques and even the explicit themes were still present (as in his versions of *Don Juan* and *Turandot*). The relentless pursuit of argument in *Galileo,* for instance, does lend itself to verses, songs, placards, even satire of the churchmen, but there is no flavor of the commedia in Brecht's Venice, modernist or otherwise. But then, by 1938–1939, much of the spirit of commedia modernism had been drained from theater in general.

The French

Much has been said of Cocteau's commedia theater, and about the peculiarly intimate and tenacious commedia modernism of the French. It is the French who have managed to maintain a version of modern commedia, in mime most obviously but also in other theater, by reverting to the Watteau and Deburau Pierrot. Cocteau's friend, the playwright, lover, man of the theater, cineast, *boulevardier,* Sacha Guitry, wrote a "comédie," *Deburau,* on the life of that "cher grand Pierrot sublime." His wife and protégée Yvonne Printemps played the heroine, and also the son of the great, sad mime. The play, which opened in 1918 at the Théâtre du Vaudeville in Paris, had been preceded by the first big Printemps-Guitry triumph, *L'Illusioniste* (1917), which had a good deal of circus commedia in it itself, beginning as it does with twenty minutes of acrobats, cyclists, singers, before Guitry appears with a conjuring act. *Parade,* Cocteau's first piece of theater, also premiered in 1917; it was "modern" in ways that Guitry could never be, but clearly these artists drank from the same spring. *Deburau* seems to radiate an air of sentiment quite like that of the great commedia film of wartime France, Carné's *Children of Paradise,* with the immortal pantomime of Jean-Louis Barrault.

Guitry's popular commedia and Cocteau's modernist commedia had as their contemporary the commedia of Jacques Copeau, the pioneer of the bare stage and the use of multiple stages layered upon one another. The *tréteau nu* put a great deal of emphasis upon the movements and gestures of the actors upon that naked expanse; in several famous productions, particularly *Twelfth Night* (1914) and Molière's *The Tricks of Scapin* (1920), both with Louis Jouvet, those movements were cast specifically in the mold of commedia dell'arte. In the latter, Copeau himself played the part of Scapin, dressed in a harlequin cloak and tam-o'-shanter, dancing through a multitude of guises—servant, penitent, ruler, actor—all in the tradition of the multifaceted Harlequin. He also emphasized the elements of farce in *Twelfth Night* and, like Meyerhold, believed deeply in the power of farce to evoke elemental relations and emotions. (Paterson, pp. 37–51.)

There is another line through the French theatrical heritage that is the most influential and productive of all in contemporary theater, a line connected vitally to the commedia, also to Pirandello, to Brecht, tangentially to Meyerhold and to other forms of theatricalism, and certainly to the existentialist impulse in modernism. The source, at least one source, is Jarry and his creatively demented Ubu plays; Antonin Artaud was the most fruitful, intelligent transmitter of the line to the modern era, particularly in his writings on the film comedians and in his vigorous campaign for an elemental theatricalism in *The Theater and Its Double* (1931–1936):

In our theater, which lives under the exclusive dictatorship of speech, this language of signs and mimicry, this silent pantomime, these attitudes, these gestures in space, these objective intonations—in short, everything I regard as specifically theatrical in the theater—all these elements, when they exist outside the text, are universally regarded as the inferior aspect of theater, are dismissed as "stage business." . . . I maintain that insofar as this language begins with the stage, draws its power from its spontaneous creation on stage, and struggles directly with the stage without resorting to words . . . it is *mise en scène* that is theater, much more than the written and spoken play.

(Sontag, pp. 233–34.)

Artaud was the teacher of Roger Blin, who was chosen by Samuel Beckett to create *Waiting for Godot* for the stage—and "create" is not too strong a word: Vladimir and Estragon are clownlike tramps because that is the way Blin conceived of them. (Fletcher, p. 44.)

Ionesco and Dürrenmatt

It is important to note that there were other strategies for confronting a mad world developing in the theater through the middle of the century, strategies that had their own vital commedic connections. Eugene Ionesco's theatrical mission was "to push everything to paroxysm, to the point where the sources of the tragic lie." (Esslin, p. 91.) In his most pugnacious theatrical polemic, *Improvisation, or The Shepherd's Chameleon* (1955), Ionesco put himself on the stage as a comic playwright visited by three pompously bedecked Dottore figures, Bartholomeus I, II, and III, who come out of the commedia dell'arte via Molière. He explains that he once saw a young shepherd embracing a chameleon: "It was such a touching scene, I decided to turn it into a tragic farce." (*Ibid.*, p. 115.) In this work, indeed throughout his career, Ionesco demonstrated a kinship to the dynamic, challenging new commedia of Meyerhold and then Brecht. At the same time, his is a very different line of approach, running in deep opposition to Brecht in his epic theater and his acting theories. What they share they share most clearly in the realm of commedic theatricality. The curious mid-fifties *The Picture*, which Ionesco called a *guignolade*, opens with a fat, ugly capitalist haggling with a painter about the price of a picture. It is obvious, absurdist social criticism (the painter ends up paying the rich man to store the picture), and it would fit comfortably into the world of *Mahagonny*—or of *Mystery-Bouffe*. Ionesco's instructions summon up the ghost of Meyerhold:

In fact, this Punch and Judy play must by acted by circus clowns in the most childish, exaggerated, idiotic manner possible. . . . It is only by an extreme simplification . . . that the meaning of this farce can be brought out and become acceptable through its very inacceptability and idiocy.

(*Ibid.*, p. 13.)

Punch and Judy, the simplicity of the basic patterns in traditional roles, gave the commedia modernists the vivid, overt physicality and theatricality with which they conducted their assault on traditional forms. For Ionesco, farce could no longer be the "battering ram" that it was for Blok and Meyerhold, because the world had changed—his *guignolade* was a failure. But these basic dramatic patterns still had their use in the theater. More than the schematic clarity, there remains the power to confront the new, changed world—a mad world:

Tragedy presupposes guilt, despair, moderation, lucidity, vision, a sense of responsibility. In the Punch-and-Judy show of our century, in this backsliding of the white race, there are neither guilty nor responsible individuals anymore. . . . Comedy is the only thing that can still reach us. Our world has led to the grotesque as well as to the atom bomb. . . . And yet, the grotesque is only a way of expressing in a tangible manner, of making us perceive physically the paradoxical; it is the form of the unformed, the visage of a faceless world.

(Dürrenmatt, p. 255.)

In *The Physicists* (1962) the Swiss playwright Friedrich Dürrenmatt created a grotesque tragicomedy in which he attempted to render the madness of the world visible by naming it, by pursuing the paradoxes of a rational madness—"a drama about physicists must be paradoxical." (*Ibid.*, p. 156.) His Punch and Judy characters are the three nuclear physicists, all pretending to be mad, two of them, as "Newton" and "Einstein" seeking out the secrets of ultimate power discovered by the third, Möbius. They are captive of Dr. von Zahnd, the director of the sanitorium housing them, who has stolen the secret and is building empires with it—and who really is mad. (We are reminded of *Dr. Caligari*.) The masks, the absurd murders committed to preserve them, and the blurring of madness and sanity all work to expose the paradox at the center of modern existence, the face of the faceless world:

Just as our thinking today seems to be unable to do without the concept of the paradox, so also art and our world, which still exist only because the atom bomb exists: out of fear of the bomb.

(*Ibid.*, p. 255.)

Dürrenmatt's way with the masks of madness echoes that of Pirandello, especially in *Henry IV*, but he writes of a more intense madness, and more insistently than Pirandello, he makes his masks mirror the real world, there being no invention more powerful than the real paradox of the Punch and Judy atomic age. This is not to say that every modernist with a streak of commedia in him conceives of the world's madness in terms of the Bomb. But its shadow is inescapable, and we catch fleeting glimpses of it even in those, like Beckett and Pinter, (the *Dumb Waiter* side of him) who reduce theater to basic theatricality. One of the two voices, "A" and "B," in Beckett's *Theatre II*, one of his "Roughs for Theatre and Radio" from the mid-seventies, refers in passing to an "unfinished game of chess with a correspondent in Tasmania . . . hope not dead of living to see the extermination of the species." (Beckett, p. 90.) The most famous modernist waiting game is, of course, that of Vladimir and Estragon, Beckett's tramp clowns. They are not waiting for the extermination of the species, but the world around them is certainly bereft of civilization, except for a few unseen marauders, a boy, and Pozzo the unmasterful master and his unlucky Lucky. The commedic echoes around the name Godot have long been meat for speculation: Godot the diminutive of God, as Pierrot of Pierre, and Charlot, the name the French universally apply to Charlie Chaplin.

It is not too much to claim Beckett for the modern commedia—or Pinter, Dürrenmatt, and Ionesco, whatever their vast differences. Their dramas insist on a new reality upon the stage, even as Meyerhold and Pirandello, and Jarry before them, by stripping the theater to essentials and playing, farcically and tragically, with the illusions they expose. They claim the power of illusion only to celebrate it as illusion to render it transparent—even when, in their ironic, ambiguous sophistication, they have nothing to put in its place. Blok's battering ram, the spirit of farce, hovers in their work for the simple reason that the commedia dell'arte reasserted itself in the twentieth century as the bright, irreducible, irrepressible essence of theater. Harlequin and Pierrot and Columbine shine with a special life against a dark background.

Chapter 5.

CHAPLIN, CALIGARI, HOLLYWOOD, AND HARLEQUIN

When one examines the history of the characters, situations, and routines of classical farce it is impossible to avoid the conclusion that slapstick cinema gave it a sudden and dazzling rebirth. The "flesh and blood farce," on its way out since the seventeenth century, survived, highly specialized and transformed, only in the circus and in certain kinds of music hall. That is to say precisely in these places where the Hollywood producers of slapstick films went for their actors.

(Bazin, p. 80.)

T HE COMMEDIA DELL'ARTE can claim the movies, especially those of the silent decades, on several grounds. Many of these connections are obvious, at least in their broad outlines: The players, directors, and the entrepreneurs of early film did come out of the popular theater, for the most part; and they brought with them the acrobatic and melodramatic skills needed to improvise and to communicate across the silence or the music by way of gesture and pantomime. But the new medium was more than an extension of theater; it offered a wealth of new possibilities for expression, and in a few important hands, for specifically modernist expression. There are great differences in intention and in achievement between the cinema clowns and the aesthetic revolutionaries of the film and other media; however, there was also much traffic between them—or at least traffic one way, because the images and antics of Chaplin, Keaton, and the Keystone Kops imprinted themselves vividly on the imagination of the avant-garde.

The Pioneers

By the turn of the century, film was for many the most fascinating part of the new technology, the engine of its image making, of the endless self-consciousness of that new world. In the mid-1890s, the Lumières, father and son, took the *cinématographe* on the road and made of it a worldwide fad. They concentrated for the most part on giving their audiences a strange new glimpse of the life around them: the mail train arriving, a baby's meal, the Diamond Jubilee procession; the mere recreation of such events in moving, flickering light on a screen was transformation enough.

But the Lumière team also toyed with story lines, and one of their most popular items, *L'Arroseur arrosé (The Sprinkler Sprinkled)*, has with some justice been called the first film farce. The plot in its entirety was described in an admiring *New York Dramatic Mirror* review of July 4, 1896:

The . . . picture showed a lawn with a gardener using a hose to sprinkle it. A bad boy steps on the hose, causing the water to squirt into the gardener's face. He drops the hose, runs after the boy, and gives him a sound thrashing.

(Pratt, pp. 16–17.)

The Lumière *cinématographe* had been preceded in the public's affections by Edison's kinetoscope, which did manage to present moving-picture humor, if not a full-fledged plot. This first recorded bit of film humor was *Fred Ott's Sneeze,* which is nothing more than the cleverly excruciating buildup to a sneeze, which finally occurs in resounding silence just as the reel ends.

From the start, then, the short, conveniently broad and cleanly resolved gags of the music hall comedian served the time-and-light-bound pioneers of film well. And from the start the entrepreneurs of the moving picture sought their audiences in the same places they found their performers and their gags. The new entertainment was working-class fare everywhere. It was a risky, wide-open business that lived on innovation and sensation, both in its rapidly evolving seat-of-the-pants technology and in the films ground out by that technology. It was suited to the less respectable:

The tricksters, the fast talkers, the cranks, the defeated; all of them took part in the gold rush to invent the cinema. Yet for years the cinema was more likely to lose your fortune than to make it. It hovered between life and death in the nether world of the fairground, the second-class music hall, the beer garden, the penny arcades and the church social.

(Rhode, p. 25.)

Leaving out the church social, this is a description not only of the world of the film aborning, but also of the breeding ground of the modern commedia. The technological and the aesthetic revolution grew most vigorously in the places where hardship and pressing poverty lived with enough emotional freedom and social fluidity to give rise to creative unrest. The cinema and the commedia thrived on necessity and disrepute—and of course they also had each other.

Georges Méliès was a gifted magician and a producer of considerable skill, one of the more successful inhabitants of this nether world. He was also present at one of the first showings given by the Lumières in Paris. Within a year of this enlightenment he was making his own films. Méliès occupies an honored place in the development of cinema because he immediately understood its unique potential for illusion. In the words of André Bazin:

Méliès . . . saw the cinema as basically nothing more than a refinement of the marvels of the theater. Special effects were for him simply a further evolution of conjuring.

(Bazin, p. 78.)

It is inevitable, then, that Méliès would employ a static camera and pour his invention into designing spectacles, costumes, and tricks to take place before its lens. Experiment and accident soon led him to multiple exposures, dissolves, and especially the simple expedient of stopping the film, changing the scene in front of it, and restarting, thus producing all kinds of magical transformations. The sensibility of the music hall and the conjurer with a brilliant new trick are combined in many of his films. His most famous film, the 1902 A Trip to the Moon, is based loosely on H. G. Wells and on Jules Verne's From the Earth to the Moon. It is best known for its science-fiction effects, but it is still essentially filmed popular theater:

The moon harbors a grimacing man in the moon and the stars are bull's-eyes studded with the pretty faces of music hall girls . . . his actors bowed to the audience, as if they performed on the stage.

(Kracauer, Theory, p. 33.)

Méliès made of the cinema more than a device for recording the real world; he demonstrated that it could make new worlds and put new frameworks around depictions of the old. Whereas a Lumière film occasionally ran backward to catch an effect only possible in film, Méliès built his special effects into the very fabric of his narratives. Méliès reinvented the theater for the new medium, along lines that were to fascinate and to suggest much to the other artists who were exploiting the traditions of the music hall and the circus. Such a line can be followed without much difficulty to the surrealists, for instance to Buñuel's classic surrealist film statement, *Un Chien andalou* (1928); more obviously to the witty trickery and theatricality of René Clair's *Entr'acte* (1924); and to the theater and films of Cocteau, for whom the camera was "the image-making machine." (Cocteau, p. 13.)

However, in the first decade of cinema, the commedia and its analogues were most vividly alive in the mainstream of popular entertainment. In the days of the melodrama and the comic "chase" film, when the nickelodeons were attracting daily audiences of millions and, according to a 1906 *Billboard,* "Every up-to-date vaudeville theatre included moving pictures as part of the performance," the commedia was present in the comic gestures, in the expressions, and in the "business" displayed by the vaudeville-trained film actors.

In 1908 David Wark Griffith joined the Biograph company, after having tried his hand as a writer and actor for vaudeville and for stock companies. Between 1908 and 1913 he directed some four hundred films for Biograph, which laid the groundwork for a career that was to revolutionize virtually every visual aspect of film, even while his taste in plots remained firmly rooted in the melodrama. One of the many successes of 1909 was a melodrama that showed its commedia affinities with unusual clarity. This was *A Fool's Revenge,* a one-reel version of *Rigoletto.* A reviewer revealed the commedic stamp on Griffith's art, referring to the court fool Rigoletto himself:

The clear facial expressions as well as the natural but intensely suggestive gestures and poses of the character approach perfection in pantomimic art.

(Pratt, p. 57.)

In February 1909, a month before the above review, a film of Charles Pathé based literally on a pantomime by the French actor Séverin opened in New York. The pantomime enjoyed a vogue in the vaudeville houses under the title *Conscience;* in the film the scene moved from the street to a Parisian cabaret, and Séverin recreated his role under the title *Incriminating Evidence.* (*Ibid.*, p. 113.) In 1908, Sarah Bernhardt starred in the filmed *La Tosca* and Réjane appeared in *Britannicus.* (The last-named especially excelled in pantomime.)

The Coming of the Clowns

But these theatrical imports must yield place, in terms of influence, to the film comics. Two who had large followings in the prewar years,

John Bunny and Alkali Ike (formerly Gus Carney in vaudeville) were Americans. Bunny was forty-seven years old, with a generation of vaudeville and stage comedy behind him when he began his film career. He was the first American comic to win worldwide fame. His character humor distanced him from the more commedic screen clowns, but pictures reveal a wonderful comic face that surely functioned in a way similar to their comic masks. The jowls and nose and bright eyes were clearly antecedent to the characteristic mask of W. C. Fields.

The most important comics to parade their wares on film in these years were not, however, Americans. The first of the European clowns to win a large following via film—one writer called him "the motion picture's first truly international star" (Bermel, p. 143.)—was Max Linder, who, true to form, had developed a career in Parisian cabarets. Linder started with Pathé, doing many small parts until he was discovered by Ferdinand Zecca, a Pathé director whose career and talents roughly paralleled those of Méliès. His forte was the farce, especially the chase comedy, and it has been argued very plausibly that many of the routines of the Keystone Kops and their brothers had their origins in Zecca. In 1907 he cast Linder in his first leading role in *The Legend of Polichinelle*, a comedy that shows by its title that it owes much to the commedia. In the four hundred and more that followed that first film in the years up to World War I (where he suffered a wound and disease that put a permanent crimp in his art and his career), Linder played a vast number of characters in a broad range of comic predicaments anticipating the gags and plots of all of the golden-age film farceurs.

Linder also took up directing in this period, in the mode of Zecca, and he had among his actors the young Abel Gance (later famous for his *Napoleon*) and Maurice Chevalier. The line of comic tradition is seen in René Clair's 1947 *Le Silence est d'or*, a loving re-creation of the early French cinema of Méliès and Zecca. The central character is a pioneer filmmaker who speaks with the voice of Clair: "I like happy endings," and is played by Maurice Chevalier. (Mast, *Comic*, p. 228.)

Max, as the world knew him, created for himself a vivid central personality that shone through an infinite variety of characters and plots. As a trickster he was especially triumphant, as in *Max Leads Them a Novel Chase*, in which he simply steals a necklace from a woman at a ball and is chased by the crowd, then by a few "Pathé policemen," then by everyone in various configurations, until he escapes in a balloon. A New York reviewer set the great screen clown in the fraternity of Harlequins, eternally lawless, but eternally exempt from judgment.

This writer is not partial to stories of this character in motion pictures, although they should be no more harmful than when presented in type in newspapers and magazines. However, we all know that Max isn't that kind of chap, and we forgive him this time.

(Pratt, p. 115.)

In *A Prince of Worth,* Linder plays a prince who falls in love with a strolling singer and marries her instead of the woman his parents have chosen for him. Ejected by his family, the couple hits the road to earn their way as acrobats, eventually to become vaudeville headliners who perform before an audience that happens to include the noble papa, whose heart melts, and the family is reunited.

Linder's ability to project a personality, a comic character that was more than the sum of countless gags and predicaments, is the essence of his link to the commedia—and also to Chaplin. It is common to list Linder among the important influences upon Chaplin; early in his career, Chaplin acknowledged his debt to Linder but he later denied it, and there is no mention of Linder in his autobiography. Critics have pointed to certain of Linder's roles, especially that of the seedy dandy, as predecessors of the Tramp. Individual routines and even the dandy image were thoroughly familiar to both the Frenchman and the Englishman by way of their vaudeville training; however, they are very different characters on the screen.

Linder was a close student of Chaplin. In an early twenties interview with Louis Delluc he said Chaplin "calls me his teacher, but, for my part, I have been lucky to get lessons at his school." (McCaffrey, pp. 55, 57–58.) His appreciation of film comedy stresses a discipline like that which gave meaning to the "dell'arte" in commedia dell'arte, the mastery and precise calculation that was the (paradoxical) foundation of true comic improvisation. The technical mastery enabled Linder, Chaplin, Keaton, and others, with varying degrees of success, to make not only comedy but also character out of their "capers." Indeed, it is very likely that the implacable demands of the new medium made the spirit of commedia more important and apparent in the comic silents than it was in the vaudeville that helped spawn them. Bazin's "sudden and dazzling rebirth" of the farce came about only when the creators of slapstick cinema transformed the looser, more segmented, and more verbal theater of vaudeville into something that was, for all its improvisation, far more structured. This was a new commedia, created at a remove from the audience, without the opportunity for change and elaboration from performance to performance. The comic turns, the surprises and the off-guard moments, had to be fixed forever. When these farceurs rose to the occasion, they made of those comic moments something eternal, much as the clowns and Pierrots and Harlequins before them played out their comedy on a framework that was ageless and deathless.

In an article in *Arts Magazine* in 1923, Vadim Uraneff argued that the parallels between the original commedia and American vaudeville were such that "in America the spirit and the art of Commedia dell'Arte could be reproduced better than anywhere else by emphasizing certain qualities already present in the American theater." (Uraneff, p. 321.) Using Gordon Craig's call for a twentieth-century revival of "this independent spirit of the Theatre" as his starting point, and adding to Craig's the voices of Copeau and Meyerhold, Uraneff very usefully located this nascent commedic impulse in:

that branch of the purely commercial theatre which has grown up in response to the demands of the great American public and which appeals directly to popular audiences. The most typical, vital, and perfect expression of that theatre is Vaudeville.

(*Ibid.*, pp. 321–22.)

Sounding very like Craig, Uraneff argued a vital connection between the audience and its entertainment in the original commedia and in vaudeville:

The most important factor in [the commedia's] evolution was that for centuries it had developed entirely by pressure of popular taste, in a theatre where the primitive spectator was the ultimate judge. The primitive spectator, having no knowledge of other forms of art, is always a peculiarly sensitive critic of the theatre, because a feeling for the essentially theatric is not dulled in him by influences and associations foreign to histrionic art. There can be no doubt of the supreme value of such a process of "natural selection" in type, story and setting, as a foundation for a National Theatre, in developing theatrical traditions and as a basis for a technique in acting.

(*Ibid.*, p. 323.)

Despite its rather elevated view of public taste, this passage certainly reflects the reality of popular comedy. All of the successful movie comedians shared an intense preoccupation with the audience's response. When Theodore Dreiser asked Mack Sennett about his "artistic reason for being," the answer was a philosophy of that audience relationship: "Everyone wants to laugh at something. Mostly at other people's troubles, if they're not too rough." (Pratt, p. 186.) And his response to those who objected to things being "too rough"—too many hot stoves, shootings, tumbles down the stairs or out the window—was in the same vein: "You've got to get the laughs, haven't you? . . . You couldn't reach the crowd by refined comedy."

Chaplin and Slapstick

The memoirs and other accounts of the early days of slapstick are full of evidence that the popular sense of humor was a primary shaping force. When Chaplin, a new arrival at the Keystone studio, first tried out the freshly improvised baggy pants, big shoes, derby, and mustache costume on Sennett, the latter responded as the world audience was to do, at least by Chaplin's own account:

The secret of Mack Sennett's success was his enthusiasm. He was a great audience and laughed genuinely at what he thought was funny. He stood and giggled until his body began to shake.

(Chaplin, p. 150.)

Again, this kind of audience sense is widespread and is to be found in the advertising executives who have made the Tramp the central character in a highly successful series of television ads for IBM. Applied to vaudeville farce, however, the popular pressure described by Uraneff can be seen as a transforming engine, turning the simple intrigues and chase sequences into something richer, intrigues and chases conducted by figures made palpable, human, by means of their individual comic identities.

The mixture of personal vision, English music hall background, and the new medium's possibilities—and necessities—often made for a commedic change. An obvious example (true for Linder and other European actors as well as for Chaplin) is in film pantomime technique in comedy. Again, Chaplin:

There was a lot Keystone taught me and a lot I taught Keystone. In those days they knew little about technique, stagecraft or movement, which I brought to them from the theatre. They also knew little about natural pantomime. In blocking a scene, a director would have three or four actors blatantly stand in a straight line facing the camera, and, with the broadest gestures, one would pantomime "I-want-to-marry-your-daughter" by pointing to himself, then to his ring finger, then to the girl. Their miming dealt little with subtlety or effectiveness, so I stood out in contrast. In those early movies, I knew I had many advantages, and that, like a geologist, I was entering a rich, unexpected field.

(Ibid., p. 161.)

Uraneff included Chaplin among his principal examples of "our own Commedia dell'Arte"; indeed, he gave him the palm as:

one incomparable American artist who, being the most representative of the spirit of Commedia dell'Arte, needs no comparison with it. Charlie Chaplin, with his extraordinary technique, with his power of getting the most subtle things over to the most primitive audience, with his instantaneous appeal, has nothing to learn from the history of Commedia dell'Arte. Although his tricks and situations are never twice the same, his mask-like make-up and his char- acterisitic walk are unvarying. In other words, he is always true to the great school of acting of the Italian improvisational comedy.

                    (Uraneff, p. 328.)

When these words were written, Chaplin had had almost a decade to make himself an American institution—his first films were made at Keystone in February 1914—but clearly his contribution to "our" com- media was founded upon training in the English popular theater as much as in his unique way with the film. But Uraneff can be forgiven his en- thusiasm for the American aspect of his subject; most of his parallels between ancient and modern commedia focus on American vaudeville, musical comedy, farce, burlesque, and moving pictures. The renais- sance he sought could not, at least by 1923, be enacted on the vaude ville stage alone.

In his *Harlequin's Stick, Charlie's Cane* (1975), David Madden could hardly share Uraneff's hope for a "brilliant revival" of the commedia. The essence of his argument does, however, stand as at least a partial confirmation of Uraneff's belief that the revival would be realized through "native American productions with scenarios constructed from the ma- terial now in use in American vaudeville." (*Op. cit.*) Madden's own list of parallels gives pride of commedic place, once again, to Charlie, and goes on to draw from an impressive list of vaudeville-trained film stars: John Bunny, W. C. Fields, Oliver Hardy, the Marx Brothers, and so on.

The particular significance of Chaplin in this commedia scheme of things has been noted by nearly everyone with an interest in the com- media. Madden's book is essentially devoted to arguing that significance (although he takes care to mention Allardyce Nicoll's vehement denial thereof); it provides much detailed support for the commedia connec- tion, drawing not only on the content of the films but on the milieu of their creation. Madden (and others) focuses on the Harlequin side of Charlie, however, and it is important to note that the vital essence of the Tramp has at least as much of Pierrot in it:

You know this fellow is many-sided, a tramp, a gentleman, a poet, a dreamer, a lonely fellow, always hopeful of romance and adventure. He would have you believe he is a scientist, a musician, a duke, a polo player. However, he is not above picking up cigarette butts or robbing a baby of its candy. And, of course, if the occasion warrants it, he will kick a lady in the rear—but only in extreme anger!

(Chaplin, p. 150.)

Chaplin is quoting himself to Sennett, and there must be a large dose of hindsight laid on here (and through much of the early part of the autobiography, published in 1964). The point stands, however, that there is more than Harlequin in this Tramp—and not merely in the sense, which Madden allows, that the modern versions of the old comic types show the effects of considerable reshuffling and accretion. Harlequin is indeed there in Charlie, and it is important to admit that in order to make the larger point. Of the many descriptions of the enigmatic Harlequin collected by Duchartre, that by Marmontel in the eighteenth century is most usefully general and also, perhaps, most supportive of Madden's argument:

His character is a mixture of ignorance, *naïveté*, wit, stupidity, and grace. He is both a rake and an overgrown boy with occasional gleams of intelligence, and his mistakes and clumsiness often have a wayward charm. His acting is patterned on the lithe, agile grace of a young cat, and he has a superficial coarseness which makes his performance all the more amusing. . . . He is eternally amorous, and is constantly in difficulties either on his own or on his master's account. He is hurt and comforted in turn as easily as a child, and his grief is almost as comic as his joy.

(Duchartre, p. 132.)

Harlequin the "chameleon" (from another eighteenth-century description) can take on many roles and disguises and therefore many of the traits of other commedia figures, which is certainly true of the Tramp, as well. But there is an essential ingredient to the Tramp's character, most visible in his face and gestures, very often reflected in his actions, that is missing, for the most part, from Harlequin. Charlie is, as he says himself, a dreamer, a vulnerable and sensitive romantic for whom the world is a place full of mystery—and sometimes a cruel or callous maze— more than a place full of opportunity, as it is for Harlequin. Duchartre describes Pedrolino, the commedia servant who first appeared in the second half of the sixteenth century, in ways that better suit this aspect of the Tramp:

He differs radically from the other valets of the commedia dell'arte: he is a young, personable, and trustworthy individual who can be a charming lover if necessary. . . . Pedrolino has such engaging simplicity and elegance that one is tempted to think of him as having sprung from the charming fantasy of Watteau or of Marivaux. . . . He was, none the less, a comic character. When Franceschina deceived him outrageously he shoulders the blame and dissolves into tears of self-reproach for sins he has never committed. And when Pedrolino is induced by Harlequin to play tricks on Pantaloon or the Doctor he is inevitably the only one ever caught and punished.

(*Ibid.*, p. 251.)

Thus, even in his earliest guise, before his transformation at the hands of Watteau and then of Deburau, Pedrolino, or Pierro or Piero, was a more elegant and sensitive creature than Harlequin. Unlike Harlequin, he wore no mask and was instead heavily powdered. He is hollow-cheeked, haunted by rejection, a creature born to suffer. The face was therefore central to the communication of thoughts and feelings in a way that it could not be for Harlequin, and yet it had the power of recognition and expression associated with the mask, also. The face of the Tramp is the perfect union of these dramatic qualities. The range of love and sentiment conveyed by Pedrolino, his successors Gilles and Pierrot, and Charlie, is quite beyond Harlequin's eternal amorousness. Doubters are directed to the final scene of the 1931 *City Lights*.

Pedrolino-like, the Tramp has gone to jail for the crime of others, and having just been released, he comes upon the flower shop of the young woman (Virginia Cherrill) whose sight has been restored with the help of money provided by way of his sacrifice. The look of radiant joy that suffuses the face of the buffeted and bedraggled benefactor when the woman recognizes him is purest sentimentality. It is more than sentimentality, however, because the intense purity of the expression, the perfect innocence of the emotion in the face, belongs to Pierrot. This Pierrot appears in the face of Harry Langdon, of Stan Laurel, and often Harpo Marx, though nowhere does it glow so steadily, so significantly, as in the Tramp.

This is not just a matter of facial expression; it applies also to the litheness, even the delicacy of much of Chaplin's pantomime, popping up again and again in the two-reeler as well as in the features, not only in *City Lights*, but in his famous first full-length work, *The Kid* (1921), in *The Circus* (1924), which is replete with commedic images, and in *The Gold Rush* of the following year, with its unequaled eating sequences. The snowbound and starving Charlie devours a shoe as if it were a turkey, shoelaces as spaghetti, a candle as a fine delicacy—all these mad gourmet transformations accomplished with an art that redefined film pantomime. Donald McCaffrey has noted the Pierrot in this display:

The twentieth century, after *The Gold Rush*, seemed to house the reincarnation of the famous eighteenth-century French clown, Jean-Gaspard Deburau, a renowned Pierrot, blended with all the rollicking good spirit of the clown created by the English music hall's favorite comedian, Grimaldi.

(McCaffrey, p. 87.)

This film scholar must be forgiven for placing Deburau in the wrong century, because he has hit upon the right mix of clowns. Chaplin got his start as a serious professional with the great English music hall company of Fred Karno (his half-brother Sydney and Stan Laurel, among others, were also associated with Karno). There is abundant evidence, in Chaplin's memoirs and elsewhere, of the vigorous and high-spirited pantomime that was basic to this company of clowns. Like the original commedia troupes, and like Chaplin's own Hollywood company, Fred Karno's troupe trained as an ensemble and developed a repertoire of pantomimed bits and—as it were—*lazzi*, all serving as the basic grid upon which improvisation was built.

In his 1928 review of *The Circus*, in *Nation*, Alexander Bakshy also established the Pierrot connection:

Through all these mirth-provoking scenes there flits the unforgettable image which has so endeared itself to the world—the image of a childishly simple and quixotically noble Pierrot who occasionally borrows the impishness of Harlequin.

(*Ibid.*, p. 131.)

The labels would not be important, certainly the issue of whether there is more Pierrot or more Harlequin in the Tramp would not be important—roles do shift, and even the great Harlequin, Picasso, seems to have detected a Pierrot in himself—except that it is the Pierrot in Chaplin that brings him in his particular way into the modern commedia.

The aesthetic sophisticates, the makers of the avant-garde, embraced film precisely at the time that it became commedic, the heyday of slapstick cinema and especially Chaplin. By the teens these artists, especially Picasso, Stravinsky, Cocteau, and Apollinaire, had very nearly succeeded in redefining, not entirely unintentionally, just what it meant to be a "man of taste." The old form thereof was rapidly becoming merely traditionalist or conservative, while the new version became forever tangled up with notions of commitment to the avant-garde. This is an ironic side effect to the major point that the commedia was a vital connecting link between the most sophisticated of artists and the film. Diaghilev and Stravinsky went together to see Chaplin films, and Stravinsky says somewhere that for him in those early years Chaplin *was* cinema. (The two seriously considered collaborating for a time in the thirties. Chaplin suggested doing a film together about a "decadent night club" at which the floor show was the Crucifixion. A businessman explains to his wife, who finds it depressing, that "It's good entertainment" and edifying into the bargain. When a drunk gets upset—"Look, they're crucifying Him! And nobody cares!"—he is thrown out. Chaplin relates that Stravinsky's grave response was, "But that's sacrilegious!" This embarrassed him, but he later received a letter indicating the maestro was still interested.) (Chaplin, pp. 429–30.)

One of the creators of this new sophistication most deeply impressed by Chaplin was Meyerhold. His application of slapstick film techniques in his productions of Mayakovsky and Gogol demonstrated just how close they were to his central conception of commedia and the grotesque, and his writings leave evidence of his admiration for Chaplin in particular as an embodiment of this vision. Like Chaplin himself, he regarded the coming of sound as the surrender of the essential communicative power of film:

A Chaplin, who today is understood not only in America but in the Netherlands and the U.S.S.R., becomes incomprehensible the moment he starts to speak English. A Russian peasant will refuse to accept Chaplin as an Englishman. Only so long as he limits himself to mime does Chaplin remain familiar and comprehensible.

(Braun, *Meyerhold*, p. 255.)

In the thirties, Meyerhold made a number of remarks that indicate that he found Chaplin's art very close to his own. A comment on Blok's *Fairground Booth* (or *The Puppet Show*) is very expressive, because it was that famous 1906 collaboration with Blok that proved to be seminal to Meyerhold's theatrical revolution:

Now I would be able to put on Blok's *The Puppet Show* as a *sui generis* theatrical Chapliniad. Read *The Puppet Show*, and you will see in it all the elements of Chaplinesque plots, only the wrappings of everyday life are different. Heine is also akin to Chaplin and *The Puppet Show*. In great art, there is such a complex kinship.

(Field, p. 313.)

The kinship is based upon the primal theatricality of pantomime, of the German romantic tradition of puppets and puppet masters, of Punch and Petrushka of the fairs, and of the eternal variations played out by Harlequin, Pierrot, and Columbine. For Meyerhold, the key figure was Pierrot, and in his most extended meditation upon Chaplin, the 1936 lecture, "Chaplin and Chaplinism" (Braun, *Meyerhold*, pp. 311–24.), he gives an account of the career and significance of Chaplin that reflects a belief that Chaplin, too, based his comedy on the deeper yearnings of a Pierrot. For the Russian, the "clowning" in the early Chaplin did not rise to the level of "humor," a word that for Meyerhold had a "profundity" because of the influence of Pushkin. But with *A Night in the Show,* of late 1915, "Chaplin clearly eliminated all excessive hyperbole and sheer knockout comedy from his clowning." The "first traces of pathos" and "the Chaplin with a predilection for monumental subjects" appear the next year, especially in *The Vagabond:* "Through the comedy one glimpses elements of tragedy. Equally significant is the absence of the acrobatic tricks which played such an important part in his earlier comedies."

It may seem paradoxical that a director for whom biomechanics, his system of acrobatic training, was so important would find this last a sign of growth. He did approve of the acrobatics as fundamental to Chaplin's development:

In discovering the means he employed to develop his monumental art, I find that he, too, realized the necessity for acrobatic training to the actor's education.

It soon became clear that it is not the stunts themselves but their dramatic meaning that is important, while "knockabout comedy" without that meaning, without "humor," is what predominated in the early Chaplin. Later, describing his work with Eisenstein and in his biomechanics studio, he describes his goal as "the maximum exploitation of the expressive power of movement":

Observe how Chaplin deploys his body in space to maximum effect; study, as we do, the movements of gymnasts and blacksmiths.

The commedia actors were, of course, acrobats to varying degrees who put their skills to the service of their comedy, often mixing sheer displays of tumbling and juggling prowess with their plots. A famous example of Chaplin's ability to turn such a display to dramatic/comic effect occurs well into the talkie period (it would have suited Meyerhold perfectly, had he lived to see it); in his role as the Hitler parody Hynkel in *The Great Dictator,* Chaplin puts on a small acrobatic show, which Gerald Mast describes vividly:

Hynkel, indulging in his dreams of world conquest, lifts the globe from its wooden stand and then tosses it about in space to suit his fancies. He flings it into the air, catches it, tosses it again, leaps effortlessly onto his desk to continue the game, bats the balloon-globe with his feet, his head, his rear. The dictator and his world are transformed into a performing seal with a ball, a child with a toy, a "specialty" dancer with her bubble. . . . The dream ends when Hynkel leaps to grasp the balloon and it bursts in his arms.

(Mast, *Comic,* p. 116.)

This routine has its parallel in a number of pantomime skits, Pierrot with bubbles, a ball, the moon—although the Pierrot-Hitler incongruity is almost too great for irony.

Acrobats and acrobatic feats, even divorced from any dramatic context, exerted an enormous fascination upon the modernists. One need only remember the saltimbanques of Picasso and the poetic response of Rilke, the circus figures of so many prewar painters, the denizens of *Parade,* to realize that these performers, with their lives built upon uncertainty, communality, and relationships both intimate and theatrical with others and with their own bodies, held a privileged place in the heart of the artist confronting the modern age. The vaudevillians who learned their trade under very similar circumstances and then took that training to the movies also knew or learned quickly how to make it count there. Pantomime aside, Chaplin had a number of equals, and betters, in the use of filmed acrobatics. Harold Lloyd's building-scaling feats in *Safety Last* are perhaps most celebrated. Lloyd was inspired in this by the human-fly act of Bill Strothers (who billed himself as "The Human Spider"), but this sort of thing has honorable precedents, not only in the circus but also in the proscenium-climbing antics of several early Harlequins.

Buster Keaton was, many believe, the greatest of the stunt-devisers and executors. With his indelible deadpan mask, his acute sense of the powers of illusion and theatricality in film, and his abilities in comic timing and pantomime, he is arguably as rich a subject for commedia sleuths as Chaplin himself. Much of Keaton's achievement is indeed more cinematic than acrobatic, as in the 1921 masterpiece of visual wit, *The Playhouse,* a film of a minstrel show in which Keaton plays every part, onstage, backstage, in the lobby, and in the audience. Sitting in a box in the audience, Keaton in a tuxedo peruses the program, announcing everyone from Bones, Sambo, and the Quartette, to Scenery Painter and Dance Arranger, as "Buster Keaton"; he turns to his companion, a drag Keaton in an evening dress, and says, via subtitle, "This fellow Keaton seems to be the whole show." (Blesh, p. 164.) But in such masterpieces as *Sherlock Jr.*, with its multiple dilemmas produced in a film-within-film framework, there is a generous mix of physical and cinematic virtuosity.

Keaton had a very acute sense of the nature of film acrobatics, based on practical experience. He asserted that he was "only a half acrobat, at most" who, like Chaplin, Lloyd, and Fairbanks, was taught how to take a fall as a child and then learned a few acrobatic tricks for the sake of his comedy routines, as well as a basic familiarity with movement: "What I do know about is body control." (Keaton, p. 149.)

Keaton took fierce pride in his stunts, very much in the circus daredevil tradition—his father was a friend of and colleague in the same medicine show as Harry Houdini, who gave the young Keaton the nickname Buster. (Bermel, p. 179.) The most appalling stunts, thread-the-needle dives, deep falls, even a ride on the handlebars of a motorcycle over a gap in a highway overpass filled at precisely the right moment by two passing trucks, were filmed in long takes that encompassed the events in their entirety. This was the acrobat-showman asserting himself against the film farceur; the saltimbanque over the illusionist. In the fifties, Keaton was invited to perform at the Cirque Médrano, the Parisian circus that had given so much commedic life to Picasso and his friends. Paul Gallico wrote about his appearance for *Esquire,* describing the "sad-faced little fellow wearing a flat, pork-pie hat, string tie, too-big clothes, and flap shoes" in terms laden with nostalgia and also with ancient comic connections:

He never once spoke a word, nor ever changed the expression on his face, for his name was Buster Keaton . . . the Buster Keaton of my youth, who sixty-ish, could still fall backwards off a bench, or trip on the ring's edge and end up in a flying forward somersault. This was my dead-pan boy, hero of a hundred movies, Frustration's Mime, pursued, put-upon, persecuted by humans as well as objects suddenly possessed of a malevolent life and will of their own.

(Blesh, p. 360.)

Keaton's last silent film was actually made in 1965. It was a short, one-character work, meant to be the first part of a trilogy, and entitled simply *Film.* The old man performed no acrobatic feats for it. It is essentially a series of close-ups of that deadpan face, with age, more masklike than ever. Its creator, working with director Alan Schneider, is another commedia modernist of the theater, Samuel Beckett.

In Gallico's and, implicitly, Beckett's appreciation of the mask and identity of the Great Stone Face, there lurks the basic principle of dramatic life in the comic character of the screen as enunciated by Meyerhold. Referring to one of Chaplin's accounts of the origins of the Tramp in which he tells of observing a drunken London cabby "who showed me the way to that character which I finally found within myself," he points to the identification in that last phrase:

This "blending" of the cabby with Chaplin was possible only because Chaplin made no attempt to "requisition" him, but discovered him *within himself*. That is absolutely typical of Chaplin! It contains the clue to the solution of the problem of the mask in the cinema, which is a question of great importance.

(Braun, *Meyerhold*, p. 314.)

In order to make true comedy, drama that, in Pushkin's formula, is "the master of man's soul and man's passions," it is necessary to find this mask, or a number of masks, which have taken root in the self:

It is no use looking for just any mask; we must discover the mask which is closest to us and closest to the people for whom the film was intended.

(*Ibid.*, p. 315.)

Whatever else the "mask" might be in this context, it means that at this late date Meyerhold had found a way to combine the Stanislavskian imperative of the actor's identification with a character with his own vision of a modern commedia. The mask must live by the soul which animates it, a truth as valid for the great players of Harlequin and Pierrot as for Lloyd and Linder—both noted by Meyerhold—and Chaplin. Chaplin's late (1952) *Limelight* is a curious and occasionally brilliant failure set in the London music halls of the teens. It includes a pantomime sequence on "The Death of Columbine," but most of its energy is directed to more implicit commedic sentiment—and sentimentality. Chaplin plays Calvero, an old comedian who has gone from music hall stardom to the inevitable status of drunken has-been. He rescues a young dancer grown suicidal because of a mysterious, and psychological, paralysis of her legs; he cures her with his support and ad hoc psychoanalysis and sets her on the road to stardom, meanwhile enduring a total career collapse himself. In desperation he becomes a street musician (as in *The Vagabond* of four decades before), but the now-famous dancer rescues him and arranges a gala benefit for him, including an opportunity for the old clown to make a comeback.

What follows, given the sentimental framework, is inevitable, but there is something to Gerald Mast's overstatement that it is "the most overpoweringly emotional moment in the whole Chaplin canon." (Mast, *Comic*, p. 123.) To the astonishment of everybody, including the contemptuous stagehands and the audience larded with carefully prepared claques, Calvero is genuinely, masterfully, funny. The act closes with a madcap duet with Buster Keaton, playing another has-been (at that point perilously close to the truth), Charlie as violinist, Buster as a near-sighted pianist. In a frenzied finale Calvero falls into the pit, landing in the bass drum, and is carried off stuck in the drum, still fiddling. He has, however, suffered a heart attack in the fall, and, concealing the seriousness of his condition from his protégée-rescuer, he watches—dying, of course—from the wings as she dances in the limelight.

Of all the clowns, Charlie the Tramp was the most universal object of love, fascination, imitation, adaptation, exploitation through the first third of the century and beyond. For him this burden of meaning was especially large, and it was peculiarly personal in its universality; the forces of identification and attraction that drew people to him were, at bottom, more intimate than those that made Fairbanks, Valentino, the Barrymores objects of adulation. Perhaps the fascination with another creature of the mask, Garbo, is comparable in this way, except that she, and her image, created a distance very different from the Chaplin mystique. For Charlie as for all the major film comedians, the laughter was, obviously, an essential, and very public, part of the image, but for him more than any other the farce, the comedy that was the overt, shared ingredient of that fascination, was rooted in the pathos, the private vulnerability of the individual. This is the Pierrot in the Tramp.

One of the simplest reasons for Chaplin's success with every level of audience was his principal and most enduring choice of subject matter: beyond all the tricks, dilemmas, and turns, the subject is Charlie himself. Just as Pierrot's pantomimic energies are devoted to the expression of his inner life, so is the inner Charlie the source of deepest fascination, however Harlequinesque his array of comic skills. Chaplin had his predecessors in this creation of comic personality, as we have seen, but no one, comic or otherwise, realized the potential of the screen for conveying emotional life so fully as he in its first decades. Even the great Griffith, master of the close-up, exploited his device chiefly to give meaning to events and relationships, rather than to create a personality.

Expressionism

If filmmakers were slow to relinquish their preoccupation with external action—and most, of course, never did—there were a few who began very early to see the primary purpose of filmed action to be the expression of intense emotion. The Swedish directors Victor Sjöstrom and Mauritz Stiller—a decade later the "creator" of Greta Garbo—applied the techniques of Griffith in a search for a film language of personal emotion. The Italian director Negroni spoke a promising prececessor of this language in the pleasantly intimate (and commedic) *Story of a Pierrot* (1913), and it is said to be used with fluency by the immortal Duse in *Ashes* (1916). She seems to have been unique among the great "legitimate" actresses in her ability to translate an intensely expressive stage personality to the early screen.

Throughout the second decade of the century there were scattered efforts to deepen the relationship between film and individual personality, although except for Chaplin the majority in the business seem in effect to have chosen something like the path indicated by D'Annunzio in 1914:

The cinema must give to the spectators fantastic visions, lyric catastrophes, marvels born of the most sturdy imagination, as in the epic poem it must bring back the marvellous, the super-marvellous of today and tomorrow.

(O'Leary, p. 30.)

It is not difficult to find the commedia in such films, rooted as they are in theatrical traditions of all kinds: the circus and the grand festival are certainly visible in such epic productions as Pastrone's *Cabiria* and Griffith's *Intolerance*. The most vital line of exploration, both in terms of commedic modernism and for the purpose of depicting the human psyche on film, came from another quarter, however.

The revolution in perception that affected the other arts struck this fledgling art most forcefully by way of German expressionism. The development of a modernist focus upon the personality and its masks was by no means the enterprise only of those who came under the sway of the expressionists, but they made the earliest and most profound impact upon the film. Many of those associated with this founding period in German film came out of the theater and, as they did elsewhere, brought their stage assumptions with them. To name a few vital to our commedic purposes, Ernst von Wolzogen, impresario of the Berlin *Überbrettl* and the cabaret, wrote film scenarios in a first flush of enthusiasm, but then rejected the enterprise on the grounds that the public was attracted only to the banal on the screen; Hugo von Hofmannsthal wrote a fantastic "dream-play" film script for *Das Fremde Mädchen* (*The Strange Girl*), released in 1913. Max Reinhardt himself turned his hand to motion pictures, but as was demonstrated most pointedly in his filming of his own pantomime *Sumurun* in 1910, he shared the general inability to see the difference in the demands of the new medium and the old. The film was an exact, static replication of the stage play. Reinhardt did manage to make one film that preserved in reasonably cinematic form his brilliant theatrical vision. This was his famous Hollywood rococo version of *A Midsummer Night's Dream* (1935).

A remarkable number of film directors and actors associated with the various currents of expressionism were also trained or directed by Reinhardt; they did not learn from his filmmaking, but all were marked by his inventive freedom, his gift for stylization, his technical prowess, and his search for a heightened expressivity. Paul Wegener, F. W. Murnau, Ernst Lubitsch, Paul Leni, Emil Jannings, Werner Krauss, Marlene Dietrich, Conrad Veidt, and many others took their Reinhardt education into this new kind of cinema. They were affected not only by Reinhardt's particular theatricality, but by theatricalism in general, the revolt against naturalism in favor of assertively self-conscious stylization carried out most triumphantly by Meyerhold and by Brecht.

As to just what expressionism is when the term (vague in any case) is applied to film, John Barlow provided a useful half dozen criteria, all related to the larger notion of expressionism as antinaturalistic and preoccupied with the examination and portrayal of intense emotion. Ideally, the expressionist film "would use a fantastic set, one that represented as emotional landscape, a projection of the intense feelings of the main character." Also, dramatic conflict would be sacrificed to a principal focus upon that main character. "Third, the acting would be exaggerated and at an extreme degree of emotional intensity." Fourth, in the black-and-white world of the early cinema "there would be considerable contrasts between light and shadow" parallel to the bright colors favored by expressionist painters and set designers for the stage (these filmmakers don't seem to have had an interest in the experiments in hand-tinting and painting of film tried by a few contemporary pioneers, Abel Gance among them). "Feverish acting would be a silent visual replacement of the outcry and exclamation of expressionist poetry and theater." A similar parallel would be sharp, "even violent" camera movements and shot angles; and finally, "the films would inevitably deal with extreme situations or excessive, overwhelming responses to everyday situations." (Barlow, p. 25.)

Only one of these expected features, according to Barlow, is not in fact common in these films: the use of sharp camera movements and angles. He conceded its presence in Murnau's *The Last Laugh,* but there principally to represent drunkenness and dreaming. Unusual and unsettling camera positions are, however, easily found elsewhere in this particular canon. They are in Lang's Dr. Mabuse films and *Metropolis,* and looking beyond these works, to Eisenstein for example, it is clear that the angular, "violent" camera often has an expressionist effect, even within films not on expressionist errands. Incidentally, Eisenstein, despite the similarity of many of his techniques, regarded these effects, and *Caligari* in particular, as anathema to good filmmaking, a "barbaric carnival of the destruction of the healthy human infancy of our art. (*Ibid.,* p. 29.)

The point of presenting this definition of expressionism is not to appropriate it wholly into commedia modernism; expressionism clearly involves other strategies, other preoccupations. But the fragmentation, the framing devices, and also versions of the irony and parody common in the commedia were also tools of the expressionists. Even more to the point, they also used many commedia themes and exploited many of the same images out of the world of popular entertainment.

One highly visible parallel line is the recurrent puppet-master and puppet theme, with rich variations. As in the modern theater, this approach to the crises of fragmentation and power facing the modern artist had roots deep in romanticism. It is not surprising, therefore, that the 1913 forerunner of high expressionism, *The Student of Prague,* directed by Stellan Rye but with a good deal of help from the principal actor, Paul Wegener, is redolent of *Faust,* E. T. A. Hoffmann, and Edgar Allan Poe. Baldwin, a poor young student, is in love with the duke's daughter. In order to move into her social sphere, he accepts a large sum of money from the Mephisto figure who turns up handily, a strange old man named Scapinelli, who wants nothing in return except something out of Baldwin's modest room. That something turns out to be the student's own reflection in the mirror, who emerges to become Baldwin's fatally menacing double.

This primitive trick is a long way from a theater full of Buster Keatons, but it is the beginning of film's uniquely palpable exploration of the fragmented self. The later expressionists saw enough potential in this for two remakes of *The Student of Prague,* in 1926 and 1935. Both of the later versions were designed by Herman Warm, who as a painter was a member of the Berlin Sturm group of expressionists. He took an openly antirealistic stance in his film designs—"Films must be drawings brought to life"—which was demonstrated most brilliantly in his work for *The Cabinet of Doctor Caligari*.

For the most part, a small group of figures were responsible for the creative dominance of German film in the years after World War I, and even a brief survey of the titles associated with them and their colleagues reveals the importance of familiar commedic themes. Werner Krauss broke into the movies in 1916 via two films by another relevant figure, Richard Oswald: *Tales of Hoffmann* and *Circus Blood*. Oswald was probably more an opportunist than an expressionist—he also used Krauss in *Es werde Licht (Let There Be Light)*, a lurid account of the dangers of syphilis, and the scandalous *Prostitution* (1919). But he also made a version of Schnitzler's *Reigen (La Ronde)* with Asta Nielsen and Conrad Veidt. Krauss was also a literal puppet master in Robert Wiene's 1923 *Puppenmacher von Kiangning*. It is not prima facie evidence of expressionist or commedic pedigree that such actors as Krauss, Veidt, Jannings, and Wegener turn up repeatedly in these films; they were all famous actors with deep Reinhardt connections and a serious commitment to the new. Krauss and Jannings were particularly legendary. The imperious eccentricity of the latter was the subject of countless tales, and of the former Jean Renoir said, "It was Werner Krauss who taught me to understand the importance of actors." (Renoir, p. 81.) He used him in his most significant early film, *Nana*, described by Paul Rotha as "a mixture of the *can-can*, Lautrec back-stage and Offenbach." (Rotha, p. 310.)

Krauss, Veidt, Jannings, and William Dieterle all were present in Paul Leni's *Wachsfigurenkabinett (Waxworks)*, released in 1924. Produced on an extremely limited budget of money and time, this small landmark of film modernism is an excellent demonstration of the intensity with which all involved in its making immersed themselves in the fantastic atmosphere and the psychological extremes of expressionism. True to the commedia connection, there is a framing device enclosing three stories within Henrik Galeen's script. The scene is a fairground booth, which contains an exhibit of wax figures. Its final episode is a Jack the Ripper chase sequence which, despite its brevity and bareness (both dictated by finances, according to Rotha), explodes with expressionist force within a commedic setting. The fair through which the murderer chases his intended victims has been transformed into what Kracauer describes as "a deserted hunting ground for specters":

Expressionist canvases, ingenious lighting effects and many other devices . . . have been used to create this eerie phantasmagoria. . . . Disparate architectural fragments form pell-mell complexes, doors open of their own accord and all proportions and relations depart from the normal. Much as the episode recalls *Caligari*, it goes beyond its model in stressing the role of the fair: the fair that in *Caligari* merely served as a background is here the very scene of action. In the course of their flight, the poet and the girl hurry past the constantly circling merry-go-round, while Jack-the-Ripper . . . pursues them on miraculous dream paths, hovering through a gigantic Ferris wheel that also turns without pause.

(Kracauer, *Caligari*, p. 87.)

Chaos, fragmentation, carnival, murder all locate the film in commedia modernism, the dark side thereof, erupting with the energies of the street and of revolt. Jack the Ripper had long exerted a fascination on the modern artist, perhaps, in our terms, as a ghastly, murderous Harlequin: Lulu, Frank Wedekind's fatally seductive Columbine (she appears first in a Pierrot costume) meets her death at his hands, and G. W. Pabst dramatized this pursuit in a dark and shadowed staircase scene in his version of the Lulu plays, *Pandora's Box* (*Die Büchse der Pandora*, 1928–1929). Its Lulu was that epitome of American Jazz Age sexiness, Louise Brooks, complete with her sensual Pierrot look.

Violence and Surrealism

1929 was, among other things, also the year of the appearance of *Un Chien andalou*, the most famous surrealist film. In their pursuit of the absurd and the extreme, the surrealists often had recourse to commedia images, bright emblems of defiant unseriousness. For not unrelated reasons, they were also attracted to images of violence. In its prologue, *Andalusian Dog* presents the most notoriously explicit example of violence in all of serious art. There are a multitude of aesthetic challenges set loose when a man casually slices a woman's eye with a carefully honed razor; after all, the surrealists did demand above all a new way of seeing. But before the metaphors the viewer is forced to witness a gruesome act of cool violence. There are also other scenes of mutilation (and also, for our purposes, a bawdy character in a jester's costume). Images of extreme violence were also vital elements in the other work of Dali and Buñuel, the makers of *Un Chien andalou* (as well as to Artaud, Breton, and other members of this branch of the avant-garde). Buñuel himself described the film in 1932 as a "desperate call for murder." (Thiher, p. 37.) Physical violence and aesthetic rebellion clearly embrace, at least in the creative arsenal of the modernists. And in commedia modernism, as in the commedia dell'arte, the link between art and violence is not merely casual.

Physical and aesthetic violence are inextricably linked in *The Cabinet of Dr. Caligari* (1919–20). *Caligari* conforms in a number of ways to the patterns of modern commedia, and its imprint is on many more commedic films. There is above all the overt theatricality of the film, emphasized by the painted sets with crazily angled street, walls, and windows, a strange world of two-dimensional flats inhabited by three-dimensional people. Even the people, or the two central figures, Caligari and Cesare (Krauss and Veidt) behave in an ominous, unreal manner more in keeping with the expressionist sets than the humanity around them.

This emotion-laden displacement of the natural world, and the blatant staginess with which this is accomplished, are both modes of revolution found in commedia modernism. A more explicit connection is the fact that the madman's story has a fair, with its tents and booths and eager crowds, as important background. The evil Dr. Caligari and his assistant Cesare appear as a sideshow in this fair, with Cesare as a somnambulist who answers questions put to him while he is in a trance. The scenes in the fair are generally introduced by a recurrent iris-in shot of an organ grinder, his arm constantly turning the crank of his instrument while a merry-go-round spins behind him. Such circular movements, whether literal as they are here or in the face of Pierrot and his moon, or metaphorical, as in such circular plotting as is found in the serial love affairs of Schnitzler's *Reigen,* are beloved by commedists. Kracauer finds this particular set of circles "a symbol of chaos," the circle representing a whirlpool into which the self is in danger of plunging. In the unsettled world of the film, and the filmmakers, such whirling may indeed have evoked disorder. That is certainly the effect of the Ferris wheel *cum* Jack the Ripper in *Waxworks;* the huge circular gong calling the workers to their shifts and the countless circles interacting in giant machinery paradoxically produce this effect in the dehumanized world of Lang's *Metropolis,* and similar wheels menace Charlie Chaplin in *Modern Times.* There is also the glittering hint of chaos in an ever-revolving hotel door in *The Last Laugh.*

Another rich commedic parallel is to be found in the relationship between Caligari and Cesare. A central element of Kracauer's thesis is that the malevolent and powerfully hypnotic Caligari is a premonition of Hitler, and he finds nothing in the environment of the makers of *Caligari* to explain their choice of such a villain except "one of those dark impulses which . . . sometimes engender true visions." (Kracauer, p. 73.) If, however, we see the Caligari-Cesare relationship in the light of the commedic puppet-master-and-puppet theme, we can place the character of Caligari in the midst of an already well-established modernist preoccupation.

In addition to other films already cited, the most important manifestations of this are the Golem films of Paul Wegener: *The Golem* (1914), *The Golem and the Dancer* (1917), and, most successfully, *The Golem— How He Came into the World* (1920).

Another important variation on the theme, with origins in *Faust* rather than Jewish legend, was Otto Rippert's *Homunculus,* a six-part serial made in 1916 that was enormously popular in Germany during the war. Like the Golem, Homunculus is created by a smart person in a laboratory, but unlike that lumpish creation, Homunculus is a brilliant, magnetic figure in romantically stylish attire (which is said to have influenced high fashion in Berlin during the war). He has every splendid quality except humanity. When he discovers that he is an artificial product, he is plunged into that deep alienation and hopeless yearning that is the fine tradition from the earliest Golem through all the Frankensteins to Ridley Scott's recent, arresting science fiction film *Blade Runner,* about a group of near-human robots driven by the urge to transcend their human-imposed limitations. (There is a wonderfully eerie, very commedic sequence involving mechanical dolls and literally murderous acrobatics in this film.) As is the fate of everyone else in the tradition, Homunculus finds himself rejected by the race which created him and, refused love, he responds finally with all-consuming hatred and, being highly gifted, comes closer than most of his unhappy brethren to destroying the world. In the end, it takes a thunderbolt to stop him.

Again, the puppet master creates a puppet that is too much for him, but this is not always the case. (Petrushka himself, commedia modernism's quintessential yearning, suffering puppet, cannot stand against his master, although he can, in the end, offer a moment of expressive defiance.) Kracauer himself makes note of an American film that was also shown in Germany during the war, *Trilby,* based on George Du Maurier's very popular novel about the hynotic Svengali and his "creation," Trilby. Another puppet, in a lighter romantic vein (Kracauer calls it "a sort of film operetta") is the mechanical doll of *Die Puppe* (1919) of Ernst Lubitsch, in which a young man whose fear of women has put him in a monastery is presented with a mechanical version to marry in order to fulfill the terms of a legacy. All ends healthily when a young woman slyly replaces the doll with her seductive self.

Murnau and Mayer

Murnau's Nosferatu, the first (and for many still the best) film Dracula, is not himself a puppet; indeed he has a puppet master's power over mere human beings—and things, as with the famous flying coffins. The script of *Nosferatu* was by Henrik Galeen, author of the first *Golem* script. There are brilliant touches of commedia in several of Murnau's films, especially his most admired *The Last Laugh* (originally *Der Letzte Mann, The Last Man*), of 1924, with Jannings; and his versions of Molière's *Tartuffe* (1925) and Goethe's *Faust* (1926). Murnau certainly experienced the correct *rites de passage:* his brother remembers the young Wilhelm staging the fairy tales of Grimm and Andersen in the puppet theater he had been given as a Christmas present. (Eisner, pp. 14–15.)

Murnau's most important collaborator was Carl Mayer, the writer of the scripts for, among others, *The Hunchback and the Dancer* (a lost, and apparently very commedic, film), *The Last Laugh, Tartuffe,* and *The Four Devils* (1928—a circus drama based on a novel by Hermann Bang, an author also used by Meyerhold). Mayer's importance to this whole avant-garde endeavor can hardly be overestimated. The great cinematographer Karl Freund's praise is typical: "If one man should ever be given credit for the best film-work to come from Germany, it would have to be Carl Mayer." (Rotha, p. 717.) Mayer's grasp of the medium as a new form of theater, with utterly new potentialities, placed him in the midst of the modernist movement. His hand is on much that is commedic as well as expressionist.

Mayer's first film, after work as a painter and in theater, was *Caligari,* conceived and written with Hans Janowitz, who also was to write for Murnau. Janowitz introduced Mayer to the creative possibilities of the new medium, having been inspired himself by the films of Paul Wegener. Both young men were pacifists. Young Carl kept out of the army by feigning madness. To these broader influences, Mayer and Janowitz added more specific experience, with richly commedic flavoring, to the impetus of *Caligari.*

Janowitz believed that he had once been witness, by chance, to the shadowy aftermath of a vicious sex murder near a fair in Hamburg. The experience, in all its horror and ambiguity, remained with him, and when he and Mayer became friends after the war, it became an element on the film project that they had decided to realize as their means of expressing thier revolutionary, antiauthoritarian beliefs. The film's gestation took place in part in a fair in Berlin, where the young pair often strolled after their work. It was there that Mayer stumbled upon a strongman act in which the man performed his feats in an apparently hyp-notized state while making strange, prophetic utterances. (Kracauer, pp. 61–62.) *Caligari* is one of the most discussed and fought over of all films. It is sufficient here to say that many of the qualities we have associated with the twentieth century's use of commedia are remarkably visible in both the genesis and realization of this work. The carnival, bright and hectic escape from a fragmented, threatening reality; insane authority and dead truths; sensuality and murder. In the world of postwar Germany (and not only Germany) these were the stuff of commedia as well as life.

Carl Mayer's best-known script, after *Caligari,* is that for Murnau's *The Last Laugh.* The focus on the hotel porter's uniform, with its shin-ing buttons, is full of ironic commedia, especially when the wearer struts proudly in it to the admiration of his neighbors. The loss of the uniform comes about as a superficially reasonable act: The old man has become too weak for the lugging duties of a porter. But to lose one's uniform is to lose, utterly, the respect of self and others. There are many brilliant commedic touches in the course of this petty tragedy, but the sudden and obviously arbitrary happy ending, the "last laugh" itself, stands out. The thoroughly broken old man, winding toward death in his uniform-less ignominy as lavatory attendant, suddenly comes into a fortune, a turn often damned as an aesthetically disastrous act of appeasement toward officials who demanded the happy ending. Whether or not Murnau and Mayer were making a virtue of necessity, they did commit a virtuous deed of commedic art in creating a film sequence that is both overtly theatrical, artificially "happy," and genuinely moving, a comic opera touch crossed with the suffering that preceded it.

The success of this balancing act is due in considerable part to the performance of Emil Jannings as the porter. Jannings had many other dramatic strengths, of course, but he often projected a unique mixture of histrionic bluster and keenly felt emotion that put him in a direct line from the Pantalones, Dottores, and Capitanos of old without rob-bing him of his large tragic potential. He managed this combination in E.A. Dupont's remarkable *Vaudeville* (1925), one of the greatest of the many dramas of life and love among variety performers. He also pro-jected the mixed image well in different proportions as Tartuffe and Mephisto. But today he is surely best known for accomplishing this as Professor Unrat in *The Blue Angel.*

The Blue Angel and Dietrich

Josef von Sternberg's version of Heinrich Mann's novel about the rigid *Gymnasium* professor who falls ruinously for the cabaret tart, is probably still the most famous German talkie (it was made in 1929–30). Jannings's performance as a clown imitating a crowing rooster and his ensuing display of madness as, still in his clown makeup, he attempts to strangle his Lola-Lola, is surely one of the most vivid stretches of screen commedia. The Austrian-born Sternberg was invited back from Hollywood to direct the film. He came by his commedia honestly. In his frank autobiography, *Fun in a Chinese Laundry,* he expresses a good deal of nostalgia for the Prater, Vienna's enormous amusement park, for the giant Ferris wheel that dominates it and the sounds of its hurdy-gurdies and calliopes.

The Blue Angel's initial notoriety and enduring fame rest but secondarily on the excellences contributed to it by Jannings and Sternberg. Its primary source was the beautiful—often called "too beautiful"—young woman who played Lola-Lola, a promising Reinhardt actress named Marlene Dietrich. Sternberg lured her away from the stage specifically for this role: "You have to play it. . . . You *have* a beautiful face which lives—really lives." (Frewin, pp. 42–43.) This discovery and the relationship between the director and his star constitute one of the prototypical Hollywood legends, never mind that it began in Berlin and its first fruit was a very German movie. The director very deliberately set about creating a specifically visual, cinematic figure of mythic proportions:

Von Sternberg worked assiduously to capture in Lola-Lola the image of a classic temptress; he bathed Dietrich in an unrelenting erotic atmosphere, to which everything—costume, lighting, backgrounds, camera angles—contributed. . . . Most memorable of all was Lola-Lola on the cabaret stage . . . in her high heels and black silk tights, plumes waving round her neck and, perversely, a silk top hat on her head.

(*Ibid.,* p. 43.)

Dietrich became, in very short order, a world-class femme fatale, her masklike, cool, faintly amused, covertly passionate visage gracing all the appropriate covers, her life (actually rather quiet) the object of all the appropriate press fascination, her dress (the "Dietrich style": masculine jacket and pants, felt hat, and slouch) a fashion imperative in Europe and America. Kracauer described her Lola-Lola as "a new incarnation of sex." (Kracauer, p. 217.) Sternberg made six films with

Dietrich in the next five years: *Morocco, Dishonored, Shanghai Express, Blonde Venus, The Scarlet Empress,* and *The Devil Is a Woman.* He focused obsessively on the Dietrich myth as the films became progressively less dynamic, increasingly static, and abstractly visual, with Dietrich always the centerpiece. The director's dominance over his star caused them several times to be called Svengali and Trilby, although after Paramount finally broke up the duo Dietrich certainly proved herself capable of a broader range of parts. (But the gifted and obsessive Sternberg showed himself more the prisoner of his role. Hired by MGM to guide the career of the young and promising Hedy Lamarr, he was soon fired because he attempted to make her over in the Dietrich mold.) (Rotha, p. 475.)

Garbo

This real-life puppet-master-and-puppet relationship was also a salient feature of the career of Greta Garbo. Garbo and Dietrich were the screen goddesses of greatest, most mythically pregnant fame in the thirties, and from this distance, at least, the Garbo legend was and is even larger than the Dietrich legend. They were different personalities who played very different parts, of course, but certain broad similarities are very suggestive: For both the beautiful mask, impassive but deeply provocative, was paramount. The face of Garbo, more than that of Dietrich (or anyone else in the history of mass media, most probably) had the power to fascinate. The image, like that of Dietrich, promised to conceal a secret, never to be revealed, but it also radiated a purity—not a conventional moral purity, but an aesthetic transcendence: "Garbo manages, because she is a supremely beautiful woman, to make beauty look like a mark of religion," runs one contemporary accolade. (Bainbridge, p. 15.) Cecil Beaton found this kind of transcendence in her eyes:

Her eyes seem to offer a special compassion for each of us. Inexhaustible spiritual assets highlight the sensitivity and delicacy of these features, continually hinting at every nuance of all that she is feeling, and giving the specator the tenuous and remarkable impression that he is witnessing the remotest depths in a human face.

(*Ibid.*, p. 16.)

Her legendary reclusiveness, her life as "the Swedish Sphinx," "the shy Valkyrie," "the dazzling enigma," "the Swedish swan," and myriad other press inventions, only added to the allure.

The Garbo legend began in the mind of the director Mauritz Stiller.

Even more thoroughly than Sternberg, he created the figure he wanted. Before Stiller she was Greta Gustafsson, an energetic young thing with bit parts, some filmed advertisements, and a "Bathing Beauty" role in the Sennett-like Swedish comedy *Peter the Tramp* to her credit. Stiller discovered her, changed her name, changed *her*. "You know," he said to doubting friends, "she receives instruction excellently, follows directions closely. She is like wax in my hands. Greta will be all right. I believe in her." And Greta would have been the first to agree.

The point here is not to deny that Garbo, or Dietrich, for that matter, had their own inner resources; both proved in their different ways that they did. Stiller died in 1928, at the age of forty-five, having directed Garbo only in *Gösta Berling's Saga*, in which she was only embryonically "Garbo," and part of *The Temptress*; even while Stiller was alive, she did her best work for another great molder of woman actresses, G.W. Pabst (*The Joyless Street*, 1925), and for others, including Victor Sjöstrom (*The Divine Woman*, 1928). It is highly significant, however, that Garbo, "the face of the century," was, as a purely theatrical image, the creation of Stiller. Any examination of her pre-Stiller photographs easily bears this out. In this specific sense, she, and Dietrich, were the work of dominant, devoted puppet masters, and it is very possible to argue that this phenomenon in the movies, like the parallel relationships in ballet, is part of commedia modernism.

The Garbo fascination was a form of worship enhanced by mystery divorced from any real life lived by the wearer of that mask—distinct even from her accomplishments as an actress. Any serious assessment of her acting always seems utterly unrelated to Garbo the myth (though she could be quite skillful—and even commedic in normal theatrical terms, as in Lubitsch's *Ninotchka*, of 1939). This ultimate "Star" and, in the nature of things, most of Hollywood's legends, fit the pattern of commedia, because for the most part they, or their legends, were indeed puppet creations. They were the work of the furious collective energy that is Hollywood, the "image industry" rather than the products of one puppet master, but in the end, beyond their acting abilities, their actual lives, failures, accomplishments, they *were* their faces, their masks, marinated in fantasy and collective desire. Their lives off the screen were often as thoroughly shaped by these theatrical identities as their roles on the screen—even a complete break from that life did not free Garbo from this fate.

Given the array of legendary masks, it is not hard to find some who do bear traces, at least, of the old commedic roles. It is neither possible nor relevant to make the argument that the connections are deliberate, but it can be illuminating because it says something about the emotional power of the theatrical mask, old or new, and the gestures and images that come under its sway. Certainly one can see the strength of vivid comic, tragic, and melodramatic types in such Hollywood studio star parades as *Grand Hotel* and *Dinner at Eight*. The sleek and spectacular costuming add often to the impression of "types" come to life, Pantalones and Dottores into put-upon businessmen husbands (Wallace Berry, say, or Lionel Barrymore on occasion); the Columbines can be hard (Jean Harlow) or soft (Carole Lombard); there are, of course, young lovers aplenty. A good film for the purposes of this game is *Gone With the Wind*, with Clark Gable as a brusque and masculine Harlequin; Leslie Howard as a proper Pierrot in look and manner; and Vivien Leigh, Scarlett O'Hara, a tough Columbine. This Columbine is more deeply attached to Pierrot than to Harlequin, but the pattern still has emotional force.

Such patterns call up the particularly potent theatricality of these Hollywood divinities. Whatever the weaknesses and frauds of the Hollywood studio star system, the tenacity of its grip on the popular imagination attests to the endurance of the myths constructed by its puppet masters.

Clair and Renoir

The film modernists did not, for the most part, thrive in Hollywood, at least as modernists, but they did share Hollywood's belief in an essentially visual theatricality. Two such figures, both French, both masters of commedia, both employed by Hollywood, are relevant here because they understood this visual power and connected it in work and in words to the commedia. They also, because of their influence on the next generations of filmmakers, serve as a reminder that the commedia remains a vital force in those next generations. In 1970, René Clair recalled his commitment, in 1923, to the purely visual:

It is time to have done with words. . . . Real cinema cannot be put into words. But just try to get that across to people—you, myself, and the rest—who have been twisted by thirty-odd centuries of chatter: poetry, the theater, the novel. . . . They must learn again to see with the eyes of a savage, of a child less interested in the plot of a Punch and Judy show than in the drubbings the puppets give each other with their sticks.

(Clair, p. 15.)

Clair never completely achieved his goal—and for the extent of his compromise, see *his* Marlene Dietrich film, *The Flame of New Orleans*, made for Universal in 1940. However, he did make some of the most brilliant, insistently visual of all the revolutionary films, including the commedic satire *The Italian Straw Hat* (1927), the witty patterns of which sprout from the supposedly simple destruction of the object in the title.

Clair also made *Entr'acte*, in 1924, which does indeed approach the visual radicalism he called for in the previous year. He made it for the Ballets Suédois of Rolf de Maré, described by Clair as "the most Parisian of all dance troupes." (*Ibid.*, p. 9.) The young Clair was at that time a novice with little to recommend him as a director besides his deep love of Méliès. The scenario, to which Clair added much, had been scrawled on a sheet of Maxim's stationery by Francis Picabia, who was the guiding genius behind and set designer for the ballet *Relâche*. Picabia wanted the film to serve as entertainment between the acts of the ballet, after the practice of pre–World War I *café-concerts*. For the purposes of commedia modernism, *Entr'acte* was certainly born under an auspicious constellation: music by Satie, who created the first original music written "in perfect synchronization with a film" (*Ibid.*, p. 10.); ballet and film scenario and sets by Picabia; choreography by *premier danseur* Jean Börlin.

Clair provided a film prologue as well as *Entr'acte*. It shows the authors "descending from heaven in slow motion" and firing a cannon to signal the beginning of the performance. It includes "an unforgettable view of Satie: white wispy beard, pince-nez, derby and umbrella" (*Ibid.*, p. 11.), surely the archetypal vision of the ironic modernist. The film itself lives up to Clair's declaration written for it:

Here now is *Entr'acte*, which claims to give a new value to the image. It was up to Francis Picabia, who has done so much for the liberation of the word, to liberate the image. In *Entr'acte* the image, "having been diverted from its obligation to mean something," is born to a concrete existence.

Having been prepared by an onrushing slow-motion cannon ball in the Prologue, the audience is confronted with the new, although its roots in Méliès, in *Parade*, and in other contemporary surrealism are clear enough. Boxing gloves, perhaps inherited from the boxer in Picasso's *Parade* curtain, box away entirely on their own; matches dance on a head of hair that (of course) catches fire; Marcel Duchamp and Man Ray play chess on a rooftop—and the Place de la Concorde is superimposed on the chessboard; a self-propelled hearse bedecked with sausages flees madly from its mourners, arriving finally at a roller coaster;

and, the most famous gag: the pirouetting legs of a graceful ballerina turn out to belong to a bearded, mustachioed, bespectacled male. Picabia wrote for the *Relâche* program, "I would rather hear them yell than applaud," (*Op. Cit.*) and he, and Clair, got their wish. With considerable satisfaction, Clair quoted the reaction of Alexandre Arnoux after he had seen the film again after many decades: "This film is still young. Even today you feel like hissing it." (*Ibid.*, p. 12.)

This is the essence of avant-gardism, the commitment to the perpetually unexpected. The irony, the surrealist parody, self- and otherwise, and the thoroughgoing fragmentation of narrative and other forms of logic, are all abundantly present in *Entr'acte*. The images, steeped in the world of the carnival, playing on the tensions between high culture and low comedy, are as much the fruit of commedia consciousness as the techniques employed in stringing them together.

The other great Frenchman, Jean Renoir, growing up in the charged atmosphere surrounding his father, had as deep a commitment to the new as Clair, but his commedia was considerably gentler. His love of the images and patterns that we have identified as commedic was just as deep, however, and readily apparent in his most significant films. His memoirs provide some useful and well-turned glimpses into the shaping of that love, and his experience, despite his unique circumstances, was shared by many of our artists. When he was very young he was taken often to the *guignol*, the French version of the Punch and Judy show, at the Champs-Elysées and in the Tuileries. He quickly developed a lifelong attachment to this form of theater, although his childishly fierce commitment to all things masculine made him distrust anything that might have been considered effeminate about that world. A life-size Polichinelle doll given him as a Christmas present precipitated a tantrum because of its shiny satin and ribbons. (Renoir, p. 29.) This may be a clue to his wonderful way with masculine Harlequin types, Georges Darnoux in *Une Partie de campagne* (1936), Jean Gabin in *La Bête humaine* (1938), and most clearly, the outrageously anarchic, bawdy Boudu of Michel Simon in *Boudu sauvé des eaux* (1932), Boudu the tramp saved from drowning only to show himself to be, in Renoir's words, "the perfect hippy" (*Ibid.*, p. 116.), disrupting utterly the settled bourgeois existence of his saviors in pursuit of women and freedom.

Renoir's commedia extends well beyond this, however; it is at the root of his clear, elegant theatricality that manages to wed ornament and artifice with the deepest humanity. "Guignol . . . endowed me with a fondness for simple tales and a profound mistrust for what is generally called psychology," he writes (*Ibid.*, p. 30.), and even in the most tragic tangles of error and illusion he finds the clear play of forms. The aristocratic officer Boeldieu in *La Grande Illusion* (1937) as a prisoner of war sees German children "playing at being soldiers," while his own soldiers, fellow prisoners, "play at being children." (Thiher, p. 96.) The make-believe takes the form of a soldier dressing up as a woman in fun, but the illusion is too real to the long-deprived fellow prisoners; the impromptu bit of theater provides pain instead of escape. The illusions of nationalism, class, religion, patriotism—all are tested in such play. Even the escape from the prison camp, with its tragic consequences for its organizer, is planned and executed as an overtly theatrical event, and the doomed aristocrat, distracting the German soldiers, plays the fife for his own suicide, forcing another aristocrat to shoot him.

La Règle du jeu (1939) plays with the complicated games of a society dying of its own rules and empty forms. The commedia is present in rococo elegance, the spirits of Marivaux and Beaumarchais and Mozart filtered through the romantic imagination of Musset, the author of the source play (*Les Caprices de Marianne*). But Renoir conveys the human suffering and waste behind the collapsing forms. An absurd, mistaken murder takes place against a background of an evening party with theatrical entertainment. The death interrupts, but does not stop the party, which continues in its splendid setting, its order, however hollow, still preserved.

Renoir caught his passion for theater at the *Guignol,* and he conveyed it with a unique directness by creating films in which life was theater, in which life's deep magic was revealed by theater. He remembers his uncontrollable excitement as a child when the introductory music of the *guignol* accordion began:

I got so excited that I sometimes greeted the rise of the curtain by wetting my pants. . . . Even today I find that moment of suspense before the curtain rises, if the performance promises to be a good one, deliciously exciting. My father told me that he felt the same during Mozart's overture to *Don Giovanni.* For my part, I know that this sensation is the infallible sign of a masterpiece, and the one which for me falls most instantly into the diuretic class is Stravinsky's *Petrushka.*

(Renoir, p. 30.)

That is Renoir the commedia modernist: ironic, aesthetic, playful, theatrical, obsessed with the human expressiveness of form. (Renoir even made a film about a commedia troupe touring in South America in the eighteenth century; *The Golden Coach* (1952) features Anna Magnani as an unlikely leading Columbine, and the story drags, but there is much energy in the theatrical moments.)

Film Commedia in the Modern Era

Early in Renoir's *La Chienne* (1931) a marionette delivers a little speech about the drama that is to follow: "The characters are neither heroes nor villains. They are poor people like me, like you. There are three principals: he, she, and the other one, as always." (Insdorf, p. 69.) Ingmar Bergman's *A Lesson in Love* (1954) opens with a shot of a music box, an exquisite porcelain device with three dolls, two men and a woman moving back and forth from one man to the other. The narrator's voice tells us that "This could have been a tragedy, but the gods were kind." (Livingston, p. 130.) Like Renoir—in most respects an utterly different sort of artist—Bergman was fascinated by puppets as a child. Like Murnau, Buñuel, Benois, and so many others, he had his own puppet theater and built several elaborate puppet and marionette theaters.

The point here is not that Renoir and Bergman reduce their actors to marionettes, but that they and other dominant film directors of the past half century have continued to be fascinated with the art of the fairground, the fixed patterns of laughter and love played by puppets, clowns, and their commedia relatives. Indeed, in the film medium if no other, it can be argued that these patterns have retained their grip upon the imagination of modern directors with something like the strength they showed in our chosen period. The relationship between these images and modernism has, perhaps, become more problematic—so has the whole notion of an avant-garde, after all. But it can be clearly demonstrated that very different directors, chief shapers of the new cinema, have approached the problems of human relationships and their own identity as modern artists by way of the forms and tactics of commedia.

To return to Renoir and Bergman—an instructive pairing just because of the great, bleak distances between them—they both resort to the techniques of overt theatricality and to literal images of the dance, the theater, and the circus and commedia in order to preserve the visibility of the basic human games of love and war. Every modern filmmaker focuses on such games. There is nothing exclusively commedic about, for instance, the eternal triangle, and there are powerful strains in modernist film narrative that perform similar reductions to basic patterns with quite uncommedic results. The most renowned example, perhaps, is the Robbe-Grillet/Resnais reduction of the triangle to the husband (maybe) M, the woman A, and the stranger X, in *Last Year at Marienbad* (1961). In commedia the steps of the dance are always somehow visible; here the patterns are made visible, only to be dissolved before our eyes.

If *Last Year at Marienbad* is one icon of narrative-straining modernism, then *Persona* (1966) is surely another. And one of the things that makes these two assaults on identity and personality so different from one another is that Bergman preserves in visible forms the signs and techniques of theatricality, while Resnais deliberately seeks to explode any such perspective. Bergman forces the distinctions between man and mask, or woman and mask/persona, even between the boundaries of identity of two women, to the collapsing point, but one of his women is Elisabeth Vogler, a famous actress, the other woman responds to her among many other ways, as to an actress. "There's something extremely fascinating to me about these people exchanging masks and suddenly sharing one between them," was Bergman's statement (Björkman, p. 202.) of the simple, fundamentally theatrical driving notion of the relationship. The framing and the distancing of theater are part of the film's essential proposition; the famous take constructing a woman's face out of half of Bibi Andersson's and half of Liv Ullmann's is a clearly framed statement about the human mask, its simplicity made resonant by all the mounting stress upon and fragmentation of the identities behind those masks. To express this fragmentation, Bergman has resorted, as in so many of his films, to his commedia arsenal.

Fellini

Bergman offers one kind of modernism with commedia; Fellini makes another, often out of a similar world of the circus and the theater, utterly different and arguably more fully of the commedia than the work of Bergman or, for that matter, any of his peers. The most obvious expression of this is Fellini's long fascination with clowns. There is nothing intrinsically modernist about this, of course; the director's love of the circus is as simple and wholehearted as he keeps telling us it is, and its roots are as much in childhood as the similar attachments of many another commedist, from Stravinsky to Bergman. But while Bergman often sees the artist typified by his commedia figures, Fellini goes beyond this to see all of humanity in clown terms. This has the effect of casting his modernism, his experiments with perception and received truths, in figures of bright fantasy, playful masks, and the grotesque.

The vivid grotesques of Fellini's *Satyricon* (1969) and the similarly arresting and varied creatures who dip in and out of *La Dolce Vita* (1960), 8½ (1963), *Juliet of the Spirits* (1965), and *Amarcord* (1974), are not often literal clowns, but they have the exaggerated features and the lively extremes of movement and character that give them the power of clowns:

Fellini convincingly demonstrates that clowns can project a full range of human feeling. To caricature someone as a clown is not to stereotype him, but to concentrate his qualities, to intensify him.

(Rosenthal, p. 97.)

But Fellini carries this artist's strategy with him into life—or brings it from his vision of life—because his characters are not caricatures in the sense that they are stereotypes; they are fully human *and* clowns. This applies to his fullest characters, most notably to Giulietta Masina, who with her bright, round, open face, creates an aura of Pierrot/clown innocence in several roles: as the trouper Melina Amour in Fellini's first feature, *Variety Lights* (1950); as the naive and star-struck Cabiria in *The White Sheik* (1952); as the perpetually betrayed and perpetually hopeful little prostitute of the title role in *Nights of Cabiria* (1956); and as the repressed, dream-struck Giulietta, the (again) betrayed spouse in *Juliet of the Spirits*. Her most famous clown role, in which she literally plays a clown, is that of Gelsomina, the simpleminded and simplehearted girl sold by her family to a brutish and lonely traveling strong man to serve as his cook, servant, clown-act come-on, and concubine. *La Strada* (1954) is suffused with commedia images, as the strong man Zampano and his female clown travel the circuit of country fairs and village weddings in a rattling motorcycle-cum-trailer. The ultimately fatal clash between the barrel-chested Zampano (Anthony Quinn) and the more subtle, mocking Matto, the circus high-wire artist and Fool (Richard Basehart), has in it much of the rough comedy and the violence of the old commedic patterns—and this violence leads inadvertently to the death of the Fool, to the sorrow of the little towheaded clown, and to the final discovery by Zampano of his own self-made desolation. Gelsomina, with her brilliantly Chaplinesque pantomime and what Zampano calls her "artichoke" face, manages to embody all of the purity of which the human heart is capable as she serves, clowns, and suffers. In the moments of her best, bright mugging and miming, she is both Chaplin and Pierrot.

That Fellini can see all of humanity through clown eyes is perhaps clearest in his literal celebration of the clown, the film made originally for Italian television called simply *The Clowns* (1970). In his introduction to the published screenplay of this mixture of documentary, fic-tionalized autobiography, and fantasy-spectacle, Fellini summarizes the two essential, opposing clown types and their relationship to one an-other. The White Clown looks a bit like Pierrot and Punchinello, but he is a harder, more ambitious and rigidly self-righteous creature. His opposite, his comic foil and source of irritation and rebellion, is Auguste, the sloppy, broadly painted funny-faced clown whose features are most familiarly and sentimentally associated with the basic notion of the cir-cus clown. Auguste is as free-spirited and bumbling (even when he is sullen or sad) as the White Clown is rigid and judgmental, and for Fellini they both reside deep in the human character. He classifies fellow di-rectors Pasolini and Visconti as White Clowns and Antonioni as a sul-len version of Auguste. Hitler was a White Clown, Mussolini an Auguste:

The game is so real that if you have a white clown in front of you, you are forced to act as an Auguste, and vice versa.

(Rosenthal, p. 98.)

The two personalities are in everyone; they certainly inhabit many of Fellini's film characters, though seldom in simple mixtures. Auguste and the White Clown collide in various ways in *The Clowns*, and in the end they are together in the circus ring making music:

The film ends with the two figures . . . meeting and going off together. Why does such a situation move one so much? Because the two figures embody a myth that is basic to each of us: the reconciliation of opposites, the singleness of being.

(*Op. cit.*)

Bergman

Bergman's feeling for the clown and the circus also runs deep, but it is not warmed by the same easy intimacy that characterizes Fellini's at-tachment. In a conversation about the making of *The Seventh Seal*, Bergman described the genesis of the white-faced figure of Death:

We decided to make death as a clown. You know, the white clown. *Not* the beautiful clown, but the white clown, because for us, as children, when we were at the circus, the white clown always frightened us.

(Jones, p. 33.)

The use to which each director put his experience of these characters is markedly different. Alienation, separation from the common lot, persecution, menace: these are clown associations that recur in Bergman's films. While their Fellinian counterparts often have a rough time of it, they are not singled out by their suffering, but rather are confirmed in their humanity thereby—we are one with the weeping Gelsomina.

The striking, stylized Death who confronts the Knight in *The Seventh Seal* does not seem to us to have anything of the clown in him, at least at first, despite his mask face. But there are signals. Skat, one of the figures in the little band of players wandering from town to town over the plague-ridden countryside, plays the clown literally in a death mask that closely resembles the face of Death. When not in use, that clown's version of death hangs on a branch or on a post in the camp, grinning vacantly in the background. And when Skat does meet his death at the hands of Death, it is in a stylized bit of clown humor: Death saws down the tree which the clown has climbed to escape.

The Seventh Seal is not a film about clowns, but it is a film about life as a theatrical, picturesque epic. Every character, from the questing knight to the suffering "witch," embodies an image from a broad tapestry of medieval life. The self-conscious rhetoric and visual symbolism derive their tremendous power from old, resonant patterns with overtly theatrical, religious, and simply "picturesque" meanings. The most famous sequence, the climactic Dance of Death along the horizon, combines all of these associations. The fact that it was the result of ten minutes' worth of improvisation (Björkman, p. 115.) prompted by the appearance of an evening cloud only confirms the director's film preconception of the kind of image that fits this canvas. The literal theatrics, the performance of the troupe on their tiny stage, with Jof as the cuckolded husband, Skat as the seducer, and Mia prancing between them, has the same kind of visual power. It is the timeless dance of the old commedia out of the music box in *A Lesson in Love*, this time dressed in motley, this time reflected in the "real-life" offstage cuckolding of the blacksmith by the onstage seducer-clown.

Life onstage and offstage continually play off one another in Bergman's films, and if he constantly gives us vivid glimpses of the basic patterns, as in the primitive medieval theater, he also builds elaborate frames for those patterns and exploits to the fullest the ambiguities and oscillations between art and life, artist and role. In *Smiles of a Summer Night* (1955), a film with a gently rueful tolerance for the games people play that recalls Renoir, the elegantly rococo structures of plot and setting move between theater lives, life imitating theater, and life's energies asserting themselves and mocking all the pretensions of form.

In the years before *Smiles* there are some especially commedic moments. In the most poignant of them, Marie, the ballet dancer in *Summer Interlude* (1951—also called *Illicit Interlude*), examines her life as she peels away her makeup at a mirror, while the ballet master, her "Doctor Coppelius" in clown makeup, crouches in the semidarkness behind her, guiding her toward an acceptance of her lot as artist.

Bergman's view of clowns is much grimmer than Fellini's, as is revealed most strikingly in his other vividly commedic work of this period, his one movie that is indeed about clowns, *Sawdust and Tinsel* (1953—also called *The Naked Night*, although *Gycklarnas afton* translates literally as "Evening of the Clowns"). Again, Bergman's circus and theater people do not as a rule enjoy the place in the center of warm humanity that Fellini's clowns and grotesques do. For all their oppressed condition, however, the members of the Cirkus Alberti do carry their full weight as yearning, dreaming, disappointed human beings. They are also very much of their trade, and Bergman scrupulously grounds his tale in the circus.

The frustrations and humiliations, principally sexual, that make up the core events of the film are mirrored in the *lazzi* of the clowns in performance under the Big Top, which are all of the slapstick-humiliation and comic-beating variety, and they give way at a key moment to real violence when Albert the ringmaster attacks the mocking seducer of his woman, first by knocking his hat off with his whip. The sexual betrayal is foreshadowed early in the film by another clown scene, the stark and painful flashback of the story of the clown Frost and his wife, Alma, who betrays him by cavorting naked in the ocean with a troop of military men. Frost, alerted to the event, runs from the circus, still in his full white clown garb (complete with a grinning sun face painted on the groin area), to the scene of his humiliation. The depth of his horror and shame is expressed in abrupt, angular montage that emphasizes his utter aloneness, as he clutches his naked and scornful wife amid a sea of mocking faces. The vividness of the sequence seems all out of proportion with subsequent events, as painful as they are—Albert and Anne betray each other, then find one another again—but the image of the broken white clown is so powerful as to make its own desolate truth.

Bergman has often expressed his admiration for Fellini, and it is true that the detailed, tactile treatment of his clowns and theater people and their milieu is similar, despite all the important dissimilarities, to the lovingly physical approach of Fellini. Both directors make strikingly theatrical events out of dreams and visions also, another expression of this physicality. They share a sense of theatricality, and a love of the literal images of the circus and the theater.

In the midst of the travail of Johan in *The Hour of the Wolf* we see a puppet-theater performance of a fragment of *The Magic Flute*, as presided over by the "worst" of Johan's demons, the Birdman, an evil version of Papageno. Johan's suffering becomes a dark and futile version of Tamino's trials; Alma, the wife who bears his madness with him, is associated explicitly with Pamina. To go from this translated, framed, distorted Mozart to Bergman's film of the opera (1975) is to see the breadth of his commedia modernism. The lush, exquisitely detailed rococo of the opera, complete with smoke-belching stage dragon and angelic, pink-cheeked boys, is more than a faithful rendering of the opera. It is one more examination of a vivid theatricality, as well as a display of it. There is an interplay between the faces of the audience and the action on stage; it is not so insistent as the relationships between audience and performers in the circus in *Sawdust and Tinsel,* the traveling show in *The Seventh Seal,* or the play scenes in *The Magician,* but this interplay in the opera film is enough to create the self-reflective framework that is the hallmark of Bergman's theatricality.

Truffaut and Buñuel

When the French New Wave broke, it carried with it important commedic flotsam of its own. One of the brightest figures of this movement, the director closest to both its founding spirit, André Bazin, and to its strongest inspirational predecessor in French cinema, Jean Renoir, was François Truffaut. Truffaut located the source of Renoir's genius in his sympathy for his characters:

It is thanks to sympathy that Renoir has succeeded in creating the most alive films in the history of the cinema, films which breathe forty years after they were made.

(Insdorf, p. 69.)

As Annette Insdorf points out, this sympathy is also a salient feature of Truffaut's work, and it aligns him with Renoir in the "lyrical" tradition of French film. Truffaut does not avail himself of commedia or its analogues to the degree that the older master did, and much less than Fellini or Bergman. He is impulsive, given to allusive, fragmentary narrative and to sometimes black, sometimes crazy ironies. When he applies this temperament to his love of silent comedies or to his preoccupation with the framing and illusion-making processes of filmmaking itself—an interest that is perhaps the only thing in him close to Bergman—the result is both new and commedic.

Truffaut's great love-triangle film, *Jules and Jim* (1961), flirts with the ghosts of Harlequin, Pierrot, and Columbine in Jim, Jules, and Catherine. The playful/serious layering, the deliberately loose and many-threaded narrative, and the constant ironic self-reflection, humorous up to and beyond the brink of tragedy, all are analogous to the ways of commedia modernism. The improvisatory moments include a comic chase, with Catherine (Jeanne Moreau) imitating Chaplin, complete with mustache; we also see a painting of Jules as Mozart; throughout we are treated to endless stories, which the principals tell one another as they, especially the men, shape their lives for art, and Catherine constantly reorders her life according to images from art—and intermittently throws herself into the Seine.

This complex of distancing techniques and displays of close, sometimes heartbreaking sympathy recalls Renoir. But Truffaut's vast film buff's knowledge and allusiveness are very much his own, as bits of Hitchcock (especially), and Welles, Renoir, Keaton, Chaplin, and many American adventure/gangster movies surface, often in contexts that make them very ironic. In *Shoot the Piano Player* (1960) the American *film noir* trappings are present in force, but there is a comic thread, even to the melodrama, that constantly insists on the illusion as an illusion, as if Charles Aznavour were reminding us, on a deliberate, if subterranean level, that both he *and* Bogart are creatures of celluloid.

Another modernist director given to deep and multiple ironies and fragmentation—of a very tightly controlled variety, unlike the more loose-reined Truffaut--is Buñuel, one of the old masters of surrealism in the late twenties. The commedic credentials he exhibited then appear sporadically but significantly in the films of his later career. Buñuel's obsessions, as familiar as those of the other obsessive masters, Bergman and Fellini, remain also: his cripples and beggars and grotesques (a darker, more hunted lot than those of Fellini), his insects, his focus on shoes, feet, parts of the body, his use of the iconography of the church. Surrealism and the often inextricable intermingling of fantasy and "reality" remain central to his repertoire throughout his career. The Buñuel social consciousness usually dictated choices in subject matter and attitude quite alien to commedia modernism; his ironies are often too savage for any distancing or framing effects, and even when the frames are entirely visible, as in the travesty Last Supper beggars' banquet of *Viridiana*, the effect is to increase the political voltage of the satire.

But Buñuel did have deep commedic allegiances that expressed themselves throughout his work, not just in the revolutionary days of *Chien andalou* and *L'Age d'or*. After all, he did, in his childhood, conform to a now-familiar pattern: his parents bought him a toy theater in Paris, with cardboard figures of king, queen, court jester, and knights, and the young Luis and chosen family members put on elaborate shows, moving the figures by wire. He also had an early attachment to the films of Max Linder and of Méliès. (Buñuel, pp. 35–36.) A striking example of his ability to inject discomfitting irony that does force reflection about the medium itself is in the late (1977) *That Obscure Object of Desire*. He achieves his odd distancing by using two actresses, distinctly different types, to play the woman Concha, the tormenting object of desire. They alternate in the part according to no perceivable plan, and the viewer is left to his own devices to adjust himself to something that no one on the screen seems to notice. This film is based upon the same novel that is behind a radically different work, Josef von Sternberg's *The Devil Is a Woman*, the last of his Marlene Dietrich films, in which she is the manipulative beauty par excellence. That common origin is Louÿs's *La Femme et le pantin* (*The Woman and the Puppet*) (Horton, p. 329.), an exquisite and overheated tale of 1898, about a beautiful young Spaniard who gradually enters into a twisted relationship with the older, hopelessly enamored Don Mateo. The principal feature of the relationship seems to be his beating her and thereupon suffering humiliation as a romantic nobleman forced into the distasteful business of whipping a woman. Sternberg's version of this male's tale has many commedia touches—a carnival, masks—and the imperious seductress serves by her mere presence as a disinfectant for all those sado-masochistic impulses. The fact that the male is the puppet is an ironic reversal of the Sternberg-Dietrich relationship, but then, this was the last gasp of that relationship.

Buñuel is much more faithful to the Louÿs novel; the author was an early favorite of the surrealists. But he plays games that call attention to the film as film, most obviously in the case of the double-cast heroine. Buñuel creates an oddly comic framework out of the original narrative device of the novel. This was originally a warning tale told by Don Mateo to a younger man in love with Concha. Buñuel makes it into a casual story told by Mathieu to a group of fellow train travelers, who have just seen him dump a bucket of water on the head of Concha and are naturally curious. Later, she reappears to dump a bucket of water on him.

This slapstick turn of events is parallel to many grotesquely funny juxtapositions in Buñuel's films. When they are not howls of anger, they often have something of the commedic in them. *The Discreet Charm of the Bourgeoisie* relies on absurdity to render all kinds of pretensions and assumption visible and then comic—even a terrorist machine-gunning scene is a comic dinner party event.

It would be straining our definitions a good deal to claim Buñuel as a commedia modernist, but he is another of the great figures of film modernism who burlesqued and fragmented the received notions of storytelling on film, as well as the whole enterprise of moral and rational realism. He belongs here less because some of his tricks are in fact commedic than because they, and his whole art, are strongly analogous to the art of the more obvious commedia modernists. His righteous anger and his private obsessions both militate against this connection, but his aesthetic commitment to irony, fragmentation, to the power of dreams and fantasy, and the theater, kept him on a parallel course.

A very similar constellation of commitments lies near the center of the art of another important modernist. Jean-Luc Godard is a modern revolutionary who has made significant use of the literal commedia and its analogues. He is a radical whose radicalism engulfs his art and craft as a filmmaker and places him, for all his acknowledged mastery, on the fringe. He is a great director, but not yet an "old master" of modern film, not in the mainstream, however diverse and vague a thing that is, marked out by such revolutionaries as Fellini, Bergman, Truffaut and Buñuel, each with his own way of defying aesthetic traditions. The commedic radicalism of Godard is a vital part of contemporary artistic expression and as such is best discussed in the final chapter. There he can be most clearly arrayed with those who have found that the most arresting quality of contemporary civilization is its absurdity.

Chapter 6.

HARLEQUIN, PIERROT, PICASSO

I
T DOESN'T take much straining after the point to find the commedia dell'arte in Paris of *la belle époque*. The most casual stroll through the cafés and the parks, Montmartre and the circuses, through the lives and the works of Cézanne and Degas, Manet and Toulouse-Lautrec, uncovers its images in abundance. The French roots of the commedia are deep, going back to the Italian *saltimbanco* troupes— the name deriving, apparently, from *saltare* (to leap) and *banco* (bench), thus, an acrobat whose stage was a portable bench. In Watteau's hands the traditional coarseness and vulgarity of the Italian originals were transmuted into a refined, wistful playfulness. Indeed, this transformation began before the career of Watteau, before that of his teacher, Claude Gillot. All three of the most familiar commedia figures, Harlequin, Columbine, and Pierrot, are essentially Parisian inventions; their familiar forms were developed in large measure by the Italian actors themselves to suit the taste of French high society.

In the eighteenth century, after its fall from grace, the commedia dell'arte returned to its wandering state, thereafter to be captured in various stages of gaiety and poignant poverty by Watteau, Tiepolo, Adolphe Roehn, and Daumier. The theme of the artist's identification with his commedic subjects announced itself in Watteau's *Gilles*, later in Daumier's wandering *Saltimbanques* of the mid–nineteenth century, and a decade or so later in Manet's *The Old Musician*. Daumier's paintings and studies also reflect the process by which the commedia troupes, still primarily theatrical in calling, merged with the other wandering entertainers, the acrobats and the jugglers, as the commedia and the circus blended in their iconography, a mélange exploited thoroughly by Seurat and Toulouse-Lautrec, and by Degas, who in 1884 put a balletic Harlequin and Columbine on stage, complete with Harlequin's stick.

Picasso's Early Career

But to confront the commedia as a force truly central to the sensibility of a visual artist, we must turn to Picasso. In 1901, during his second

163

sojourn in Paris, the young denizen of Montmartre painted *The Two Saltimbanques*, subtitled *Harlequin and His Companion*, and another substantial early work, called simply *Harlequin*. This was in the autumn, after he had begun to make important connections, with the dealer Vollard, who was to play a vital role in the career of Rouault and so many others, and with Max Jacob, who first encountered the nineteen-year-old Picasso at his first showing, which had been arranged by Vollard. This was also a dark time, however, after the suicide of his close friend Casagemas, after the paintings inspired by that death, a time of emotional and financial hardship that was to culminate in Picasso's retreat to Barcelona, where he would plunge into the Blue Period.

This pair of Harlequin paintings was not Picasso's first use of this imagery. There is, for example, a clown for a carnival handbill of the previous year in Barcelona. But they were his first ambitious commedia projects. In all likelihood Cézanne provided the impulse for the choice of subject. According to Penrose (Penrose, p. 108.), Picasso first encountered Cézanne's work in Vollard's gallery, in the form of his brilliant *Mardi Gras* (1888), a Pierrot dressed in a bluish white ruffled costume with a carnival hat and a Harlequin in checkered red and blue. Apart from the vivid colors and, perhaps, something of the detachment in their expressions, Picasso's early commedia figures are very different from Cézanne's—this was well before he was ready to absorb any of the revolutionary stylistic implications of that master's work. Picasso later claimed that Cézanne "was my one and only master" (O'Brian, p. 138.), and he was loath to admit the influence of anyone, crediting almost no one else besides Cézanne and van Gogh at any time. There seems to be, however, something of Degas in another early Picasso commedia picture, *The Blue Dancer*, in which the title figure is joined center stage by a Pierrot.

These early works were the products of a young man voraciously devouring the styles around him. His "passionate surge forward had not yet left him the leisure to forge for himself a personal style," in the words of the review by Felicien Fagus of that first show. But there is a personal stamp upon them that binds them to Picasso's later uses of the commedia. The vivid colors and the brusque outlining of *Harlequin* must descend from van Gogh, and the pose has been traced to van Gogh's *L'Arlésienne*, but there is an odd, feline twist to his posture, a touch of the ironic. The *Two Saltimbanques* hunched together create something of the same effect with their hands, an ironic grace when taken together with their vacant expressions. That combination of vacancy and intimacy anticipates the saltimbanques to come.

Irony did not play a large part in the commedia of Picasso, young or not young; he exploited its imagery in ways that were uniquely affirming, and drew upon the ties of friendship and family that he saw in the lives of those clowns. Still, he also knew how to exploit the ironic associations that had gathered about these circus lives; he could paint a detachment into his celebration of them. Even at the time of his Paris beginnings, he showed signs of seeing the circus with new eyes.

In 1904 Picasso returned to Paris, this time determined to remain. He moved into a ramshackle building on the slope of Montmartre, named Bateau-Lavoir by Max Jacob after the laundry barges anchored nearby. At first he struggled, sold few works for little money, and shared the poverty of those around him. But he made friends, among them Apollinaire and Gertrude and Leo Stein; in the summer *la belle Fernande,* the green-eyed Fernande Olivier, moved in with him. Ochre and rose and light began to encroach upon the blue in his painting. The Medrano Circus, especially beloved of the group that had come to be known as *la bande à Picasso,* was another source of light.

"I was really under the spell of the circus," Picasso recalled. "Sometimes I came there three or four nights in one week." (Carmean, p. 39.) He was especially attracted to life behind the scenes and managed to develop real friendships there. Olivier recalled that Picasso and his friends, especially Jacob and Apollinaire, "felt very flattered because they could be intimate with the clowns, the jugglers, the horses and their riders," and that Picasso "admired them and had real sympathy for them." (Carmean, p. 40.) The large body of commedia works that emerged suddenly, mostly in the early months of 1905, relied heavily upon the circus people as models. However, when the artist chose to invest these figures with individuality, he drew most upon his images of himself and his friends. Fernande probably figures in *Pierrette's Wedding* (1904), which has Harlequin blowing a farewell kiss to Pierrette, who is in the process of marrying someone in a top hat who looks rich and sinister. There is an odd mix of poignancy and melodrama in this painting, which Reff, perhaps the most perceptive student of Picasso's commedia, argues to be a good deal more enigmatic than the simple title—not by Picasso— suggests. (*Ibid.*, pp. 28–29.)

Max Jacob, idealized, may be the model for Picasso's first major piece of sculpture (1905), the cryptically amused bronze *Jester.* Certainly Jacob was a jester, a "creature of fantasy" who "had a strange and unspoilt innocence" (Harding, p. 165.), despite his extravagant homosexuality and his insistent theatricality. He was a Pierrot in his childlike play of mind and his openhearted adoration of Picasso—and a Harlequin in his love of malicious gossip and his ability to mimic anyone worth the mimicking and to hold sway over dinner-table conversation.

Apollinaire and Friends

Apollinaire, who was an authority figure as well as a friend, also took an important place in many of the paintings and drawings of this period. In a bookplate that Picasso created for him, he is a fat jester dressed as a king, with wineglass raised for a royal toast. In an interview long afterward the artist described it "as representing Apollinaire as king among poets and as a jester—i.e., amuser of painters—among art critics." (Gedo, p. 64.) This jester resembles the more specifically commedic figure, the large buffoon who carries an air of benign, wise authority through several works and sketches, culminating in the *Family of Saltimbanques*. He has been called "the understander," and because of this role and his appearance, is an Apollinaire figure; so, too, is another circus figure, the large, young strong man. The literal caricatures of Apollinaire as a muscle-bound athlete play on the absurdity that this pear-shaped *gourmande* with an aversion to exercise had found work as editor of a physical-culture magazine. But Picasso was genuinely impressed by his size and the aura of confident strength about him. Thus, the friend, critic, and interpreter, who was himself to be the celebrant of commedia figures in his poetry, stands behind two figures of strength in the Harlequin period:

Apollinaire *was* Picasso's understander, the good mirror, whose vision of the painter reflected his best and truest self, and interpreted to the world (and perhaps even to Picasso himself) the iconography of his paintings.

(Op. cit.)

While this identification of Apollinaire and the saltimbanques is too literal, there is important truth to it, because Picasso was translating his personal experience very purposefully into a harlequinade. Apollinaire was a source of strength, but he was also a poseur; he was an authority, but he was also something of a fraud, and he put an awareness of this into his own style. Picasso, like generations of artists before him, loved the Medrano Circus, but he also had this literal harlequinade dancing before him, in Jacob, Apollinaire, the pistol-packing, ether-sipping Alfred Jarry, and in the other theatrical personalities of the avant-garde to whom they introduced him:

Throughout the Circus period Harlequin dominates the scene. He is seen off stage, lithe and sensitive in physique, with his family and their attendant pets.

In intimacy he nurses a baby while his wife stands nude arranging her hair. In the *Family of Acrobats with a Monkey* he watches the young mother with her child. . . . He appears at times a small boy or wanders in open country with an acrobat and a dog, or again he stands in thought looking into the blind face of one of his companions.

(Penrose, p. 108.)

If Picasso easily found the pose, the playful irony, and the buffoonery of the commedia in those around him, he also found its images within; it is in his act of joining the harlequinade of his work, in his identification with Harlequin himself, that Picasso makes most intimate and creative use of these images. Many critics have noted the identification, and in doing so they sound many of the basic themes of the modern artist's relation to the commedia:

The preference that Picasso shows, particularly in early life, for Harlequin suggests that analogies must exist between him and this legendary character. Picasso's Harlequin is not the elegant flirtatious entertainer loved by Watteau, nor Cézanne's proud youth in fancy dress, nor is he a buffoon. Though he may be a jester he speaks the truth, and though he may be wearing a disguise we detect him by his mercurial nature and his elusive ways. It would be legitimate to interpret this Harlequin, with his diamond coat of many colours, as the power to juggle with everything while remaining evasive and irresponsible. . . . His game is ambitious; it is a test of strength with the established order.

(*Op. cit.*)

Symbolist art often possessed . . . a confessional element, and this is plainly the case with the pictures in which the figure of Harlequin appears. The melancholy jester who was also an eternal outsider clearly aroused in Picasso strong feelings of self-identification.

(Lucie-Smith, pp. 204–205.)

Mary Gedo constructed a chronology of Picasso's inner struggle and maturation from the successive Harlequins of this period, from the lonely, bitter figure among the jaded customers, *Au Lapin Agile* onward. There must be a well of autobiographical emotion in this painting, however one views the progression overall. The Lapin Agile was a Montmartre café that was a favorite hangout of Picasso's band. Picasso himself is the obvious model for the Harlequin, and the artist has identified the woman with him as having been modeled upon Germaine, the model for whom his friend Casagemas killed himself. (Carmean, p. 29.) Carmean suggests that Germaine may have been the person who introduced Picasso to the circus because, in Gertrude Stein's words, "there were many other tales of Germaine Pichot and the circus where she found her lovers."

Gedo traces a development through Picasso's many unhappy, isolated little boy Harlequins, through the achievement of serenity and confidence in the *Family of Saltimbanques*, to the culminating urge "to relinquish this alter-ego" in *The Death of Harlequin*. A brief comparison of this last painting with the work that may have suggested it (Blunt and Pool, p. 135.) demonstrates the degree to which Picasso had eschewed the light sophistication of much contemporary commedia in favor of the attempt at grand emotions in the same dress. That work, Aubrey Beardsley's illustration to Dowson's *The Pierrot of the Minute*, puts the sickbed figure very much in the background, while the carnival figures mince past the bed with a playful, conspiratorial air. Picasso's dead Harlequin lies in state, hands in the approved position of prayer, with the impassive faces of two mourners vividly highlighted. The mood of tragedy almost completely subdues the Harlequin imagery.

Whatever the specific psychological import of this Rose Period preoccupation with Harlequin and Company, it is clear that the artist used the figures to explore his own identity as a man and as an artist. If this robbed the characters of frivolity and comedy, it did not tear them from their origins; the costumes and colors and poses are intact in their nineteenth-century guises. For all the celebration and study of the family, it is never just a family, or even a circus family; the diamonds of Harlequin and his three-cornered hat, the jester's cap, the ruffles and the tights, all worn with a strange, pervading grace, play too vivid a part in the whole.

It is significant that this paradoxical blend of the spirit of the commedia with the sense of family intimacy on the one hand and quiet, sad isolation on the other is best comprehended by Picasso's "understander." In a 1927 "souvenir" of Picasso for *Cahiers d'Art*, Max Jacob wrote:

Picasso and Apollinaire understood one another marvellously. Picasso painted harlequins and saltimbanques; Apollinaire put them in his poems.

(McCully, p. 55.)

In late February and early March of 1905 Picasso took part in an exhibition at Galéries Serrurier at which he showed his first Rose Period paintings, including eight saltimbanques. (Rubin, p. 57.) Apollinaire's review in *La Plume* is more than criticism; it is poetic re-creation:

The harlequins go in splendid rags while the painting is gathering, warming or whitening its colours to express the strength and duration of the passions, while the lines, delimited by the tight curves, intersect or flow impetuously. . . . In a square room paternity transfigures the harlequin, whose wife bathes with cold water and admires her figure, as frail and slim as her husband, the puppet. . . . Love is good when it is set off. . . . Some harlequins match the splendour of the women, whom they resemble, being neither male nor female. . . . Placed at the frontiers of life, the animals are human, and the sexes are indistinct . . . taciturn harlequins have their cheeks and foreheads paled by morbid sensibility.

His insistence on the difference between these figures and actors is related to the argument Meyerhold was making for the power of improvisatory farce at approximately the same time. Apollinaire continues:

You cannot confuse these saltimbanques with actors. The spectator must be pious for they are celebrating silent rites with a difficult agility . . . here virility is beardless, but shows itself in the sinews of thin arms, in the flat planes of the face, and the animals are mysterious.

(McCully, pp. 52–53.)

These lines lead to his famous judgment, "More than all the poets, sculptors and the other painters, this Spaniard scathes us like a sudden chill." Much has been made of Apollinaire's lack of real understanding of the paintings that he interpreted and promoted so valuably. Steegmuller gathers the testimony of Braque, Villon, and Picasso himself, among others, to that effect. (Steegmuller, pp. 140–43.) However, in the matter of the Harlequins Apollinaire spoke with the authority of one who was himself an *arlequiniste*. When, in 1965, Daix and Boudaille showed Picasso a copy of the *La Plume* review, he read it with great emotion, and in his last days he was much preoccupied with the memory of his old friend. This may not argue the interpretive authority that Gedo thinks it does (Gedo, p. 62.), but it joins other indications that Picasso regarded this period as one of sensitivity, even vulnerability in his development. In a late interview, he refused to talk about it, claiming, "All that was just sentiment."

Sentiment plays about these works, flirting with a heavier sentimentality, as it does in Apollinaire:

> The little saltimbanques turned a cart-wheel
> With so much harmony
> That the organ stopped playing

And the organist hid his face in his hands
With fingers like descendants of his destiny
Small foetuses which came out of his beard
New Indian cries
The angelic music of trees
The disappearance of the child

The saltimbanques lifted the great dumb-bells in their arms
And juggled with the weights

But each spectator looked in himself for the miraculous child
Century O century of clouds.

> ("Phantom of the Clouds,"
> Apollinaire, p. 165.)

But the sentiment is supported, enhanced, by the mystery and grace of the play of images:

> Grazed by the shadows of the dead
> Where day expires on the grass
> The columbine takes off her clothes
> Looks at her body in the pool.

> ("Twilight," Apollinaire, p. 61.)

This *arlequine* could be the wife "who bathes in cold water and admires her figure" of Apollinaire's *La Plume* description of *The Harlequin's Family;* there is even a similar air of isolation about Picasso's woman, despite Harlequin's admiring gaze:

> The blind man rocks a lovely child
> The roe walks by with all her fauns
> The dwarf regards with sad demean
> The magic growth of harlequin

> (*Op. cit.* [*arlequin trismégiste* in the original].)

Harlequin Trismegistus, the thrice greatest, is linked by way of Apollinaire's cryptic phrase to Hermes Trismegistus, the god to whom the Neoplatonists and sundry mystics through the ages assigned the greatest of magical powers. André Salmon linked the harlequins of his friends by describing Picasso's "acrobats that were also metaphysicians" and "sorcerer clowns" as "figures like Apollinaire's *arlequin trismégiste.*" (McCully, p. 55.) Clearly, for both artists there was a seriousness to the magic of Harlequins and Columbines and saltimbanques because it was, for them, a power of tranformation very close to the heart of the artist's vocation.

[RIGHT] Garbo in *Inspiration*
[BELOW] Masina in *La Strada*

[ABOVE] Keaton and Chaplin in
Limelight
[LEFT] Jannings in *The Blue Angel*

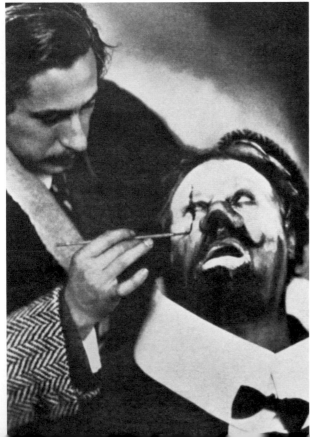

Dietrich in *The Blue Angel*

Bergman's *Sawdust and Tinsel*

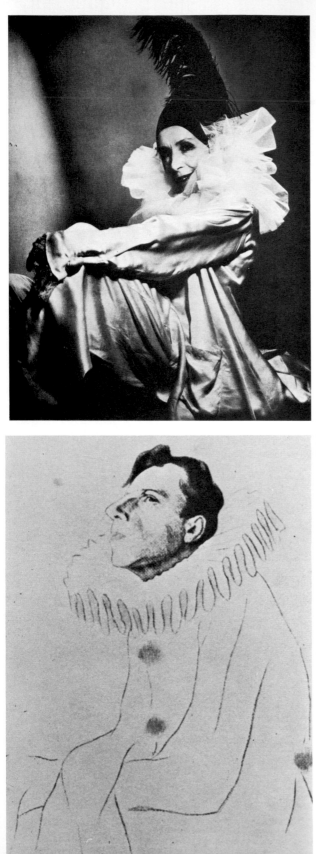

Dinesen as Pierrot

Meyerhold as Pierrot (drawing by Ulyanov)

Wedekind with Maria Orska
as his Lulu

Orska as Lulu

Proust

Virginia Woolf

Isak Dinesen in old age

Edith Sitwell

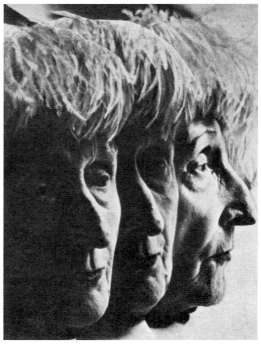

Family of Saltimbanques

The strongest evocation of this magic came in the spring of 1905 with the *Family of Saltimbanques*. In the words of Barr, "Every few years throughout his career Picasso has had the conviction and energy to concentrate in one large canvas the motives and problems of a whole period of his work." (Barr, p. 36.) Measuring about seven by seven and a half feet, this was the artist's first really big work. It was not the last of his Rose Period circus paintings, but it was the culmination of the images and the energies generated in the hundreds of harlequins, acrobats, weight lifters, clowns, and circus families sketched and painted in the 1903–1905 period.

The autobiographical dimension of the work has been enthusiastically probed by many critics. Besides Apollinaire as the fat clown "understander" and Harlequin as Picasso himself, the boy tumblers may, according to Theodore Reff, be André Salmon and Max Jacob. (Carmean, p. 50.) Beyond this particularity (which is less convincing in the case of the boys), more generalized artist-as-performer metaphors hover about the painting. It has been suggested that, since *arlequin* often means simply "acrobat" to the French, Picasso may have been influenced by the long line of French poets, beginning with Gautier and including Banville and the Goncourts, who applied the image of the high-wire artist to their own poetic activity. (The metaphor remains common currency— Ferlinghetti uses it, for instance.) Manet's *Old Musician*, which Picasso would likely have seen at a 1905 exhibition, and Daumier's *Mountebanks* (or Saltimbanques) *on the Move*, shown in Paris in 1901, have been cited as important influences upon the painting; certainly the isolation and melancholy of Manet's and Daumier's performers is present in Picasso's.

Rilke and the Saltimbanques

Apollinaire the friend is a figure of strength and connection within this scene of stillness and isolation, and Apollinaire the poet made very similar links between the circus and the human condition. But it was another poet, a war and most of a generation away, who captured, for his own purposes, the heart of this commedia. In 1922, Rilke wrote to Lou Andreas-Salome:

I had intended to make a copy of the other three Elegies for you today, since it is already Sunday again. But now—imagine!—in a radiant afterstorm, another elegy has been added, the "Saltimbanques." It is the most wonderful

completion; only now does the circle of the Elegies seem to me truly closed.
. . . And so now the "Saltimbanques" too exist, who even from my very first
year in Paris affected me so absolutely and have haunted me ever since.

(Rilke, pp. 324–25.)

Indeed, Rilke had been so thoroughly haunted that he wrote to Hertha
Koenig, who had bought the Picasso in 1914, to request that she allow
him to stay in her Munich home during the summer of 1915, while she
was away, in order that he could live with the "glorious Picasso." The
request was granted; she eventually became the dedicatee of the Fifth
Duino Elegy. Like Apollinaire, whose "Phantom of the Clouds" resembles the later work in many ways, Rilke also had his own experience of
the circus folk to draw from, especially the troupe of the sad, old, once-
famous Père Rollin and his troupe whom Rilke watched and then described in touching detail in 1907. And again, there is a tradition of
the poet finding himself in the sad, superannuated clown, established
in Baudelaire's "Le Vieux Saltimbanque." That Picasso himself was deeply
aware of this strain, the artist who has lost his art, is reflected occasionally in flashes of wretchedness among the Harlequin works, but in another way in his play with the images of clown and king, in which the
jester's cap and the king's crown grow into one another, a theme older
than *King Lear*. This is most striking in Picasso's *The Organ Grinder (Old
Jester and Harlequin)*, a painting of an old man as a clown holding a
crank organ, with a boy Harlequin sitting at his feet. The clown-king
theme is implicit in the pose; there is humor in the treatment, but the
Baudelaire edge is there also, a sense that such artist-clown-kings are a
disregarded, discarded breed of royalty.

But old musicians and old acrobats aside, the real power of the commedia in the elegy, as in the painting, is in the freedom and the skill,
the endurance and the quiet devotion to a theatrical, noisy art (muted
here in color and in words) that asserts itself against the modern world,
even as it lives in its hire. In the fragment appended to the elegies,
Rilke asked a question:

> Once poets resounded over the battlefield; what voice
> can outshout the rattle of this metallic age
> that is struggling on toward its careening future?

(*Ibid.*, p. 215.)

The answer is nothing—except, someday, some "greatness . . . lying
in ambush." In his Fifth Elegy, the suggestion of an answer catches him
up and prompts the basic question:

But tell me, who *are* they, these wanderers, even more
transient than we ourselves, who from their earliest days
are savagely wrung out
by a never-satisfied will (for *whose* sake)?

(*Ibid.*, p. 175.)

This is the old linking of the acrobats' art with sacrifice and ultimately
with death (Madame Lamort, the milliner who "twists and winds the
restless paths of the earth . . . for the cheap winter bonnets of Fate").
But Rilke's questions are not answered by reference to an act of simple
sacrifice, any more than the other clowns of modern art are simply or
(with the possible exception of Rouault) even primarily sacrificial. The
questions relate too sharply to the artist himself, and the implications
in the clown-artist identifications are too critical.

"Art is superfluous," Rilke said to Katharina Kippenberg, and he put
more questions: "Can art heal wounds, can it rob death of its bitterness? It does not calm despair, does not feed the hungry, does not clothe
the freezing." (Heerikhuizen, p. 328.) These are not only the charges
of the artist against himself, of course; they only echo those of the "metallic age" in general. If the questions which the artist asks to open the
Fifth Elegy have answers, they must also address these charges. The answers have to do with the rituals designed to conquer death that lie at
the root of art. The magic and the ritual are expressed in Apollinaire's
arlequin trismégiste, but also, with added emphasis upon the artist's agility, in Cocteau's 1919 "Ode to Picasso":

Nothing in his sleeves   Nothing in his pockets
            Would some gentleman
lend his hat
to the harlequin from Port-Royal.

(Cocteau, p. 174.)

But if these powers and these burdens are borne by Picasso's saltimbanques, they are not the primary focus of attention for either the
painter or the poet. They are motionless, these acrobats, standing together in their curious isolation, gazing and not gazing at the one seated
figure, the mother of the young boy, perhaps, placed apart from the group.
Somewhere Picasso said that his purpose was not to capture motion but
to stop it; here he has done that, and Rilke has seized this moment after
they have landed:

on the threadbare carpet, worn constantly thinner
by their perpetual leaping, this carpet that is lost
in infinite space.

(diesem verlorenen Teppich im Weltall.)

Motion, quickness, and graceful (or skillfully comic) agility are essential
to commeida, but even more than Apollinaire, Rilke concentrates, in
this stopped moment, on the life behind that motion. The melancholy
of the circus life at the center of "the rose of Onlooking" performing to
"the unconscious/gaping faces, their thin/surfaces glossy with boredom's
specious half-smile," is as familiar as the nostalgic sadness about the
"shriveled-up, wrinkled weight lifter." The poet invests the gaze from the
boy to the woman with another melancholy:

sometimes, during brief pauses, a loving look
toward your seldom affectionate mother tries to be born
in your expression; but it gets lost along the way,
your body consumes it, that timid
scarcely-attempted face.

(Rilke, p. 177.)

And this glimpse of circus condition as human condition is interrupted
with the characteristic gesture of circus/commedia:

the man is clapping his hands for your leap, and before
a pain can become more distinct near your constantly racing
heart, the stinging in your soles rushes ahead of
that other pain, chasing a pair
of physical tears quickly into your eyes.

(Op. cit.)

Rilke converts the relentless movement, the "perpetual leaping" of his
subjects into emotional movement, even transcendence. With an attitude akin to that of Apollinaire ("The spectator must be pious for they
are celebrating silent rites with a difficult agility"), Rilke takes his scene
back to the time before "equanimity," before the difficulties had been
conquered:

Oh where is the place—I carry, it is in my heart—,
where they still were far from mastery, still fell apart
from each other, like mating cattle that someone
has badly paired;—

(Ibid., p. 179.)

Here are images of the pratfalls that precede the art, "where the weights
are still heavy" and "the plates still wobble and drop" from "vainly twirling
sticks." We feel the struggle in order to feel its resolution:

And suddenly in this laborious nowhere, suddenly
the unsayable spot where the pure Too-little is transformed
incomprehensibly—, leaps around and changes
into that empty Too-much;
where the difficult calculation
becomes numberless and resolved.

(Op. cit.)

The achievement of this freedom is ambiguous, *jenes leere Zuviel*, "that
empty Too-much," and it is mocked by its setting, Madame Lamort's
Paris, "infinite showplace" bedecked with her "new bows, frills, flowers,
ruffles, artificial fruits"—but the achieved serenity is real enough, and
the vision it inspires is itself a perfectly executed turn, from the acrobatics of the body to those of the heart:

Angel! If there were a place that we didn't know of, and there,
on some unsayable carpet, lovers displayed
what they never could bring to mastery here—the bold
exploits of their high-flying hearts,
their towers of pleasures, their ladders
that have long since been standing where there was no ground, leaning
just on each other, trembling,—and could *master* all this,
before the surrounding spectators, the innumerable soundless dead:

(Op. cit.)

With this enormous conditional clause addressed to the Angel, Rilke
encompasses much of the emotional power of these commedial figures
for the modern artist, the freedom, the sense of communion, even the
fascination of the difficult. But this large "If" is resolved with an
expression of yearning for a happiness, "final, forever saved-up, forever
hidden, unknown to us, eternally valid." This is beyond commedia,
certainly beyond Picasso's troupe, still stranded, even in their serenity,
upon the *verlorenen Teppich im Weltall,* rather than partaking in Rilke's
final vision of the "at last/genuinely smiling pair on the grati-
fied/carpet." *(Ibid.*, p. 181.)

In this Rilke is like many artists of this period who were not psychologically or spiritually drawn to the world of the commedia as a source
of creative identity, but who still felt the fascination of its image. Whether
he had any deeper sympathy for the theatricality, the play of quick mo-
tions and emotions of the commedia, Rilke caught this particular man-

ifestation, this phase of Picasso's commedia, with precision, even as he put it very much to his own use. For Picasso this world was a part of his identity: the *Family of Saltimbanques* represents a culmination of one aspect of his growth as an artist—and as a commedia artist—but he was to return to these themes with similarly intense self-identification again and again.

From Rose Commedia to Revolution

In what Barr called "the first 'classic' period," from mid 1905 to mid 1906, the serenity that had become more and more evident through the Rose Period expressed itself in a series of compositions imbued with a "Greek" litheness and impersonal grace that show their kinship with the previous Harlequins, but are also very likely reflections of a new interest in classical figures. The many youths with horses in this period bear a strong resemblance to the young circus figures, and the circus remained a literal subject also, as in the drypoint *At the Circus,* in which two figures are poised on pointe on the back of an oddly dominant "classical" horse. There has been a change, as Barr notes: "the intimate, offstage life of the acrobats and their families is forgotten. In the classic, impersonal grace of these nymphs riding bareback there is no smell of the tanbark." (Barr, p. 40.)

In his trips to Holland and then (especially) to Gosol, in the Spanish Pyrenees, in his encounters with the Fauves and with African and ancient Iberian art during this 1905–1906 time of ferment, the young Picasso absorbed and labored. Beyond all the significant work of this time, the peasants, the portraits of Gertrude Stein and of himself, the dynamic *Composition* showing his discovery of El Greco, and the massive, archaic *Two Nudes,* there was one great, concentrated effort gathering. Like the *Family of Saltimbanques,* it was to be a group of figures, and like it, a huge painting, around a foot longer in each dimension than that work and larger than anything that had come before it.

Never was labor less repaid with obvious joy, and it was without his earlier youthful enthusiasm that Picasso set about applying to the great nudes of the *Demoiselles d'Avignon,* begun in the spirit of the Rose Period, the first results of a research strictly dictated by the calm examination of all that had preceded it. There is never any break of continuity in Picasso's work, although a single moment in it was the signal for the Cubist revolution, which was a revolution indeed. Picasso subjected his genius to the cold light of Reason. When he gave it wings again, he stood immortal at the center of a transfigured universe.

(Salmon, in McCully, p. 140.)

It was Salmon who, for better or worse, gave this composition of five whores its title. This description, by one of the closest observers of Picasso's life and art, captures the elements of discipline, concentration, painful growth, and, finally, freedom that went into the revolution that both connects and separates the Harlequins and the *Demoiselles*. It is also arguably the quintessential description of the commedia artist in the twentieth century; it would apply in large measure to the wedding of improvisation and tradition, freedom and discipline, emotion and "the cold light of Reason" that was to take Stravinsky from *Firebird* to *Petrushka* to *Le Sacre*, and thence to *Les Noces*, then to *Pulcinella*; it is the same fierce absorption and transformation that was to make Meyerhold wring an entirely new symbolist theater out of realism and farce. And that same power of the cold light, the power of disinterested self-analysis (as directed at art, if not life), was to enable Picasso himself to turn from his invention, play with, and "betray" cubism. Salmon goes on, in this essay of 1920, to "describe the curve of Picasso's genius" with an aphorism that encompasses both the working and the accomplished work:

> Wide and white, the sleeves of Pierrot are not
> those of a conjuror.
> They contain only two bare arms.

> (McCully, p. 141.)

Was Picasso Cocteau's Harlequin or Salmon's Pierrot? He was, of course, both. He was the conjurer and the trickster and also the voracious recipient of others' tricks, which he poured into his inventions, transformed, not by magic but by the work of "two bare arms."

The *Demoiselles* remains perhaps the most famous, most influential, most revolutionary work in twentieth-century painting; the tale of its difficult early life does not belong here, but it is relevant to point to small matters that connect the great opening statement of cubism with the commedia that preceded it. It has been noted (Penrose, p. 124.) that the melon rind among the fruit in the lower center of the picture is in the shape of a harlequin's hat upside down. It is a rather bold slice of melon, accentuating the already somewhat surprising presence of the fruit (which is all that remains of a sailor who accompanied the fruit and gradually disappeared in the course of the seventeen composition sketches that went into the final product); as a Harlequin hat it seems most like those of Cézanne. In the momentous reordering of the geometry of reality that occurs in this painting, Cézanne is, of course, much more significant than this—and because the master had died in October

1906 he was more than ever in the mind and in the exhibitions—but it is not entirely impossible that this is a modest icon cast at the feet of the new world to preserve a connection with the old. It is not impossible, too, that the famous masklike faces of the two women on the right, whatever their much-disputed African/Iberian ancestry, owe something to the masks of the commedia and the circus, and that the bold display of arms, torsos, and legs is related to the thrusting assurance of the acrobats.

In any case, Picasso took the commedia with him into his new world, turning once again to his harlequins in 1908 and 1909. The cubist *Carnival at the Bistro,* based on Cézanne's *Card Players,* evolved from several studies depicting Harlequin and Pierrot and others seated at a table; the *Woman with Fan* of the spring of 1909 is wearing what looks very much like Harlequin's hat (Rubin, p. 127.), and from 1909 there is also a cubist *Harlequin.* In June 1910 Fernande Olivier wrote to Gertrude Stein that she and Picasso "have made great friends with some clowns, acrobats, circus riders and tightrope-walkers, whom we met at the Cafe and spend all our evenings with." (McCully, p. 67.) This is confirmation that he was not merely reworking old material; the fascination with the circus remained. Carmean argues, however, that "the sense of autobiography" so strong in the earlier commedia pictures is missing in these and the synthetic cubist works of 1912–1914. "Picasso was interested primarily in the formal qualities of the imagery." (Carmean, p. 56.)

When he and Fernande finally moved out of the happy squalor of the Bateau-Lavoir in 1909, Picasso continued the intense, exhausting experimentation in which he and others, especially Braque (whom the *Demoiselles* had converted, at first much against his will) developed a more and more daring and rigorous cubism. If the commedia images did not figure importantly as subjects in themselves, fragments of the circus life did, for Braque and Juan Gris as well as Picasso. It is true that the recurrent mandolins, violins, and guitars must have been fascinating primarily for the possibilities offered by their graceful and peculiar geometries, but they shared the atmosphere of the circus for these young men, as did the accordion player, transformed into the brilliant, gay energies of cubist abstraction in the summer of 1911 at Céret. It is well to remember that whatever objects were enlisted in the cause at this time, their communicative power outside the group was limited: as his old friend Manolo, living at Céret, said of the *Accordionist,* "What would you say, Picasso, if your parents were to come and fetch you in the station at Barcelona and found you with such a fright?" (Barr, p. 74.)

There was a spirit of play as well as of concentration in these developments, as Picasso and Braque turned their inventive wit to the creation of the new art form in the midst of their abstration, the collage; again, the mandolin and the violin became constructions in cardboard, chalk, wood, and paint. The connections with the commedia assert themselves in the literal sense with the Céret oil, *Harlequin,* of 1913. The *Man with the Guitar,* of the same year in Paris, also has many qualities of the Harlequin, suggested in part by the multicolored panels which seem to absorb the figure. The Paris *Harlequin* of 1915 still uses the simple rectangular forms, but the tall, vivid figure is more obviously the smiling Harlequin—we see a smile and a bright eye, and the diamond suit is back—and the rectangles are set off one another at jaunty angles to make the figure dance. As the cubism became less austere, the commedia began to breathe more freely. This Harlequin is regarded by Rubin (p. 179.) as "the major work in a long series on this theme," a "starkly geometric" masterpiece that initiates a development within "Synthetic Cubism" that is to culminate in the *Three Musicians* of 1921. This belies somewhat the playfulness of the piece—and Rubin even feels that "His toothy smile seems almost sinister"—but it underscores the fact that once again, Picasso has chosen a commedia subject as the vehicle for concentrated work. The work itself belies its creator's mental state, because it was painted during the fatal illness of Eva Gouel, Picasso's "Ma Jolie," for whom he had broken off his deteriorating relationship with Fernande in 1911. In December 1915 Picasso wrote to Gertrude Stein:

My life is hell. Eva becomes more and more ill each day. I go to the hospital and spend most of the time in the Metro. . . . However, I have made a picture of a harlequin that, to my way of thinking and to that of many others, is the best thing I have ever done.

(Rubin, p. 179.)

This is the stance of the commedia artist who has mastered the separation of the man who suffers and the mind which creates (to borrow the formulation of another artist, T. S. Eliot, who had learned much from the commedia).

It was this Harlequin which, when freshly painted, caught the attention of the young Cocteau.

Shifting Styles

These are the years in which Picasso demonstrated his sovereignty over any aesthetic system, especially his own, first by reintroducing realism into his cubist work, then by dismaying his cubist friends and confusing his critics with a series of exquisite, graceful portraits in the style Barr dubbed "Back to Ingres" because the evidence of Picasso's admiration of that master is very much present in their line and proportion. He alternated freely between cubist experimentation and work in this style, further discomfitting those for whom cubism had become law.

There is a meticulous and expressive portrait of Apollinaire in this style, showing him in uniform with the bandages of his head wound showing beneath his cap; for all the signs of soldierly heroism—Apollinaire had volunteered for service on the Western Front although he was not a French citizen—there is still something irreverent about the figure. There is a broader wit in an ink-and-watercolor mock war poster that Picasso tossed off in 1914, which depicts Apollinaire in a heroic pose, sword in hand, pipe in mouth, dressed in his artilleryman's uniform, and standing before a cannon labeled in bold letters, "Guillaume de Kostrowitsky, Artilleur, 1914." According to Brown (*Theater*, p. 135.), Picasso regarded the war as "a stupid embroilment absolutely no concern of his." As a foreigner, Picasso did not have to fight, either, and he didn't; considering his future statements against war, there is remarkably little notice of it in his art of this time. Braque, Derain, Salmon, and Cocteau all did service in the French army, and another close friend, the dealer Kahnweiler, was forced because of his German origins to close his gallery for the duration. It was in part Picasso's relationship with Kahnweiler and another German patron, Thannhauser, that inspired those hostile to cubism to associate it with *les Boches,* an accusation that was to emerge again during the *Parade* scandal. It is consistent with his commedia spirit that Picasso saw little in this war worthy of his art besides the bandages and uniform of his friend (Apollinaire was to die of influenza complicated by these shrapnel wounds in 1918).

Cocteau and the Ballet

An art which only now became important to him was the ballet, specifically the Ballets Russes, which Diaghilev kept together in the face of the difficulties of the war by means of heroic panache and tours of the Americas and such parts of Europe as could afford the distraction. True again to the commedia in him, and also true to his Left Bank social sense, Picasso had heretofore confined his interest in theater and dance to the popular forms of entertainment, especially as artist and intimate of the circus, and most vitally of its more downtrodden aspects. The elegant extravagance of the Ballets Russes, and even the quieter, high-culture equipoise of the dancers of Degas, held little attraction for him.

It was Cocteau who introduced Picasso to the world of the ballet, and Edgard Varèse who introduced Cocteau to Picasso. There were a number of avant-garde artists in Cocteau's circle, most of them minor cubists such as Albert Gleizes and André Lhote, who inhabited Montparnasse. According to Cocteau, Varèse took him to Picasso's studio: "How can I ever forget that visit? . . . It was a meeting written in the stars." (Brown, *Impersonation*, pp. 136–37.) According to Brown, however, Varèse actually took Picasso to visit the undramatically prostrate Cocteau, who was bedridden with a bad cold. Cocteau's enhancement of this first encounter was no doubt the result of his being utterly smitten with the young Spaniard.

Like Max Jacob and Apollinaire, and to a much greater degree, Cocteau embodied the theatricality, the flamboyant costumed and masked life, and this emerged with especially vivid self-consciousness in Montparnasse, where even Lenin tried to make a living as a model. Cocteau said of his own uniform, a combination of high-laced, yellow aviator-style boots, red jodhpurs, black tunic, and purple steel helmet, "If I make an issue of costume, it's because costumes were an issue in Montparnasse, and some became legendary." (*Ibid.*, p. 139.) Picasso, however, did not take part in this style; for the most part he chose his work over the gay life. But he watched, and he absorbed. He needed Cocteau in very different ways, therefore, than Cocteau needed him:

Picasso wanted poets near at hand to serve him as lightning rods and like his women, they rotated in accordance with his cyclical self. Cocteau first appeared shortly before Olga Kohklova, and reappeared with Jacqueline Roche, like an epiphenomenon of the bourgeois phases in Picasso's life. (*Ibid.*, p. 138.)

When they met, Apollinaire was away at the war; Eva was about to die.

Cocteau knew of Picasso's preoccupation with Harlequins; he had seen the great *Harlequin* just finished in late 1915, before it was sold. Thus, in the spring of 1916 Cocteau visited Picasso wearing a Harlequin's costume beneath his trenchcoat (it is said that Picasso had told Cocteau he wanted to paint him in a Harlequin's costume, but as this was apparently only their second meeting, this was still remarkably harlequinesque behavior). Picasso did paint Cocteau on that May 1, but it rapidly became a strenuously cubist exercise in which Cocteau is not to be found. Cocteau left the costume behind with Picasso, who twice painted his friend, the painter Jacinto Salvado, wearing it in 1923—two of his most elegantly realistic Harlequins.

But Cocteau was not merely a passive tool in this relationship. Cocteau knew ballet and in his way knew the new music very well; he had been more or less closely associated with Diaghilev and the Ballets Russes since its first Paris season; for some time he had wanted to mount a ballet on the subject of David, which would feature a peculiarly modern commedia twist:

An acrobat was to do the parade for "David," a big spectacle which was supposed to be taking place inside; a clown, who subsequently became a box, a theatrical version of the phonograph at a fair, a modern equivalent of the mask of the ancients, was to sing through a megaphone the prowess of David and implore the public to enter to see the piece inside.

(*Cock and Harlequin*, Cocteau, p. 326.)

Cocteau called this, "in a sense, the first sketch of *Parade*, but uselessly complicated by the Bible and a text."

By 1916 Cocteau had refined his idea and had also acquired important backing. He wanted to forge a collaboration between himself, Erik Satie, and Picasso for the Ballets Russes. At first he faced powerful resistance from Picasso and his friends, a resistance that reflected the difference between his "outer" and Picasso's "inner" commedia. Writing of the *Sacre* premiere, Cocteau noted the absence of the young painters and their masters, due in part to "social prejudices":

This condemnation of luxury, which Picasso professes like a cult, has its merits and demerits. I fling myself upon this cult as upon an antidote, but it may be that it restricts the horizon of certain artists who avoid contact with luxury from motives of envious hatred rather than conviction. In any case, Montparnasse is still ignorant of the *Sacre du Printemps*.

(Cocteau, p. 324.)

Montparnasse, and especially the cubists and Picasso's friends, indeed wanted nothing to do with this extravagance. Uneasy as they were with Picasso's willingness to turn from the faith and paint like Ingres, the notion of painting a ballet set and creating its costumes was positively sacrilegious—"God *hates* Cocteau," wrote the recent Catholic convert Max Jacob to Jacques Maritain. (O'Brian, p. 219.) As Cocteau put it in his book *Picasso* in 1923:

A dictatorship weighed upon Montmartre and Montparnasse. We were crossing the austere period of Cubism. . . . To paint a setting, and above all for the Russian Ballet . . . constituted a crime. . . . The worst was that we had to rejoin Serge Diaghilev in Rome and the cubist code forbade all journeys except that from north to south between the place des Abbesses and the boulevard Raspail.

(McCully, p. 119.)

But it was also true that "Cocteau could scarcely have invented a piece better calculated to overcome Picasso's left-bank prejudices." (Barr, p. 98.) His *ballet réaliste* was to be based upon the gestures and the aesthetic of the music hall and vaudeville, with a healthy dose of the circus, the popular entertainment so close to Picasso's heart. In late May, 1916, Cocteau brought Diaghilev to Picasso's studio to aid in the campaign to bring him into the project. Diaghilev helped his cause not a little by purchasing dozens of paintings by Picasso and fellow cubists at very persuasive prices. Finally, in the next winter, in the words of Gertrude Stein, "One day Picasso came in and with him leaning on his shoulder was a slim elegant youth. It is Jean, announced Pablo, Jean Cocteau, and we are leaving for Italy." (O'Brian, p. 219.)

This was a difficult wartime trip, and the choice of Rome was in part dictated by efficiency: it was the point of the return for the Ballets Russes from its American tours. Picasso had never seen a ballet, and he had never seen Italy. This trip was a major event in his life for many reasons, not the least of which was his encounter with the birthplace of commedia. And the *Parade* collaboration was a major event for many reasons, but it ought not to be overlooked that for Picasso it was also part of the continuum of his work as a commedia artist, especially during this period through the early twenties, when Harlequin and Pierrot made their appearance repeatedly in major composition.

Parade

Much has been written and reported about this gathering of talents, their arduous preparation, their quarrels, their unity, and most of all the scandal of the premiere. Such a gathering there has seldom been, with Massine (to choreograph and to dance), Diaghilev and his company (among them Olga Khokhlova, the lovely but mediocre dancer who in short order won Picasso's heart and hand) all residing in the elegant Palazzo Theodori—even Stravinsky was there with Diaghilev's company, composing a circus-related opus of his own, the *Feu d'artifice*. The principal creators had their difficulties, Satie (who refused to travel to Rome anyway) refusing at one point to go on with the score, Picasso asserting himself to force major changes in the original conception, Cocteau "moping at home and threatening suicide." (Brown, *Impersonation*, p. 142.) However, Picasso, in his complete ignorance of any received notions of the "higher" theater, did indeed conceive and execute a whole new kind of set and costume design; Cocteau, who adored Picasso anyway, had the good sense to see the strength in Picasso's ideas and allowed them to prevail in ways that enhanced his original vision of a burlesque, not only of the music hall but of the whole play of illusion and reality that had been the theater. Meanwhile, Satie created music that fit, music described by Cocteau somewhat misleadingly as "like an inspired village band." (Barr, p. 98.) Cocteau attributed to it a multifaceted vision that would also suit the cubist aspects of the show:

Gradually there came to birth a score in which Satie seems to have discovered an unknown dimension, thanks to which one can listen simultaneously both to the *Parade* and the show going on inside.

(Cocteau, p. 327.)

Considering the aural equivalent to a cubist collage, which Cocteau marshaled in his assault on theatrical reality—typewriters, firing revolvers, lottery wheels, pipes, a "bottlephone," treble and bass sirens, as well as drums, clappers, cymbals, a tom-tom, xylophone, and triangle—Satie's own remarks about his music, while characteristically arch, don't seem far from the point: "I have composed a background to certain noises that Cocteau considers necessary to create the atmosphere of his characters." (Templier, p. 86.) Cocteau's response to this was, "Satie exaggerates," but he conceded that "noises certainly played an important part," despite the fact that "material difficulties" hindered the effect of some of these "ear-deceivers," which Cocteau employed "with the same object as the 'eye-deceivers'—newspapers, cornices, imitation woodwork, which the painters use." (Cocteau, p. 329.) The music has retained a place in the repertoire, a witty, melodic suite of circus "turns" with a sly, restrained buffoonery and a grace that belies the famous ruckus the show was originally accorded.

Parade was put together in about two months of prodigious labor in Rome, including Picasso's designs and preliminary sketches for the costumes and the decor. It has already been discussed from a ballet perspective in the third chapter, but its importance to many of our central characters is such that it deserves treatment in the context of Picasso's career. He also found time in this period for Naples, Pompeii, and Olga, and for elegant drawings and caricatures of Diaghilev, Stravinsky, Bakst, Massine, a cubist *Harlequin and Woman with Necklace*, and much else.

In the early spring of 1917 the whole troupe returned to Paris to prepare for the May premiere, and Picasso and assistants set to work on the drop curtain. A photograph of him with his assistant scene painters sitting on that curtain provides an inkling of the scale of the work: the artist and two other men fit easily into the lap of the seated Harlequin, who is himself only a small part of a scene that as a full curtain measured over 35 feet by 57 feet. (Rubin, p. 197.) Not surprisingly, this was Picasso's largest composition to date, and as with his other "biggest" pieces, he brought to it several significant changes in style. Barr provides the most pointed description of it as a commedia scene:

At first glance, it carries us back to the circus and vaudeville pictures of 1905. . . . Here again are the bareback rider on her horse, the acrobat's ball, the harlequins and guitarists. But the style is cruder and more mannered, a skillful parody of popular scene painting. The colors are mostly heavy reds and greens and there is none of the sentimental melancholy and nervous refinement of the early work—Pegasus backstage is a mare suckling her foal, her wings held on by a strap, and the harlequins are smiling and well fed.

(Barr, p. 98.)

There is rather more continuity with the earlier harlequins than this suggests, and "parody" is misleading—there is too much about this mix of Roman ruins, drapery, animals, and strangely varied people (the ensemble presumably representing a family troupe within a circus tent) that is bright and new; Picasso celebrates, transfigures, rather than parodies here. He is true to his roots in popular entertainment, so true in fact that Bakst could label the curtain passéiste. (Ibid., p. 99.)

The costume which Picasso created for Le Chinois ("Prestidigitateur Chinois" in Satie's tripping, elegantly asymmetrical, but not particularly Oriental score), danced by Massine himself, is probably his most famous theater piece; for all its chinoiserie (including the rays of the rising sun on Chinese coat), it partakes of the same commedia spirit as much else in the show—even the "Oriental" headdress is more a multilayered jester's cap than anything else. His most radical costumes, and at the time certainly the most notorious, were for the Managers, which had the function of "un-human or superhuman characters who would finally assume a false reality on the stage and reduce the real dancers to the stature of puppets." (Cocteau, p. 327.) They were, again in Cocteau's words, "sort of human scenery, animated pictures by Picasso." (Op. cit.)

The French and English Managers were dancers encumbered with ten-foot-high cubist constructions, which covered them completely except for the legs, and even these had rectangular forms stuck to them.

These enormous, dominant assemblages of cones and cylinders and rectangles brought with them a new form of theater:

Their dance was an organized accident, false steps which are prolonged and interchanged with the strictness of a fugue. The awkwardness of movement underneath those wooden frames, far from hampering the choreographer, obliged him to break with ancient formulae and to seek his inspiration, not in things that move, but in things round which we move, and which move according to the rhythm of our steps.

(*Ibid.*, p. 328.)

The function of the French Manager was to introduce the Chinese conjurer after stamping out onto the stage immediately after the curtain rose, and "The Chinaman pulls out an egg from his pigtail, eats and digests it, finds it again in the toe of his shoe, spits fire, burns himself, stamps to put out the sparks, etc." (*Op. cit.*) Then the New York Manager, whose costume featured a skyscraper and cowboy boots, stamped out a dance and then broadcast through a megaphone the virtues of his particular act, the Petite Fille Américaine, who "mounts a racehorse, rides a bicycle, quivers like pictures on the screen, imitates Charile Chaplin, chases a thief with a revolver, boxes, dances a ragtime, is shipwrecked, rolls on the grass, buys a Kodak, etc." (*Op. cit.*) Massine said that in choreographing this turn, Cocteau and he had Mary Pickford in mind. She was followed by the two acrobats, "the poor, stupid, agile acrobats" whom, harking back to the Rose Period circus, "we tried to invest . . . with the melancholy of a Sunday evening after the circus." (*Op. cit.*) This was followed by a (musically modest) grand finale, with everyone taking a last "turn." The simple plot exploited the play of illusion and reality that the rest of the apparatus promoted: the performers (who were, of course, performers playing performers) show their wares in the traditional "parade," which is supposed to be the device whereby the audience (an imaginary audience within the plot, but all the gestures, of course, are to a real audience) is enticed to come "inside" and see the show. But this imaginary audience misunderstands and takes the parade for the show itself (which, again of course, is true . . .) and goes away despite vigorous pleadings on the part of the Managers, who collapse from their vain efforts. As has been noted, a final playbill is displayed just as the red curtain falls: "The drama, which did not take place for those people who stayed outside, was by Jean Cocteau, Erik Satie, Pablo Picasso" (Brown, *Impersonation*, p. 144.), which, given the premises, is, of course, true.

Apollinaire's program notes provided the theoretical underpinning, or rather a rhapsodical celebration: this *ballet réaliste* was actually to transcend reality with "a kind of sur-realism in which I see the beginning of a series of manifestations of the Esprit Nouveau, of that new state of mind which . . . cannot fail to enchant the elite and which, amid universal gaiety, intends to change our arts and customs from top to bottom, since common sense requires that they should at least keep pace with scientific and industrial advance."

This seems to have been the first use in print of the word *surrealism* by the man generally credited with coining it. But it is also a dramatic statement of a good many of the basic motivations of the modern commedia. *Parade* was the engine of revolution, and the driving force of this assertion of a new reality "amid universal gaiety" drew much from the commedia. There is evidence that *Parade*, through Cocteau's second-hand knowledge, was influenced in a general way by the theatrical innovation of Stanislavsky, Reinhardt, and Gordon Craig. (*Op. cit.*) Another possible influence, however indirect, could have been that earlier piece of revolutionary commedia, the "battering ram" that was the Blok/Meyerhold production of *The Fairground Booth.* Meyerhold had himself been in Paris four years before *Parade,* in 1913, to produce *Pisanelle* for Ida Rubinstein. He had worked on that lavish display piece with Bakst and Fokine, and he had formed a friendship with Apollinaire, and he had Ballets Russes connections that went back much further than this.

As has been well recorded, the "gaiety" fell somewhat short of "universal" the evening of the premiere of *Parade,* May 18, 1917. The crowded house had come with some preconceptions of what constitutes an evening of ballet, even with the track record of surprises behind the Ballets Russes. Satie's chorale-like opening was soothing, and Picasso's bright curtain was received with applause—but then, to the accompaniment of sirens and typewriters, the battering ram of the farce burst through, farce that asserted itself not only against the canons of ballet, but against the ordering of the players' and the watchers' realities. More to the point, all this was perpetrated with the aid of cubist monstrosities that even the more recognizably brilliant dancing of Massine could not atone for. In wartime Paris the many who regarded cubism with hostility (despite the fact that as a movement it was not only established but well past its prime) naturally regarded it as a German plot. Amid the other forms of loud disapprobation that erupted in the theater, the cry of *"sales Boches!"* was probably the most heartfelt and dangerous, because many took it upon themselves to show their disapproval of the "dirty Germans" in physical ways. From the safe vantage point of history, this farce-induced confrontation had itself strong elements of the farce. If the accounts of Cocteau and some others are to be believed—and Brown presents some evidence that there was a good deal of exaggeration afoot (*Ibid.*, p. 152.)—Picasso, Cocteau, and Satie were saved from the mob, some of whom were armed with hatpins, by none other than Apollinaire, who was in his uniform, complete with Croix de Guerre, and with all the appearance of a war hero, thanks to his bandages. He was just the man to wring forgiveness, or at least reprieve, out of the crowd, and to convince them that whatever else they were, his friends were not *Boches*. If the wounds had not been so real, it would not be difficult to see this incarnation of the New Spirit, the very embodiment of all in the new aesthetic that inspired such anger, as a commedia braggart soldier rising up to bluff on behalf of three cornered *zanni*.

The ballet was not an utter failure, even immediately—and this scene pales before the uproar occasioned four years before by *Le Sacre*, anyway. Proust was there with friends; they loved it and carried the word of this new spirit. When it was produced again after the war it was a major success with the avant-garde. And by reputation *Parade*, and the spirit of commedia so essential to it, became a reference point in the very definition of avant-garde. The principals themselves were not particularly taken aback by the reception—after their rescue, that is. (Satie was to spend a week in jail for criminal defamation, after he sent an insulting postcard to a particularly nasty critic. The trial for that event—at which even Apollinaire was called a *Boche*, Cocteau slapped the prosecutor and was himself beaten up, and all of modern art seemed to be in on the arraignment—was itself something of a farce.) They all learned much from *Parade*, especially Picasso, who was to contribute significantly to the musical theater again, with Stravinsky and de Falla as collaborators (and all the while he was never to lose his utter, and utterly unembarrassed, ignorance of and indifference to the "high-culture" music for which he made his settings).

Harlequin and Pierrot

For Picasso, in love again, and with a dancer, the immersion in the world of the theater inspired a strong interest in the possibilities of grace and movement in the human figure; the *Parade* project, being itself an expression of the artist's revived interest in the commedia, gave new impetus and new forms to that interest.

This great burst of harlequins and pierrots was accomplished in the most contrasting styles. A 1918 pencil drawing of the pair, Pierrot masked and playing the violin, Harlequin playing the guitar, is clearly from the hand of the master draftsman. It foreshadows the costume designs for the Stravinsky collaboration, *Pulcinella,* and has been called a study for that full-dress commedia, but at two years before the fact, it seems unlikely. But in the same year, 1918, in Paris, Picasso produced the great series of cubist harlequins, the rough, vigorous collection rectangles with a deliberately simple "smiley face" (*Harlequin Playing the Guitar*); a more restrained, more vertical *Harlequin;* and a beautiful exercise in texture, and in reducing violin fingering technique to cubist essentials, *Harlequin with Violin,* known also as "Si tu veux," after a title on the sheet of salon music Harlequin is holding. Edward Henning has demonstrated that there is very likely a pointedly personal dimension to this violinist:

Considering Picasso's tendency to put autobiographical images and verbal messages in his work, it is possible that the words *Si Tu Veux* (if you wish) . . . indicated his surrender to Olga's wish to legitimatize their relationship.

(Carmean, p. 57.)

He argues further that this change in marital status is reflected in commedia symbols in the painting:

There is a possibility that in this work Picasso finally joined the two figures that were closely associated pictorially in other works. . . . The black silhouetted Harlequin with a tight suit of diamond-patterned shapes to identify him is seen against a lighter gray shape suggesting the baggy white costume of Pierrot. . . . Furthermore, the white shape defining the left side (on our right) of the figure's head unmistakably refers to Pierrot's traditional hat, not Harlequin's.

(*Op. cit.*)

Harlequin Picasso, facing domestication, takes on the form of faithful (and foolish?) Pierrot.

In the midst of these cubist compositions came the realistic *Pierrot Seated,* a plaintive, expressive figure holding his mask, the face governed by the quiet, lost look of the eyes. No commedia figure since those of the Rose Period has such personal, possibly autobiographical intimacy; in the ferment of this last year of the war, Picasso married Olga, the weakened Apollinaire died of the Spanish influenza, and Cocteau published his manifesto, *Cock and Harlequin,* which celebrated and gave a definition to much in the new spirit of which Picasso was a central component. It is not surprising that the resilient little Spaniard, who was accustomed to putting himself into his bright harlequins, would turn here to a lost Pierrot for a respite and possibly, identity.

More Ballet—and a Last Burst of Commedia

In 1919–1921 Picasso acted on his *Parade* experience and became extensively involved, again, with Diaghilev and the Ballets Russes. In 1919 he went to London to design the ballet *Le Tricorne (The Three-Cornered Hat)*, by another great Spaniard, Manuel de Falla. Although there is much in the sprightly, farcical plot, based on a fable of Alarcon, that is akin to the commedia, neither the ballet nor Picasso's contribution is literally commedic. De Falla himself nurtured an interest in commedia theatrical techniques; *Tricorne* had been conceived at first as pantomime, a *farsa mimica*, and *Master Peter's Puppet Show*, the 1923 mini-opera written for the exquisite marionette theater of the Princesse de Polignac, and based on Don Quixote's famous puppet incident, was written not only for puppet principals but for a puppet audience. In 1921 Picasso collaborated with de Falla again (and Diaghilev and Massine) on *Cuadro Flamenco*, a ballet set to a suite of traditional Andalusian songs and dances arranged by the composer.

Between these Spanish-Spanish projects came the Spanish-Russian collaboration that finally brought Picasso exposure to the original Italian commedia. This was *Pulcinella*, Stravinsky's "Ballet with Song in One Act After Pergolesi"—a good deal after, in the event, for Stravinsky had breathed much of the new spirit of the age into the (still recognizable) eighteenth-century Neapolitan melodies. The studies for this production reflect Picasso's serious study of the originals; the famous costume and mask for Pulcinella himself has the characteristic Picasso draftsman's hand and flow; all of these compositions are necessarily less personal in impact than those that emerged from Picasso's own commedia. Because of several misunderstandings, Picasso was unable to realize all that he wished for *Pulcinella*, but he made do brilliantly, and the production was a major success. Stravinsky regarded Picasso's costumes and set designs as perfectly suited to the spirit of the music, and his opinion was very widely shared. Ever since the *Parade* sojourn in Italy had brought them together, there had been a genuine sympathy uniting these very different geniuses of the commedia.

Meanwhile, Picasso's own commedia continued, unaffected in any literal way by his researches into the real thing. In the summer after the May 1920 premiere of *Pulcinella*, Picasso and Olga traveled to Juan-le-Pins on the Riviera, and there the artist painted his familiars into contemporary settings, Pulcinella reading the newspapers, Pierrot and Harlequin at a café. He also created a cubist gouache of the pair—the next link in the great series of cubist commedia pictures that culminated the next year at Fontainebleau in the two versions of *Three Musicians*. These two large oils are certainly among Picasso's most familiar works. The masks, instruments, and hats of these figures seem to be consciously gathered from Picasso's private repertoire of the cubist commedia, and the same can be said of the figures themselves. In both paintings Harlequin and Pierrot make up two-thirds of the trio, and the third member, darker in both works, is a monk who, for all the difference in his apparent calling, seems to be at one with the others. Reff argues persuasively that the monk is a clue to the essentially autobiographical nature of these pictures. Picasso's old friend Max Jacob had entered a Benedictine monastery only a few months before these compositions were begun; Pierrot's costume is a French blue, and Apollinaire had once labeled Pierrot "a poet, an artist": Harlequin is, as usual, Picasso himself. Thus, as in the *Family of Saltimbanques*, the painter and his friends are assembled into a commedia troupe, this time as "a memorial to his lost friends and bohemian youth, painted at a moment when he felt that loss most keenly." (Carmean, p. 59.)

After these works Picasso seems to have stopped his pattern of returning to these themes with bursts of obsessive repetition. He exploited them often enough, however. From the year 1923 there are the realistic Harlequin portraits of Jacinto Salvado wearing the suit left behind so long before by Cocteau. Drawing upon Olga's ballet world, Picasso also painted a number of dancers in saltimbanque and Harlequin costumes, such as the *Saltimbanque Seated with Arms Crossed*, also from 1923. In 1924 Picasso's son Paulo was captured as Harlequin; the next year he was painted as Pierrot. In both cases the costumes have the look of beautiful, specially designed child's uniforms. In this same period Picasso also kept his hand in at the theater, though with only indirectly commedia results, with his collaboration with Satie and Massine (*Mercure*) and with Milhaud and Cocteau (*Le Train bleu*).

While the dance and dancers, mandolins and guitars continued to appear regularly in the late twenties and early thirties, often revealing their commedia/circus pedigree, Harlequin and Pierrot themselves fade, almost, from sight. There is a 1935 Paris *Harlequin*, very spare, a cubist head perched upon an obelisk; it is subtitled "Project for a Monument" and seems the product of an impersonal wit. There are lots of expressive acrobats, including an agonizingly contorted figure of 1930 and a series of a half dozen flying, wispily abstract circus performers of 1933. Much later, in 1954, the images return in the strange drawing, *The Monkey and the Mask*, in which a monkey and a young woman watch as a man— with some of Picasso's features, some of Pierrot's—puts on the large mask of an old man. The old Picasso chose many forms in which to express his struggle with age; this may be an old trouper's sleight of hand: old age is just another mask, albeit a heavy one.

The commedia never disappeared entirely from Picasso's work, but by about 1930 it had stopped being what it had been for him, a source of identity on the one hand, an arsenal of gay and brilliant weaponry for warfare on the old ways of seeing on the other. There are many accounts of his continued love of masks, clowns, and costumes—for instance, there is the 1951 Robert Capa photograph of Picasso wearing a clown's nose and whiskers. (Starobinski, p. 129.) He loved, and loved to imitate, Charlie Chaplin. He remained, in short, the commedia artist he had been, ever the improviser, making the new out of the familiar, always subjecting his powerful and insistent emotions to the discipline of the draftsman, and asserting the primacy of Apollinaire's new spirit, a revolution amid "universal gaiety." But in the last period of his life, Picasso, along with much of the culture he had done so much to change, seemed to have dropped his special relationship with the commedia in itself, with Harlequin and Pierrot.

Rouault and Others

The career and accomplishments of Picasso offer the most vivid and complete evidence of the influence of the commedia dell'arte on the imagination of the visual artist in the early twentieth century, but a very good case could be made by summoning a broad range of other artists who have various claims to a part in the making of modernism. Among the founding fathers of cubism there was much sharing of subjects and objects, and for the uninitiated at least, it is sometimes difficult to determine whether a particular guitar, wine bottle, or musician has been dismembered at the hands of Picasso, Braque, or Juan Gris. At first glance, this seems to be the case with a *Harlequin with a Guitar* painted by Gris in December 1917; indeed, his interest in Harlequin was sparked in part by Picasso. But a closer look at this and, among others, a *Harlequin Seated beside a Table* of eighteen months later, reveals an individual gaiety and brilliance. Gris was inspired in this by the Ballets Russes as well as by Picasso, and by the desire to relieve the austerity of his earlier work. His interest in Harlequin was aesthetic, an attraction of composition and color rather than of shared identity—he was the first to paint in a diamond floor pattern to mirror Harlequin's diamonds, in *Harlequin Seated beside a Table*. (Cooper, p. 176.)

The Italian Gino Severini was another figure active in the beginning, painting in Paris by 1906 beside Braque, Dufy, and others, in 1909 joining for a time the circle of Picasso, Apollinaire, and Max Jacob. He is perhaps best known as one of the pioneers of futurism, although he had a long and varied career. He is relevant here because he displayed a deep attachment to the commedia during much of that career, especially in his sketches and designs for the stage. He was active in several commedia revivals and adaptations in the twenties, a production of Vecchi's *Anfiparnaso* in 1938, Busoni's *Arlecchino* in 1940, and other commedia-related enterprises through the forties and fifties. Given his connections with the Diaghilev circle and others, the interest is unsurprising, but it is worth noting because Severini made a sustained and distinct commedist art out of it, in cubist, futurist, and especially in expressive and often witty representational forms. He felt that the figures of commedia allowed him to "humanize his geometry" and to express a sense of the "mysterious and fantastic" denied him by other means. (Fagiolo, pp. 5–6.)

There are impressive commedia works by Chagall, Ensor, and Klee—see Jean Starobinski's psychological meditation *Portrait de l'artiste en saltimbanque* for many others from several centuries—but the remaining major artist who demands attention in this regard is Georges Rouault. Rouault was born in Paris in the midst of the Commune uprising in 1871, a coincidence that conveniently symbolizes the spirit of anger, defiance, and sacrifice that characterizes his lonely, brooding art. His sense of social outrage crystallized early and found a focus in the work of the clown-prophet of so much in modern commedia, Alfred Jarry. Jarry's great grotesque Père Ubu, epitome of all the soulless brutality that ruled the world, was a vital figure to Rouault. Between 1916 and 1928 he produced hundreds of designs for wood engravings, etchings, and aquatints for *Les Réincarnations du Père Ubu*, a sequel to Jarry's *Ubu Roi* written by Ambroise Vollard. The great dealer, publisher, and connoisseur harbored a lifelong passion for Jarry's brilliantly scandalous marionette play and may even have been present at its 1896 premiere in the form for living actors. Rouault is faithful to Vollard's act of homage and also to Jarry's original conception (Jarry designed his own original marionette Ubu), but his Ubu characters are also comic originals, forceful cartoonlike grotesques that communicate volumes about the human condition apart from any text.

But Rouault's fascination with the mad ruler of a mythical Poland was, despite its length and intensity, secondary to the commedic devotion that was truly central to his art, his love for the clown. In the text he wrote for another of his illustrated books, *Le Cirque de l'étoile filante—The Shooting Star Circus* (1938, also commissioned by Vollard), he expressed his deep and childlike admiration:

Strolling players over all the highways of Ile-de-France, drifting from North to South, from East to West, fun-loving, peace-making conquerors who go your way in winter toward the sun, the green plain in spring or toward the ocean sea, I have always envied you, I a recluse tilling the pictorial soil as the peasant tills his field, now toward Spain you go by way of Navarre, now toward Flanders . . . far from the Venturers of the Celestial Highways; from the consortiums of the Mad Match King, . . . from the garglings of pettifogging classicists, or the latest agents of clandestine armaments for World Peace.

(Venturi, p. 21.)

Fleeing the world of power and brutality and "the hard or hostile masks of the dispirited and the withered of the heart," Rouault found refuge in the "Shooting Star Circus," and throughout his life he celebrated, mourned, identified with, and studied its inhabitants. His countless clowns, sometimes wounded, sacrificial, Christ-like, his big-eyed and expressive Pierrots, dwarfs, and circus troupes, his self-portrait in clown garb, all attest to this deep, unchanging attitude. Between, for instance, the heavy and brooding *Head of a Tragic Clown* of 1904 and the bright and winsome *Aristocrat Pierrot* of 1942, there are many differences in style, treatment, and mood, but the attitude, the sympathy, is the same.

In this attitude, and certainly in the expression of it above, Rouault is close to the essence of the appeal of the circus and commedia to the early revolutionary modernists in general. Here is the triumphant "illegitimacy," the free and improvisatory spirit of the revolutionary artist who sees through and beyond the law—and war-makers and the "pettifogging classicists." Like Picasso's Rose Period saltimbanques, Rouault's clowns often bear the weight of poverty, sacrifice, rejection—but also like them, they endure, and in the ways of the heart and the eye that mattered most to these visionaries, they triumph.

Chapter 7.
CLOWNS, PUPPETS, AND
THE NEW MUSIC

T HE SIMPLEST CASE for the importance of the commedia dell'arte to music in the twentieth century can be made by listing composers who made significant use of it: Stravinsky, Schoenberg, Strauss, Prokofiev, Satie, Busoni, Weill, Puccini, Milhaud, Ravel, Poulenc, Debussy (the *Suite Bergamesque*, Cello Sonata, songs), Berg (in *Lulu*), Nielsen (in his operatic masterpiece *Maskerade*), Hindemith (in his Berlin theater music), Szymanowski (the commedia *Mandragora*), Martinu (several commedia suites), even the unlikely Max Reger (the 1913 *Ballettsuite*). A wider casting of the net brings in de Falla, Krenek, Walton, interesting minor Englishmen Lord Berners and Granville Bantock, vital contributors to French theatrical life such as Hahn, Françaix, and Messager, and many more. There is even an argument to be made for a commedic strain in musicians who are most unpromising commedic material, in minor Sibelius (the music for the "mimic drama" *Scaramouche*) and in major Bartók (two of his three stage works, *The Wooden Prince* and *The Miraculous Mandarin*). But the catalogue must stop before all distinctions between the commedic and non-commedic are blurred.

It is not possible to generalize about the musical nature of the scores written to evoke the characters or actions of commedia. It is certainly appropriate to hear playfulness, romantic yearning, and irony in Pierrot as he is depicted, for instance, by Bantock in his "comedy overture" after Dowson's play *Pierrot of the Minute*; by Debussy in the "Serenade" movement of the Cello Sonata; and by Schoenberg in *Pierrot Lunaire*. There is a characteristic melodic and rhythmic shape associated with this last Pierrot throughout the thrice seven movements of the work, and there is a characteristic, defiant "Petrushka chord" that is a musical signal of Stravinsky's Russian Pierrot/Punch, but there is no musical connection between these motifs.

The music of the commedia flows through particular contexts—poetry, ballet, and theatrical works, which make it the music of the commedia dell'arte. But this does not mean that the fascination with the commedia in the early modern period was not a musical phenomenon; indeed, the uses to which the most influential composers put its characters and patterns were enormously fruitful, and in specifically musical ways.

Schoenberg

The power which the commedia exerted over the greatest of the musical revolutionaries becomes clear in the key works of Stravinsky and Schoenberg. The former belonged in many ways to the world of commedia in his artistic associations and outlook. Rather like Picasso, he was a clear-eyed, disciplined servant of his gifts and his work who nevertheless associated with the flamboyant and eccentric, most famously and rewardingly with the circle of Diaghilev and the Ballets Russes. Schoenberg was more relentlessly the "straight man" with virtually none of the playfulness and taste for ambiguity that characterized the more recognizably commedic personality of Stravinsky. He had a sense of humor, often rather grim, and a sharp sense of irony that was burdened more than a little by the (not unjustified) belief that he was a man with a mission who was misunderstood and persecuted. His attraction to the images of the commedia was very different from that of Stravinsky, but it was, in its moment, no less intense.

Schoenberg came to breathe the atmosphere of commedia by way of the cabaret—not the bold and brilliant phenomenon of 1920s Berlin nightlife, but the *Brettl*, the German version of the French cabaret of the 1890s. The leading entrepreneur of this new form of sophisticated popular theater was Baron Ernst von Wolzogen, writer, restless traveler, and friend of many similarly restless young Germans, including Frank Wedekind and Richard Strauss (he wrote the libretto for Strauss's early opera *Feuersnot*). In 1900 his travels took him to Paris, where his experience of the Chat Noir and the Grand Guignol fanned his enthusiasm for his own project, which was further inspired by frequent and extremely successful appearances in Germany by Yvette Guilbert, immortalized by Toulouse-Lautrec, Kokoschka, and many others as the epitome of cabaret gaiety and sensuality.

Wolzogen's Buntes Theater (variety theater) opened in Berlin in January 1901 and was an immediate, enormous success. Wolzogen himself appeared in a blue tailcoat and addressed the audience as "My noble lords"; Christian Morgenstern performed a satire; Otto Julius Bierbaum's poem, "Der Lustige Ehemann" ("The Happy Bridegroom"), with music by the company's musical director, Oscar Straus, was a particular

hit. This elegant dance was later published with a fashionable Art Nouveau cover featuring a laughing but melancholy clown playing a guitar.
(Stuckenschmidt, p. 53.) Of his *Überbrettl* company—so called because
its immeasurable superiority to other popular theater earned it, in the
director's eyes, the right to that *über*—Wolzogen was later to write:

I indeed wanted to teach the German bear to dance, and without pain, for its
own pleasure—so I could not use the old cruel method of putting this bear on
a hot grill, but I preferred to use the mild and as it were proven method of
education by arousing its ambition of imitation by presenting other animals which
by nature are able to dance.

(Ibid., p. 52.)

This chimes well with another call for liberation, from Bierbaum's introduction to his *Deutsche Chansons*, subtitled "Brettl-Lieder":

We are firmly convinced that the time has come for the whole of life to be
permeated by art. . . . We want to write poems that will not just be read amidst
the bliss of solitude, but that can bear singing to a crowd hungry for entertainment.

Among the devoted admirers of the *Deutsche Chansons* was the twenty-
six-year-old Arnold Schoenberg, unknown and unpublished (although
Verklärte Nacht was already behind him). In short order he concocted
musical settings for three of the "chansons," including Bierbaum's
"Gigerlette":

Fräulein Gigerlette
Invited me to tea
Her attire
Matched the snow's purity.
Just like Pierrette
Was she all decked out.
Even a monk, I'd bet,
Would covet Gigerlette
Never having doubt.

(Stein, p. 2.)

This erotic Pierrette is surely the sunny sister of Frank Wedekind's
Lulu, the "wild and true and beautiful beast . . . created to stir up great
disaster, to lure, seduce, and poison." (For a discussion of Wedekind,
see Chapter 2.) Lulu is introduced by the Animal Trainer as a "snake"
in his "little zoo" in the circuslike Prologue to *Erdgeist*, but she first appears there and in the play proper in the costume of Pierrot. Schwarz,
the infatuated painter of her portrait in this guise, says, "Her whole body

was in such harmony with that impossible costume it seemed she had been born in it." (Wedekind, pp. 30–34.) In creating his great *Lulu* out of this play and *Die Büchse der Pandora,* Alban Berg was forced to reduce the text by some eighty percent, but he preserved the opening image of Lulu the Pierrot. Like his master Schoenberg, though in a later and very different time (the opera was unfinished at his death in 1935), Berg shared Wedekind's attraction to popular entertainment and the circus. Stuckenschmidt has noted that even the dark final scene of Berg's great first opera, *Wozzeck,* shows this: The children playing in front of the house of the just-murdered Marie sing a song that begins with the words *"Ringel, ringel, Rosenkranz,"* which are the words of the opening of the Bierbaum/*Überbrettl Happy Bridegroom.* (Stuckenschmidt, p. 54.) They were added to Büchner's play text by Berg himself.

Wedekind appears, naturally, in the *Deutsche Chansons,* and he was one of the contributors whom Schoenberg already admired, along with Dehmel and Liliencron, poets he had already mined for songs before his own *Brettl-Lieder,* his name for the eight songs he composed in this cabaret style. In the years around the turn of the century, Schoenberg struggled to earn a living chiefly by orchestrating and copying out the parts of other people's operettas. It is estimated that he churned out some six thousand pages of scores in this occupation, and while one could forgivably assume that this would kill any affection for the form, especially in so "serious" a soul as Schoenberg, in fact it only increased what was already a considerable intimacy with the operetta. As an adolescent he had composed a few pieces for friends in this style; the Viennese waltz and other dance forms make important appearances in his "serious" music; and well into his career he was not above making careful and skillful transcriptions for chamber ensemble of Strauss waltzes, among them "Roses from the South" and the "Emperor Waltz" (1925), the latter arranged specifically to be performed after *Pierrot Lunaire* during a Spanish concert tour with the Pierrot ensemble.

Thus, Schoenberg's friendship with fellow Viennese Oscar Straus, composer for Wolzogen's company and then creator of the *Waltz Dream* (1907) and countless other Viennese bonbons, was not as incongruous as it might appear. It was Straus who brought Schoenberg into the *Überbrettl* company, first as a last-minute replacement for himself, then as a regular conductor. He joined the company in December of 1901 and stayed with it until 1903. This intensive exposure to the atmosphere of popular entertainment and the *Brettl* style contrasted sharply with his "real" work at the time. The money he earned in Wolzogen's company enabled him to finish his big, luxuriantly romantic symphonic poem *Pelleas und Melisande* (1903) and to make a serious start on the decade-long struggle to complete the orchestration of the epic *Gurre-Lieder*. There is certainly little in the way of light entertainment in the revolutionary works of this first decade of the century—although "Ach, Du Lieber Augustin" does make an appearance in the great Opus 10 String Quartet of 1907, and its presence is "not ironical—a real emotional significance," Schoenberg claimed. (Lessem, p. 22.) Still, the images and patterns of light theatrical entertainment, of the gay and sophisticated life on (or close to) the "boards," the *Brettl*, were undergoing a vital gestation.

Like so many other laborers in the vineyards of early modernism, Schoenberg was principally engaged in digesting, transmuting, and at the same time revolting against Wagner and the legacy of symbolism. The ghost of the master haunts his early works. The choice and treatment of subjects in *Pelleas* and the *Gurre-Lieder* reflect the influence of late, love-death romanticism in ways akin to the art of the symbolists who flourished in the shadow of the institutionalized *ennui* of the Paris of the third Napoleon and the Second Republic. In this sense, the serious work of the young composer, as well as his operetta-cabaret breadwinning, drew upon the same world that had produced the Watteau commedia of Paul Verlaine's *Fêtes galantes* and the Pierrot poet Laforgue, and the circus and cabaret that had attracted Wedekind.

One of the minor figures who chose the exquisitely sensitive Pierrot as his subject was the Belgian Albert Giraud, a member of La Jeune Belgique, led by progressive symbolists Max Waller and Emile Verhaeren. In 1884 he published a collection of fifty poems, redolent with already overfamiliar decadent images and the refined, narcissist longings and ironies of Pierrot. The derivative nature of the verses and their flat and labored rhythms prevented their success much beyond the Jeune Belgique, but they attracted the attention of Otto Erich Hartleben, friend of Dehmel and associate of the Wolzogen circle, dilettante cabaret poet and *littérateur*, who translated them very freely into German in 1892 and recited them with much success to cabaret audiences. Hartleben's liberties were apparently all to the good, injecting a lighter perfume and a quieter, wittier irony. It has been said (Lessem, p. 124.) that Hartleben transformed Pierrot into the clown familiar in German romanticism, but this overstates the case. Layers of irony and reflection conceal and reveal this creature:

> Horse-doctor of souls,
> Snowman of lyrics,

Moon's maharajah,
Pierrot . . .

("Prayer to Pierrot," in Perle.)

They put him at a considerable remove from the Fasching prankster of
the earlier time, however lovelorn he may have been.

In 1912 a Frau Dr. Albertine Zehme proposed to commission
Schoenberg to compose a cycle of recitations on the Giraud-Hartleben
poems. After hearing the proposal, Schoenberg wrote in his diary:

Have read the preface, looked at the poems, am enthusiastic. A marvellous
idea, quite right for me. Would do it even without a fee.

(Stuckenschmidt, p. 195.)

The poems have much in them to attract both the late romantic symbolist and the *Brettl* entertainer in Schoenberg, and Frau Zehme was
herself a fascinating product of the culture which contained both of the
strains. She was a Viennese actress in her fifties when she met
Schoenberg. She had studied with Cosima Wagner at Bayreuth, and she
had enjoyed great successes in such roles as Desdemona, chiefly at the
Leipzig Stadttheater. She gave up her career to marry the lawyer Felix
Zehme, who achieved large fame and wealth for his part in a comic
opera–style scandal around 1900. (The Saxon Crown Princess Louise
had fallen in love with the young Enrico Toselli, a popular violinist and
composer—his "Serenade" is a once-ubiquitous salon piece—and it was
only through the machinations of lawyer Zehme that her most royal and
Catholic marriage was dissolved in Rome. His triumph and subsequent
success allowed Zehme to build the palatial Villa Albertine for his wife.)
Albertine Zehme returned to the stage in 1904, still in Leipzig, with
the major Ibsen roles and then as a proponent of the melodrama, a form
of theater piece in which a narrator speaks/acts a script with musical
accompaniment. The melodrama enjoyed a considerable vogue in
Germany and France around this time.

Albertine Zehme was a singer as well as an actress (she had studied
the parts of Venus in *Tannhäuser* and the Brünnhildes at Bayreuth), and
she had performed some of the *Pierrot Lunaire* settings by another composer, Otto Vrieslander, who wrote them in 1904. In 1908 she performed successful recitations of romantic poetry to the music of Chopin
and Liszt, and her peculiar combination of talents, interests, and dramatic presence must have influenced Schoenberg greatly in his creation
of "a new kind of expression," as he called it in his diary:

The sounds become an almost too animal and immediate expression of sensual and spiritual emotions. Almost as if everything was translated directly. I am curious to see how it goes on.

(*Ibid.*, p. 198.)

"Sensual and spiritual" are terms as appropriate as they are paradoxical, not only to the song cycle but to the image of Pierrot hovering about it. And Schoenberg responded to the artificial formal sophistication of poems with his own formal manipulation. He chose twenty-one of the poems to correspond to the opus number he intended to assign to the work. The *Dreimal sieben Gedichte* comprising Opus 21 conjure up a dream world of commedic images and "decadent yearnings, guilts, delights, and fears." They are, of course, both familiar and utterly new, and there has been a critical tradition of ignoring "this show of sentimental puppets," as Carl Engel called the lyrics (Lessem, p. 125.), and concentrating upon the music.

Stravinsky was present at an early performance of the work. He remembered it as "the great event in my life then," speculating that his enthusiasm was the reason for Debussy's letter to a friend expressing the fear that "Stravinsky is inclining dangerously *du côté de* Schoenberg." (Stravinsky, *Expositions*, p. 78.) But Stravinsky's enthusiasm did not embrace Schoenberg's commedia:

Albertine Zehme, the *Sprechstimme* artist, wore a Pierrot costume and accompanied her epiglottal sounds with a small amount of pantomime. I remember that and the fact that the musicians were seated behind a curtain, but I was too occupied with the copy of the score Schoenberg had given me to notice anything else. I also remember that the audience was quiet and attentive and that I wanted Frau Zehme to be quiet too, so that I could hear the *music*. Diaghilev and I were equally impressed with Pierrot, though he dubbed it a product of the *Jugendstil* movement, aesthetically.

(Stravinsky, *Dialogues*, p. 53.)

Diaghilev had arranged a meeting between himself, Stravinsky, and Schoenberg at that time—they also attended a performance of *Petrushka* together—because he wanted to commission Schoenberg (nothing came of the intention, it turned out). His and Stravinsky's distaste for *Jugendstil*, the ornamental aestheticism of the German art nouveau that they saw in *Pierrot*, may seem ironic in light of the perfumed splendor of Diaghilev's productions, but this is actually expressive of important differences in the two composers' attraction to commedia. Stravinsky's Pierrot, his

Petrushka, has his dreams, but he is not a creature of dreams. As we shall see, Stravinsky's commedia is of the dance and daylight; Schoenberg's expressionism is often a thing of moonlight and shadows.

Alan Lessem has offered a detailed and often compelling argument for the modernism of Schoenberg's approach to the commedia, including a detailed structural and thematic analysis of the methods by which the composer both underlines and sets in an ironic framework the poetic texts. He demonstrates that Schoenberg mimics "the play of surface qualities and stylistic mannerisms drawn from the musical traditions of the past" (Lessem, p. 126.):

Familiar or all-too-familiar idioms, procedures, genres and forms, so irrevocably an aspect of the *déjà vu,* are as intrinsic to the work as is the sense of their incongruity. The subject of absurd stylistic exaggeration or, conversely, allusive understatement, they are recomposed in such a way as to become witness to their own disintegration. Pierrot does go back, finally, to "die liebe Welt," rejoicing in his anticipation of pleasures too long despised; yet the composer cannot join the clown, for his conscience . . . had denied him a too easy earthly happiness.

(*Ibid.,* p. 163.)

This is useful because it offers a way of contrasting Schoenberg's ironic, disintegrative recomposition of his chosen commedia themes with Stravinsky's neoclassic renovation of his commedia in *Pulcinella,* which is often witty, even broadly humorous, as in the original Italian comedy, but never ironic about its sources. But if Schoenberg is operating at some ironic distance from his Pierrot, his Columbine, the moon-drunk poet and their moonbeams, the separation was not nearly so sustained as Lessem suggests. Schoenberg once described the basis of the original conception as "a light, ironic, and satirical tone" (Reich, p. 74.), but neither in the work's performance indications nor in the 1940 recording led by the composer himself, does this tone emerge as self-alienating. It is rather the soft-contoured, self-absorbed irony of Pierrot:

> Pierrot, with waxen complexion,
> Stands musing, and thinks: How shall I today make up?
> He shoves aside rouge and the Oriental green,
> And he daubs his face in dignified style
> With moonbeams so weird and fantastic.

These lines, from the third song of the first group of seven, "Der Dandy," present "the taciturn dandy from Bergamo" in vaulting, sliding con-

tours, by turns ecstatic and coy, the voice accompanied in a richly inventive counterpoint by piccolo and clarinet as well as piano. And the
voice, that famous *Sprechstimme,* both radically new and yet immediately expressive, somehow descended from the *diseuse* of the melodrama
and the café, sings-speaks with lush tones and with whispers by insin-
uating *portamenti* that create a fascination stronger than any parody.
Schoenberg's instructions for his "speech melody" are precise (although
they have left a rich legacy of controversy and performance problems).
The performer is to be "well aware of the distinction between *singing
tone* and *speaking tone:* singing tone maintains the pitch . . . speaking
tone does, certainly, announce it, only to quit it again immediately, in
either a downward or an upward direction." (*Ibid.,* p. 76.)

In "Der Mondfleck," from the last of the three groups, Pierrot is
suddenly disturbed by something on his clothes; he turns about and discovers a spot of white on his back. Thinking it a spot of plaster, he tries
to remove it:

> Whisks and whisks, yet he cannot remove it.
> So he goes on, full of spleen and fury,
> Rubs and rubs until the early morning
> A spot of white, of shining moonlight.

> (Perle.)

The voice, with piano, piccolo, clarinet, violin, and cello, rushes *pian-
issimo* at a light but furious pace, grows loud with the desperation of the
futile rubbing, then dies away on "of shining moonlight" (*des hellen
Mondes,* literally "the bright moon") as the early morning meets the
moonlight. And the whole of this brief, magical piece of music is constructed upon a mirror principle, a retrograde canon with four of the
instruments, linked in pairs, going forward to the point at which Pierrot
twists around and sees the spot, and then following their lines backward. This artificial, brilliant display of polyphony imbedded in a new
tonal language is a good example of what so enthralled Stravinsky the
modernist, but that artistic success is in part rooted in the composer's
identification, even momentary, and not free of irony, with the images
and gestures of his Pierrot.

The program book for the first performance of *Pierrot Lunaire* contained the texts of the poems preceded by a quotation from the mystical, intensely subjective pre-Romantic German poet Novalis:

One can imagine tales where there would be no coherence, and yet associations—like dreams; poems that are simply euphonious and full of beautiful words,

but with no meaning or coherence whatever. . . . Such true poesy can have, at most, an allegorical meaning, as a whole, and an indirect effect, like music.

(Reich, p. 78.)

This is prophetic, encompassing the whole repertoire of the century that rediscovered, among other things, "the crystal sighing from the old Italian pantomime." (Schoenberg, "Pierrot Lunaire," No. 15: "Homesickness.") But in this context it is also a particular expression of the aesthetic nature of the commedia heritage shared by the composer and the actress. It may have been the last great gasp (or sigh) of that symbolist clown, but his spirit was preserved alive inside the new music that had been made for him.

Stravinsky and Pierrot

Stravinsky set to work on his principal commedia, *Petrushka,* shortly after the brilliant first success of *The Firebird,* in June of 1910, and with *The Rite of Spring* already seething within him. Still, with the revolution aborning in him as surely as in Schoenberg, Stravinsky began *Petrushka* with an explicitly romantic notion:

My first idea for *Petrushka* was to compose a *Konzertstück,* a sort of combat between the piano and the orchestra. . . . In that first vision I saw a man in evening dress, with long hair; the musician or the poet of romantic tradition. He placed several heteroclite objects on the keyboard and rolled them up and down. At this the orchestra exploded with the most vehement protestations— hammer blows, in fact.

(Vera Stravinsky, p. 66.)

When the idea matured, and Diaghilev had indicated his determination to have a new ballet from his new discovery for his 1911 season, the character of the work changed:

For me the piece had the character of a burlesque for piano and orchestra, each with an equal role . . . the real subject was the droll, ugly, sentimental, shifting personage who was always in an explosion of revolt . . . a sort of guignol called Pierrot in France, Kasperle in Germany, and Petrushka in Russia. . . . I began to meditate an entire poem in the form of choreographic scenes . . . of the mysterious life of Petrushka, his birth, his death, his double existence— which is the key to the enigma, a key not possessed by the one who believes that he has given him life, the Magician.

(*Op. cit.*)

In his *Chronicle* (White, *Stravinsky*, p. 256.) Stravinsky put less of the brash *guignol* into his description: "The eternal and unhappy hero of every fairground." Although the final version of the character exhibits a good deal of fiery energy, it is this latter, more romantic image that prevails. In either case, it is clear that Stravinsky's commedia is something quite different from Schoenberg's moonstruck descendant of Watteau's troupers. It is equally clear, however, that they do have some elements characteristic of the modern commedia in common. Most important is the presence of the music and atmosphere of popular entertainment. In Stravinsky, unlike Schoenberg, this melodic presence is more than a matter of allusions and distortions; it is literal. When he dipped into Vienna's past, it was to quote two Joseph Lanner waltz tunes directly; an opportune hearing of a hurdy-gurdy led to the introduction of its melody, a French *chanson*, into the First Tableau (as it turned out, this popular tune had a composer who later demanded and got royalties from Stravinsky). There are a number of Russian folksongs woven into the score, but their presence reflects this same desire to project a popular, carnival-like atmosphere, rather than any Bartok-like devotion to folk roots:

I was not attracted by any folklore element in *Petrushka*, always being tempted, in the life of things, by something very different from that.

(Vera Stravinsky, p. 66.)

This is the tone of a commedia modernist, dismissing the earnest, concentrated search beneath the layers of cultural sophistication but embracing the totality of popular life that is rooted beneath those layers. In December 1910, he wrote to Andrey Rimsky-Korsakov, the son of his teacher, Nikolay:

My last trip to Petersburg did me much good, and the final scene is shaping up excitingly . . . quick tempos, concertinas, major keys . . . smells of Russian food—*shchi*—and of sweat and glistening leather boots.

(*Ibid.*, p. 67.)

This is the Russia of the St. Petersburg *bon vivant*, not the cossack or the peasant. But the Petrushka of the fairs and the people was certainly the common childhood experience of the collaborators, Diaghilev, Fokine, Nijinsky, and Benois. It was Stravinsky who suggested that Petrushka was the subject of his "burlesque" for piano and orchestra, but once proposed, the puppet was common property. The commedia patterns in *Petrushka* are revealed most fully in light of the ballet aspect of the work (see Chapter 3), particularly as reflected in the art of Nijinsky and his relationship with Diaghilev. Stravinsky, however, was deeply involved in the dance and theatrical aspect of the collaboration. As Benois remembered, "One of the binding links between us, besides music, was Stravinsky's cult of the theatre and his interest in the plastic arts. . . . Discussion with him was very valuable to us, for he 'reacted' to everything for which we lived." (White, *Stravinsky*, p. 17.) Benois had been particularly devoted to puppet theater throughout his life; Nijinsky had played at being the fairground Petrushka with great intensity as a child. (Nijinska, pp. 33–34.) The primary impetus, the music, was conceived in commedic imagery with the same feeling of cultural ownership that went into Benois's scenario and painting of commedia and Nijinsky's dancing of his role within it.

In another version of the work's gestation, in his *Chronicle*, Stravinsky described something of the direct translation of that imagery into music:

I had in my mind a distinct picture of a puppet, suddenly endowed with life, exasperating the patience of the orchestra with diabolical cascades of *arpeggi.* The orchestra in turn retaliates with menacing trumpet-blasts. The outcome is a terrific noise which reaches its climax and ends in the sorrowful and querulous collapse of the poor puppet.

(White, *Stravinsky*, p. 156.)

This piano-orchestra episode eventually became the Second Tableau of four, its original title, "Petrushka's Cry," changed to the simple "In Petrushka's Cell." The fact that this scene was about a puppet before it was about *the* puppet is significant, because the puppet nature of this manifestation of Pierrot is essential to his human dimension in ways not shared by the Pierrot of Laforgue and Giraud. This puppet nature was, of course, central to Nijinsky's unequaled realization of the character— unequaled because, as Cyril Beaumont put it, "He suggested a puppet that sometimes aped a human being, whereas all the other interpreters conveyed a dancer imitating a puppet." (Hamm, p. 191.) This puppet is signified in the music most clearly by that "Petrushka chord," the superimposition (in various inversions) of C-major and F-sharp-major triads, a major white-key chord coupled with the major black-key chord, sounds that clash most expressively, separated as they are by a diminished fifth, the tritone, the anciently troubling *diabolus in musica.*

There is a natural emphasis upon the aspect of the suffering, trapped soul in Petrushka, helped along no doubt by the original Showman-Diaghilev, Petrushka-Nijinsky parallels. They inevitably result in a more

Pierrot-like Petrushka, certainly much more than human puppet. Edith Sitwell summons up Laforgue and the fate of the artist in her peroration on Petrushka's humanity: "the anguished beat of the clown's heart as he makes his endless battle against materialism," the clown, who, after his death, represents "our own poor wisp of a soul that is weeping so pitifully to us from the top of the booth." (*Ibid.*, p. 189.) But Petrushka is not weeping from the top of the booth; he is, on the contrary, triumphantly mocking the crowd and frightening the Showman-magician. There is certainly much room for commedia artist Sitwell's vision of the commedia artist in Petrushka, but Stravinsky was not so prey to easy sentiment as to cry out for pity for the poor clown.

For Stravinsky, who was after all coauthor of the scenario with Benois, brash defiance was far too important an element of Petrushka to be dissolved in the end by tears. The immortal laughter of the puppet-man at the expense of the human hypocrites, bullies, and fools who preside over his demise changes its essential tone. Stravinsky saw his Petrushka chord not as a divided, ambiguous thing, but as an expression of that mocking laughter:

The resurrection of Petroushka's ghost was my idea, not Benois's. I had conceived of the music in two keys in the second tableau as Petroushka's insult to the public, and I wanted the dialogue for trumpets in two keys at the end to show that his ghost is still insulting the public. I was, and am, more proud of these last pages than of anything else in the score.

(Stravinsky, *Expositions*, p. 156.)

This is from 1962. In 1958, he had expressed this in another, but consistent set of images:

The "ghost" at the end is the real Petrushka . . . the character in the [preceding] play only a doll. The "ghost's" gesture is . . . not so much one of triumph as a nose-thumbing to the magician.

(Vera Stravinsky, p. 67.)

Neither easy triumphs nor easy tears. The music is infinitely various, colorful, and responsive to the characters and action. It can indeed yearn, struggle, and die with Petrushka, just as it can swagger and can kill with the Blackamoor, flirt and sing pretty, inane melodies with the Ballerina, command and mock with the Showman. But for all the warmth and intensity of each succeeding passage, the work as a whole is held together in emotional equipoise by a sure, restless forward momentum. In the words of the perceptive and sharp-eared H. T. Parker, writing in Boston in 1916, this is music "that can summon and maintain the illusion of a puppet tragedy in all its grotesque externals and all its inner ironies." (Hamm, p. 197.) The equipoise is that of *puppet* tragedy, essentially conditioned by the masks, the dance, the puppet nature of the hero—the quintessential commedia tragedy of the modernist. It is tragedy because the love and the death are made real musically and dramatically; it is commedia because, again musically and dramatically, the actions and the suffering are puppet actions and suffering—and puppet-like, Petrushka lives again. But, of course, his resurrection is more than a matter of restuffing the sawdust—it is a frightening, mocking revival of the spirit, the "real Petrushka," transcending both his human and his puppet fate. In this he gives the lie both to the Showman and to the tragedy.

The final brash independence of Petrushka represents an important difference in stance between Stravinsky's commedia and that of the Romantic fascination with the puppet theater. For E. T. A. Hoffmann and Richard Wagner, it is the puppet master himself who is the object of that fascination. Wagner saw in the Kasperltheater, the puppet theater of the markets and carnivals, that the Showman is no deluded pretender to power, but the master of the *Gesammtkunstwerk*, the total work of art. The puppet master is improvising poet, theater director, and actor all in one. Kasperl is given life by the Showman; he cannot transcend him. This focusing of power remains important in the theater of Appia, of Gordon Craig (as in his theory of the actor replaced by *Übermarionette*), in the work of Meyerhold, in the role, and attitude, of the ballet master, and in the world which Diaghilev created about him. But in *Petrushka*, great product of that world, at the specific insistence of Stravinsky, that power is mocked. Like Picasso, Stravinsky was an artist of enormous self-sufficiency; like him, he could be the perfect autocrat about his art, and in it he expressed and radiated great power. But neither had the remotest interest in gathering disciples, even pupils. *Petrushka* is no cry for freedom—the puppet loves, dies, and jeers; he does not lead a revolution—but he does, for the space of one Shrovetide carnival day, make an illusion stronger than any bondage. Again like Picasso, Stravinsky celebrated the stuff of the illusion, the forms, dances, puppets, masks; to reveal it as illusion was to express the essence of art, not to undermine it.

Stravinsky's Other Commedia

The world of illusion, the spectacle of gilt and masks, processions and rituals, circuses and festival events, provided the locus of dramatic imagination for much of Stravinsky's work in the first decades of the century. In 1930, in his first book on Stravinsky, published by the Woolfs, Eric Walter White could make the parallel with Picasso and his subject, drawing on milestones in Stravinsky's development:

A similar love of fairs, with their temporary stages and puppet shows, is shown early by Stravinsky in his *Petrushka*, and traces of it occur later in *Renard*, *The Soldier's Tale*, *Pulcinella* and *The Fairy's Kiss*.

(White, *Stravinsky's Sacrifice*, p. 78.)

In many vital respects Stravinsky put the fair and the commedia to very different uses from those of Picasso—certainly there is nothing parallel to the persistent identification of the Spaniard with Harlequin—but it is still true that in Stravinsky as well as Picasso it is possible to range widely among his works and find the images and techniques of commedia used with an intensity of purpose that belies the argument that they are present merely as bright decorations, just as the common observation that harlequins lend themselves to cubism is scarcely sufficient to account for Picasso's continued fascination.

Referring to White's short list, *Renard* was written in 1915 for the Princesse de Polignac, the Singer Sewing Machine heiress. *Renard* is based upon Russian folktales about the cunning fox brought to account by other animals, in this case a cat and a goat who plays a *guzla*, a one-stringed violin-like folk instrument. But once again, this is not folk-rooted music; it is music of lightly sophisticated formality, even in the guise of what the composer called a "barnyard fable":

I planned the staging myself, and always with the consideration that *Renard* should not be confounded with opera. The players are to be dancing acrobats, and the singers are not to be identified with them.

(Stravinsky, *Expositions*, pp. 138–39.)

The short opera, *The Nightingale*, begun in 1908, the year before *Firebird*, and finally completed in 1914 after a number of delays and false turns, was another Benois-Diaghilev collaboration. It used a similar arrangement of offstage performers and onstage miming dancers; it is not literally commedia, but the abundant chinoiserie in the music and the drama, the brilliant artificiality of the Emperor's court, and elaborate dance rituals (especially as realized in Meyerhold's production) all retain that sense of framed illusion that is central to Stravinsky's commedia. Like another of the works of White's list, *The Fairy's Kiss*, written in 1928 for Ida Rubinstein in homage to Tchaikovsky, it is based on Hans Christian Andersen. The childhood feeling for the marvelous seems to have been essential to the grown-up composer's projection of these beautifully organized illusions. Indeed, his memory of that childhood feeling links the fairy-tale ballets and the puppet ballet with the same place:

St. Petersburg was also a city of large, open piazzas. One of these, the Champs de Mars, might have been the scene of *Petroushka*. The Mardi Gras festivities were centered there, and as puppet shows were part of the carnival entertainment, it was there that I saw my first *Petroushka*. . . . The whole populace came there to sleigh, but a more beautiful spectacle was that of sleighs drawn by elks. These elegant creatures were brought to the city in carnival season by Finnish peasants, who used them to sell rides. They were part of a realistic fairy-tale world whose lost beauty I have tried to rediscover later in life, especially in Hans Christian Andersen.

(*Ibid.*, p. 35.)

Stravinsky did not intend to recreate childhood experience; as in his use of folk material, he subjected his material to elaborate translation. Even the great "Russian" masterpiece of that translation process, *Les Noces,* was conceived and to a degree carried out as work in which the folk wedding elements fit visibly into a commedia framework. In his *Chronicle* the composer was quite explicit about this:

It was not my intention to reproduce the ritual of peasant weddings, and I paid little heed to ethnological considerations. . . . I took my inspiration from those customs, but reserved to myself the right to use them with absolute freedom. I wanted all my instrumental apparatus to be visible side by side with the actors or dancers . . . I wished to place the orchestra on the stage itself, letting the actors move on the space remaining free. The fact that the actors would wear uniform Russian-style costumes while the musicians would be in evening dress not only did not embarrass me, but, on the contrary, was perfectly in keeping with my idea of a *divertissement* of the masquerade type.

(White, *Stravinsky,* pp. 220–21.)

This conception is strikingly similar to the exploitation of jostling styles in explicitly *divertissement* fashion—and explicitly commedia—in the Strauss-Hofmannsthal *Ariadne auf Naxos* of 1912.

It is easy to survey the dramatic works and find the patterns and techniques which underline, even celebrate, the illusion, the artistic framework. They are present in important ways in *The Soldier's Tale* (1918), with its imitations of jazz, its deliberately small stage, and use of acting and dancing; they are vital to the neoclassic "fable" of 1951, the Stravinsky-Auden *Rake's Progress*. Of the many other works, early and late, to which this applies, one short nondramatic opus is of interest: *The Three Pieces for String Quartet* (1914). These are short, pungent movements, the second of which acquired the title "Eccentric" in its orchestral guise.

This movement was actually inspired by an outward event, indeed by the same unique commedia/vaudeville artist who so attracted Nijinsky:

I had been fascinated by the movements of Little Tich, whom I had seen in London in 1914, and the jerky, spastic movement, the ups and downs, the rhythm—even the mood or joke of the music—which I later called *Eccentric*, was suggested by the art of this great clown.

(Stravinsky, Memories, p. 89.)

He saw these pieces as looking ahead to his *Three Easy Pieces* for piano duet, of the following year, and to "my so aberrant 'neoclassicism.'" Those Easy Pieces have the commedia stamp on them in their air of light popularity. The *Polka*, the last of them, was dedicated to Diaghilev, and Stravinsky told him that in composing it he had imagined him as a "ring-master in evening dress and top-hat, cracking his whip and urging on a rider on horseback." (White, *Stravinsky*, pp. 199–200.) Stravinsky also recounts that Diaghilev was at first put out by this image, before giving in to laughter. It is certainly a picture that could have offended the great ringmaster of modernism. In 1942 Stravinsky returned to this circus theme with a similar approach when a commission came his way via Balanchine from the Barnum and Bailey Circus. The choreographer had been called upon to construct a ballet for elephants; Stravinsky agreed to write the music with the understanding that he was doing it for "very young" elephants. Despite the fact that the beasts were apparently troubled and even frightened by Stravinsky's nonstandard (for elephants) rhythms, the act enjoyed a run of some 425 performances. (*Ibid.*, p. 375.)

A small and curious demonstration of the connection between these vaudeville and circus images and their commedia roots is recorded in Amy Lowell's response to a performance of the string quartet pieces, which she heard not long after their premiere performance under the title "Grotesques." In a poem attempting to translate the experience of the music into the sounds and movement of poetry, and possibly given clues by some now-lost program notes, she managed to convert the Little Tich movement into something resembling *Pierrot Lunaire*:

Pale violin music whiffs across the moon,
. . . .
Cherry petals fall and flutter,
And the white Pierrot,
Wreathed in the smoke of the violins,
. . . .
Claws a grave for himself in the fresh earth
With his fingernails.

Like Picasso (and nearly everyone else growing into modernism out of the late romantic heritage), Stravinsky's commedia was essentially this collection of characters and patterns filtered through the circus and the puppet show and (to a much lesser extent than Schoenberg) the Watteau line through the symbolists. However, also like Picasso, and for the same occasion, he turned once, very importantly, to the original Italian product.

Pulcinella

The idea that eventually bore fruit in *Pulcinella* originated with Diaghilev, who was himself inspired to reach back to the preromantic commedia by an earlier success along this line. Massine's first ballet, *The Good-Humored Ladies*, had premiered in 1917 and was an enormous success. The action was based upon a Goldoni love-intrigue-at-carnival-time comedy, set to the harpsichord works of Domenico Scarlatti orchestrated with an impeccable sense of lightness and restraint by the Roman composer, Vincenzo Tommasini. The rediscovery of the musical riches of the baroque and even earlier eras was very much in the air at this time. The principal crusaders, people like the Dolmetsches, Schweitzer, and Landowska, breathed a very different air from that of the Diaghilev circle. One would look in vain for Pierrot and Columbine in the personalities of Albert Schweitzer and Wanda Landowska, but their performances and editorial labors attracted much attention.

Although driven by passions other than those motivating these apostles of purity and original instruments, Diaghilev was himself extremely good at creative cultural exhumation, as he had demonstrated in his great portrait exhibition and other labors for Russian art in his early career. He showed this ability again, by searching in a number of libraries and conservatories for forgotten masterpieces. It is not clear how much of the material he turned up was actually unpublished (all the music finally used in *Pulcinella* came from published sources) but he did exercise his characteristically superb taste in selecting it and was very effective in making a case for Pergolesi—or what was thought at the time to be Pergolesi: many of the works once attributed to this short-lived (1710–1736) Neapolitan genius have in the intervening decades been shown to be the work of largely anonymous others. Diaghilev's efforts also paid off for the good name of the excellent Venetian Domenico Cimarosa, whose opera *Le astuzie femminili* he successfully revived in 1920 in Paris and London, and music from which he presented as a "ballet divertissement" *Cimarosiana*, by Massine, in 1924. The Cimarosa is genuine Cimarosa, while the Pergolesi of *Pulcinella* is a mixture of the genuine, the dubious, and the fake—all, however, truly old, and beautiful.

Diaghilev presented his Pergolesi manuscripts to Stravinsky partly with the intention of luring him back into the fold with an attractive new project. There had been a minor rupture between the composer and the entrepreneur, caused in part by wartime separation and by the unforgivably large success of *The Soldier's Tale*, a project in which the ever-jealous Diaghilev had no part. According to Stravinsky, he agreed to look at Diaghilev's proffered "delightful eighteenth-century music" with skepticism, but "I looked, and fell in love." (Stravinsky, *Expositions*, p. 127.) He was clearly responding as a creative musician to a new source of inspiration, a breath of fresh lyricism, rather than to anything specifically commedic. The brilliant Russian critic Boris Asaf'yev described this aspect of *Pulcinella* with perspicacious understatement in his 1929 *A Book About Stravinsky*:

Despite obvious identity of material, Stravinsky's fragrant material is neither repetitive nor slavishly imitative of Pergolesi. In *Pulcinella*, as in any genuinely contemporary work, there is economy—even asceticism—in the choice of expressive means, and a continuing attempt to speak not in the intricate schemes of abstraction but in an unaffected musical language that is melodic, alive, and heart-warming. . . . But the principal delight of *Pulcinella* lies in the fact that again (and again, moreover, by a Russian composer, following the lead of Glinka and Tchaikovsky) the beautiful plasticity of Italian melody—eternally alive, eternally fascinating—is treated with love and tenderness.

(Asaf'yev, p. 188.)

Asaf'yev (a disciple whom Stravinsky rejected utterly, mostly on the grounds of his Soviet Communist atheism, it seems) describes the legacy of Italian melody as "a kind of universal reserve—a musical 'central heating system' " for European music, and the image is useful also for this aspect of the appeal of commedia. It was the bright, energetic warmth of the original characters and plots and patterns that Diaghilev, Massine, the composer, and then Picasso sought to translate into modern thea-

ter; the effect of this older melodic warmth, even in its very recognizably "modern" guise, is quite different from either romantic commedia
or carnival/circus images through the nineteenth century. (Which may
be a reason for Picasso's difficulties in adjusting to the kind of commedia projected by his collaborators, steeped as he was in that of the circus.) The plot of the work came from the product of another Diaghilev
excavation, an old manuscript containing Pulcinella stories, dating from
1700, particularly the story, "The Four Pulcinellas." The plot was an
important consideration in Stravinsky's selection of music and its order
because, as he put it, "*Pulcinella* is more an *action dansant* than a ballet." (Stravinsky, *Expositions*, p. 127.)

That plot is a standard commedia round of love and mixed identities, with four little Pulcinellas as well as an original, a magician-double
of the original, a Pimpinella, a Dottore and assorted lovers. The only
essential commedia ingredient missing was true improvisation; it is clear
that Diaghilev was seeking a re-creation of that original commedic pattern of acrobatic complexity and jaunty emotional simplicity. This gave
him problems with his composer:

A stylish orchestration was what Diaghilev wanted, and nothing more, and my
music so shocked him that he went about for a long time with a look that
suggested The Offended Eighteenth Century.

(*Op. cit.*)

He also had to contend with a painter who insisted on being faithful to
the original only in his own modern way:

Picasso accepted the commission to design the *decors* for the same reason that
I agreed to arrange the music—for the fun of it—and Diaghilev was as shocked
with his set as he was with my sounds.

(*Ibid.*, pp. 127–28.)

Picasso's six Pulcinellas in baggy white costumes and masks do represent
a compromise from his original sketches, a move toward the original
commedia, just as Stravinsky's music in the end preserves the melodies
of the original sources quite intact and even respects the harmonies to
the important extent that they are recomposed with the original bass
very much in mind. It is the orchestration that marks the work most
vividly as Stravinsky and modern. Even there, however, where the in-
strumentation is most "modern," as in the saucy, swaggering *duetto* for
trombone and bass, the insolence and freedom of the old Harlequin is
refreshingly visible.

Pulcinella was for Picasso a masterful achievement but finally something of a detour from the main road of his creative output (a road full of turns, to be sure). His swarms of other commedia sketches and paintings from the same period are personal Picasso in ways that his Pulcinellas are not. Stravinsky, on the other hand, for all his attention to the original, made something wholly personal, wholly Stravinsky:

Pulcinella was my discovery of the past, the epiphany through which the whole of my late work became possible. It as a backward look, of course—the first of many love affairs in that direction—but it was a look in the mirror, too.

(*Ibid.*, p. 129.)

This is not to say that the composer's celebrated neoclassicism came to flower in this work. He was still struggling with the orchestration of the great "Russian" masterpiece, *Les Noces*, not to be premiered until the next year, 1921, the same year that saw the composition of *Mavra*. This is a little comic opera after Pushkin, the commedia elements of which have a strong Russian flavor, as in *Petrushka* (the handsome young hussar disguises himself as a woman, Mavra the cook, in order to gain access to his beloved; he is unmasked when he is caught in the act of shaving). *Pulcinella* may have set its composer on the path of neoclassicism, but the truly neoclassic works to come were not founded on the impulse (and commission) to "recompose" but were intentionally original works that drew on the forms and techniques of the baroque. The sound and "feel" of this literal commedia are different, as important as it was to Stravinsky's neoclassicism. It is a vital commedia re-creation, a very personal homage of a very sophisticated modernist to the roots of commedia.

The place of *Pulcinella* in the modernist return to these roots is different just because it was a return, for all the transformations wrought by Stravinsky and Picasso; it was this difference that was captured by Boris Kochno's remark, "With *Pulcinella* comedy returned to Europe." (*Stravinsky and the Dance*, p. 47.) Indeed, the only "scandal" occasioned by this work in its (extremely successful) early performances in 1920 came directly out of the old comedy and related to the modern context only in the inability of the modern audience to accept the touch of scatological vulgarity that was part of that older comic repertoire. At opening night in London, when the commedia women rejected their suitors by dumping sand from chamber pots onto them from a balcony, the consternation expressed by the audience was such that the chamber pots were replaced with plain pitchers by the next performance. The forms of the past could be threatening as well as reassuring.

Busoni

There is a pleasant anecdote in which the Shah of Persia, during a visit to foggy London, was asked whether it was true that they prayed to the sun in his country. The Shah is said to have replied: "If you knew the sun you would also pray to it." Stravinsky told me once, through a third person, that he found it strange to hear that I admired the German classical composers. Whereupon I commissioned the third person to reply to Stravinsky that if he knew the classical composers he would also value them.

(Busoni, p. 26.)

Ferruccio Busoni was for the most part distrustful of the man he once described as "the Russian acrobat of sound" (*Ibid.*, p. 42.), although he was open enough to overcome his hostility to his art when it touched him, as in his response to *The Soldier's Tale*, "One had become a child again; one forgot music and literature, one was simply moved." (White, *Stravinsky*, p. 65.)

Busoni, the great all-encompassing virtuoso, teacher, theorist, and seeker after his own form of modernism, was a neoclassicist long before Stravinsky, in fact, the only composer who deserved the name before Stravinsky. In the above exchange he is rather too hard on Stravinsky, who did know and love "German classical composers," but his remark does underline the difference in their commitment to the past. Busoni was not a commedia personality, not a commedia modernist, not even, except as a theorist, a modernist when set beside Stravinsky. His neo-classicism was as serious as his formalist personality; in his search for modern transformations of classic proportions, harmonies, and counterpoint, he managed to find a remarkably personal, transparent texture and an oddly expressive voice, never to be confused with the creations of the rearguard. And in *Arlecchino* he created a modern commedia that is, in these terms, an almost perfect work of art.

Busoni's sense of classical proportion was one of the constants in a complex, paradoxical nature: "I am a worshipper of Form! I have remained sufficiently a Latin for that." (Busoni, p. 18.) He liked nothing of Verdi except that perfection of comic grace that is *Falstaff*. Like Diaghilev and other more characteristic modernists, he much admired early eighteenth-century opera and the lighter Rossini, a composer much exploited in these circles, most successfully in the Rossini-Respighi revolt-in-a-toy-shop ballet *La Boutique Fantasque* (1919), by Massine for Diaghilev, and by later treatments of Rossini's many short, comic works by Respighi and by Britten.

Like Stravinsky, he cherished early memories of puppet theater, especially a *teatro mecanico* that he saw while he and his mother lived alone in Trieste. In later life he again became fascinated with this form of theater, around the time he was seeking models for viable modern dramatic form in the past, in Mozart and in early Italian comedy. According to the conductor Vittorio Gui, the idea for creating his own commedia occurred to Busoni after he attended a performance of the seventeenth-century comedy *L'Inutil precauzione* in Bologna in 1912 (Gui, p. 1.), and Busoni himself coupled this and his experience of puppet theater as dual inspiration:

I got the idea for *Arlecchino* from the masterly performance of an Italian actor (Piccello, if I remember rightly) who tried to reintroduce the old *commedia dell'arte,* and in it he spoke and played the role of my hero surpassingly well. At the same time I got to know the Roman marionette theatre and their performance of the little comic opera written by Rossini when he was twenty (*The Travelling Bag or Opportunity Makes the Thief*) left a deep impression on me. My *Theatralisches Capriccio* arose out of these two experiences. The first of them exercised an appreciable influence on the poetry, the second on the composition.

(Busoni, pp. 62–63.)

Gozzi and *Turandot*

In the early years of the century Busoni expressed his interest in the images of the commedia in another way, by taking up, as subject of a concert suite, incidental music, and then an opera, Carlo Gozzi's famous *Turandot* of 1762. Gozzi himself called his play a "tragicomical theatrical Chinese fairy tale." *Turandot,* the old tale of the ice-hearted princess who poses cruel tests to her suitors and is finally won by the exiled Calaf, was the most popular of Gozzi's works, both in its own exotic and colorful right and because of Schiller's revision and translation. Busoni disregarded Schiller's adaptation because of the German's failure to capture the original's sense of fantasy and the power of the commedia characters and masks.

Puccini and his librettists did not create their version of *Turandot* out of Schiller, either, but Puccini's last, unfinished burst of lyricism and high melodrama has much less of the feeling of the commedia in it than Gozzi or Busoni, and Puccini's own comments to a journalist on the subject of these masks indicate the difference in his approach. Speaking of the decision to replace the Venetian Masks with Ping, Pang, and Pong, he said:

There is a semicomic element in *Turandot*. Instead of our usual Masks, I have introduced Chinese masks. This exoticism will also serve to justify a task I assign to these three figures. In the opera, they represent good sense.

(Greenfield, p. 269.)

Puccini's *Turandot* is certainly not devoid of the "continuous gaily-coloured change of passion and make-believe, of reality and unreality, of the commonplace and the fantastically exotic" (Busoni, p. 61.) that Busoni so prized in Gozzi, but it really offers a much more familiar theatrical embrace in its love-overcoming-trial plot and in the full-throated romantic appeal of the music.

The Love for Three Oranges

Another major Gozzi adaptation of this same period, based on his *Fiable dell'amore delle tre melarance* of 1761, did make for more vigorous use of the commedia, but it too projected a dramatic atmosphere different from that of Busoni. In 1914 Meyerhold and his cohorts in his part of the Russian dramatic avant-garde published a scenario of the play in *Dr. Dapertutto's Journal*. The scenario, and the theatrical entertainment constructed about it, so attracted the young Serge Prokofiev that he set about making his own libretto and music, and by 1919 *The Love for Three Oranges* was completed, although it was to endure a series of delays before its premiere in Chicago in 1921. Satire and irony are strong elements in much of Prokofiev's art, often nestled beside the most glowing lyricism, and there are many scattered moments that could be regarded as indebted to the commedia (his 1915 ballet *Le Chout*, or *The Buffoon*, based on Russian folktales and taken up by Diaghilev in 1920, is a good contemporary example). This, his first opera to be staged, is, however, the one literally commedic work, with extensive use of the theatrical framing techniques of commedia as well as its characters.

It opens with crowds of Tragedians (who want tragedy, of course), Comedians (calling for comedy), Lyricists (demanding lyric drama), Empty Heads (wanting "Farces! Farces!"), and Eccentrics ("Silence! Silence!") who fight among one another until the Eccentrics manage to force them to take their places as audience in tower balconies at the side of a grand proscenium. The use of the curtain, set within this proscenium frame, has something of the multilevel quality of the *Parade* curtains. The "play" so actively witnessed and commented upon by this "audience" is an absurdity revolving around the illness ("insuperable hypochondriac condition") of the son of the King of Clubs, with plots spun by a Prime Minister and the witch Fata Morgana, and a panoply of commedia characters, the courtier Pantaloon, jester Truffaldino, a Smeraldina, even a devil, Farfarello. The music includes some of the most popular of all Prokofiev, indeed two of the segments, a Scherzo and especially a March, having long since separated themselves from the opera to become classical "hits." Although it must always be said that there is no such thing as intrinsically commedic music, this March, a blend of pomp and self-mockery, an immediately attractive melody with a whiff of exoticism and a deftly clumsy profile, is probably the closest thing to it, even thoroughly divorced as it is from its original context.

But for all its debt to the old comedy, *The Love for Three Oranges* is more an absurdist adventure/romance, heavily laced with satire. There is magic, there are princesses hidden in giant oranges, and the fantasy, faithful to Gozzi and to Meyerhold as it is, is more a modernist fairy tale than modern commedia. Still, the opera deserves its place here because it is, after the works of Stravinsky and Schoenberg, the best known and, in theatrical terms, most successful evidence of a leading modernist musician's fascination with the commedia.

Arlecchino

It is admittedly misleading to treat Busoni, in so many ways the epitome of noncommedic high seriousness, as a standard for true commitment to modern commedia. In this particular comparison with Prokofiev and with Puccini, Busoni stands with Stravinsky. This is not because Stravinsky, the very type of the commedia modernist in music, was like Busoni—as they both knew, they were utterly unlike—but because in their different ways they built their commedia into the essence of their work, rather than only into the decoration.

In Busoni it is the companion piece to his *Turandot*, premiered the same evening in 1917, that most clearly reveals this essence. *Arlecchino* fully embodies Busoni's commitment to the commedia. More than this, it is his most complete realization of his classical impulse, as well as his belief in artistic freedom that, for him, accompanied the mastery of form. As Stravinsky found *Pulcinella* to be a "look in the mirror" as well as a look into the past, Busoni put much of himself into *Arlecchino*, and in more extensive and personal ways. This is most vividly true of the title character, a speaking role. The action takes place in Bergamo, traditional home of Harlequin, and this particular Harlequin stands out in every dramatic sense, transcending that action as well as playing at the center of it, the only non-singing role:

his dress is motley and his nature bold, he loves, he fights, and laughs,
he flies and sings and is like one possessed with the devil of truth.

(Busoni, pp. 69–70.)

Arlecchino serves as master of ceremonies, delivering a prologue:

> This play is meant neither for children [nor for] gods,
> It does address itself to human understanding
> · · · · · · · · · · · · · · · ·
> Old scenes in proverbs couched are being re-enacted
> As played since ancient times on stages of all lands.
>
> A husband, though deceived, stays blind to the occurrence,
> Some rivals are at odds to win a second, a mate,
> A bloody duel is fought and followed by a sequence
> Of common gossip, talk, and local wisdom's say.
> · · · in the small the small world is reflected,
> The living truth appears as though pretense.

(Busoni, *Arlecchino*.)

The four episodes depict the hero as "the rogue," "the swordsman," "the
husband," and "the victor." In the end, his own wife Colombina elopes
with Leandro (a parody of the grand opera tenor), and Arlecchino himself is about to run off with the pretty young wife of Ser Matteo, the
Pantalone-Philistine figure (who however reads from the *Divine Comedy*
and quotes from *Don Giovanni*, both among the most cherished icons
of the high-serious Busoni). Arlecchino doffs his mask and sums it all
up with an epilogue that fulfills Busoni's claim that "the title role gives
my own confessions" (Busoni, p. 66.):

. . . Does not everything eternally repeat itself in the same circle? . . .
Who conquers? Who falls? And who in the end is right?
He who, confirmed within himself, awake in mind, lets his heart
find the straightest way to follow.
Good night, ladies and gentlemen! (this followed by a brief, lively dance per-
formed by the hero and his new lover)

Most of this opera was composed in Zurich in 1915–1917, during
the period in which Busoni deliberately refused to perform in or otherwise aid the war effort of any of the fighting countries. The declaration
of the victory of the individual who chooses to make himself free, ut-
tered by the freest and brightest of the commedia figures, aligns Busoni
with the greatest of these Harlequin artists, Picasso, who also refused
firmly to have anything to do with the war. This action is a most eloquent component of the revolt against the traditional values of man and

state that fueled the modernist revolution. The most intensely personal aspect of Busoni's commedia modernism derives from the fact that it is the work of a deeply serious, classic humanist who found himself at odds with much of what the modern world was doing in the name of the humanist traditions he himself embodied:

I have been reproached for *Arlecchino* because it is considered scornful and in-human: nevertheless, this creation arose from an impulse completely opposed to such feelings—namely, out of sympathy for men who make life harder for one another than it should and might be, through egoism, through inveterate prejudices, and through convention when it is opposed to feeling! Therefore, in *Arlecchino* one comes (and this aim is attained) only to a painful laugh. . . . After that of *The Magic Flute* (which I value highly) it is the most moral li-bretto there is.

(letter to Margarete Klinckerfuss, 1918, in Busoni, p. 66.)

Paul Feyerabend quotes this passage in part, calling it "very close to the circle of ideas expressed in Brecht's *Mother Courage*" (Dent) but free of the fetters of ideology. Claiming Busoni as the originator of the idea of "distantiation" (*Verfremdung*) so important in the theater of Brecht, Ionesco, Weiss, and others, he points to Busoni's desire that the spectator not confuse theater with reality, in Busoni's words, "lest the artistic enjoyment deteriorate into human compassion." The real goal of theatrical communication ought to be a deeper self-knowledge. Again, Feyerabend:

The spectator who participates in the conflict depicted on the stage does so in order to enrich his own petty life. . . . He savours second hand what would be dangerous to experience from close by. . . . Distantiation breaks down this process of emotional masturbation and forces the audience to think. Of course, it cannot do so without repercussions: Busoni's *Arlecchino* which quite con-sciously undercuts any possibility of self-gratification was called sadistic and in-human.

Kurt Weill

Busoni's commedia theater did anticipate the theatrical techniques of the revolutionaries of the next two decades, and *Arlecchino* was partic-ularly important to the young man who was his most famous pupil and who was to become the most successful of Brecht's collaborators, Kurt Weill. As Weill himself often said, his Berlin years as one of the dis-ciples of Busoni and his "young classicism" were decisive. Among the master's works, it was *Arlecchino* that was particularly influential. Weill's

1925 opera *Der Protagonist*, with play-within-play structure and a pan-tomime, showed his understanding of the distancing theatricality of Busoni's commedia, and his early works have more than a little of the sound of *Arlecchino* in them. But even after Weill matured and chose a different path from that of his classicist mentor, the influence of Busoni's sense of musical proportion and theatrical clarity was felt in the pungent directness of his music and, of course, in the ever-present ironic framework of Brecht/Weill theater. As one recent critic put it:

Busoni once taunted him with wishing to become "a Verdi for the poor," which he may justly be said to have become, though it is seldom recognized how much the transformation of the "advanced" idiom of the Symphony No. 1 and the Violin Concerto into the deceptive simplicity of *Mahagonny* and *Die Dreigroschenoper* owed to the *junge Klassizität* ideals of transparency and formal concision.

(Corleonis, p. 103.)

Berlin and Reinhardt

There was a lot happening in Berlin of the 1920s that in one way or another involved circus and commedia images and techniques, and it would not do to ascribe it all to the influence of Busoni and *Arlecchino*. Although in a much different phase of life than the prewar *Brettl* of Schoenberg and Wolzogen, the dance hall and cabaret were in full flower. The operettas of Lehár and Oscar Straus, as performed by the likes of Richard Tauber and Fritzi Massary, were enormously popular, and the fantasies of adventure, comedy, and coquetry which they celebrated borrowed lavishly from commedia—the saucy, kittenish Massary, queen of the operetta, was surely a Colombina for the multitudes of inflation-dizzied devotees of light entertainment; for the revolutionaries there was Lulu. Weill was only one of several creators of a different sort of people's music, related distantly to the Strauss-Lanner-descended melodies of Lehár, but more demanding, more agitated, and in service of very different theater. Hindemith was also creating this music, more "classical," never "Verdi for the poor," but at times very close, as in his little farce-with-murder, *Hin und Zurück*, based on an English revue sketch. This premiered the same year, 1927, that saw the sensational advent of Ernst Krenek's *Jonny Spielt Auf*, in which jazzman Jonny, the black hero (a startling innovation), disports himself as a triumphant Jazz Age Harlequin.

The Berlin of these years of runaway inflation and decadence was still the Berlin of Max Reinhardt, after two decades still the reigning genius of the theater, although he was being challenged by such revolutionaries as Piscator and Toller and Brecht. Reinhardt harbored a genuine interest in Weill that continued for decades. In New York in the thirties he collaborated with him on the musical-biblical epic, *The Eternal Road.*

Reinhardt did, of course, devote much creative effort to the commedia in those earlier decades, and the most enduring commedic work associated with him is in the realm of opera. In 1910 Reinhardt went to Dresden at the behest of the well-nigh distracted Hugo von Hofmannsthal and Richard Strauss in order to rescue their "comedy for music," *Der Rosenkavalier,* the immense demands of which had proven too much for the resident director. Reinhardt saved the day with a lavish and brilliant version of the Vienna of Maria Theresa, framing perfectly the gilded atmosphere of waltzes, tender sentiment, and comic intrigue created by the composer and the poet. (The not inconsiderable commedic aspect of *Rosenkavalier* itself is demonstrated indirectly by its place as a symbol for lost beauty and grace in Osbert Sitwell's novel of the early decades of the century in England, *Those Were the Days.*) The undying gratitude thus earned by Reinhardt, gratitude enhanced by the enormous and continued success of the production, inspired Hofmannsthal with the notion that he and Strauss ought to write a work especially for him.

Strauss, Hofmannsthal, Zerbinetta

The work which the poet had in mind first appears in a letter to Strauss in March 1911, with the success of *Rosenkavalier* still two months fresh. Significantly, it appears in a parenthesis, as a project of distinctly secondary importance, a sideline to a proposal to work on "something big," which after long struggle became something huge, the vast, morally ambitious *Die Frau ohne Schatten.* The unimportant "thirty minute opera . . . as good as complete in my head:

. . . is called *Ariadne auf Naxos* and is made up of a combination of heroic mythological figures in 18th-century costume with hooped skirts and ostrich feathers and, interwoven in it, characters from the commedia dell'arte; harlequins and scaramouches representing the buffoon element which is throughout interwoven with the heroic.

(Hammelmann, p. 76.)

As Busoni called his *Arlecchino* "less than a challenge and more than a jest" (Busoni, p. 68.), so the same urge to keep the stakes below those of high seriousness remain here part of the appeal of commedia, its sense of freedom. This freedom survives in the finished product as unique playfulness, unique because it rises out of, depends upon, the enormous technical sophistication of both the music and the libretto. The complexity of its plotting, added to the additional complication that it is formally a "divertissement" to follow a production of Molière's *Le Bourgeois Gentilhomme,* creates a highly visible, deliberately self-conscious theatricality. There are in effect three overlapping casts of characters; those in the Prelude are musicians and attendants and others engaged in preparations for a performance in a palatial early eighteenth-century residence; the second cast, made up of the Tenor, the Prima Donna, and other singers from the first cast, is that of the "opera," Ariadne, Bacchus, Naiad, Dryad, Echo; the third, also drawn from the first, is that of the Intermezzo, and this is the commedia group, Zerbinetta, Arlecchino, Scaramuccio, Truffaldino, Brighella.

The Prelude is devoted to bustling preparations for the theatrical event, which will ostensibly consist of the *opera seria Ariadne,* followed by the comedy. Much discussion and haggling involving the Music Master, the Composer, and the members of both casts follow. The Prima Donna calls the comedy vulgar; the beautiful coloratura playing Zerbinetta complains that the opera is boring; the Composer, though very much of the high-serious view ("Music is a holy art!") falls in love with Zerbinetta. Suddenly the Major Domo appears, accompanied by rolls from the tympani, to announce a change of plans ordered by his master: instead of one following the other, the Dance Masquerade will be played simultaneously with the Tragedy of Ariadne, the whole not to last any longer than the tragedy, "for on the stroke of nine o'clock a display of fireworks is commanded to begin in the garden."

This naturally causes much consternation, much argument, feverish cutting of and negotiating about the enforced union. It also brings about, in the "opera" proper, abundant opportunity for a clashing of the two worlds and for play between the parallel themes, play that is part of the parodic nature of the comic characters in the first place. In a famous letter of mid-July 1911, responding to Strauss's cool, insufficiently appreciative reception of his finished libretto, Hofmannsthal set forth his understanding of the relationship between these casts:

What it is about is one of the straightforward and stupendous problems of life: fidelity; whether to hold fast to that which is lost, to cling to it even unto

death—or to live, to live on, to get over it, to transform oneself, to sacrifice
the integrity of the soul and yet in this transmutation to preserve one's essence, to remain a human being and not to sink to the level of the beast, which
is without recollection. . . . We have the group of heroes, demi-gods, gods—
Ariadne, Bacchus . . . facing the human, the merely human group consisting
of the frivolous Zerbinetta and her companions, all of them base figures in life's
masquerade. Zerbinetta is in her element, drifting out of the arms of one man
into the arms of another; Ariadne could be the wife or mistress of *one* man
only. . . . One thing, however, is still left even for her: the miracle, the God.
To him she gives herself, for she believes him to be Death: he is both Death
and Life at once. . . .
But what to divine souls is a real miracle, is to the earth-bound nature of
Zerbinetta just an everyday love-affair. She sees in Adriadne's experience the
only thing she *can* see: the exchange of an old lover for a new one. And so
these two spiritual worlds are in the end ironically brought together in the only
way in which they can be brought together: in non-comprehension.

(Hammelmann, pp. 93–94.)

As is clear in this description, Zerbinetta carries rather more than
her share of the noncomprehension; she remains loose, frivolous, un-
transformed, and uncomprehending, while Ariadne undergoes ecstatic
rebirth. This denies Zerbinetta (and her companions) her native re-
source and wit, and more importantly, her dramatic stature as an ironic,
brilliant counterbalance to the tragic Ariadne. This does, however, seem
to be Hofmannsthal's view of her in general.

On the part of Strauss, the practical musician who generally left the
philosophy to his collaborator, this view prevails—to a degree. That is,
in the end glowing music of love and Schubertian tenderness accompanies the departure of the united Ariadne and Bacchus, while Zerbinetta
can do little more than look on from the wings. In the original 1912
version of the opera the dramatic illusion was broken in the end by a
reassertion of the original theatrical framework, but the final, 1916 version sustains the illusion and the mood to the end, with no further reference to the almost *Parade*-like self/audience–reflecting theatricality of
the Prelude. As William Mann cleverly put it, "as we have it *Adriadne
II* starts by pricking the balloon and then blows it up to full size."
(Forsythe, p. 108.) In this respect, the opera steps away from a commedic
structure, that of *Arlecchino* or of *Petrushka*, toward Puccini's *Turandot*
or even *Love for Three Oranges*, which also begins by constructing theater within theater and then also gradually sheds the framework in favor
of the fantasy.

But if the sure dramatic instincts of Strauss induced him to resolve the opera in favor of unironic love, they also led him to make much more of the commedia, particularly Zerbinetta, than his librettist had envisioned. This is most evident in the great scene in which Zerbinetta confronts the grieving Ariadne, "Grossmächtige Prinzessin," in an attempt to impose a more practical, earthbound perspective on her sorrows:

> Are we not women, both of us,
> And does not in each bosom beat a heart—
> a woman's heart—that passeth understanding?

The words are indeed earthbound, cheerfully unencumbered with Ariadne's nobility, reveling in the ways of the merely human and the flesh:

> Full oft when I think that for ever unshaken
> My constancy every attack will repel
> Strange promptings assail me, that in me awaken
> A longing for liberty long lost, a yearning—
> . . . So it was with Pagliacco
> And with Mezzetino!
> Then followed Cavicchio,
> Then Burattino,
> Then Pasquariello,
> Can I believe it?— . . .

The music, however, soars into coloratura heaven. In both technical and purely musical terms, it is one of the most perfectly realized virtuoso set pieces in all opera; into it Strauss poured all of his musical and dramatic inventiveness, and the result is a rich, brilliant portrait of a Columbine. She is as much a Viennese soubrette, the epitome of the operetta coloratura, as an Italian comedienne, and she is not "modern" in the way of Petrushka or Pierrot Lunaire—Strauss rooted himself too deeply in the music and the Vienna of the past to disturb her outlook or her dramatic shape in any radical way. But Zerbinetta does, with all of this, embody the spirit of the commedia, and if her words fail—"it seems the lady and I do not understand each other's language"—the manner of their musical presentation is triumphant. This scene has been called the musical axis of the whole opera (Daviau, p. 184.); musically and dramatically it is certainly the moment most eagerly awaited by the audience, a significant point, considering the very audience-wise composer. Forsyth argues that Zerbinetta descends from Colombine (p. 141.), and she goes on to argue for a richly ironic erotic consciousness in the character, even detecting Schnitzler-like libidinous ironies in the world view of this gay soubrette. (*Ibid.*, p. 143.) There is something interesting in this notion of a hyperconscious Freudian commedia mingling with a relatively unconscious *opera seria* (Zerbinetta "is in this a more complicated and more interesting character than Ariadne," argues Forsyth, but it is finally unconvincing dramatically.

What gives Zerbinetta her magnetism, her utterly arresting presence, is not her "interesting" complexity but her brilliant simplicity. It is not the merely vulgar simplicity that Hofmannsthal envisioned, perhaps, but to an important degree she does remain his creation. It is Strauss's music that gives her the requisite stature, that makes her simplicity something unforgettable. Once again, his means are technical, extremely sophisticated (terrifyingly so to generations of ambitious coloraturas); in this he is true to the traditions of the commedia: nothing is so simple dramatically and at the same time so complex technically as first-rate acrobatics. There is much more, of course, in the way of careful attention to orchestration (for instance, the consistent use of piano to accompany the commedia characters), in subtle delineation of character, in exquisite placement of telling motifs, but the unique accomplishment in the whole is this vivid musical presence. Commedia gestures, like operetta gestures, appear occasionally in Strauss operas after this, as they did before in *Rosenkavalier*—they are easily visible in *Arabella*, *Intermezzo*, subtly in *Capriccio*—but nothing else, perhaps nothing else in all of music, so completely embodies the brilliant and playful side of the commedia dell'arte, the comedy of skill, as the dazzling Zerbinetta.

Strauss's version of twentieth-century commedia did not play the part in creating modernism that the versions of Schoenberg and Stravinsky, and to a lesser extent, Busoni, Weill, and Prokofiev did. It is not the frank embrace of the old grand opera that is Puccini's *Turandot*, but like the rest of Strauss it is a conservative's compromise, modern in its distancing and its sophisticated use of traditional language, but also a rejection of the modern in its complete refusal to turn against that language.

Satie

The other creator of the modernist commedia in musical terms, Erik Satie, has been treated, mostly in connection with *Parade*, in the chapters on ballet and painting; considered only as a composer, Satie has never been accorded much of a place among the creators of modern music. For our purposes, he is best seen in the *Parade* context because his place in it represents his most vital contribution here. His spare, graceful, witty music, the sometimes outrageous titles thereof aside, has seldom been appreciated as "modern" in itself, certainly not as avant-garde. It could be argued that his critical reputation bears an inverse relation to that of Strauss. That is, he wanted, it is believed, very much to be a serious, radical modernist, but he lacked the talent and training and technique to become this, while the immensely talented and accomplished Strauss was able to use his gifts and skills to avoid becoming modern. This assessment of Satie's music was not that of one of his principal collaborators in the invention of modernism, Cocteau, who saw in the *Parade* music something like musical cubism.

Satie's own assessment (referred to in Chapter 6) takes no such claim for his lovely circus music:

I have composed a background to certain noises that Cocteau considers necessary to create the atmosphere of his characters.

(Templier, p. 86.)

But the dryly witty, direct cast of mind that this statement (and many similar remarks) reveals is evidence that Satie was indeed making something new.

In 1923, Satie wrote a short appreciation of Stravinsky for *Vanity Fair*, which, as in everything he wrote, contains much that applies directly to himself:

I have always said—and I shall keep on saying it long after my death—that there is no such thing as Artistic Truth (no unique Truth, that is). . . . My illustrious friend Igor Stravinsky . . . is the living proof of this; and he is the most precise, the most real, the most perfect example.

(Satie, pp. 102–103.)

It may well be that Satie's own rejection of absolutes, even in a life full of privation and yearning for acceptance, constituted an alienation more radical, more avant-gardiste than the very professional Stravinsky could conceive. As one who lived under the spell of Wagner much as did his Symbolist compatriots, he went in for the perfumed decadence born under that spell. But even in this early phase his path was original; even then he was concocting his own private mixture of esoteric mysticism and cabaret gaiety—he earned something like a living playing piano at the Chat Noir and then at the Auberge de Clou and elsewhere in Montmartre. The ingredients were there for a Laforgue Pierrot or Giraud/Schoenberg commedia, perhaps, but Satie made his own use of the cabaret. His characteristically arch melodic lines carry with them something of the cabaret *chanson* throughout his career, but his spare abstraction makes of them something fresh.

It is easy to find gestures appropriate to the commedia throughout that career. There are the three absurd but utterly serious self-nominations for the ultimate honor accorded the established French artist, membership in the French Academy, in 1892, 1894, and 1896, pursued with relentless, if polite tenacity by the poor, obscure young man, complete with elaborate protocols and immense self-inflation. (Shattuck, p. 125.) In his music there is his penchant for parody. For instance, he and his friends concocted a parody ballet of the popular Diaghilev *Schéhérazade* to Satie's *Trois morceaux en forme de poire*, a four-hand piano work that acquired its odd title—it consists of seven pieces not particularly shaped like a pear—in response to the complaint of Debussy, for some three decades his best friend, that his music was deficient in "form." Even a brief look at Satie's theatrical work shows a commedia modernist sensibility hard at work: his 1899 *Geneviève de Brabant*, a puppet play collaboration with Contamine de Latour, in which the chorus reminds the audience that they are made out of cardboard (Harding, p. 84.); his Jarry-style absurdist parody *Le Piège de Meduse*, featuring "a beautiful giant monkey stuffed by a master hand" (Satie, p. 140.); his *Cinq Grimaces pour le Songe d'une Nuit d'été*, for "circus" ensemble, all that was realized of a project conceived by Cocteau; a version of *Midsummer Night's Dream* for the Medrano Circus and the Fratellini brothers, the great clown family (the project was to have involved Schmitt, Ravel, and Stravinsky, as well as the young Edgard Varèse); *Relâche*, a 1924 work for the Ballets Suédois, with sets by Picabia the film *Entr'acte*, by René Clair and large inscriptions reading, "Erik Satie is the greatest musician in the world" and, "If you don't like it, the box office will sell you whistles for two cents" (Templier, p. 51.); the ballet *Mercure* (also 1924), with brilliant costumes and sets by Picasso, and Massine dancing the title role; and, above all, the earlier collaboration of these men with Cocteau, *Parade*.

The self-enclosing, protective irony, the refusal to follow or to lead, and the deep isolation of the master of Arcueil all have more complicated origins than can be explained with reference to a commedic sensibility, but in the general rediscovery of Satie it is becoming clear that these qualities are essential to his role as a founding father of the modern artistic sensibility. Alan Gillmor argues that Satie embodied the spirit of the avant-garde by applying Renato Poggioli's *The Theory of the Avante-Garde*:

Sometimes the artist ends up by considering the state of alienation as a disgraceful condemnation, a moral ghetto, and seeking to react against that oppressive feeling finds no way out but the grotesque one of self-caricature and self-mockery. Conscious of the fact that bourgeois society considers him nothing but a charlatan, he voluntarily and ostentatiously assumes the role of comic actor.

(Poggioli, in Gillmor, p. 116.)

Gilmor directs this insight to Satie in such a way that he becomes the very type of the commedia modernist:

Satie's irreverent attitude toward art and life, his very refusal, in fact, to differentiate the one from the other, is the primary quality which defines his importance, and it is precisely those aspects of his work which can be identified as avant-gardistic which explain, to a great extent, his relevance and his ultimate historical significance. If Satie did in fact wear a mask, as many would claim, its function was not to conceal his own alleged inadequacy, but rather, in the words of Peter Dickinson, "to cloak a spiritual crisis which he sensed well before this century."

(Ibid., p. 119.)

Other Musical Commedia

Satie's influence upon many other composers, especially upon Les Six, is well known, and it is not incidental that many of them turned to specifically commedic themes and attitudes. They did this not out of discipleship—Satie would have nothing to do with such a relationship, and in any case the clashes of personality made for very different artistic identities. Rather, they absorbed something of his irony, it seems, especially that refusal to take oneself as artist so seriously as to elevate the artist above the man; they also loved the theater and the circus and the cabaret. This was most obviously true of Darius Milhaud, the only one of the Six who was so invincibly amiable that he never had a falling out with Satie. He wrote his Le Boeuf sur le toit in Paris in 1919, shortly after returning from a stint as attaché to the ministry of his friend Paul Claudel in Rio. It is essentially his tribute, one of several, to the popular music and dances of Brazil (the title comes from a Brazilian popular song), and he called it a "Cinema-Symphonie," hoping that it would be suitable as accompaniment for a Charlie Chaplin silent. (Milhaud, p. 102.) However, Cocteau took possession of it and provided it with a pantomime scenario for the Fratellinis, among others, with slow-motion choreography to contrast strangely with the lively music. Milhaud loved carnival music and wrote several suites of it; in fact the piano-and-orchestra suite Carnaval d'Aix began life in 1924 as the ballet *Salade*, based on a commedia dell'arte episode, with Massine as Punchinello and scenery by Braque. (Harding, p. 210.)

1924 was also the year of the premiere of the first important work of another of the Six, Francis Poulenc. *Les Biches* (roughly, "sweet things"—literally "does"), written for Diaghilev, with choreography by Bronislava Nijinska, is not literally a work of commedia, but commedia is distinctly in the air. Sixteen lovely coquettes lounge around an immense sofa, and three muscular young men dressed in bathing suits leap in to flirt and play games. Poulenc referred to the work as:

a ballet in which you may see nothing at all or into which you may read the worst. . . . In this ballet, as in certain of Watteau's pictures, there is an atmosphere of wantonness which you sense if you are corrupted but which an innocent-minded girl would not be conscious of.

(Rostand.)

Marie Laurencin's soft, sexy sketches for her costumes rather incline us to suspect the worst of her kittenish *biches*, but the overall impression is still of soft-edged, safe indulgence.

Again, images and echoes of the commedia abound in this generation, and they continue to appear into the present. For example, Peter Schickele—best known as the "discoverer" of P. D. Q. Bach, the scapegrace son of the great J. S.—wrote a *Commedia* for winds (1979) under his own name, which includes musical portraits of Pantalone, Doctor Graziano, and Arlecchino. A leading Dutch composer, Oscar van Hemel, has done a suite of character pieces entitled simply *About Commedia dell'Arte*, and in the seventies the Englishman Richard Rodney Bennett composed a series of chamber works called *Commedia*.

The most significant recent example of "serious" musical commedia is probably the opera *Punch and Judy* (1966–1967) by another Englishman, Harrison Birtwistle. With his brilliant contemporary Peter Maxwell Davies, Birtwistle also formed the Pierrot Players, an important chamber music group consisting, with additions, of the forces required for performance of *Pierrot Lunaire*. Davies and Birtwistle and others have composed a number of striking experimental works with flamboyant dramatic effects which transform this and similar ensembles into theatrical as well as musical troupes. Their use of masks, dancing, lighting tricks and musical improvisation call up something of the spirit of commedia.

In general, however, the legacy of the commedia has become increasingly matter for decoration, as in *Les Biches*, and understandably so, as the basic notion of an avant-garde has lost much of its sharpness.

When Stravinsky, Schoenberg, Satie, Busoni, and Weill turned to the circus and the cabaret and the old Italian comedy, they could find there more than a flood of images; they found ways of creating new relationships in music and theater, of making something new and enclosing it in a new frame. For all their radical will, they could draw upon their roots to make something new in ways denied to the uprooted generations that followed them.

Chapter 8.

LITERATURE AND THE COMMEDIA

WHO are the great novelists we should salute as commedic? They are not so easy to spot as the great performers in arts like painting and ballet, who can, if they wish, present us with versions of the traditional characters. There are strong pressures to prevent a writer from building a book-length narrative around a Pierrot and a Harlequin. These pressures derive from the novel's commitment to values we sum up as realism. In the nineteenth century, nearly all the great fiction writers were realists; and in the twentieth century their successors have to offer something that, if not itself realistic, exceeds and outdoes realism.

Nevertheless, there has been a change. In the field of fiction, modernism can be described as a revolt against realism. Realism must then be split between the formal and the moral varieties. Formal realism refers to the plausible imitation of time and place, and of social and psychological fact, while moral realism has to do with judgment—a plausible balance in the writer between enthusiasm and skepticism, sympathy and severity. Separable though the two realisms are, they cooperate to glorify a middle-of-the-road imaginative policy, which endorses moderate values like manliness and womanliness. Modernism is therefore to be associated with the opposite qualitites, with implausibility of plot and motive, with extremism of mood, and with an attack on moderate values.

The most important single case is Vladimir Nabokov (1899–1977) whose work was both truly brilliant and truly pan-European. It derived from, or touched upon, all five of the countries we toured in Chapter 2. His commedic sensibility was formed in Russia, in Silver Age St. Petersburg, and bears many traces of that early nurture but had an episode in England, developed in Germany and France, and finally blossomed most completely in America.

We will look first at his last novel, *Look at the Harlequins* (1974), which carries the most direct reference to the commedia in its title, and which represents and reflects on Nabokov's whole career as a novelist. Of course, it is not overtly autobiographical. Nabokov's feeling for fic-

233

tion—one might say, the commedia feeling—forbids any simple or direct transposition of fact into fiction. The central character, like Nabokov, is a novelist, but has a radically different history of personal relations: an "atrocious childhood," a gambler father who died before he was born, and a series of unfortunate marriages. But all these changes merely bring out the underlying similarity between the two careers and the single identity which stamps the work the two novelists produced.

The title derives from an exhortation the boy Vadim gets from the great-aunt who brings him up. She urges him not to yield to his melancholy and self-destructive urge. She gives him a specific against that, which becomes his life-motto. "Stop moping!" she says. "Look at the harlequins . . . everywhere. All around you. Trees are harlequins, words are harlequins. So are situations and sums. Put two things together—jokes, images—and you get a triple harlequin. Play! Invent the world! Invent reality!" (Nabokov, *Harlequins*, pp. 8–9.) This is what Vadim does from then on; he begins by inventing *her*, he tells us (a typical authorial insolence, reminding the reader that Nabokov holds the strings of all his puppets) and that is what Nabokov did in his life and work.

Like other Nabokov heroes, Vadim is insomniac, subject to hallucinations, and always threatened by insanity. In crises, his "flayed consciousness" of reality pushes aside his playfulness, and he finds life intolerable. But he manages to survive, and to create significant works of art, by means of allowing the Harlequins to shape his vision of the world as much as possible.

He rebels against ordinary reality and realism. He rebels, for instance, against the laws of nature. The law of gravity, he says, is an infernal and humiliating contribution to our perceptual world because of its irreversibility. (*Ibid.*, p. 85.) He claims the right to reverse all laws, by imposing his imagination on everything. His second wife, Annette, complains that he is unlike the other men she has known—who were decent military men, who spoke to her of dangers and duties, of "bivouacs in the steppes," and who never made unchaste jokes or horrid weird comparisons (i.e., Harlequins). Vadim is not manly; he has perceptions and feelings which "real men" lack, and vice versa; he is as unlike "real men" as if he wore Pierrot makeup and costume and moved in Pierrot's world. He says to her, "Look at that harlequin," pointing to a butterfly. She sees the insect, but not the Harlequin. (*Ibid.*, p. 108.)

Harlequins, and other commedia figures, appear throughout the book. The American motels Vadim stops in (like the ones Humbert Humbert visits, in *Lolita*) are Harlequins. (*Ibid.*, p. 156.) The poets whose works he puts in his daughter's room (Keats, Yeats, Coleridge, Blake) are "dear, bespangled mimes with wands of painted lath." (*Ibid.*, p. 163.) He uses the acronym LATH (for *Look At The Harlequins*) throughout the book, as a slogan. He calls the novels he has written Harlequins, "followed by a tiger or two, scarlet-tongued, and a libbelula girl on an elephant." (*Ibid.*, p. 228.)

And behind or beneath these explicit references lies the fundamental theatricality of Nabokov's world view, which is his deepest debt to the commedia. He has worked out an artist's metaphysic of invented reality (the opposite of found fact), which constitutes a remarkable objective correlative for the commedic sensibility, in philosophic terms. The novel's first sentence refers to the "main plotter" of his life story (God or Fate) who has made many "inept moves." Vadim has frustrated these moves, and risen above factuality. He says, "My battle with factual, respectable life still consisted of sudden delusions, sudden reshufflings—kaleidoscopic, stained glass reshufflings—of fragmented space."

Nabokov's autobiography, *Conclusive Evidence* (later reissued as *Speak, Memory*), carries the same insignia, if more discreetly. The book is organized around the theme of memory, but that very playful and theatrical memory—not the servant of sober purposefulness, but a rebel against it—which we can take to be usually the ally of fanciful imagination, and therefore an instrument of the commedia in fiction. (In Proust's great novel, the Pierrot-narrator builds his art and thought around such memory.) Nabokov tells us that his first memory is of seeing his father wearing his Horse Guards uniform, which, since Prince Nabokov had long before left that regiment, must have been a "festive joke" on his part. "To a joke, then, I owe my first gleam of complete consciousness." (Nabokov, *Evidence*, p. 4.)

His narrator-persona announces itself as commedic. "I am now going to do something quite difficult, a kind of double somersault with a Welsh Waggle (old acrobats will know what I mean), and I want complete silence, please." (*Ibid.*, p. 142.) And he signals to us the commedic character of his various environments. When his family fled St. Petersburg after the Revolution, they went to Yalta, in the Crimea. Under the rule of the White Russian forces, Yalta then had "the kind of brash, hectic gaiety associated with White-held towns. . . . Cafés did a wonderful business. All kinds of theatre thrived." (*Ibid.*, p. 181.) Hunting butterflies outside the town, the young Nabokov met a furious "outlaw" (in fact, a film star, in the makeup and costume of Hadji Murad) whose horse had carried him away from the film set—a slice of dream life in daylight. And the émigré cultural life, in Berlin and Paris, was all a bit like that. It was characterized by its Lilliputian scale, by fierce factions and mutual competitions, and by publishing firms of "hectic, unstable, and slightly illegal appearance." (*Ibid.*, p. 210.)

He was, while still in Russia and still at school, marked out as an aesthete or a decadent. Teachers at his school reproached him for being apolitical and antisocial, unlike his liberal politician father. His father was their hero, and they were disappointed that he had an aesthete for a son. Nabokov says, "My father was, indeed, a very active man, but I viewed his activities through a prism of my own, which split into many enchanting colours the rather austere light my teachers glimpsed." (*Ibid.*, p. 131.) His father's liberal politics split up into acts of fantasy, kinds of fun, arts of paradox. He describes himself, on the way to Yalta, as a "brittle young fop," with his coral-knobbed cane. (*Ibid.*, p. 177.)

He talks often of things that he would later call Harlequins—for instance, of his sense of the colors of various vowels, in various languages. He talks of the stained-glass window through which he looked at the garden at home. "But the most constant source of enchantment during those readings came from the harlequin pattern of coloured panes inset in a whitewashed framework on either side of the veranda. . . . If one looked through blue glass, the sand turned to cinders while inky trees swam in a tropical sky. The yellow created an amber world." (*Ibid.*, p. 168.) He talks of playing with his mother's jewels while lying in her bed (and similar childhood scenes are described by other commedia writers—in Osbert Sitwell's memoirs, and Cecil Beaton's). (*Ibid.*, p. 17.) He tells of the garnet egg he wrapped in a wet sheet, to see the deep red color seep through—"the closest I ever got to feeding upon beauty." (*Ibid.*, p. 6.)

This sort of thing can of course be called aestheticism, and in fact Nabokov calls his theory of colored sounds "the confessions of a synaesthete"; which will remind us of French Decadents Laforgue knew—of Huysmans' hero, Des Esseintes, and of Baudelaire's *correspondances*. Synaesthesia, dandyism, and the commedia are linked to one another in many times and places.

Another element in the complex is Nabokov's flaunted "heartlessness," his indifference to ordinary moral and emotional claims. (We put the word in quotes because the author, by drawing our attention to his affront to our feelings, expresses a paradoxical compunction.) He describes a family friend, General Kuropatkin, who amused the boy Nabokov with matchstick tricks in St. Petersburg, and who, after the Revolution, selling matches, met Prince Nabokov when both were escaping from the Bolsheviks. Nabokov says, "Whether or not old Kuropatkin, in his rustic disguise, managed to evade Soviet imprisonment, is immaterial. What pleases me is the evolution of the match theme." (Nabokov, *Evidence,* p. 9.) And later in the book he describes having lunch with another Russian émigré author in Paris, Ivan Bunin, who tried to get Nabokov to engage in a "heart to heart talk." When Nabokov fastidiously refused the gambit, Bunin told him bitterly that he would "die in dreadful pain and complete isolation." (*Ibid.,* pp. 215–16.) But outside the restaurant, as the two men stiffly put on their coats, to part, a commedia scene developed between them. Bunin found that his overcoat had had Nabokov's long scarf stuffed into its sleeve (by the hat-check girl) and the two had to cooperate to pull it out, inch by inch, revolving around each other in silent, angry ballet.

Nabokov was devoted to butterflies in real life as well as in his books, and his butterfly hunting can be called commedic; both because of *their* fluttering colorfulness, and because of *his* comic pursuit of them—the absurdity of the butterfly-hunter image, which attracted to him the scorn of philistines. As a boy he was mocked by family visitors and elderly relatives: "Can't you enjoy yourself like a normal boy?" and in America, "from cars passing me on the highway have come wild howls of derision." (*Ibid.,* pp. 86–87.) (In many commedia performances, including *Les Enfants du Paradis,* Pierrot is a butterfly hunter.)

Nabokov's sensibility also included the commedic touch of horror. Of a pretty park in a St. Petersburg square he writes, "In one of its linden trees an ear and a finger had been found one day—remnants of a terrorist whose hand had slipped while . . . those same trees (a pattern of silver filigree in a mother-of-pearl mist out of which the bronze dome of St. Isaac's arose in the background) had also seen children shot down at random from the branches. (*Ibid.,* p. 128.) In *Invitation to a Beheading* and *Bend Sinister,* he applied this gruesome commedia art to political themes in full-length novels.

But he did not yield completely to the commedia and fantasy view of life. Like Proust, he affirmed an allegiance to quite opposite values also, such as marriage, parenthood, decency, and culture. One of his critics, Julian Moynahan, is able to say with some justice that all his work is a celebration of married love. In *Look at the Harlequins,* Vadim's last wife is identified with reality, and that sort of connection, between marriage and truth, is made in various other novels. In the autobiography, Nabokov describes his sexual promiscuity during the decade 1915 to 1925, which ended with his marriage, and dismisses that period of his life as "talentless and derivative." (*Ibid.,* p. 183.) Married life is better because talented and tasteful.

This complex pattern of conflicting tendencies can be seen everywhere in his work. In *Lolita* we have a remarkable version of Columbine in the girl herself, and in Humbert Humbert we have an equally remarkable combination or alternation of Pierrot and Harlequin. (We also have a showier, more expressionist pairing of Humbert and Quilty as Pierrot and Harlequin.) But this is counterpointed by Nabokov's strongly sustained feeling for the joys and virtues of romantic love, and even for decency and moral realism. One might say that *Lolita* combines the romantic love novel with its commedia/surrealist opposite, and that that combination is the source or the form of its greatest distinction.

It seems to have been in the 1930s that Nabokov gradually developed this highly original fictionalization of the commedia. He began where Proust left off. A short story, "The Leonardo" (1933), begins, "The objects that are being summoned assemble, draw near from different spots; in doing so, some of them have to overcome not only the distance of space but that of time. . . . Here comes the ovate little poplar, all punctuated with April greenery, and takes its stand where told, namely by the tall brick wall, imported in one piece from another city. Facing it, there grows up a dreary and dingy tenement house, with mean little balconies pulled out one by one like drawers. . . . All this is only sketched and much has to be added and finished, and two live people— Gustav and his brother Anton—already come out on their tiny balcony." (Nabokov, *Beauty*, p. 11.) This is certainly a Proust-like fantasy, but Proust attributes the "creative" power to unconscious memory, while Nabokov claims it entirely for the arbitrary artist.

Gustav and Anton, two coarse and brutal philistines, torment and finally kill their lodger, Romantovski, merely because he is "different." He has a conspicuous and defenseless Adam's apple; "long-faced and pale, with quivering eyelashes, he sat in a complicated pose, partly doubled up, partly bent out." He is, we see, a Pierrot. He is also, Nabokov tells us, a Leonardo, which means a counterfeiter. This gives the story its small surprise at the end, but does not break the rules of the commedia genre. The last lines are "My poor Romantovski! And I who believed with them you were indeed someone exceptional. I believed, let me confess, that you were a remarkable poet." (*Ibid.*, p. 23.) But for Pierrot to be a remarkable poet would be too sentimental; he must be a criminal as well as a victim.

"Spring in Fialta" (1938) is a beautiful story built around the poster of a traveling circus, a commedic poster that recurs throughout the narrative; "a feathered Indian on a rearing horse in the act of lassoing a boldly eudemic zebra, while some thoroughly fooled elephants sat brooding upon their star-spangled thrones." (Nabokov, *Dozen*, p. 9.) (This is a literary version of Picasso's commedia curtain for the ballet *Parade*.) The woman in the story is a light-minded Columbine who forgets everything that passes between her and the narrator immediately after it happens. She is totally promiscuous, and yet loyal to her heartless and immoral Harlequin husband, and yet delicate and charming. The narrator gradually realizes that through her Columbine promiscuity, attractive though that is, "something lovely, delicate, and unrepeatable was being wasted. . . . [he realizes] the lies, the futility, the gibberish of that life." (*Ibid.*, p. 23.) This is a classic commedia story. And *Laughter in the Dark*, a novel also of 1938, is a surrealist or expressionist version of the Pierrot/Harlequin/Columbine story that foreshadows *Lolita*.

Nabokov's connection with the kind of Russian commedia we have discussed already is suggested most clearly in two chapters of an unfinished novel, written in 1939–1940, the last of his works written in Russian. These two chapters, "Ultima Thule" and "Solus Rex," prefigure *Pale Fire*, for they involve, like that novel, a framed story about a Ruritanian king with whom the central character identifies. What particularly concerns us is that this king (the Nabokov hero in a dream disguise) comes to the thone when his degenerate aesthete cousin, Prince Adulf, is assassinated. The Nabokov figure displaces the degenerate cousin. The relation between the two men (mutual admiration, kinship, revulsion, separation) follows the lines of the relation between Nabokov representatives and their decadent aesthete twins in other novels. But in this case Nabokov gives us a very interesting clue to his aesthetic politics, by saying that he based Prince Adulf on Diaghilev. (To be exact, he says the physical aspect was Diaghilev's, but I think we may enlarge on that hint.)

Adulf is described as having a broad pelvis, a big-cheeked, evenly pink face, and fine, bulging eyes; but his lips are fat and greasy, and he has a nasty little mustache. (This all fits Diaghilev.) He is a man of sensibility, always ready to help others, but always inadvertently causes them a deeper pain than any he himself could experience. He is merely an aesthete. "He wept profusely while listening to the melting violin of the great Perelmon, and shed the same tears while picking up the shards of a favourite cup." (Nabokov, *Beauty*, pp. 191–92.) He was a "*charmeur*, defying one not to recognize his charm." (*Ibid.*, p. 193.) All this fixes the resemblance to Diaghilev (and to Kuzmin).

What is more important is the way the author relates him to the king-hero. The latter agrees with Adulf's ideas (for instance, the idea that the power of a king—an artist—is rooted in magic) and is attracted to him as to a personality much more brilliant than his own; but is fundamentally afraid of him, and makes excuses not to spend time with him. Adulf says, "Only don't be so bashful with me, I won't bite you, I simply can't stand lads *qui se tiennent toujours sur leurs gardes.*" (*Ibid.*, p. 200.) We can perhaps take this as a hint as to what Nabokov heard Diaghilev saying to him in his imagination.

The young man goes to a party given by Adulf, which is recognizably a ballet party, an assembling of Diaghilev's entourage, including a beautiful acrobat, Guldving, who represents Diaghilev's dancer lovers. The young Nabokov admires the simplicity of the group's manners, and recognizes in them a certain kindliness that he "who himself did not possess it, recognized in all of life's phenomena." (*Ibid.*, p. 203.) This is an important concession for Nabokov to make—to concede a moral superiority, a life superiority, to his rival. But then, equally serenely, Adulf calls over Guldving, unbuttons his trousers, and begins to play with his genitals in full view of everyone. The young Nabokov runs out of the room, appalled. He decides that Adulf is "really a savage, a self-taught oaf, lacking real culture . . . a prurient ruffian." (*Ibid.*, p. 204.) He sticks to the vocabulary of culture, but clearly he uses it to mean a moral judgment.

What this suggests is how powerful a presence Nabokov felt Diaghilev to be. Other members of Nabokov's family, like his brother Sergei and his cousin Nikolai, were close to Diaghilev. (And there are many indications that the Nabokov family belonged to the world of the Petersburg poets we discussed before: his strong feeling for that city and landscape, for example, and the family portraits by *The World of Art* painters.) And if Diaghilev represented the commedia, then a resistance to him would involve seeking an alternative to the commedic values. Perhaps Nabokov found that alternative in marriage. We would guess that more than anything else, his own marriage saved him from what repelled him in Diaghilev; which helps explain the celebration of marriage in his novels, the connection of marriage with truth. There is no reason to believe that Nabokov felt in any simple sense endangered by Diaghilev's homosexuality, but sexual panic and disgust are certainly among the feelings evoked. But the rich colors and wild humors of Nabokov's art come from a commedia source, as much as Diaghilev's ballets did, and he is as a whole clearly a commedia artist.

Another striking case to consider is the Danish novelist, Isak Dinesen (1885–1962), who lived in a British colony in Africa and found her first success with an English reading audience. This international character to her work and its audience is worth noting. International writers like her and Nabokov feel an affinity with the commedia; they are not rooted in a national culture as other writers are.

She is far from being as brilliant a writer as Nabokov, but she is equally a commedia writer, and in certain ways more directly so. She actually dressed up as Pierrot—in her later years too—and went to visit people wearing that costume. We can hardly imagine Nabokov doing that. Dinesen's early writings included several literally commedic scripts (Copenhagen had a strong theatrical tradition, and something of an intellectual tradition, of commedia art) and some of them were adapted to become major fiction later.

The most striking example of this is her story "Carnival," written as fiction in the late 1920s, and at the time intended to be one of her *Seven Gothic Tales*. (She used the word Gothic in an eighteenth-century way, to suggest the playful-fantastic revival of old artistic forms.) This is a story set in Copenhagen in February 1925, on the night of the Opera Carnival, and it is about the spirit of the times.

Four men and four women meet for dinner, wearing commedia costumes, some of them tranvestite. Of the women, one is a Camelia, but the others are dressed as men; a Watteau Pierrot, an Arlecchino, and a Kierkegaard (who is described as "that brilliant, deep, and desperate Danish philosopher of the 1840s, a sort of macabre dandy"). (Dinesen, *Carnival*, p. 57.) The girl dressed as Kierkegaard is a modernist poet, but she will live in fame not for her verse but for her beauty—"in her case the spirit will be transient, the flesh immortal." (*Ibid.*, p. 58.) While of the Camelia we are told, "at whatever place—throat, arm, waist, or knee—you cut her slim body through with a sharp knife, you would have got a perfectly circular transverse incision." (*Ibid.*, p. 57.) The epigrammatic prose, and the touch of defiant sadism, declare the narrator herself to belong to the commedia and the twenties.

The other two women are sisters. They are "a little more spare of build, and had darker eyes and redder mouths than the others, as if the vitality within them had come out less in plain matter and more in colour and brightness [and they had] the placid and slightly mocking expression of Japanese dolls." (*Ibid.*, p. 58.) Arlecchino is a dancer, and so full of herself that when kissed she does not feel the man's hot, dry lips but her own coolness and freshness. She (like Nabokov) declares the law of gravity done away with, and she and Pierrot dance together, both very light, straight, and supple, coming to a halt in front of a mirror. She is in love with her sister's lover, but her strongest feelings still seem oriented toward her sister. And her highest praise for the latter is that she does not merely wear a Pierrot costume but *is* a Pierrot.

The latter warns Arlecchino against love. She herself is in love with her husband and this ruins her life; it deprives her of her independence. Moreover, he does not want her love—he wants her to run parallel with him, not toward him. She pretends to do so—becoming his rival as a pilot, driving a racing car alongside him—but secretly and shamefully she wants only to be his shadow. "Never had a little ruined and lost Pierrot looked more tragic." (*Ibid.*, p. 64.) All these details correspond to a commedic psychology and philosophy.

The men are dressed as a Venetian lady, a Chinese sage, a Harlequin, and a magenta Domino. (The taste governing all this variety can be called eighteenth century—a point which is made within the story— and Dinesen in general works in that eighteenth-century extension of the commedia that included Gothic and chinoiserie.) Of these the most important is the Chinese sage, who is really a famous Danish painter, Rosendaal. He is (whether in costume or not) one of the hermaphrodite commedia masks, with a pink full-moon face with no features, hair, or expression, "like a baby's bottom." (*Ibid.*, p. 59.) His pupils say his face and bottom must be reversed, and he must have a radiant and expressive face on the other end of his body. He is the group's philosopher, and talks to them, for instance, about the thinness of 1920s women as a form of moral heroism. More important, he tells his young friends that their lives are insipid ("flat and greasy") because they are all painted in pastel colors, with no touch of black.

That is, people in the 1920s have no sense of sin, and no capacity for passionate jealousy. In the old days, "With the torture chamber and the iron cages beneath you [you really relished] the ecstasies of the wine and the beauty of your young naked courtesans and boys." (*Ibid.*, p. 80.) This line of thought we might call an 1890s commedic decadence, reminiscent of Oscar Wilde or Péladan; here contrasted with the 1920s kind exemplified by the young people.

The actual 1920s scene is presented as a version of the commedia. Sexuality is hectic and confused. Modern women are said to be like Athenian boys, and half the world is masked and transvestite. Marriage no longer makes sense—or not sacred sense. One of the men, who owns a shipping company, recalls how his skippers' wives wait for them on the quay as the ships come in: "Those were the people who knew how to be married, and he admired them." (*Op. cit.*) His friends do not. They have all quarreled with their parents and turned away from family life. (These ideas can remind one of England's Children of the Sun, and in fact Dinesen's lover in Kenya, Denys Finch-Hatton, was a much admired member of that generation of Englishmen.)

In order to introduce some blackness, some spice of danger, into their lives, the young people devise a lottery, which will give the winner the combined incomes of all the participants for one year; the others will live out the year temporarily penniless, except that the winner will choose one of them to be the companion of his/her pleasures. It is a commedia-drama situation.

Then they are interrupted by a man in a black mask and black makeup (the touch of black Rosendaal asked for). He is in fact an assistant in an antiques store they all know, owned by a Russian called Madame Rubinstein, and he is dressed for the Carnival as Zamor, Madame du Barry's black page. (The Negro page was a famous motif of eighteenth- and ninetheenth-century rococo. We meet it among the Russians, but it was too blatant for Nabokov to use.) He tells them he has killed his benefactor and employer, and demands money from them at the point of a gun. He of course represents the danger and evil they needed to complete their life picture; and he is persuaded to let the lottery proceed. Arlecchino wins it, and chooses him to be her year's companion—her artificial shadow.

In this story we see the commedia claiming to be the spirit of the twenties, in life as well as in art. Another overtly commedic story by Dinesen is "Anna," written as late as the early 1950s, which begins with a ballet impresario like Diaghilev who goes to Bergamo (the hometown of Harlequin in the original commedia) to find a new dancer to reinvigorate ballet. The story would in fact make a ballet scenario.

But much of Dinesen's writing works within subject areas allied to, and settings favored by, the commedia; for instance, the short novel *Ehrengard*, about a rococo German court and intrigues of seduction. Indeed, all the *Seven Gothic Tales* are demonstrably commedic, in various ways. "The Roads Around Pisa" includes a marionette play, a transvestite heroine, and a sinisterly fat and painted prince. "Deluge at Norderney" is a philosophical conversation in a house about to collapse into a flood, involving—amongst others—a fake cardinal and a mad aristocratic spinster, and others, all defying reality. "The Dreamers" is a Hoffmannesque story about a virtuoso soprano beauty (controlled by her Jewish manager) and all the men who have known her and loved her under a variety of names.

As I have indicated, Dinesen identified herself in real life with the commedia. She cherished china figures of Pierrot and Columbine, about which she wove fantasies; and in the plays she wrote when young, she always acted Pierrot, her sisters Columbine and Harlequin. In Africa she identified herself rather as aristocrat and adventurer, but her versions of those ideas were closely allied to that of the commedia artist. And in later life she dressed up as Pierrot for an emotional scene with the young poet Thorkild Bjornvig. But she gradually came to resemble a different sort of mask, especially in her last decade. She stylized herself both by costume and cosmetics, and by manners and behavior (claiming for instance to have made a Faustian compact to pay with her syphilis for her artistic powers) to the point where she ceased to be assimilable to ordinary human norms. She became a witch.

In that way she can remind us of another woman writer who also began in commedia playfulness and ended up as something of a witch— Edith Sitwell; also overweening in her claims on others, extraordinary in her looks and manner, and appalling in her (potent or impotent) malevolence. (The two women were aware of each other, and of the similarity in their roles.) The final phase of the Sitwells' life story was commedic in the gruesome sense. When their father finally died, after World War II, he left them little money, and they suspected the friend of his last years of embezzling his fortune and murdering him. However, Osbert did then inherit, and go to inhabit, the great castle of Montegufoni in Italy, which was itself a fantastic or commedic version of a home. (When Sir George Sitwell bought it, three hundred people were living within its walls.) But it became the setting for black comedy scenes involving the trio.

Edith fell and injured herself there more than once. It was felt to have a sinister atmosphere. But the most gruesome incident involved Osbert's long-term lover, David Hornby, who had begun to neglect Osbert as the latter gradually succumbed to Parkinson's disease and was confined to a wheelchair. Hornby seemed to have the secret of perpetual youth and beauty, and spent more and more time with other friends. Edith in particular grew privately furious with him, and in letters and conversations cursed him to death. Then one night at Montegufoni, Hornby fell (he felt himself pushed) down a long flight of stone steps and nearly died. He was confined to a wheelchair for a long time, during which Osbert gave his affections to a Maltese manservant instead.

And there were other ugly, pathetic, grotesque disharmonies among the aging trio. Sacheverell became seriously alienated from the other two, and allied himself in memory with their long-mocked parents, against Edith and Osbert. Thus the liberating rebellion of their youth turned into Grand Guignol conflict in their old age.

Edith began as a poet with a profusion of commedia names and symbols, ribboned mandolins, and gilded furniture. Even then some of her
most striking effects were the grotesque. In *Sleeping Beauty* (1924) the
fairy Laidronette's pet apes beg her, when she goes to bed:

> That she will leave uncurtained that Roc's egg
> Her head, a mount of diamonds bald and big
> In the ostrich feathers that compose her wig . . .
> And ancient satyrs whose wry wig of roses
> Nothing but little rotting shames discloses

However, in those days her art seemed to be rooted in the trio's mutual
support, or mutual flattery, in the battle against their family's and their
caste's coarse stupidity; as in "Colonel Fantock," which was dedicated
to Osbert and Sacheverell:

> But Dagobert and Peregrine and I
> Were children then; we walked like shy gazelles
> Among the music of the thin flower bells . . .
> All day within the straw-roofed arabesque
> Of the towered castle and the sleepy gardens wandered
> We; those delicate paladins the waves
> Told us fantastic legends that we pondered.

Such poetry is not in the literal sense commedic, but can perhaps
be called pre-commedic: it portrays the prelapsarian fairy-tale innocence to which Pierrot and Harlequin may be imagined to look back,
from the painful and sordid absurdities of their later lives.

By 1929, with *Gold Coast Customs*, she was striving for something
more substantial, though she could only lamely imitate the Eliot of *The
Hollow Men* and *Ash Wednesday*. It was after the war, with *Three Poems
for the Atomic Age*, "Dirge for the New Sunrise," "The Shadow of Cain,"
and "The Canticle of the Rose," that she began to find an impressive
voice that could name the preoccupations of her contemporaries with
ceremonial dignity. It is worth noting that in this late work she relied
on the symbolism and ceremonial of the Roman Catholic Church, which
she entered in 1955, thus conforming to the general pattern we have
suggested: turning away from the commedia of this world to become the
severe guardian of other-worldly values. Indeed, the grandly symbolist
manner of these poems could also be compared with that of Wagner's
operas, for instance, *Parsifal*. The playful episode of the commedia was
over, and modernism returned to an earlier grandeur.

T. S. Elliot was a keen observer of the Sitwells' promotion of the
commedia taste from the beginning. In 1918, in *The Egoist*, he said,

"Instead of rainbows, cuckoos, daffodils, and timid hares, they give us garden gods, guitars, and mandolins." (Glendinning, p. 60.) Eliot was himself a commedia poet, but a subtler one. He was able to treat other values, notably religious ones, more seriously than they could. In 1921, in the first issue of *The Tyro*, he wrote, "The poets who consider themselves most opposed to Georgianism, and who know a little French [Edith Sitwell knew a *very* little French] are mostly such as could imagine the Last Judgment only as a lavish display of Bengal lights, Roman candles, catherine wheels, and inflammable fire balloons." (*Ibid*, p. 4.)

In Eliot's early verse there was a more subtle appropriation of the commedia images. (One might compare Eliot with Nabokov in this regard, and Sitwell with Dinesen.) We recognize a Pierrot figure in Prufrock, but the stereotype is blended with other images of modern ordinariness:

> And indeed there will be time
> To wonder, 'Do I dare?' and 'Do I dare?'
> Time to turn back and descend the stair—
> (They will say: 'How his hair is growing thin!')
>
>   (Eliot, *Prufrock*.)

How many stage and screen Pierrots we have seen (for instance, Stan Laurel in formal dress) striking in theater the lyric-ironic note that Eliot goes on to strike in poetry:

> My morningcoat, my collar mounting firmly to the chin,
> My necktie rich and modest, but asserted by a simple pin—
> (They will say: 'But how his arms and legs are thin!')
> Do I dare
> Disturb the universe?

Equally of the commedia is the self-parody, which is also the parody of the tragic hero:

> No! I am not Prince Hamlet, nor was meant to be.

This Hamlet reference reminds us of Laforgue, who defined himself as a Hamlet who was yet only a parody of Shakespeare's hero. But Laforgue's non-Hamlet was perhaps more of a Harlequin, while Eliot's was a Pierrot. *His* Harlequin or Moor is to be seen in the coarsely animal Sweeney:

> Apeneck Sweeney spreads his knees
> Letting his hands hang down to laugh,

> The zebra stripes along his jaw
> Swelling to maculate giraffe.
>
> (Eliot, *Sweeney*.)

Eliot was of course a great master of parody, irony, and fragmentation, the three major commedia techniques, and the major key in which commedia art is played is heard in poems like "Rhapsody on a Windy Night" or "Preludes." From the first:

> Twelve o'clock.
> Along the reaches of the street
> Held in a lunar synthesis,
> Whispering lunar incantations
> Dissolve the floors of memory
> And all its clear relations,
> . . . .
> And through the spaces of the dark
> Midnight shakes the memory
> As a madman shakes a dead geranium.

And later we are told that the moon, like a commedia actress or ballet dancer:

> [She] smooths the hair of the grass.
> The moon has lost her memory.
> A washed-out smallpox cracks her face,
> Her hand twists a paper rose,
> That smells of dust and eau de Cologne . . .

When we come to *The Waste Land,* as early as 1922, we find Eliot blending these commedia images with more symbolist techniques, in order to build a larger form. There are still vignettes (for instance, the seduction of the typist, and the conversation in the pub) that we can imagine as commedia episodes by Chaplin or Marceau (Eliot is never so simply portentous as Sitwell), but we find also much to remind us of the first wave of modernism. We find the Upanishads and Baudelaire, and even several quotations from and allusions to Wagner himself.

In 1927 Eliot became a member of the Anglican Church, declaring himself royalist, Catholic, and classical in his sympathies. At about the same time, his poetry began to lean upon the dogma and traditions of orthodoxy—primarily Christian but also cultural. Like Stravinsky, he reformulated symbolism, and divided its heritage between religion and art. The splendid pictures of *Ash Wednesday* draw their far horizons of meaning from the poet's faith in his Catholic heritage. But his persona is still intermittently commedic. One can locate that persona in, for instance, *The Hollow Men*, which strikingly prefigures Beckett's plays.

Of the English-language poets we must mention also Wallace Stevens, who can remind us of both Eliot and Nabokov. His point of departure as a poet was close to Eliot's (they were both at Harvard and in the same decade), and Eliot remained an impressive and daunting precursor for Stevens. The latter once said that reading Elliot was like having a Giotto in one's breakfast nook, and that Eliot "remains an upright ascetic in a world that has grown exceedingly floppy and is growing floppier." (Fuchs, p. 27.) This perhaps applies primarily to the older and Christian Eliot, but it is not inappropriate to his younger, commedic phase. Both stances were morally severe in a way alien to Stevens. The poems by Eliot that most resemble Stevens's were those early extrovert exercises in bravura like "The Hippopotamus" and "Mr. Eliot's Sunday Morning Service," which have least of that other character element, the nervous melancholy that drove Eliot along his path of development.

Stevens passed from *his* earliest gaudiest exuberance straight to metaphysical reflections of the human mind. Even in *The Commedian as the Letter* C, though Crispin is a commedia character, the stock buffoon of French comedy, the poem is about the imaginative man's relation to the phenomenal world. (*Ibid.*, p. 33.) The commedia figure is as merely decorative as the Harlequins of Picasso's cubist period. He is not felt as a commedic presence. But Stevens said that while Crispin is an everyday man, whose life includes no adventures, the poem reproduces both his everyday plainness and the contrasting "plush of the stage." (*Op. Cit.*) Clearly, the commedic sensibility is felt in that plush, in the verse, and in Stevens's "hypercivilized, perverse, confusing, and erudite wit." (*Ibid,* p. 29.) As he became the philosopher, he did not cease to be the dandy; he did not submit, as Eliot did, to an ideology that outlawed his commedic freedoms.

In this he can remind us of Nabokov, so much more defiant than Eliot, the Nabokov who called one of his early novels, which remained a favorite, "this bright brute." Some of Stevens's early poems, like "The Emperor of Ice Cream," are also "bright brutes." He and Nabokov seem to find the Christian virtues irrelevant, and their sense of evil is metaphysical rather than ethical. (The difference between the two is that Nabokov is more grossly insulting to our ethical sensibility, but makes an emotional affirmation of the virtues of domesticity, and also—a related matter—Nabokov's art is full of people about whom we care and in whom we are interested, while Stevens's poetry is notably abstract.)

Among those associated with Stevens as American dandy writers were novelists like Elinor Wylie and James Branch Cabell, who were fairly overt in their use of commedia motifs. But the most important employments of that material in English-language novels were more concealed. Of the novels of the 1920s we might take *The Great Gatsby* (1925) first. Its commedic emotional pattern is clearly focused in Daisy (Columbine), Tom (Harlequin), and Gatsby (Pierrot). Tom is primarily the brutal philistine. He is described in terms of power and size; as having been a powerful end at Yale, and as being enormously wealthy. (Fitzgerald, p. 6.) We see him standing with his legs apart in riding clothes on his front porch, leaning forward, showing his body's "enormous power," and we are told of his hard mouth, arrogant eyes, and supercilious manner. But there is an even more commedic touch in the wistfulness with which he always seeks to win the approval of the narrator—"some harsh defiant wistfulness of his own." (*Ibid.*, p. 7.) The narrator is another Pierrot, and Harlequin is dependent in his way on Pierrot.

Daisy is straightforwardly glamorous. Her face is "sad and lovely, with bright things in it," and she has a low, thrilling voice. (*Ibid.*, p. 9.) The narrator seems to respond uncritically to a magazine image; but he stresses also the fragility and the instability in her poise, which leaves her complicit with Tom after the car accident in which she killed Myrtle Wilson but let Gatsby take the blame. She is a faithless Columbine. The narrator, watching Tom and Daisy through a window, afterward, finds they have an air of natural intimacy, as if they were conspiring together. (*Ibid.*, p. 146.) While Gatsby, on the other hand, is seen watching her house all night after the accident, to see if she needs him. His feeling for her is not intimate but idealistic. He has rented his enormous house just so he can watch hers across the Sound. He is a Pierrot image of silent yearning and hopeless devotion.

Of course, we rightly think of *The Great Gatsby* as a picture of its time, a study of contemporary manners and morals. Much of the art of such fiction consists in the skill with which the commedia stereotypes are adapted to contemporary life, and vice versa; to give the reader a satisfying sense of pattern, the souce of which is hidden from him. As compared with Dinesen, Fitzgerald is less the Muse of the commedia and more the chronicler of the Jazz Age. But the commedic mode is easily detectable in his chronicle. He gives us contrastive scenes of elegant fantasy at the Buchanans, of gaudy pantomime at Gatsby's parties, of sordidness at the Valley of Ashes, of poetic meditation in the night hours on the shore of Long Island Sound. All this scene setting functions like the backdrops, costuming, and dancing of theatrical commedia. Fitzgerald's way of describing places turns them into theater. We first see Daisy lying with her friend on an enormous couch, on which they are "buoyed up as though upon an anchored balloon." (*Ibid.*, p. 8.) "They were both in white, and their dresses were rippling and fluttering as if they had just been blown back in after a short flight around the house." While on the other hand the Valley of Ashes is "a fantastic farm where ashes grow like wheat into ridges and hills and grotesque garden" (*Ibid.*, p. 23.); a wasteland overlooked by the enormous eyes of Dr. T. J. Eckleburg.

If we turn now to Hemingway's *Fiesta (The Sun Also Rises)*, we can perhaps take for granted the author's similar adaptation of the Paris expatriate and nightclub scene to the commedia stereotypes. *Fiesta*, as its British title makes clear, is another carnival novel, like Fitzgerald's. Brett is a Columbine/Muse, Cohn is a Pierrot, Mike is a Harlequin. Moreover, the people of the Paris background he described were commedic types, in fact involved in the cult of commedia modernism. Hemingway's task, in which he succeeded brilliantly, was to draw out of the commedia images their 1920s café-and-bullring equivalents, their contemporary manifestations, and to create a novel whose surface was wholly realistic but whose depths were archetypal.

What is more striking is Hemingway's partial transformation and transvaluation of Pierrot and Harlequin; a transvaluation in which he was followed by later novelists. In the triangular relationship of Jake, Brett, and Romero, Jake is clearly Pierrot to the others' Columbine and Harlequin; he is Brett's true love, but he is impotent; the coarser bond of sexuality unites her and Romero, and Jake can only stand in the wings of their love affair and wait to be of use to her. This is the familiar pattern. However, in the triangle of Jake, Brett, and Cohn, it is Cohn who is Pierrot. He is the yearning, sentimental, suffering adorer; but he is mocked by the novel for his pains. This time Pierrot does not win the audience's sympathy. (Of course, we do not *simply* mock, but we do, if we accept the terms of readership offered us, feel Cohn/Pierrot to be in the wrong.) Harlequin's triumph over Pierrot, in its cruder aspect, goes to Mike, but Jake joins forces with him against Cohn; and the reader follows Jake. We choose Harlequin to represent us, not Pierrot. This is an important innovation, but of course it occurs within the limitations of the commedia—it is a reshuffling of the same pack of cards.

The other important development Hemingway offers is the assimilation of the bullring and the bullfighter to the commedia stage. Of course the bullring is not a stage on which Jake, Cohn, and Brett can act. Only Romero can enter it, and he is too large to be a commedia figure—he appears in the novel as a shadow thrown by someone outside it, who lives in a larger, brighter, nobler world.

But we have seen how eagerly commedia art accommodates that multidimensional imposing of illusion upon illusion, of theater upon theater. The bullring is felt as a greater theater beyond, of which the theater we see is the ignoble travesty. We are told at the beginning that "Nobody ever lives their lives all the way up except bullfighters." (Hemingway, p. 10.) It is made clear, in the conversation between Romero and "the critic," that bullfighting is a supreme art. (*Ibid.*, p. 174.) But it is an art that involves the artist's risking his life; an art that is also a priesthood, and a heroic priesthood. Thus Hemingway offered the commedic genre of fiction two important extensions of its scope. (Bullfighting and fishing are of course very unlike commedia acting; it is Hemingway's stylization of them that makes us call them extensions of the commedia.)

A third, and English, example of commedia fiction is to be found in Evelyn Waugh's entertainments: *Decline and Fall* (1928), *Vile Bodies* (1931), *Black Mischief* (1932), *Scoop* (1938), and *Put Out More Flags* (1942). These are works of humor, primarily, and so are different from *The Great Gatsby* and *The Sun Also Rises.* But Waugh makes just as striking use of commedia stereotypes. His leading women characters are Columbines (Margot in his first novel and Nina in the second, up to Sonia in the last one named.) His central men are usually Pierrots; though Paul and Adam, in the first two novels, are not psychologically developed. Like Hemingway, Waugh introduces Harlequin figures with whom the reader is encouraged to identify and who get rougher and tougher in each succeeding novel. The most striking case of this is Basil Seal, who appears in *Scoop* and *Put Out More Flags.* In the last-named novel, the most perfect of Waugh's works, a full-blown Harlequin contends with a full-blown Pierrot (Ambrose Silk), and they bore and betray each other, mutually dependent, helplessly entangled together.

Again the triumph of this art lies in the mutual adjustment of the stereotypes to the social scene, and vice versa. Basil (Harlequin) belongs to the rebellious generation of England's Children of the Sun. The perfect "brilliant" undergraduate, he cannot develop past that stage; he belongs with the famous scapegraces of that generation, Burgess, Maclean, and Philby. Ambrose, a genuinely gifted artist, is a Jew, a homosexual, and an aesthete. He represents (in the form of Pierrot) the sad fate of the literary intellectuals of that generation, too fragile to sustain the posture of rebellion they took up in their youth, or even to find another ideology, let alone a mode of action, once Communism had let them down. These bold equivalences between the social-historical drama of 1930s England and the commedia stereotypes are brilliant both as fictional art and as historical interpretation.

In the 1920s even more strikingly, D. H. Lawrence, a novelist of genius who had committed himself to opposite values and modes of imagination, fell under the commedic influence so strong just after World War I and produced in *Aaron's Rod* (1922) some brilliant chapters of commedic fiction. In this novel, despite Lawrence's famous celebrations of love and marriage in earlier work, the domestic life of Aaron Sisson is made to seem very small beer and dull stuff, in the first chapters. The people Aaron meets in London—commedic types—are much more vivid. One of them, Josephine Ford is a "cameo-like girl with neat black hair done tight and bright in the French mode. She had strangely drawn eyebrows, and her colour was brilliant." (Lawrence, p. 23.) In Florence, Aaron meets two of the most vivid 1920s dandies in fiction, Francis and Angus.

"Their hair was brushed straight back from their foreheads, making the sweep of the head bright and impeccable, and leaving both the young faces clear as if in cameo." (*Ibid.*, p. 184.) We see Angus, looking like a white owl, his monocle beaming with bliss, making tea in a railway carriage, "with his feet under him, in the authentic Buddha fashion, and on his face the queer, rapt, alert look, half a smile." (*Ibid.*, p. 200.) And we see Francis, "in fine, coloured silk pyjamas, perched on a small upper balcony, turning away from the river towards the bedroom again, his hand lifted to his lips, as if to catch there his cry of delight. The whole pose was classic and effective; and very amusing. How the Italians would love it!" (*Ibid.*, p. 203.)

All this is commedia writing, about commedia types. Both young men are absorbed in their own performances—so completely absorbed that they are no longer substantially men. And the woman in the novel, the American Marchesa, who has lost her gift of singing, is a silenced and sinister Muse:

She seemed like a demon, her hair on her brows, her terrible modern elegance. She wore a wonderful gown of thin blue velvet, of a lovely colour, with some kind of gauzy gold-threaded filiment down the sides. It was terribly modern, short, and showed her legs and her shoulders and breast and all her beautiful white arms. Round her throat was a collar of dark-blue sapphires. Her hair was done low, almost to the brows, and heavy, like an Aubrey Beardsley drawing.

(*Ibid.*, p. 241.)

In other words, she was an image out of the Bakst-Diaghilev ballets, a fantasy of erotic luxury; the opposite of the Lawrentian woman:

She was most carefully made up—yet with that touch of exaggeration, lips slightly too red, which was quite intentional, and which frightened Aaron. He thought her wonderful and sinister. She affected him with a touch of horror. She sat down opposite him, and her beautifully shapen legs, in frail, goldish stockings, seemed to glisten metallic, thrust out from out of the wonderful, wonderful skin—like periwinkle-blue velvet. She had tapestry shoes, blue and gold; and almost one could see her toes; metallic naked. The gold-threaded gauze slipped at her side. Aaron could not help watching the naked-seeming arch of her foot. It was as if she were dusted with dark gold dust upon her marvellous nudity.

(*Op. cit.*)

Here we see Lawrence compelled by the spirit of the times to create a commedic goddess of love (a Marlene Dietrich figure) alien though that image was to his erotic philosophy.

That spirit was indeed compelling and pervasive. "For I feel that, broadly and essentially," wrote Thomas Mann in 1926, "the striking feature of modern art is that it has ceased to recognize the categories of tragic and comic, or the dramatic classifications, tragedy and comedy. It sees life as tragicomedy, with the result that the grotesque is its most genuine style." Mann wrote that in an introduction to a German translation of *The Secret Agent*, and what he says applies to both his own German fiction, and Conrad's Polish/French/English variety. There is indeed much grotesque farce in Conrad, which is sometimes explicitly commedic (e.g., in the Harlequin figure in *The Heart of Darkness*).

Of other literatures, the one that most importantly embodied the spirit of the commedia, at least from the Anglo-Saxon point of view, was the French. German literature deserves some mention, Russian can be entirely neglected, but French commedia influenced the rest of the world, in many forms. Englishmen like Cyril Connolly tell us that in the 1920s and 1930s they went to Paris as to the city of Pierrot. And the most important embodiments of Pierrot were in Marcel Proust and his great autobiographical novel, *À la recherche du temps perdu*. It is striking how many autobiographies by Englishmen of the interwar years refer to the way the authors saw their friends as Proust's characters, as Verdurins or Guermantes, and interpreted their experiences into Proust's terms.

One cause of his enormous influence was that rebellion of his against manhood, which was repeated by so many young men of the interwar generation. Proust does not seem literally to have hated his father, but he refused to enter into the heritage, the cultural form, of father-hood/manhood/masterfulness. His father was in fact both a genial head of household and a highly successful doctor, a friend of ministers of state and an authority on the international control of cholera. In the novel the narrator says that as a boy he implicitly relied on his father to re-solve all the family's problems, and to win them privileges. "He was so powerful, in such high favour with people in office, that he made it possible for us to transgress laws which Françoise had taught me to re-gard as ineluctable." And the boy is confident that "if I had been cap-tured by brigands, my father's understanding with the supreme powers" would have saved him. (Proust, p. 223.)

But the narrator (like Proust himself) from earliest childhood re-fuses to take the route that would lead *him* to manhood. The family calls this "developing willpower." He often hears himself accused of failing at this, and he agrees with the diagnosis. His grandmother disapproves of his being allowed to read so much. " 'That is not the way to make him strong and active,' she would say sadly. 'Especially this little man, who needs all the strength and will-power that he can get.' " (*Ibid.*, p. 11.) Everyone around was concerned "to reduce my nervous sensibility and strengthen my will." (*Ibid.*, p. 40.) In the real life of the Proust family, moreover, there was another boy, Robert, who was indeed manly and became a doctor and a husband and a father, just like Dr. Proust.

On the night his parents yield to his pleading, against their better judgment, and let his mother spend the night in his room, he for the first time hears his mother ascribe his behavior to "nerves," and so give it and him a medical excuse. Proust then developed (in his novel as well as in his personality) traits of sensibility that we can compare with the Pierrot persona in the way they differ from the social norm or hu-man average of manhood. One such trait was a valetudinarian hyper-sensitiveness, developed into a refinement of both feeling and analysis. Another was a hypertrophy of memory and nostalgia, developed into a theory of unconscious memory as the key to a reality which actual ex-perience missed. "When he tasted the madeleine dipped in lime tea, a shudder ran through him, and exquisite pleasure invaded his senses, he was filled with a precious essence—no, that essence *was* him." (*Ibid.*, p. 54.) This contact with the unconscious was the *symboliste* element in Proust, and the root of his art. The commedia element is most ob-vious in the grotesque comedy of the Verdurins.

Within the field of the psychology of love, he developed the motif of erotic obsession, which had been there in Balzac and Flaubert, but which Proust—in, for instance, the story of Albertine—developed into the form in which Nabokov was to use it. We can draw a clear distinction between this form of love and what we find in D. H. Lawrence. It is the Pierrot/Harlequin/Columbine triangle, and commedic art in general, that presents love in the form of obsession.

Other kinds of weakness or wound in Proust—his Jewishness, his homosexuality, his snobbery, his susceptibility to high society—also help to make him a Pierrot, partly because he presents them as weaknesses. They ingratiate him with the reader just as the signs of Pierrot's unmanliness—his hairless face, blank expression, floppy white costume—ingratiate him with the theater audience. While Proust's sentimental piety about high bourgeois values—his love for Françoise, his mother, his grandmother, his appreciation for their cooking, their housekeeping, their gardening, their gentle and loving manners—remind the readers that he is on their side at heart.

No doubt it is for all those reasons that Proust became a *representative* artist of the 1920s and 1930s, one who subsumes, as an image of the writer, such figures as Rilke and Kafka. At the root of the sensibility of both of the latter we see a comparable rebellion against manliness. Rilke was sent to a military academy, with a brutally male-chauvinist ethos, after his mother deserted the family. Deeply wounded by his experience, he developed a cult of virginity in his early stories, about pure young girls yielding themselves reluctantly to gross old men. In his poem "Requiem for a Friend," he accuses "the male" in general. And like Proust, he was excited by the idea of aristocracy and developed an elaborate mystique of art. All these reactions against reality and realism are symbolized by the figure of Pierrot.

Kafka had an extreme case of the father problem, analyzed at length in his "Letter to my Father," and an equally clear refusal of the masculine role. He told his friend Max Brod, "I shall never grow up to be a man, from being a child I shall immediately become a white-haired ancient." (Brod, p. 37.) His father was a Prague butcher and property owner, loud, confident, and masterful, while the boy preferred his mother's family of scholars, dreamers, and eccentrics.

As a (weak and delicate) child, he had, according to Brod, big questioning eyes, a dour tight-lipped mouth, and limp hands. He wrote plays for his sisters to perform, but would not act himself. Brod compares the Kafka family atmosphere, the distribution of roles between men and women, the *importance* of the family circle, and the resultant pressure the son felt, with the atmosphere in the Proust family. He also points to a similar meticulous love of detail in both writers' work, a detail that baffled and confused their readers because it implied a denial of "reality and realism"—an assertion of a counterreality. And, like Proust, Kafka continued to the end of his life to feel his need for his father's approval as "a load of fear, weakness, and self-contempt." (*Ibid.*, p. 23.)

As for the commedia aspect of his work, we can take as an example the last chapter of his novel *The Trial.* It begins:

On the evening before K's thirty-first birthday—it was about nine o'clock, the time when a hush falls on the streets—two men came to his lodging. In frock coats, pallid and plump, with top hats that were apparently irremovable. After some exchange of formalities regarding precedence at the front door, they repeated the same ceremony more elaborately before K's door."

(Kafka, p. 279.)

This is practically a commedia script.

K, meanwhile, is presented to us as dressed all in black, and slowly pulling on a pair of tight-fitting gloves. "The two gentlemen bowed, each indicating the other with the hand that held the top hat. . . . 'Tenth rate old actors they send for me,' said K to himself. . . . 'What theatre are you playing at?' " (*Ibid.*, p. 280.) And when they get him outside, they take hold of him with commedic, though sinister, expertise. "They kept their shoulders close behind his and instead of crooking their elbows, wound their arms around his at full length, holding his hands in a methodical, practised, irresistible grip. [Throughout the novel, Kafka sketches postures and gestures with a Chaplin eye.] K walked rigidly between them, the three of them were interlocked in a unity which would have brought all three down together had one of them been knocked over. . . . 'Perhaps they are tenors,' he thought, as he studied their fat double-chins. He was repelled by the painful cleanliness of their faces. One could literally see that the cleansing hand had been at work in the corners of their eyes, rubbing the upper lip, scrubbing out the furrows at the chin." (*Ibid.*, p. 281.) A similar pair come to arrest K at the beginning of the novel; and in *The Castle* another couple act as the Land Surveyor's assistants. These are versions of the commedia's zanies, who will remind us of Samuel Beckett's pairs, in, for instance, *Waiting for Godot.*

The Trial has of course tragic and indeed realistic elements, which are well known. But the literary convention that complements and holds together this realism and this tragedy derives from the commedia, in several of its aspects, comic, romantic, and sinister. After the two "gentlemen" have arrested K, they cross a bridge in the moonlight, over water glittering and trembling beneath them—there is a suggestion of a Watteau landscape. Then they remove K's coat, waistcoat, and shirt, prop him up against a boulder, and settle his head upon it, like a marionette's. When one produces a long, thin, double-edged butcher's knife, K knows that he is supposed to take it himself and plunge it into his own heart. But he "could not completely rise to the occasion." (*Ibid.*, p. 285.) So they do it—"thrust the knife deep into his heart and turned it there twice. With failing eyes K could still see the two of them immediately before him, cheek leaning against cheek, watching the final act. (*Ibid.*, p. 286.) This is one of the most brilliant and moving pieces of commedia fiction we have.

And there are also striking likenesses between Kafka's fiction (particularly the short pieces) and mime performances by, for example, Marcel Marceau; those pale enigmas of pure line are all manifestations of Pierrot. Looking at the photographs of the writers of the 1920s, we are struck by how often the Pierrot mask appears, the large-eyed, gaunt-faced, androgynous mask of intelligent suffering. And surely the three most eloquent faces of them all belong to Kafka, Proust, and Rilke—though Virginia Woolf is a close rival.

In terms of sheer sensibility and originality, Proust can perhaps claim no advantage over the others. But he is particularly interesting to us in our argument, because he had so much to say about and against earlier ideas of art and society. In *Contre Sainte-Beuve*, he reproached the nineteenth-century critic for allying himself with the general reader and not with the rebellious artist; he reproached his master in aesthetics, Ruskin, for confusing art with morality; and (in his novel) he taught his mother to overcome her prejudiced preference for "generosity and moral distinction" in art. (Proust, p. 51.)

Thus it was Proust who turned away most consciously from the great figures of nineteenth-century humanist art. And it was he who welcomed the Diaghilev ballets, that harbinger of twentieth-century commedia art, to Paris. George Painter writes, "In June (1910) Proust was lured from solitude by a new revelation of high art. Diaghilev and the Russian Ballet had first exploded upon Paris for an all-too-brief season in May 1909. In 1910 all Paris had awaited them for a year, and their triumph was instant and tremendous." (Painter, p. 160.) Proust said he had never seen anything so beautiful as when the curtain went up on *Schéhérazade*, showing a dazzling green tent with shadowy blue doors and a vast orange carpet. He got to know Nijinsky, Rubinstein, and others, and his friends Cocteau and Hahn created a new ballet for the company. "Already the camp following of artists and intellectuals which formed an indispensable part of the Diaghilev circus was beginning to gather . . . the incessant cross-fertilization, devised by the strange and cunning genius of Diaghilev." (*Ibid.*, p. 161.)

Proust triumphed as a writer after the War. À *l'ombre des jeunes filles en fleur* came out in 1919 and won him the Prix Goncourt. The day after the award, twenty-seven articles about Proust appeared in the press, and by the end of that year, a hundred. In its enthusiasm for Proust, France repudiated nineteenth-century humanism, and, implicitly, the patriotic heroics of the war. In May 1922, on the first night of Stravinsky's ballet *Renard,* Sydney and Violet Schiff gave a party, to which they invited the ballet company and the four greatest artists of the day, James Joyce, Stravinsky, Picasso, and Proust—an event that can symbolize the triumph of Proust, and of the commedia.

Associated with Proust in his enthusiasm for the ballet and related matters was Cocteau, who went on to have an important career as artist and taste-maker in the France of the 1920s and 1930s. But the influence of the commedia movement was also strong on French writers as unlike Cocteau as Sartre and de Beauvoir, in the 1930s.

Sartre's autobiography, *Les Mots,* is a brilliant exposition of the rebellion against manhood that we have met in Proust and the others. "There is no good father, that is the rule. Don't lay the blame on men but on the bond of paternity, which is rotten." (Sartre, p. 19.) To his refusal of manhood he ascribes his "incredible levity. I am not a leader, nor do I aspire to become one. Command, obey, it's all one. The bossiest of men commands in the name of another—his father—and transmits the abstract acts of violence which he puts up with. Never in my life have I given an order without laughing, without making others laugh. It is because I am not consumed by the canker of power; I was not taught obedience." (*Ibid.*, p. 21.) At the very end, he says, "I became a traitor and have remained one. . . . I'll repudiate myself in a moment, I know I will, I want to." (*Ibid.*, p. 238.) This is a commedic prose, worthy of Scapin or Sganarelle.

In fact, Sartre never knew his father, and it was his grandfather he had to react against. This man appears in his memoir as an embodiment of nineteenth-century culture. "He was a man of the nineteenth century who took himself for Victor Hugo, as did so many others, including Victor Hugo himself." (*Ibid.*, p. 24.) This might be Laforgue speaking.

In another place, Sartre says his grandfather so resembled God the

Father that he was often mistaken for Him. (*Ibid.*, p. 22.) However, he was not a man of religion, but a humanist:

Stained glass windows, flying buttresses, sculpted portals, elaborate cruicifix-ions carved in wood or stone. Meditations in verse or poetic Harmonies: these Humanities led us straight to the Divine, all the more in that added to them were the beauties of Nature. The works of God and the great achievements of man were shaped by one and the same impulse; the same rainbow shone in the spray of waterfalls, shimmered between the lines of Flaubert, gleamed in the chiaroscuro of Rembrandt; it was the Spirit. . . . In certain exceptional cir-cumstances—when a storm broke on a mountain, when Victor Hugo was in-spired—one could attain that sublime point where the Good, the True, and the Beautiful blended into one.

(*Ibid.*, p. 57.)

One can think of Proust as well as Laforgue; for Madame Verdurin re-garded Rembrandt's *The Night Watch,* together with Beethoven's Ninth Symphony and the Winged Victory, as the supreme masterpieces of the universe.

Satre says, after expounding the humanism his grandfather taught him, "I had found my religion." (*Ibid.*, p. 57.) But the Sartre we read in fact devised for himself a cult quite opposite in character to his grandfather's; one which in its early phases had elements of the commedic.

Simone de Beauvoir has much to tell us, in her memoirs, of the im-portance of play and fantasy in the group to which she and Sartre be-longed as students. Sartre in those days composed a constant stream of humorous ballads, epigrams, and poems, which featured puns, allitera-tion, and other verbal tricks. He set himself to disguise life's mediocrity with lying fantasies. (de Beauvoir, *Life*, pp. 20–21.) They took from Cocteau the fantasy cosmology of *Le Potomak.* At that time Sartre lived to write. "Society as then constituted we opposed. But there was noth-ing sour about this enmity: it carried an implication of robust optimism. Man was to be remolded, and the process would be partly our doing. We did not not envisage contributing to the change except by way of books: public affairs bored us." (de Beauvoir, *Daughter*, p. 18.) Later she tells us that his faith was in beauty, which he treated as inseparable from art. (de Beauvoir, *Life*, p. 21.)

De Beauvoir's memories of family and friends are, like Sartre's, full of commedia perceptions and types—full of the 1920s. It seems that her father saw himself as commedic. She compares him with Pierrot and with Sarah Bernhardt. He went clean-shaven, unlike others in his social class, in order to look like an actor, and he and her mother (though the latter was religiously pious) spent three weeks every year with a group of amateur actors at Divonne-les-Bains, where the director of the Grand Hotel gave them free room for entertaining the other guests. He subscribed to the theatrical journal *Commedia* and took a special delight in makeup. He could escape from himself in wig and false mustache. (*Ibid.*, p. 37.) Simone adored her father, whom she describes as aristocratic, epicurean, irreligious, but above all theatrical. She was thus well prepared for the first man she fell in love with, her self-dramatizing cousin Jacques, who inducted her into modern literature with gifts of Cocteau and Gide. Like Sartre, her first values were commedic.

During World War II, both changed. Sartre came back from German prison camp disconcerting in the stringency of his moral demands, she says—hitherto, duty had repelled him. And she turned her old distaste for social piety into indignation against the Vichy regime of General Pétain. Pétain, accepting France's defeat by Germany, blamed French intellectuals and their irresponsibility. De Beauvoir writes, "The crawling hypocrisy of the man who had the nerve to assert his loathing for 'the lies which have done us such terrible harm' put me in a blazing temper. . . . Henceforth (said Pétain) the family would be the sovereign unit, the reign of virtue was at hand, and God would be spoken of respectfully in the schools." (*Ibid.*, p. 370.) She (and Sartre) set out to create a truer morality.

In this new tone of moralism, after the war, she and Sartre denounced the surrealists; the latter, heavily influenced by the commedic mood, continued to play after Sartre had renounced playfulness in favor of Marxist Existentialism. He now submitted to a political and philosophical rigor that put an end to the commedic phase of modernism. His art, and that of his allies (we could cite Frantz Fanon's books of ideas, and Jean Genet's fiction and drama), was typical of the third phase of modernism, in which rigorism in politics combined with and controlled boldness of imagination and speculation.

Chapter 9.

SOME CONTEMPORARY IMAGES

T HE TRIUMPH of Pierrot occurred between the years 1890 and 1930. In the half century of artistic history that has passed since 1930, other image sets have exerted more power over the imaginations of our painters, poets, and dancers. Comparatively speaking, the Pierrott/Harlequin/Columbine figures have retreated and the claims of ideology, religious or political, have reasserted themselves against the insouciance of the commedia. A balance between all the rival claims similar to that prevailing before 1890 has now reasserted itself, a balance that we are therefore prone to call normal.

But the commedia has not disappeared from the imaginative scene. As our chapters on literature and film made clear, we found much after 1930 that deserved discussion. Here and now and for any foreseeable future—and the same is true for any discoverable past, as the names of Baudelaire and Watteau will remind us—there will always be important artists who are inspired by the commedia tradition. There will also always be forms of popular entertainment in which we recognize the commedia spirit as important.

Let us begin with the great traditional artists. They are traditional because they belong in the mainstream of European art since the Renaissance, although they are also modernists, and seemed like aesthetic radicals when we first met their work; and they are traditional also because of the sophisticated uses they make of the commedia material. There were some striking examples in the chapters on literature and film. We discussed Evelyn Waugh and Vladimir Nabokov and alluded to several other writers whose uneasiness about the functions of art in this rich and guilty civilization finds a natural expression in commedic images. These are contemporary writers who are still widely read today. They represent one strain in contemporary sensibility, and a clearly commedic one. But perhaps we cannot think of them as expressing the "here and now."

The films of Bergman and Fellini have stronger claims to contemporaneity, because the two directors are still alive—Bergman offered us his examination of man-woman relationships, *From the Life of the Marionettes*, in 1980—and because their films are continually publicized and shown. Clearly Bergman and Fellini return to the theater and the circus, to clowns and marionettes and grotesques, all the time—more than other filmmakers. The physical images derived from the popular forms of theater, from the fairground, have more personal meaning to them and remain more intimately a part of their growth and self-conception as artists—and the profound differences between them make this all the more striking. Fellini's Rome, as Pauline Kael said, "more familiar to us by now than Rome itself," is a "big-top city," a commedia concept. (Kael, p. 51.) An equal familiarity and an equal flamboyance accrue to the actors in Bergman's films and their emotions. We may not quite understand the amusing/fascinating/menacing marionette sequence in *Fanny and Alexander*, but we certainly recognize the mix of emotions, and we've been there before.

Other films have made vital use of the same images, of course. Indeed, the most sustained film commedia of all emerged at the end of World War II, between the heyday of the slapstick and expressionist comedians and the rise of Fellini and Bergman.

However, the Prévert-Carné *Children of Paradise* may be Marcel Carné's direct response to his own experience—Carné "platonically observing the melancholy masquerade of life, the riddle of truth and illusion, the chimeras of *la comédie humaine*," as Bosley Crowther put it after the American premiere. (Amberg, p. 226.) But it is also a historical study of the loving and suffering of Jean-Gaspard Deburau, both in and out of his role as the great Pierrot. It contains exquisite footage of Jean-Louis Barrault in pantomime, and the mime sequences manage to sum up the beauty and pathos of the lives of those who must play to the galleries (*le paradis*)—a perfect vision, in other words, of nineteenth-century commedia, the art of Deburau. This, in fact, is what the film is, a long-lined, slow, and exquisitely wrought re-creation of romantic commedia. It is not the work of film modernists; like Chaplin's *Limelight* of a few years later, it summons up a past of clowns and actors, rather than using them to make something new.

Hockney

But besides these nostalgic artists of film and literature, there is a brilliant modernist painter who loves the commedia, has made undeniably new things out of it, and who can indeed claim to be a kind of revolutionary.

In 1960, David Hockney, a young Yorkshireman doing postgraduate work at the Royal College of Art, went to a large Picasso exhibition at the Tate Gallery. He went, by his own count, about eight times, and in the abundant mixture of styles and media he saw in Picasso, especially in the magisterial disregard for consistency and homogeneity, even within a single canvas, Hockney found a sense of liberation:

Style is something you can use, and you can be like a magpie, just taking what you want.

(Livingstone, p. 23.)

In other words, Picasso taught him the uses of parody, irony, and fragmentation.

The magpie trait was, of course, strong in many of the original commedia modernists, Stravinsky, Meyerhold, Cocteau, but especially Picasso, and in discovering this tendency in Picasso, Hockney also affirmed it in himself. Like them, he uses disguise as a way to strip off ordinary coverings and stand naked. Few artists on the contemporary scene have been so various in so public, frank, and autobiographical a way as Picasso and Hockney; no one else in the history of art has exposed himself so openly, playfully, seriously, in so many different styles and media as Hockney and Picasso.

These similar temperaments touch, appropriately, in a shared taste for the commedia. Twenty years after that Tate exhibition, Hockney went to the Walker Art Center in Minneapolis to study another major Picasso exhibition, and that same year he pursued Picasso to the monumental Museum of Modern Art retrospective. Included in this were reconstructions of some of Picasso's 1917 *Parade* costumes, which had been prepared for the 1973 Joffrey Ballet revival. They were of particular interest to Hockney because he was designing a *Parade* himself, for the Met. True to both Picasso and his own magpie nature, Hockney managed to borrow distinctive features from the Picasso costume designs, but the achievement as a whole was thoroughly characteristic Hockney. As with so much of his other work, he drew from many other sources, especially Matisse, Dufy, and others of the early twentieth-century Mediterranean bent.

Hockney's earlier stage work had demonstrated both his cheerful cannibalism and his deep loyalty to the modernist commedia line. In 1966 he designed the Royal Court production of *Ubu Roi*, Jarry's grand progenitor of so much modernist farce; he entered into the anarchic spirit of the thing by creating naturalistic figures alongside slapdash abstractions and by placing letters on stage that spelled out locations and that, naturally, dispensed with the need for "real" sets. The Polish army was two childishly uniformed men bound together by a banner, which read "Polish Army." In 1974 Hockney took on the role of designer again, this time for *The Rake's Progress* at Glyndebourne. For this, Hockney made extensive use of crosshatched pen lines in imitation of the Hogarth engravings of his own *Rake's Progress*, applying the technique to clothing and makeup as well as scenery and emphasizing the engraving effect with stylized eighteenth-century structures—until the final madness scene, the scene in Bedlam, for which the artist created walls covered with Miróesque fantasies and, on the floor, a grid of partitions with a figure in each box, each an inmate whose mental state was dramatized by the mask he or she wore, most of which were strongly reminiscent of commedia masks.

In the 1980 project for the Met this literally commedic strain burst into full flower. This was not only because of *Parade*, but because of the demands, and the inspiration, of the other two works that shared the stage with the Satie ballet, *Les Mamelles de Tirésias* of Poulenc and Ravel's *L'Enfant et les sortilèges*. Both of these small operas sprang out of the modernist fairground and circus of the century's first decades, the balloon-breasted Tirésias representing the arch, elegantly absurd strain; Ravel's naughty child and his abused, angry belongings representing the childlike, yet artfully grotesque side of this fascination. *Les Mamelles* was not composed until 1944, but was based on a play of Apollinaire written around 1903. *L'Enfant* was based upon a poem written by Colette during the war and composed in 1920–1925. The triple bill, called *Parade, An Evening of French Music Theatre*, was originally conceived by John Dexter; he brought Hockney into the project, and it was he who directed Hockney to the original commedia dell'arte as the source of unifying imagery for the productions. Of course, Picasso had already played the commedia theme, which Hockney was only too glad to take up, but his *Parade* was only a seventeen-minute ballet in a three-hour evening of theater, and Hockney and Dexter needed a unifying theme.

In the midst of their search, Dexter discovered a review of an exhibition of Tiepolo's Punchinello drawings at the Frick Museum in New York. Hockney's reaction to the drawings was immediate and had the force of a major discovery:

Fantastic . . . nobody can draw like this today. Unbelievably full of life, aren't they? . . . Look at the life in them. Look at this one, the Punchinellos with the dogs and the dogs look like Punchinellos. Fantastic.

(Smith, in *Arts*, p. 88.)

Out of this grew the chorus of thirty-six bright green Punchinellos in the Ravel. The brilliant, and by all critical accounts unforgettable, color scheme that ruled in all three works found its common note in that emerald green. The soloists of *L'Enfant* also wore costumes that took their cue from the Punchinellos, and there were even Punchinello stagehands who helped with scenery changes onstage:

I gave the Met wardrobe people the Tiepolo catalogue, pointing out that each Punchinello was different. I said, "If you look closely, it's not a complete uniform. They all have a tall hat, every one wore a mask, but there are tall ones and little ones, fat and thin ones, chic and dowdy ones, babies—some with little potbellies."

(Friedman, p. 160.)

In short, Hockney immersed himself in Tiepolo's commedia; but he also remained faithful to Picasso's. Following Dexter's desire that the Great War cast its shadow on the evening, Hockney created an opening with searchlights playing over the audience, coiled barbed wire, and a crowd of soldiers, one of whom stepped from the group and stripped off his uniform and gas mask to reveal himself as a Harlequin. After this prologue a curtain appeared, a version of the original *rideau rouge*, the red curtain to which Satie's *Parade* music refers.

Hockney pursued Picasso's commedia, and that of Satie and Poulenc, in the fantastic creatures he designed for *Parade*. The most vivid of these is an enormous, grotesque woman with one large red and one large blue breast (she is so imposing that she must be danced by a man); she is carted about the stage in a baby carriage. Babies have an important place in *Les Mamelles*—the Husband of Thérèse is, by some absurdist law of symmetry, transformed into a woman when his wife becomes Tirésias, and it becomes his (her) role to populate their country, Zanzibar; accordingly, he produces thousands of infants with the help of an incubator machine. Hockney provided Punchinellos for carting babies about, and, again, he mixed the Italian and the early twentieth-century commedias by dressing the sophisticated town ladies called for by Poulenc in costumes and hairstyles modeled upon the styles of the French couturier Paul Poiret.

The work on his French evening for the Met inspired Hockney to much else in the way of commedia, and true to that magpie nature, he resorted to the commedia of the old Italian prints as well as to that of his revered Picasso. He turned out oils and prints with *Parade*-related themes, several of which contain a red-white-and-blue-striped ladder like the original Picasso drop-curtain ladders. In 1980, the time of the Met project and most of this related work, Hockney produced one of his best-known recent paintings, *Harlequin*, in which the familiar figure, patched, masked, and slightly chunky of form, is doing a handstand. Behind him is a similarly patched curtain, various brightly colored geometric forms, and that *Parade*-induced striped ladder. This painting got its widest circulation as the basis for the Met poster advertising the *Evening*.

Naturally enough, most of the commentators who have admired the work ascribe its genesis to Hockney's Picasso side. (Friedman, p. 48.) In fact, the figure of Harlequin himself, down to the patches, the pose, the mask, is a brightly colored, slightly roughened, but otherwise quite faithful copy of a Harlequin out of the *Recueil Fossard*, a seventeenth-century repository of commedia engravings of images based on presentations by Italian commedia troupes in France during the reign of Henry III. (Duchartre, p. 133.) Hockney makes the face beardless (and red) beneath the mask and provides his own background, but he borrows the quaintly serifed lettering used to identify the character "Harlequin."—including the period.

Another much-admired product of the same year, 1980, is *Punchinello on and off Stage*. Friedman also calls this "Picasso-inspired" and describes it as:

a composition in which a dwarf punchinello in long, blond curls stands in the orchestra pit and faces the audience while a scene is played on stage. The drawing is deliberately chunky, with the innocence and forcefulness of a child's vision.

(Friedman, p. 48.)

But here again, Hockney's knowledge of the old commedia is being underestimated. The painting is a version, more a translation into bright Hockney colors and forms than a copy, but still quite recognizable, of a seventeenth-century print, *Pulcinella on and off Stage*. (Duchartre, p. 218.) The Pulcinella onstage has a more stylized mask that does recall Picasso, but the dwarf in the foreground is just as chunky, innocent, and forceful in his seventeenth-century incarnation as in his twentieth.

Thus Hockney very characteristically embraced all of the commedia strain within his immediate grasp as soon as he discovered Tiepolo. And while Picasso remains central to him, Picasso's commedia is his only in the sense that Picasso's images, designs, and ideas are now in the service of Hockney's vision. Picasso himself turned to the original Italian commedia only briefly, when he, too, discovered it in connection with a stage project, his Pergolesi-inspired *Pulcinella* for Diaghilev. The autobiographical harlequins and saltimbanques and dancers that mark the first decades of Picasso's career reveal a different, and deeper, commitment to the commedia in him than in Hockney. But then, Hockney is a modernist in a new age and in a different way.

Unlike Picasso, Hockney claims to take pleasure in all the pleasures his culture recommends. It is typical that in his early days he was in love, from afar, with the pop singer Cliff Richard; he expressed this love in cryptic codes and initials in a series of early paintings that variously express his coming to terms with his homosexuality. (Livingstone, p. 23.) His familiarity with the pop world and pop styles is just as much part of the Hockney achievement (as well as of the Hockney image) as his attachment to the "classical" sources of his modernism. His exquis-itely drafted realistic paintings of swimming pools, TV, and various manifestations of modern living can be very amusing (*Mr. and Mrs. Clark and Percy*, two friends of Hockney as soulfully pouting young moderns with cat, 1970–1971); but there is often as much acceptance in these works as satire. Indeed, Hockney may be a pop modernist in the specific sense that he is at ease with the commedic strains in pop culture, in-cluding what we might call pop behavior.

Pop and Python

This final argument can be no more than suggestive and tentative. This pop commedia has little to do with television and street-corner and party mimes, although there are undoubtedly connections to be made. It is more importantly, though obliquely, related to the theatricalism of Hollywood and the star system and the commedia-like patterns in per-sonalities and in plots that grew out of that phenomenon. But pop com-media manifests itself most fully not in the movies, but in the hypertheatricalism of pop music of the seventies and eighties.

Pop culture is by definition naive, because it is defined in opposition to the sophisticated radicalism of intelligentsia culture. However, pop culture also produces figures of enormous sophistication, who can apply all of the elements of commedia, or their rough parallels, very know-ingly. This is true, for instance, of the Monty Python troupe, who have all the university degrees they need to exploit or mock any tradition or collection of values they choose. Their behavior as a company, their repertoire of stock characters and *lazzi*, their sexual humor, physicality, endless use of masks and disguises, all of these suggest many obvious parallels with the commedia. Many of their routines involve literal stages and theatrical events, and cartoons framed by multiple, ornate curtains and stages are stock features, as are mannequins (a Princess Margaret replica as well as the department store variety) and liberal applications of sexual and homosexual humor. One of the very few monographs (so far) about Monty Python puts together an appreciative, if sketchy "dossier" on the group as a purveyor of the grotesque, sometimes in the tradition of Rabelais. (Thompson.) The broad social satire also occasionally summons up the ghost of Brecht, but Monty Python goes no further than the intent to amuse when they expose and mock the pretensions, high and low, of society.

Whatever their commitments as individuals, the collective view of Monty Python is absurdist; even their expressions of towering, righteous outrage are funny, often very funny, despite the fact that outside of their particular comic constructs the objects of the outrage may be the targets of legitimate anger. It was ever thus in the world of popular theater, perhaps, but the Python group has a way of calling up extremes that suggests alienation. Their skit about the World's Funniest Joke, a joke that kills with laughter, is almost lethally funny itself. But this is a good way down the road from the let's-laugh-as-hard-as-we-can school of the twenties and Evelyn Waugh. This modern absurdist vision has as its basic subject a world or at least an age that is indeed absurd, that has conceived of grotesque absurdities in rapid succession for decades that have outstripped the imaginations of any possible surrealist avant-garde. The most knowing of the rock stars of this age share with such as Monty Python a sense of the absurd. This sense may be fitful; seldom is it so sweeping as this suggests, and it is clouded by self-absorption. But nevertheless this sense of modern life underlies the theatricality of both the rock stars and Monty Python, a sense that the world is indeed a glittering, doomed theater.

Rock Commedia

The evidence for this argument, this intuition, is a matter of certain recurring pop images, such as the masklike, impassive yet soulful Pierrot face that some popular performers assume, at least for purposes of album covers and for the stage. Performers as different as Juice Newton (*Quiet Lies*) and Pete Townshend (*Chinese Eyes*) stare out from album covers with startlingly similar faces, and the face they share is that of Pierrot. David Bowie, the king of Glitter Rock and so much else in a multitude of roles and personalities, has that look even more strikingly, and the ambivalent sexual identity to go with it. He is especially a twenties Pierrot when he adopts the slicked-hair, bowed-lips look, and because of the longevity of his stardom, he can claim to be the precursor of such androgynous creatures as Boy George ("If I have sex at home, does that

mean that I'm a homosexual?"—as quoted by Collins in *USA Today*.)
Boy George has constructed a theatrical image based on a combination
of vulnerability, flamboyance, and the grotesque—all framed, masked,
and thick with makeup. Culture Club and Kiss and so many other groups
conceive of themselves, at least for their public, in these deliberately
artificial, often mocking, ironic terms—even though they then plunge
into songs about the breaking down of barriers and throwing away of
masks. The parallels with commedia may be based only on this dominant theatricality. It is rarely deliberate, or definite, of course: the Pierrot
dolls in Prince's bedroom in *Purple Rain* do say something about this
image, but they don't make him a Pierrot.

With the sexy impudence of the "Material Girl," Madonna has a
sly self-knowledge that recalls the sauciness of Columbine, but the echo
is very distant. Even more, perhaps, than Beckett and Ionesco and their
confreres, the rock world projects a theater for the end of a civilization:
the darker elements of the commedic arsenal, the grotesquerie, a stylized decadence, all of these are present, along with the blurred (but em-
phatic) sexuality, in Bowie and other significant rock figures. And there
are many in the pop world with a sophistication about elements of this
theatricality, such as the dramatic potential in colored lights and in sound,
the projection of the larger-than-life image made possible by the rock
amplifier. To most this is merely a means for generating a blaring excitement; some, however, use it as a basis for an elemental form of
commedia.

Commedia Apocalypse

Even more than the kings, queens, and princes of rock, certain filmmakers have focused upon the absurdities that attend the actions of a
civilization that seems intent on destroying itself. Hans-Jürgen Syberberg's
epic *Hitler: A Film from Germany* is about a particular self-destructive
civilization, but in its immense philosophical and theatrical ambitious-
ness, it also encompasses Western civilization of the 1970s. Its relevance here lies in Syberberg's striking use of commedic devices. They
are basic not only to his imagery but also to the shifting levels of narrative. The techniques for emphasizing artifice, developed by the earlier
commedia modernists, are pushed to expressive extremes. At one point
the actor playing SS man Ellerkamp asks himself, "Who am I?" Is he
Ellerkamp, Hitler's projectionist, showing the Führer such favorites as
Broadway Melody, with Fred Astaire:

Or am I just one of the great entertainers? A solo performer, a circus director of a big show that's known as History and the Past?

(Syberberg, p. 108.)

The actors are visible as actors as well as characters, but they are also seen manipulating puppets. Puppets of various leading Nazis are trotted out, most vividly "Adolf, the degenerate puppet from the Punch and Judy show":

Yes, indeed, the Führer as a puppet-clown; that's it, the vengeance of hell, that they now have to live as puppet-clowns.
Adolf has to yodel, and to keep on yodeling, and Eva has to dance, forever. At the Oktoberfest. And the children will laugh, immortal figures, a big number this.

(*Ibid.*, p. 70.)

But we are reminded of the sharper message beyond the spectacle of punishment, of "the puppet-clown as the Hitler within us." Like the German expressionist commedists before him, Syberberg makes brilliant theater out of the darkest shadows in the psyche.

Another contemporary director with similar powers is Ridley Scott, as exhibited in the science fiction thriller *Alien* and particularly in *Blade Runner*, the puppet–puppet-master lineage of which has already been discussed in the film chapter. The aesthetic elegance of these films and the tense play of human against android remind one at times of the commedia. But this is end-of-the-world commedia, projected into a future darkened by our culture's present self-betrayal.

But the leading film modernist who has shown himself to be fond of dwelling commedically on the end of civilization is Jean-Luc Godard. Surely it is an enjoyment, however crazy and self-mocking, we sense percolating through the satire in *Alphaville*, the gangster movie for the end of civilization, and *Le Weekend*, Western culture's last vacation. However strong the social consciousness of Godard, he remains an ironist, fascinated with the framing powers of his medium. The frames both detach the viewer from reality and dissolve the distinctions between reality and unreality: Godard has said that in movies "the imaginary and the real are separated distinctly and yet form a single entity, like the Möbius strip, which has two sides and yet is one-sided." (Godard, *Godard*, p. 242.) Like Dürrenmatt and Beckett, Godard imposes a simplification upon his subjects, but it is of a different kind from that envisioned by the playwrights. He preserves, revels in, the choking clutter of civilization—countless characters with countless purposes or cross-purposes—

but he reduces the plot, the presumptive story line, to a point of casualness that forces us to discard all traditional notions of expectations, tension, and resolution. The story does not disappear—this is not Warhol—but it competes with the accidental, the casual, and we must seek it out, even in a gangster/adventure film such as *Breathless* (1959—written by Truffaut). This is especially true of the one Godard film that makes an overt bow toward the commedia, *Pierrot le fou* (1965).

In this film, as in *Breathless*, Jean-Paul Belmondo plays the gangster/adventurer, this time into gun-running rather than stealing cars. His name is Ferdinand, but his Marianne, Anna Karina, insists on calling him Pierrot. Indeed, she insists to the end over his objections (he is bored, alienated, modern): her last words, after he has taken revenge for her leaving him, are "I ask you to forgive me, Pierrot," to which he replies, "My name is Ferdinand . . . it's too late." (Godard, *Pierrot*, p. 103.) We never know what to make of this game, or whether we care. But we are drawn into the apartment scenes with Marianne and Ferdinand, with cheap postcard reproductions of Picasso, Renoir, and Modigliani on the walls, along with photos from *Life* and *Paris-Match*—and we get a close-up of a Picasso Pierrot. In an interview, Godard said, "I wanted to tell the story of the last romantic couple, the last descendants of *La Nouvelle Héloise*, *Werther*, and *Hermann and Dorothea*." (*Ibid.*, p. 5.) Marianne does sing of love as they lie in bed. In the end the mad Pierrot/Ferdinand paints his face with blue paint and blows himself up. Godard also said, "The whole thing was shot, let's say like in the day of Mack Sennett. . . . Watching old films, one ever gets the impression that they were bored working." (*Ibid.*, p. 7.) But whatever irritated suspicions are aroused by all this, Godard insists, and perhaps demonstrates, that he plays with purpose. It is the modernist revolutionary, as well as the aesthetic ironist, who says "*Pierrot* is not really a film. It is an attempt at cinema. And the cinema, by forcing reality to unfold itself, reminds us that we must attempt to live." (*Ibid.*, p. 244.) Pierrot is put to yet another modernist use; he is un-Pierroted, denied his framed theatricality in a sullen, unwilling incarnation, who, in the course of (Godard's notion of) the unfolding of reality, paints himself blue and destroys himself, in a burst of Pierrot madness.

Other Godard films, notably *Les Carabiniers*, are essentially postludes, entertaining sketches of the end of civilization as we know it, which preserve some recognizable elements of the old commedia interludes. And it is this use of Pierrot and Harlequin characters to deal with postnuclear possibilities which must stay in our minds as the most striking example of the commedia work of the 1980s.

Let us take our final example from literature. In the savage and primitive England of Russell Hoban's 1980 novel, *Riddley Walker,* civilization begins to piece itself together, long after nuclear-bomb devastation. "The clevver looking bloak said, 'Clevverness is gone now but littl by little itwl come back. The iron wil come back agen 1 day and when the iron comes back they wil bern chard coal in the hart of the wood.' " (Hoban, p. 4.) The primitive orthography reminds us always, sotto voce, of the primitive and rudimentary culture that has grown up among the ruins of our metropolitan centers, nuclear power plants, underground arms factories, and so on. And at the heart of this dim and uncertain process of recovery and discovery are the people who, by secret wisdom, magic, and hidden organization, can make the "connexion" to the old forgotten science. The central character, Riddley Walker, takes his name from the riddles he propounds as he walks across the few miles he knows. He makes his connections by way of his puppet performances with commedia puppets, and his pregnant questions and answers.

"Jack Ketch says, 'If a dead pig is bacon whats a dead Punch?' Punch says, *'You wont never see no dead Punch Im too old to dy.'* " (*Ibid.,* p. 137.) "Punch said, 'I am the balls of the worl I am the stoans of the worl. I am the stoans and I have my littl stick.' " (*Ibid.,* p. 172.)

The incantatory power of Hoban's Punch has roots that are older than Punch himself, older than his cousins Pierrot and Petrushka. It is these deep connections that are being awakened today. They were evidently still there in the commedia we knew so well, even in its attenuated and familiar versions. Today they are coming alive, in response to the new resonances of modern experience. If the 1980s and 1990s see a new revival of the commedia, it is likely to be a triumph of Hoban's Punch with his stick, rather than Deburau's Pierrot, with his dreams.

BIBLIOGRAPHY

Introduction

Elias, Norbert. *The Civilizing Process,* trans. E. Jephcott. New York: Urizen Books, 1978.

Green, Martin. *Children of the Sun: A Narrative of Decadence in England After 1918.* New York: Basic Books, 1976.

Huizinga, Johan. *The Waning of the Middle Ages.* Garden City, NY: Doubleday, 1954.

Leites, Edmund. *The Puritan Conscience and Modern Sexuality.* New Haven: Yale University Press, 1986.

Chapter 1

Arkell, Alan. *Looking for Laforgue.* Manchester, England: Carcanet Press, 1979.

Beaumont, Cyril. *The History of Harlequin.* New York: Arno Press, 1976.

Harding, James. *Erik Satie.* New York: Praeger, 1975.

Lea, K. M. *Italian Popular Comedy.* Oxford: Oxford University Press, 1934.

Magee, Bryan. *Aspects of Wagner.* New York: Stein & Day, 1969.

Martin, Stoddard. *Wagner to the Waste Land.* Totowa, NJ: Barnes & Noble, 1982.

Mawer, Irene. *The Art of Mime.* London: Methuen, 1932.

Nicoll, A. *The World of Harlequin.* Cambridge: Cambridge University Press, 1976.

Storey, Robert. *Pierrot: A Critical History of a Mask.* Princeton: Princeton University Press, 1978.

Chapter 2

Akhmatova, Anna. *A Poem Without a Hero,* trans. Carl R. Proffer. Ann Arbor, MI: Ardis, 1973.

Arkell, Alan. *Looking for Laforgue.* Manchester, England: Carcanet Press, 1979.

Beaton, Cecil. *Photobiography.* London: Odhams, 1951.

Brandenburg, Hans. *München Leuchtete: Jugenderinnerungen.* Munich: Neuner, 1953.

Eliot, T. S. *Introduction to Ezra Pound, Selected Poems.* London: Faber & Faber, 1928.

Glendinning, Victoria. *Edith Sitwell.* New York: Knopf, 1981.

Gould, Jean. *The Poet and Her Book.* New York: Dodd, Mead, 1969.

Kunitz, Stanley, and Max Hayward. *Poems of Akhmatova.* Boston: Atlantic Monthly Press, 1973.

Kuzmin, Mikhail. *Wings,* pref. by Vladimir Markov. Ann Arbor, MI: Ardis, 1972.

Lewis, Wyndham. *The Wild Body.* New York: Haskell House, 1927.

Magee, Bryan. *Aspects of Wagner.* New York: Stein & Day, 1969.

Markov, Valdimir. In H. W. Tjalsma, *Russian Modernism.* Ithaca: Cornell University Press, 1976.

Martin, Stoddard. *Wagner to the Waste Land.* Totowa, NJ: Barnes & Noble, 1982.

Mawer, Irene. *The Art of Mime.* London: Methuen, 1983.

Millay, Edna St. Vincent. *Collected Poems.* New York: Harpers, 1956.

Painter, George. *Proust: The Early Years.* Boston: Little, Brown, 1959.

Proust, Marcel. *Swann's Way,* trans. C. K. Scott-Moncrieff. New York: Modern Library, 1928.

Sitwell, Sacheverell. *The Cupid and the Jacaranda.* London: Macmillan, 1952.

———. *The Dance of the Quick and the Dead.* Boston: Houghton Mifflin, 1937.

———. *For Want of the Golden City.* New York: John Jay, 1973.

Tjalsma, H. W. *Russian Modernism.* Ithaca: Cornell University Press, 1976.

Trotter, David. *The Making of the Reader.* New York: St. Martins, 1984.

Wedekind, Frank. *Five Tragedies of Sex,* trans. Fawcett and Spender. New York: Theater Arts Book, n.d.

Wellek, Rene. "Russian Formalism," in H. W. Tjalsma, *Russian Modernism.* Ithaca, NY: Cornell University Press, 1976.

Wilson, Edmund. *American Earthquake.* New York: Doubleday, 1958.

———. *Axel's Castle.* New York: Scribners, 1931.

———. *Five Plays.* New York: Farrar, Straus, Young, 1954.

———. *Galahad and I Thought of Daisy.* New York: Farrar, Straus, Young, 1967.

———. *The Shores of Light.* New York: Farrar, Straus, Young, 1952.

———. *The Twenties.* New York: Farrar, Straus & Giroux, 1975.

Chapter 3

Axsom, Richard H. "Parade," *Cubism as Theater.* New York: Garland, 1979.

Buckle, Richard. *The Adventures of a Ballet Critic.* London: Cresset, 1953.

———. *Diaghilev.* New York: Athenaeum, 1979.

———. *Nijinsky.* New York: Simon & Schuster, 1971.

Cohen, S. J. *Next Week Swan Lake.* Middletown, CT: Wesleyan University Press, 1982.

Fonteyn, Margot. *The Magic of Dance.* New York: Knopf, 1979.

Gordon, Suzanne. *Off Balance.* New York: Pantheon, 1982.

Grigoriev, Sergey. *The Diaghilev Ballet 1909–1929.* London: Constable, 1953.

Hamm, Charles, ed. *Petrushka.* New York: W. W. Norton, 1967.

Haskell, Arnold. *Diaghileff.* London: Gollancz, 1935.

Kirstein, Lincoln. *Dance.* Westport, CT: Greenwood Press, 1970.

Kochno, Brois. *Diaghilev and the Ballets Russes.* New York: Harper & Row, 1970.

Lawrence, D. H. *Women in Love.* New York: Viking, 1960.

Levinson, Andre. *Ballet Old and New.* New York: Dance Horizons, 1982.

Leiven, Peter. *The Birth of the Ballets Russes,* trans. L. Zarine. New York: Dover, 1973.

Spencer, Charles, and Philip Dyer. *The World of Serge Diaghilev.* Chicago: Regnery, 1974.

Stokes, Adrian. *Tonight the Ballet.* London: Faber & Faber, 1934.

Woolf, Virginia. *The Voyage Out.* London: Duckworth, 1920.

Chapter 4

Appia, Adolphe. *The Work of Living Art: A Theory of the Theatre,* trans. H. D. Albright. Coral Gables: University of Miami Press, 1960.

Beckett, Samuel. *Ends and Odds.* New York: Grove Press, 1976.

Braun, Edward. *Meyerhold on Theatre,* trans., ed., critical commentary. New York: Hill & Wang, 1969.

————. *The Theatre of Meyerhold, Revolution of the Modern Stage.* New York: Drama Book Specialists, 1979.

Brown, Frederick. *Theatre and Revolution: The Culture of the French Stage.* New York: Viking, 1980.

Craig, Edward Gordon. *On the Art of the Theatre.* London: William Heinemann, 1911.

————. *The Theater—Advancing.* Boston: Little, Brown, 1923.

Dürrenmatt, Friedrich. *Plays and Essays,* ed. Volkmar Sander. New York: Continuum, 1982.

Esslin, Martin. *The Theatre of the Absurd.* New York: Anchor-Doubleday, 1961.

Ewen, Frederic. *Bertolt Brecht: His Life, His Art and His Times.* New York: Citadel, 1967.

Field, Andrew. *Pages from Tarusa: New Voices in Russian Writing,* ed. with intro. Boston: Little, Brown, 1963.

Fletcher, John. *Samuel Beckett's Art.* New York: Barnes & Noble, 1967.

Golub, Spencer. *Evreinov: The Theatre of Paradox and Transformation.* Ann Arbor, MI: UMI Research Press, 1984.

Gorchakov, Nikolai A. *The Theater in Soviet Russia,* trans. Edgar Lehrman. New York: Columbia University Press, 1957.

Gorelick, Mordecai. *New Theatres for Old.* New York: Octagon, 1975. (Originally published 1940.)

Guitry, Sacha. *Deburau, Comédie en vers libres.* Paris: Fasquelle, 1918.

Harding, James. *Sacha Guitry: The Last Boulevardier.* New York: Schribners, 1968.

Houghton, Norris. *Moscow Rehearsals: The Golden Age of the Soviet Theatre.* New York: Grove, 1962. (Originally published 1936.)

Kluge, Rolf-Dieter. *Westeuropa und Russland im Weltbild Aleksandr Bloks.* Munich: Verlag Otto Sagner, 1967.

Law, Alma H. "Meyerhold's The Magnanimous Cuckold," *The Drama Review* 26, no. 1 (Spring 1982): 61–86.

Leisler, Edda, and Gisela Prossnitz. *Max Reinhardt und die Welt der Commedia dell'arte.* Salzburg: Otto Muller Verlag, 1970.

Leyda, Jay. *Kino: A History of the Russian and Soviet Film.* London: Allen & Unwin, 1960.

Mead, Mary. *Through the Zani's Mask: Examining Blok's "Balagancik" and Evreinov's "Veselaja Smert."* (Thesis, Harvard University, 1975.)

Moody, C. "Vsevolod Meyerhold and the 'Commedia dell-Arte,' " *Modern Language Review* 73 (Oct. 1978): 859–869.

Nijinska, Irina, and Jean Rawlinson, trans. and ed. *Bronislava Nijinska: Early Memoirs,* intro. and consultation by Anna Kisselgoff. London: Faber & Faber, 1981.

Oxenhandler, Neal. *Scandal and Parade: The Theater of Jean Cocteau.* New Brunswick, NJ: Rutgers University Press, 1957.

Paterson, Doug. "Two Productions by Copeau: 'The Tricks of Scapin' and 'Twelfth Night,' " *The Drama Review* 28, no. 1 (Spring 1984): 37–51.

Rudnitsky, Konstantin. *Meyerhold the Director,* trans. George Petrov, ed. Sydney Schultze, intro. Ellendea Proffer. Ann Arbor, MI: Ardis, 1981.

Schmidt, Paul, ed. *Meyerhold at Work.* Austin: University of Texas Press, 1981.

Segel, Harold B. *Twentieth-Century Russian Drama: From Gorky to the Present.* New York: Columbia University Press, 1979.

Shostakovich, Dmitri. *Testimony: The Memoirs of Dmitri Shostakovich,* as related to and ed. by Solomon Volkov, trans. Antonina Boulis. New York: Harper & Row, 1979.

Sogliuzzo, A. Richard. *Luigi Pirandello, Director: The Playwright in the Theatre*. Metuchen, NJ: Scarecrow Press, 1982.

Sontag, Susan, ed. with intro. *Antonin Artaud: Selected Writings*. New York: Farrar, Straus & Giroux, 1976.

Styan, J. L. *Max Reinhardt*. New York: Cambridge University Press, 1982.

Symons, James M. *Meyerhold's Theatre of the Grotesque, Post-Revolutionary Productions, 1920–1932*. Coral Gables: University of Miami Press, 1971.

Vogel, Lucy E. *Aleksandr Blok: The Journey to Italy*. Ithaca, NY: Cornell University Press, 1973.

Volbach, Walther R. *Adolphe Appia, Prophet of the Modern Theatre: A Profile*. Middletown, CT: Wesleyan University Press, 1968.

Worrall, Nick. "Meyerhold Directs Gogol's 'Government Inspector,'" *Theatre Quarterly* 2, no. 7 (July–Sept. 1972): 75–95.

Chapter 5

Bainbridge, John. *Garbo*. Garden City, NY: Doubleday, 1955.

Barlow, John D. *German Expressionist Film*. Boston: Twayne, 1982.

Bazin, André. *What Is Cinema?*, trans. and selected by Hugh Gray. Berkeley: University of California Press, 1967.

Bermel, Albert. *Farce: A History from Aristophanes to Woody Allen*. New York: Simon & Schuster, 1982.

Björkman, Stig, Torsten Manns, and Jonas Simas. *Bergman on Bergman: Interviews with Ingmar Bergman*, trans. Paul Britten Austin. New York: Simon & Schuster, 1973.

Blesh, Rudi. *Keaton*. New York: Macmillan, 1966.

Braun, Edward, ed. *Meyerhold on Theatre*, trans. and commentary by Braun. New York: Hill & Wang, 1969.

———. *Theatre of Meyerhold, Revolution on the Modern Stage*. New York: Drama Book Specialists, 1979.

Buñuel, Luis. *My Last Sigh*, trans. Abigail Israel. New York: Knopf, 1983.

Carné, Marcel, and Jacques Prévert. *Les Enfants du Paradis*, trans. Dinah Brooke. London: Lorimer, 1967.

Chaplin, Charles. *My Autobiography*. New York: Pocket Books, 1966.

Clair, René. *Cinema Yesterday and Today*. trans. Stanley Applebaum, ed. R. C. Dale. New York: Dover, 1972.

Cocteau, Jean. *Cocteau on the Film.*, a conversation recorded by André Fraigneau, trans. Vera Trill. London: Dobson, 1954.

Crowther, Bosley. *The Great Films: Fifty Golden Years of Motion Pictures*. New York: Putnam, n.d.

Duchartre, Pierre Louis. *The Italian Comedy*, trans. Randolph T. Weaver. New York: Dover, 1966.

Durgnat, Raymond. *Luis Buñuel*. Berkeley: University of California Press, 1968.

Eisner, Lotte H. *Murnau*. Berkeley: University of California Press, 1972.

Fellini, Federico. *Juliet of the Spirits*, ed. Tullio Kezich, trans. Howard Greenfield. New York: Ballantine, 1965.

Field, Andrew, ed. *Pages from Tarusa: New Voices in Russian Writings.*, ed. with intro. Boston: Little, Brown, 1963.

Frewin, Leslie R. *Dietrich: The Story of a Star*. New York: Stein & Day, 1967.

Horton, Andrew, and Joan Magretta, eds. *Modern European Filmmakers and the Art of Adaptation*. New York: Frederick Ungar, 1981.

Insdorf, Annette. *François Truffaut*. New York: William Morrow, 1979.

Jones, G. William, ed. *Talking with Ingmar Bergman*. Dallas: Southern Methodist University Press, 1983.

Kael, Pauline. *Reeling*. New York: Warner, 1976.

Keaton, Buster. *My Wonderful World of Slapstick*, with Charles Samuels. Garden City, NY: Doubleday, 1960.

Kerr, Walter. *The Silent Clowns*. New York: Knopf, 1975.

Kracauer, Siegfried. *From Caligari to Hitler: A Psychological History of the German Film*. Princeton: Princeton University Press, 1947.

————. *Theory of Film: The Redemption of Physical Reality*. New York: Oxford University Press, 1960.

Lahue, Kalton C., and Terry Breuer. *Kops and Kustards: The Legend of the Keystone Films*. Norman: University of Oklahoma Press, 1968.

————. *World of Laughter: The Motion Picture Comedy Short, 1910–1930*. Norman: University of Oklahoma Press, 1972.

Livingston, Paisley. *Ingmar Bergman and the Rituals of Art*. Ithaca: Cornell University Press, 1982.

Lloyd, Harold, and Wesley W. Stout. *An American Comedy*. New York: Dover, 1971.

Madden, David. *Harlequin's Stick, Charlie's Cane*. Bowling Green, NC: Bowling Green University Popular Press, 1975.

Mast, Gerald. *The Comic Mind: Comedy and the Movies*. Indianapolis: Bobbs-Merrill, 1973.

————. *A Short History of the Movies*. Indianapolis: Bobbs-Merrill, 1976.

McCaffrey, Donald, ed. *Focus on Chaplin*. Englewood Cliffs, NJ: Prentice-Hall, 1971.

O'Leary, Liam. *The Silent Cinema*. New York: Dutton, 1965.

Pratt, George C. *Spellbound in Darkness: A History of the Silent Film*. Greenwich, CT: New York Graphic Society, 1973.

Renoir, Jean. *My Life and My Films*, trans. Norman Denny. New York: Athenaeum, 1974.

Rhode, Eric. *A History of the Cinema: From Its Origins to 1970*. New York: Hill & Wang, 1976.

Rosenthal, Stuart. *The Cinema of Federico Fellini*. Cranbury, NJ: A. S. Barnes, 1976.

Rotha, Paul. *The Film till Now*, 2nd rev. ed. New York: Funk & Wagnalls, 1951.

Sesonske, Alexander. *Jean Renoir, The French Films, 1924–1939*. Cambridge: Harvard University Press, 1980.

Sternberg, Josef von. *Fun in a Chinese Laundry*. New York: Macmillan, 1965.

Symons, James M. *Meyerhold's Theory of the Grotesque*. Coral Gables: University of Miami Press, 1971.

Thiher, Allen. *The Cinematic Muse: Critical Studies in the History of French Cinema*. Columbia: University of Missouri Press, 1979.

Uraneff, Vadim. "Commedia dell'arte and American Vaudeville," *Theatre Arts Magazine* 7, no. 4 (Oct. 1923).

Welsford, Emil. *The Fool: His Social and Literary History*. Garden City, NY: Doubleday, 1961.

Wood, Robin. *Ingmar Bergman*. New York: Praeger, 1969.

Chapter 6

Apollinaire, Guillaume. *Selected Writings of Guillaume Apollinaire*, ed. and trans. Roger Shattuck. New York: New Directions, 1949.

Barr, Alfred H., Jr. *Picasso: Fifty Years of His Art.* New York: Museum of Modern Art, 1946.

Blunt, Sir Anthony, and Phoebe Pool. *Picasso: The Formative Years, A Study of His Sources.* Greenwich, CT: New York Graphic Society, 1962.

Brown, Frederick. *An Impersonation of Angels, A Biography of Jean Cocteau.* New York: Viking, 1968.

———. *Theater and Revolution: The Culture of the French Stage.* New York: Viking, 1980.

Carmean, E. A., Jr. *Picasso: The Saltimbanques.* Washington, D.C.: National Gallery of Art, 1980.

Cocteau, Jean. *Cocteau's World, An Anthology of Writings by Jean Cocteau*, ed. and trans. Margaret Crosland. New York: Dodd, Mead, 1972.

Cooper, Douglas, and Gary Tinterow. *The Essential Cubism: Braque, Picasso, and Their Friends.* New York: Braziller, 1983.

Fagiolo, Maurizio, and Ester Coen. *Gino Severini.* Rome: Bulzoni, 1977.

Feld, Charles. *Picasso: His Recent Drawings.* trans. Suzanne Bruner, pref. by René Clair. New York: Abrams, 1969.

Gedo, Mary. *Picasso: Art as Autobiography.* Chicago: University of Chicago Press, 1980.

Harding, James. *Erik Satie.* New York: Praeger, 1975.

Heerikhuizen, F. W. van. *Rainer Maria Rilke, His Life and Work.* London: Routledge & Kegan Paul, 1951.

Lucie-Smith, Edward. *Symbolist Art.* New York: Oxford University Press, 1972.

McCully, Marilyn, ed. *A Picasso Anthology: Documents, Criticism, Reminiscence.* Princeton: Princeton University Press, 1982.

O'Brian, Patrick. *Pablo Ruiz Picasso: A Biography.* New York: Putnam, 1976.

Oxenhandler, Neal. *Scandal and Parade: The Theater of Jean Cocteau.* New York: Viking, 1968.

Penrose, Roland. *Picasso: His Life and Work.* New York: Schocken, 1962.

Picasso. New York: Skira, n.d.

Rilke, Rainer Maria. *Selected Poetry of Rainer Maria Rilke*, ed. and trans. Stephen Mitchell. New York: Random House, 1982.

Rubin, William, ed. *Pablo Picasso, A Retrospective*, chron. by Jane Fluegel. New York: Museum of Modern Art, 1980.

Soby, James Thrall. *Georges Rouault: Painting and Prints.* New York: Museum of Modern Art, 1947.

Starobinski, Jean. *Portrait de l'artiste en Saltimbanque.* Geneva: Editions d'Art Albert Skira, 1970.

Steegmuller, Francis. *Apollinaire: Poet Among the Painters.* New York: Farrar, Straus, 1963.

Templier, Pierre-Daniel. *Erik Satie*, trans. Elena and David French. Cambridge: MIT Press, 1969.

Venturi, Lionello. *Rouault*, trans. James Emmons. Paris: Skira, 1959.

Wertenbaker, Lael Tucker. *The World of Picasso.* New York: Time-Life, 1967.

Chapter 7

Appel, David. *Prokofiev by Prokofiev: A Composer's Memoir*, trans. Guy Daniels. New York: Doubleday, 1979.

Asaf'yev, Boris. *A Book About Stravinsky*, trans. Richard French. Ann Arbor, MI: UMI Research Press, 1982.

Axsom, Richard Hayden. *Parade: Cubism as Theater*. New York: Garland, 1979.

Best, Alan. *Frank Wedekind*. London: Oswald Wolff, 1975.

Borchmeyer, Dieter. *Das Theater Richard Wagners*. Stuttgart: Philipp Reclaim, 1982.

Busoni, Ferruccio. *The Essence of Music and Other Papers*. trans. Rosamond Ley. New York: Dover, 1965.

Carlson, Tom. "Ernst Krenek: *Jonny Spielt Auf*," essay for recording on Mace MXX 9094.

Cocteau, Jean. *Cocteau's World: An Anthology of Writings by Jean Cocteau*, Margaret Crosland, ed. and trans. New York: Dodd, Mead, 1972.

Corleonis, Adrian. "Ferruccio Busoni: Historia Abscondita," *Fanfare* (Jan–Feb 1984): 90–116.

Craft, Robert. "Pulcinella," an Essay for recording on Columbia ML 4830.

———. *Stravinsky: Selected Correspondence*, Vol. 1. New York: Knopf, 1982.

Daviau, Donald G., and George J. Buelow. *The "Ariadne auf Naxos" of Hugo von Hoffmannsthal and Richard Strauss*. Chapel Hill: University of North Carolina Press, 1975.

Dent, Edward F. "Ferruccio Busoni," and Paul Feyerabend, "Busoni's Aesthetics," essays in booklet for *Busoni Piano Concerto*, recording on Angel SBL-3719.

Forsyth, Karen. *"Ariadne auf Naxos" by Hugo von Hoffmannsthal and Richard Strauss: Its Genesis and Meaning*. Oxford: Oxford University Press, 1982.

Gee, Karolynne. "Sergei Prokofiev and the *Love for Three Oranges*," essay in booklet for recording on Angel SRBL-4109.

Gillmor, Alan. "Erik Satie and the Concept of the Avant-Garde," *The Musical Quarterly* 69, no. 1 (Winter 1983): 104–119.

Greenfield, Howard. *Puccini, A Biography*. New York: Putnam, 1980.

Gui, Vittorio. "Busoni and Arlecchino," and *Arlecchino* libretto, Busoni, trans. by Nicolai Rabeneck, booklet for Glyndebourne Festival recording of *Arlecchino*.

Hamm, Charles, ed. *Petrushka* (Norton Critical Scores). New York: Norton, 1967.

Hammelmann, Hanns, and Ewald Osers, trans. *The Correspondence Between Richard Strauss and Hugo von Hofmannsthal*. New York: Cambridge University Press, 1980.

Harding, James. *Erik Satie*. New York: Praeger, 1975.

Kowalke, Kim H. *Kurt Weill in Europe*. Ann Arbor, MI: UMI Research Press, 1979.

Lessem, Alan Philip. *Music and Text in the Works of Arnold Schoenberg, The Critical Years, 1908–1922*. Ann Arbor, MI: UMI Research Press, 1979.

Milhaud, Darius. *Notes Without Music*. New York: Da Capo, 1970.

Nijinska, Irina, and Jean Rawlinson, trans. and ed. *Bronislava Nijinska: Early Memoirs*, intro. and consultation by Anna Kisselgoff. London: Faber & Faber, 1981.

Perle, George. *"Pierrot Lunaire, Op. 21,"* essay in booklet for "The Music of Arnold Schoenberg," vol. 1, CBS recording M2S 679. Includes text and trans. of poetry by Ingolf Dahl and Carl Beier.

Pierrot Players, recording on Mainstream MS/5001, with Davies, Birtwistle, Bedford, and Orton.

Reich, Willi, and Leo Black, trans. *Schoenberg: A Critical Biography*. New York: Praeger, 1971.

Rostand, Claude. "Francis Poulenc: *Les Biches Suite*," essay for recording on Angel S 35932.

Roth, Ernst. *"Ariadne auf Naxos,"* essay, and libretto by Hugo von Hofmannsthal, trans. Alfred Kalisch (Boosey and Hawkes), booklets for recording on Angel 3532C.

Rufer, Josef. "An Unknown Side of Schoenberg," essay for "Arnold Schoenberg: 'Wien, Wien, nur du Allein . . . ,' " recording on Philips 6570 811.

Sampson, Tom. *The Music of Szymanowski*. New York: Taplinger, 1981.

Sanders, Ronald. *The Days Grow Short: The Life and Music of Kurt Weill*. New York: Holt, Rinehart & Winston, 1980.

Satie, Erik. *The Writings of Erik Satie*, ed. and trans. Nigel Wilkins. London: Eulenberg, 1980.

Schoenberg, Arnold. *Pierrot Lunaire*, score (piano reduction by Stein). Vienna: Universal, 1914.

Shattuck, Roger. *The Banquet Years: The Origins of the Avant-Garde in France, 1885 to World War I*. New York: Anchor-Doubleday, 1961.

Simpson, Robert. *Carl Nielsen, Symphonist*. New York: Taplinger, 1979.

Stein, Leonard. "Schoenberg Brettl-Lieder and Early Songs," trans. Barbara Zeisl, essay for recording on RCA ARL 1-1231.

Stravinsky, Igor, and Robert Craft. *Dialogues and a Diary*. New York: Doubleday, 1962.

———. *Expositions and Developments*. New York: Doubleday, 1962.

———. *Memories and Commentaries*. New York: Doubleday, 1960.

Stravinsky, Vera, and Robert Craft. *Stravinsky in Pictures and Documents*. New York: Simon & Schuster, 1978.

Stravinsky and the Dance: A Survey of Ballet Productions, 1910-1962. New York: Dance Collection of the New York Public Library, 1962.

Stuckenschmidt, H. H. *Schoenberg: His Life, World, and Work*, trans. Humphry Searle. New York: Schirmer-Macmillan, 1977.

Styan, J. L. *Max Reinhardt*. New York: Cambridge University Press, 1982.

Templier, Pierre-Daniel. *Erik Satie*, trans. Elena and David French. Cambridge: MIT Press, 1969.

Van den Toorn, Pieter C. *The Music of Igor Stravinsky*. New Haven: Yale University Press, 1983.

Wedekind, Frank. *The Lulu Plays*, trans. Carl Mueller. New York: Fawcett, 1967.

Wellesz, Egon. *Arnold Schoenberg*, trans. W. H. Kerridge. London: J. M. Dent, n.d.

White, Eric Walter. *Stravinsky: The Composer and His Works*. Berkeley: University of California Press, 1966.

———. *Stravinsky's Sacrifice to Apollo*. London: Hogarth Press, 1930.

Chapter 8

Beauvoir, Simone de. *Memoirs of a Dutiful Daughter*, trans. J. Kirkum. Cleveland: World Publishing, 1959.

———. *The Prime of Life*, trans. P. Green. Cleveland: World Publishing, 1962.

Brod, Max. *Franz Kafka*. New York: Schocken, 1960.

Dinesen, Isak. "Carnival," in *Carnival: Entertainments and Posthumous Tales*. Chicago: University of Chicago Press, 1977.

———. *Seven Gothic Tales*. New York: Modern Library, 1934.

Eliot, T. S. *The Complete Poems and Plays.* New York: Harcourt Brace, 1953.

Fitzgerald, F. Scott. *The Great Gatsby.* New York: Schribners, 1953.

Fuchs, Daniel. *The Comic Spirit of Wallace Stevens.* DurhamUniversity of North Carolina Press, 1963.

Hemingway, Ernest. *The Sun Also Rises.* New York: Scribners, 1926.

Kafka, Franz. *The Trial,* trans. W. and E. Muir. New York: Random House, 1969.

Lawrence, D. H. *Aaron's Rod.* New York: Viking, 1961.

Nabokov, Vladimir. *Conclusive Evidence.* New York: Grosset & Dunlap, 1951.

———. "The Leonardo," "Solus Rex," and "Ultima Thule," in *A Russian Beauty and
Other Stories.* New York: McGraw-Hill, 1973.

———. *Look at the Harlequins.* New York: McGraw-Hill, 1974.

———. "Spring in Fialta," in *Nabokov's Dozen.* New York: Avon, 1958.

Painter, George. *Proust: The Later Years.* Boston: Little, Brown, 1965.

Proust, Marcel. *Swann's Way,* trans. C. K. Scott-Moncrieff. New York: Modern Library, 1928.

Sartre, Jean-Paul. *The Words,* trans. B. Frechtman. New York: Braziller, 1964.

Sitwell, Edith. "Colonel Fantock," in *Collected Poems.* London: Duckworth, 1930.

———. *Sleeping Beauty.* London: Duckworth, 1924.

Chapter 9

Amberg, George, ed. *New York Times Film Reviews, 1913–70.* New York: Arno, 1971.

Carné, Marcel, and Jacques Prévert. *Les Enfants du Paradis,* trans. Dinah Brooke. London: Lorimer, 1967.

Claire, Vivian. *David Bowie! The King of Glitter Rock.* New York: Flash Books, 1977.

Collins, Monica. "Boy George Chats Cozily on 'Face the Nation' " in *USA Today,* June
27, 1984, p. D1.

Duchartre, Pierre Louis. *The Italian Comedy,* trans. Randolph T. Weaver. New York:
Dover, 1966.

Friedman, Martin. *Hockney Paints the Stage.* New York: Abbeville Press, 1983.

Godard, Jean-Luc. *Godard on Godard.* Jean Narboni and Tom Milne, eds., trans. Tom
Milne. New York: Viking, 1972.

———. *Pierrot le Fou,* trans. and description of action by Peter Whitehead. New York:
Touchstone-Simon & Schuster, 1969.

Hoban, Russell. *Riddley Walker.* New York: Summit, 1980.

Kael, Pauline. *Reeling.* New York: Warner, 1976.

Livingstone, Marco. *David Hockney.* New York: Holt, Rinehart & Winston, 1981.

Mussman, Toby, ed. *Jean-Luc Godard, A Critical Anthology.* New York: Dutton, 1968.

Narboni, Jean, and Tom Milne, eds., *Godard on Godard,* trans. Tom Milne. New York:
Viking, 1972.

Smith, Philip. "Sets and Costumes by David Hockney," in *Arts* magazine 55, no. 8
(April 1981): 86-91.

Stangos, Nikos, ed. *David Hockney by David Hockney.* London: Thames & Hudson, 1976.

Syberberg, Hans-Jurgen. *Hitler: A Film from Germany,* trans. Joachim Neugroschel. New
York: Farrar, Straus & Giroux, 1981.

Thompson, John O., ed. *Monty Python: Complete and Utter Theory of the Grotesque.*
London: British Film Institute, 1982.

INDEX

Grateful acknowledgment is made to the following for permission to reprint previously published material:

"A Poem Without a Hero" by Anna Akhmatova, translated by Carl R. Proffer. New York: Ardis, 1973. Reprinted by permission.

Selected Writing of Guillaume Apollinaire, edited and translated by Roger Shattuck. New York: New Directions, 1949. Reprinted by permission.

"The Fifth Elegy" by Rainer Maria Rilke, from The Selected Writings of Rainer Maria Rilke, edited and translated by Stephen Mitchell. New York: Random House, 1982. Reprinted by permission.

"Ode to Picasso" by Jean Cocteau, from Cocteau's World, edited and translated by Margaret Crosland. London: Peter Owen, 1981. Reprinted by permission.

Five Tragedies of Sex by Frank Wedekind, translated by Fawcett and Spender. New York: Theatre Arts Books, 1952. Reprinted by permission.

Pierrot Lunaire, translated by Ingold Dahl and Carl Beier. Copyright © 1962 by CBS Masterworks, New York. Reprinted by permission.

Sleeping Beauty by Edith Sitwell. London: Duckworth, 1924. Reprinted by permission.

"Colonel Fantock" by Edith Sitwell, in Sitwell's Collected Poems. London: Duckworth, 1930. Reprinted by permission.

CREDITS

Frontispiece: Harlequin (1980) by David Hockney, oil on canvas, 48" x 36", copyright © 1980 by David Hockney, courtesy David Hockney. Following page 74: Family of Saltimbanques (1905) by Pablo Picasso, oil on canvas, 83¼" x 90⅜", courtesy Chester Dale Collection, National Gallery of Art, Washington, D.C. Fokine and Fokina in Carnival (1910). Nijinsky in Schéhérazade (1911), photograph by Baron Adolphe de Meyer. Diaghilev and Cocteau (1917). Stravinsky and Nijinsky (1911). Charlie Chaplin in City Lights (1931). "Little Tich," song cover illustration, BBC Hulton Picture Library, London. Buster Keaton. Barrault as Deburau in Carne's Les Enfants du Paradis (1945). Nijinsky in Carnaval (1910), photograph by Baron Adolphe de Meyer. Old Clown (1917) by Georges Rouault, oil on canvas, 44¼" x 29⅜", Edward G. Robinson Collection. Pierrot (1911) by Georges Rouault, oil on canvas, 33¼" x 19¼", courtesy Fogg Art Museum, Harvard University, gift of Mr. and Mrs. Joseph Pulitzer, Jr. Barrault as Hamlet, photography by Roger Viollet. Barrault as a real-life Pierrot in Les Enfants du Paradis (1945). Following page 170: Greta Garbo in Inspiration (1931). Giulietta Masina in Fellini's La Strada (1956), courtesy Janus Films. Buster Keaton and Charlie Chaplin in Limelight (1952). Emil Jannings in Sternberg's The Blue Angel (1930). Marlene Dietrich in The Blue Angel. Bergman's Sawdust and Tinsel (1953), courtesy Janus Films. Karen von Blixen (Isak Dinesen) dress as Pierrot (1954), photograph by Rie Nissen, courtesy the Royal Library of Copenhagen. Vsevolod Meyerhold as Pierrot, drawing by Ulyanov, courtesy Ardis Publishers. Franz Wedekind with Maria Orsaka as Lulu, and Maria Orsaka as Lulu, both courtesy Theatermuseum der Universität zu Köln. Marcel Proust, drawing by Quennell, Biblioteque Nationale, Paris. Virginia Woolf, photograph by Roger Viollet. Isak Dinesen, photograph by Peter Beard. Edith Sitwell, photograph by Cecil Beaton. Photograph of David Hockney with his Harlequin, Penbroke Studios (1980), copyright © 1980 by David Hockney, courtesy David Hockney.